Praise for *Transforming the European Economy*

Transforming the European Economy is a timely contribution to a debate that deserves the closest attention: how to get faster economic growth so the essence of Europe's social model can be preserved against a background of a rapidly changing world. This work admirably complements the European Commission's *European Competitiveness Report* and *Internal Market Strategy Report* as well as the Sapir Report (*An Agenda for a Growing Europe*) published a year ago and offers cogent advice on the reforms needed. I warmly recommend it.

—*Romano Prodi, president of the European Commission*

This book is a stunning achievement, combining the insights of the latest macroeconomic literature on productivity growth differences across countries with the comparative microeconomic insights of the McKinsey studies in which Baily has played a central role. The authors provide a tough-minded and challenging set of policy reform objectives for Europe that provide one of the best illustrations I have ever seen that policymakers should not accept policy choices as a zero-sum game. Instead of being forced to *choose* between productivity and employment, reforms that improve efficiency and foster competition and entry could allow Europe to achieve faster growth in *both* productivity and employment.

—*Robert J. Gordon, Stanley G. Harris Professor in the Social Sciences, Northwestern University*

At a time of self-doubt, Europe needs clear thinking. It needs an analysis of where it stands, what it does well, and what it does badly. It needs to find a better way to balance its commitment to social insurance with the need for economic flexibility. It needs a clear path of reforms, free of ideology, clichés, or slogans. This remarkable book should, and I very much hope, will help.

—*Olivier Blanchard, Class of 1941 Professor of Economics, Massachusetts Institute of Technology*

Globalization is not just about the US and the Third World. What happens in Europe is also important, not just for Europeans but for everyone. This book offers an accessible and penetrating analysis of the successes and failures of the European economy, and what it must do to grow and prosper. It is also a clear-eyed look at perennial policy issues like combining equity and efficiency, getting the best results from market incentives and regulation, and stimulating productivity growth.

—*Robert M. Solow, professor emeritus of economics, Massachusetts Institute of Technology*

A lucid and in-depth study on the European economies at the turn of the century. It goes beyond rhetoric and looks at what works and what doesn't work in Europe and at how individual countries can learn from each other's reform experience. An important reading for those interested in the costs and benefits of reforms.

—*Stefano Scarpetta, lead economist and labor market adviser,*
The World Bank

Martin Baily is one of the world's most authoritative scholars on economic growth and productivity. He has carried out numerous in-depth studies of economies across the world. This book is a very balanced assessment of Europe's growth performance. It has about everything in it that is needed to understand the region's economic challenges and fortunes.

—*Bart van Ark, director of the Groningen Growth and Development Centre,*
University of Groningen

TRANSFORMING the EUROPEAN ECONOMY

INSTITUTE FOR INTERNATIONAL ECONOMICS

TRANSFORMING the EUROPEAN ECONOMY

Martin Neil Baily

Jacob Funk Kirkegaard

Washington, DC
September 2004

Martin Neil Baily, senior fellow at the Institute for International Economics, was chairman of the Council of Economic Advisers of President Clinton (1999–2001) and a member of President Clinton's cabinet. He is a senior adviser to the McKinsey Global Institute. He was a senior fellow at the Brookings Institution (1979–89) and a professor of economics at the University of Maryland (1989–96). He was an academic adviser to the Federal Reserve Board and the Congressional Budget Office. His research focuses on wage setting, macroeconomic policy, innovation, productivity, and economic growth.

Jacob Funk Kirkegaard is a research associate at the Institute for International Economics. His research focuses on European economies and reforms, offshoring, and the impact of information technologies. Before joining the Institute, he worked with the Danish Ministry of Defense and the United Nations in Iraq. In 1996 he graduated from the Danish Army's Special School of Intelligence and Linguistics with the rank of first lieutenant.

INSTITUTE FOR INTERNATIONAL ECONOMICS
1750 Massachusetts Avenue, NW
Washington, DC 20036-1903
(202) 328-9000   FAX: (202) 659-3225
www.iie.com

C. Fred Bergsten, *Director*
Valerie Norville, *Director of Publications and Web Development*
Edward Tureen, *Director of Marketing*

Typesetting by BMWW
Printing by Kirby Lithographic Company, Inc.
Cover Photo: Getty Images/Guy Vanderelst

Printed in the United States of America
06 05 04   5 4 3 2 1

Library of Congress Cataloging-in-Publication Data

Baily, Martin Neil.
  A transformation of the European economy / Martin Neil Baily, Jacob Funk Kirkegaard.
    p. cm.
  Includes bibliographical references and index.
  ISBN 0-88132-343-8
  1. Europe—Economic conditions—21st century. 2. Europe—Economic policy.
  I. Kirkegaard, Jacob F.   II. Title.

HC240.B24 2004
330.94—dc22   2004051598

The views expressed in this publication are those of the authors. This publication is part of the overall program of the Institute, as endorsed by its Board of Directors, but does not necessarily reflect the views of individual members of the Board or the Advisory Committee.

Contents

Tables

Figures

Boxes

Preface

The European Union has been plagued by high unemployment for many years. More recently, it has been unable to achieve the high productivity growth experienced in the United States since the mid-1990s. As intensified global competition and aging populations in the 21st century threaten to further increase the pressure on European labor markets and government budgets, EU leaders in 2000 in Lisbon set out a bold vision for Europe in 2010: "... *to become the most competitive and dynamic knowledge-based economy in the world*. ..." Such a Europe was to be achieved through growth-promoting policies and a modernization of the European social model.

Nearly halfway to 2010, the European Union continues to be mired in low economic growth, persistently high unemployment, and large government deficits despite a strong global economy. Why is this so? What is the right diagnosis of the problem? Is the correct cure being administered?

In this study, Senior Fellow Martin Neil Baily and Research Associate Jacob F. Kirkegaard explore why major European economies have not been able to maintain the rapid pace of economic growth and productivity increases that they experienced in the initial decades after World War II. The authors make a strong case for comprehensive reforms of Europe's social systems and product markets to generate the essential flexibility needed to fulfill the goals of the Lisbon agenda.

The study reveals that the challenges facing EU members are indeed severe but punctures the myths that Europe is doomed to perpetual economic decline or that the destruction of the European welfare states is inevitable in the reform process. Indeed, Baily and Kirkegaard show the great variety of performance among European economies, some of which—particularly smaller ones—have already carried out social reforms that have succeeded in raising employment and lowering unemployment while maintaining high levels of social protection. Similar variety exists in product markets. Baily and Kirkegaard demonstrate convincingly, using detailed industry case study evidence, that European industries have achieved strong productivity growth when faced with the correct competition-enhancing regulation. In the case of mobile telecom, for example, productivity levels in France and Germany are above those in the United States.

Building on these past European experiences, as well as results from the United States, Baily and Kirkegaard propose reforms aimed at improving the incentive structures faced by all European economic actors: workers, the unemployed, companies, and regulators. EU welfare states must provide new employment opportunities rather than protect existing jobs, and do so via realignment rather than dismantlement. EU product markets must similarly facilitate competition, innovation, and choice rather than shelter unproductive incumbents and suboptimal standards.

With macroeconomic variables playing an important supporting role in generating sustained economic growth, corresponding proposals are made for adjusting macroeconomic institutions. EU government budgets need discipline but in a way that does not unnecessarily constrain countercyclical expenditure. On the monetary side, the European Central Bank should not only be a strong and credible inflation fighter but also growth promoting, and it should recognize the costs imposed when inflation falls too low.

Baily and Kirkegaard illustrate that member states, rather than EU-level or entirely new institutions, have to be the main drivers of change. In evaluating the reform process to date in the largest EU economies, they conclude that progress is occurring albeit at an uneven, slow pace. The book offers a positive way forward for Europe—one the authors hope Europe's decision makers will choose to embrace. They conclude that standing still is not an option, given the sweeping forces of change occurring within Europe and deriving from Europe's place in the global economy.

The Institute for International Economics is a private, nonprofit institution for the study and discussion of international economic policy. Its purpose is to analyze important issues in that area and to develop and communicate practical new approaches for dealing with them. The Institute is completely nonpartisan.

The Institute is funded largely by philanthropic foundations. Major institutional grants are now being received from the William M. Keck, Jr. Foundation and the Starr Foundation. A number of other foundations, private corporations and individuals contribute to the highly diversified financial resources of the Institute. About 23 percent of the Institute's resources in our latest fiscal year were provided by contributors outside the United States, including about 8 percent from Japan. Support for this study was provided by JER Partners, reflecting its major interest in the European economy and in transatlantic economic relations.

The Board of Directors bears overall responsibility for the Institute and gives general guidance and approval to its research program, including the identification of topics that are likely to become important over the medium run (one to three years) and which should be addressed by the Institute. The director, working closely with the staff and outside Advisory Committee, is responsible for the development of particular projects and makes the final decision to publish an individual study.

The Institute hopes that its studies and other activities will contribute to building a stronger foundation for international economic policy around the world. We invite readers of these publications to let us know how they think we can best accomplish this objective.

C. FRED BERGSTEN
Director
August 2004

Acknowledgments

The authors would like to thank their colleagues at the Institute for International Economics for many helpful comments, and C. Fred Bergsten and the Institute for sustained support of this project. Bart van Ark from the University of Groningen and Stefano Scarpetta from the World Bank reviewed the book and made a number of valuable comments and suggestions. We also thank European Commission President Romano Prodi, Robert Solow and Olivier Blanchard from MIT, Robert Gordon of Northwestern University, and Paul Hofheinz and Anne Mettler from the Lisbon Council for their advice and assistance. Tamim Bayoumi of the International Monetary Fund, Hervé Carré and Moreno Bertoldi of the European Commission, William Dickens and Charles Schultze from the Brookings Institution, and Dirk Pilat and John Martin of the Organization for Economic Cooperation and Development commented on a prior draft of the book. We would like to thank Gunilla Pettersson and Pavel Trcala for their excellent research assistance, and Marla Banov, Madona Devasahayam, and Valerie Norville for their excellent and tireless assistance in editing the manuscript and preparing it for publication. The book draws extensively on work at the McKinsey Global Institute, where Martin N. Baily is a senior adviser. The opinions and any factual mistakes are the authors' own, and the views expressed do not necessarily reflect the opinions of the staff or trustees of the Institute for International Economics.

New Policies and New Goals for Changing Times

Recognize that things change and that we need to change with them, so the mere fact that a set of practices has been successful or comfortable in the past is not an argument for its maintenance into the future.

—Bradford DeLong[1]

The European economy was one of the great postwar success stories. Today the eastward-expanding European Union will become the world's largest economic region. More countries would like to join the European Union and emulate the current member states—not surprising since most Western Europeans today are living comfortably and are protected from economic losses. Yet today's affluent European economies face serious challenges if they are to maintain their current standard of living, while the newly entering countries of Eastern Europe will be able to catch up economically only if they avoid the growth-limiting policies that exist in some of the Western European economies. Transforming the European economy is a necessity. Preparing it for the challenges of the 21st century will require painful adjustments; many existing companies will fail, and many workers will lose their jobs.

Not surprisingly, there is great political resistance to serious reform efforts. Yet a transformation of the European economy—indeed a *radical* transformation—is exactly what European leaders agreed was needed at a meeting in 2000 in Lisbon. The leaders reiterated their commitment to the Lisbon goals at the March 2004 EU Council meeting in Brussels. The time has come to actually implement the reforms and achieve those goals. As the Council itself stated in March: "The challenge now is follow-up:

---

1. One of five lessons learned from David Landes' *The Wealth and Poverty of Nations;* see www.j-bradford-delong.net.

real progress towards more and better jobs must be made over the coming year."

A positive message that performance in Europe can be improved—substantially so—can drive economic reform in Europe. Europe can create an economy that combines both strong growth and a solid social safety net, though it will not be easy. Indeed, many sacred cows of social policy, labor-market policy, and product-market regulation will have to be slaughtered along the way. These changes will not be costless. But the promise of better performance does not have to be taken on faith. There are several examples within Europe of reforms that have already worked. Denmark, the Netherlands, and Sweden have made labor-market reforms that raised employment and lowered unemployment. Britain, France, and Germany all have industries that were privatized or deregulated and where productivity increased rapidly.

Positive messages are more appealing than negative ones, but economic reform in Europe also has to be driven by a stick. When the going gets tough on reform and protests abound, it is important to remember that Europe cannot simply maintain the status quo. To do so would mortgage the future of younger Europeans, who would pay the price of present-day political inaction. But even apart from the issue of generational equity, the current system is not sustainable. The days when workers stayed in the same job or with the same firm until retirement (which might begin at age 55) have gone. The world today is radically different from the postwar period, when the cornerstones of Europe's present economic and social institutions were laid. It is not just the impact of technology. It is not just the impact of trade, globalization, and the new countries entering the European Union. It is not just shifts in consumer tastes or in demographics. Rather, it is the combination of all of these. These forces inevitably will affect Europe—indeed, they have already. Europe must not only respond positively to future forces of change, but also reverse some of the adverse trends that started in the 1970s.

The book's purpose is twofold. First, it presents an analysis of economic performance in Britain, France, Germany, and—to a lesser extent—Italy. We examine how these large European economies reached their current situations and the challenges they face going forward. In addition, the book reviews labor-market developments in Denmark, the Netherlands, and Sweden to evaluate the success of their reform efforts and see what lessons they can provide to the efforts now under way in France and Germany.[2] The book also analyzes the policies of the European Central Bank (ECB) and the impact of the Stability and Growth Pact (SGP), and offers recommendations for their continued role in solving the economic challenges facing the region.

---

2. Britain's economic situation is somewhat different, while Italy has not yet undertaken a major social reform effort.

Second, the book builds on this analysis to suggest specific policies that—if adopted—would increase the core European economies' rates of productivity growth and job creation. Improved performance in these areas is the key to improving living standards, meeting the future demographic challenge of the retiring baby boom generation, and—crucially— mitigating the social exclusion that occurs with persistently high levels of unemployment and underemployment.

The most important theme of this book is that workers, companies, and policymakers must be able to adapt to change. This idea has not been accepted on either side of the Atlantic and fighting against it causes many economic battles and policy distortions.[3] As important as it is to enact new reform policies in Europe, it is even more important to alter workers' view of the economy and to articulate their role in its—and consequently their own— prosperity.

Structurally, the book sets out the factual analysis first and follows up with policy recommendations. However, this first chapter jumps the gun by providing an overview of the main policy proposals. The reason for this is obvious, but there are two dangers involved. The first danger is that the policy proposals and the priorities placed on them as presented will stand alone since the later chapters provide analysis and support. We ameliorate this problem by giving summaries of why the proposed policies are important.

The second danger occurs because many of the specific reforms proposed are designed to improve the economic incentives facing individuals and companies—we are suggesting market-oriented reforms. Since a main purpose of this book is to contribute to the policy debate in Europe, it would be unfortunate if its findings were dismissed because of a belief that they simply suggest that Europe become more like the United States. We fully understand the antipathy of Europeans toward self-congratulatory US commentators who preach the virtues of the free market while conveniently ignoring the serious economic problems facing their own country—some of which stem from US policies not following good market principles. While economic and policy problems in the United States are not addressed in this book, we are well aware of them.

At the same time, we are also impatient with European commentators who argue that the region does not face serious economic problems and therefore existing policies are adequate and major new reforms are unnecessary. We also disagree with a variation on this theme that says that Germany is the *only* economy in Europe with problems. The European

---

3. The 2004 US presidential campaign is influenced by fears of offshoring US jobs. In Germany, Chancellor Schröder has described any company that moves jobs offshore as unpatriotic, which is something of an irony since the country has run a large trade surplus for years. Many German jobs depend upon the willingness of other countries to offshore their jobs.

economies are diverse, and we acknowledge that some of these economies are performing very well. However, a number of European economies—notably the four largest—clearly need to sustain existing reforms and enact additional economic reforms.

The title of this book, *Transforming the European Economy*, is actually a modification of a landmark statement made at the 2000 Lisbon Council meeting where European leaders called for a "*radical* transformation of the European economy." They also argued that "an average economic growth rate of around 3 percent should be a realistic prospect for the coming years. . . ." Subsequent meetings set ambitious targets for increasing employment: Over 20 million jobs would be created in the European Union by 2010.[4] However, these goals should be reached while preserving an effective social safety net and sustaining the region's environment and historical legacy.

The reform proposals in this book are intended to help national policymakers and EU-level policymakers figure out how to reach the goals they have set for themselves.

The Need for Sustained Economic Reform in Europe

For most of the postwar period, Europe outpaced the United States and caught up to the US level of labor productivity (output per hour worked). After experiencing an economic slowdown in 2002–03, Europe is expected to make at least a modest recovery in 2004.[5] But reform is needed if Europe is to return to full employment and to achieve its maximum growth rate, given the pace of worldwide advances in technology and business practices. European policymakers should use neither concerns about social inclusion nor the environment as an excuse for inaction. Furthermore, they should not protect special interests at the expense of those who could be employed in a more flexible economy. Welfare systems and labor laws must provide the right incentives to Europeans to participate in the economy and not divide the population into two groups: the well-protected *insiders* who have jobs and an unsustainably large number of *outsiders* who do not.

---

4. See Presidency Conclusions, Lisbon European Council, March 23–24, 2000, http://ue.eu. int/Newsroom/LoadDoc.asp?BID=76&DID=60917&from=&LANG=1. See also European Commission (2002e, 1–3). Many additional targets for specific policy areas have since been set at the biannual European Council Summits. For an overview, see the European Commission's Lisbon Agenda Web site, www.europa.eu.int/comm/lisbon_strategy/index_en. html.

5. Although Europe did not experience the same level of job loss after 2000 that occurred in the United States, the region did suffer a significant slowdown. Hours worked per capita are down in all the major economies. To the extent that the number of jobs has increased, this is mostly from part-time work or increased job sharing.

Germany today seems to be the most troubled of the four large European economies, with unemployment around 10 percent as of mid-2004. Real GDP growth in Germany was only 1.4 percent a year over the 1993 to 2003 period. The German economy has gone from being the leader and driver of European growth to its laggard. France's real GDP growth was somewhat faster than Germany's at 2 percent a year over the same period, but its unemployment rate was also around 10 percent in 2004. In fact, unemployment in France has been chronically high for decades. Italy, at 1.5 percent per year, saw growth almost as low as Germany's from 1993 to 2003 and continues to face arguably the worst demographics of any European country—an unemployment rate close to 10 percent and a government debt to GDP ratio of more than 100 percent. In contrast, Britain's GDP growth was pretty strong from 1993 to 2003, at 2.8 percent a year, and its unemployment rate is around 5 percent. However, this follows many years of very poor performance, and even today, Britain's level of productivity is well below that of the other large European economies and of the United States and shows little sign so far of closing the gap. Despite their differences, Britain, France, Germany, and Italy all have GDP per capita of about the same level, equal to roughly three-quarters of the US figure.

On the productivity issue specifically, it seems that productivity *growth* has slowed in the large European economies in recent years.[6] This is in contrast not only to the United States, but also to Australia and some of the smaller European economies. If the large European economies could increase their rate of productivity growth they could raise their living standards, lower unemployment, and go part way toward meeting the needs of the retiring baby boomers. *Thus, the goal for Europe is to combine high and rising productivity with full employment.*

Europeans who resist economic reform argue that they are quite willing to trade off higher incomes for greater social equity, but this argument does not justify resistance to reform. First, providing greater employment opportunities is a vital part of an egalitarian society. Second, Europe could achieve many of the same social goals while improving economic incentives and economic performance. Social insurance in Europe could be redesigned to cause fewer perverse incentives for a given level of social protection. The current system in major European countries is fatal for employment. Wage rates for low-skilled workers are inflexible. Payroll taxes are very high and inflate company employment costs (along with other employer mandates). Benefit levels paid to the unemployed and to many others on a variety of social welfare programs are kept high relative to after-tax wages and are paid for prolonged periods. This system discourages employers from hiring and workers from taking jobs.

---

6. Germany is a special case because of reunification. Reunification caused a large one-time drop in average productivity as East Germany was absorbed into the total. Then growth was boosted as East Germany was modernized. We discuss Germany further in chapter 2.

In fact, the case for reform is stronger even than the above discussion suggests. Europe does not have the luxury of running in place. Inextricably linked to the global economy, Europe is facing large new challenges as rapid technological change continues, countries such as China and India emerge as new competitors in the world market, and Eastern European nations enter the union. We have already mentioned the impending internal challenge from the large aging population.

Europe's economic performance has deteriorated over time because the institutions and policies that were effective in the postwar period of rebuilding and catch-up have become increasingly dysfunctional. The key to economic growth in high-income economies is adaptability and flexibility. Only flexible economies are able to adapt to internal shifts, global developments from beyond their borders, and new technological advances, while generating productivity growth and the new jobs required to achieve true social cohesion.

Reform Progress to Date

Europe's political leaders not only embraced reform in Lisbon in 2000, they have also undertaken specific reform policies, a number of which are important moves in the right direction. Overall progress on reaching the Lisbon goals, however, has been limited. In its own recent review, the European Commission (2004c, 2) noted the following: "Indeed, in certain domains there are significant problems which hold back the entire strategy and which hinder the return of strong growth. What is more, the most important delays have been identified in three strategic domains, which are crucial for growth: knowledge and networks, industrial and service sector competitiveness, and active ageing."

Following the Council meeting in Brussels in March 2004 the leaders issued a statement that acknowledged the validity of the Commission's concerns about the reform agenda's slow progress. However, one of their proposed solutions was to convene yet another study of the situation—a very weak response.

This is particularly frustrating since the European Commission report also highlights the diversity within Europe. Some member states have already achieved many of the 2010 goals, while others have barely begun.[7] "Catch-up" economies, such as Ireland and Spain, have achieved very rapid growth. Some of the smaller European countries, such as the Netherlands, Denmark, and Sweden, have performed well in recent years, even though they were already above the European income average. These three countries have achieved high employment rates and high degrees of social

---

7. See European Commission (2003a) for a detailed progress report as of spring 2003.

insurance, and safeguarded the future with sustainable pension systems already in place. As we will show, much progress would be achieved if European countries would learn from each other's policy successes. After all, *European solutions have already been found to many of Europe's problems.*

A Framework for Transforming the European Economy

This section summarizes the specific reform measures that we believe would be most effective in improving employment and productivity growth in Europe—the top priorities for reform. We then point to some policy reforms that have been proposed but in our view are less important or in some cases even counterproductive. One of the common misconceptions in Europe—particularly in Germany—is that the labor market is the only problem. We find that both product- and labor-market reforms are important. We start by highlighting the top three policies to improve productivity and the top three policies to improve labor-market performance, before going into the complete reform framework.

Top Three Policy Priorities for Productivity.   First, reform land use policies to give decision makers greater incentives to favor economic development. Second, because European manufacturing is not fully open to global competition, the remaining trade barriers must be eliminated. Third, complete the task of service-sector liberalization and privatization that has already yielded substantial successes.

Top Three Policy Priorities for Increasing Employment.   First, sharply reduce the legal and financial barriers that prevent companies from restructuring and discourage new hiring. Second, reform social welfare policies by encouraging people to work instead of encouraging them not to work. Cut back automatic benefits, and either start a wage insurance program or institute the close monitoring of individual social benefit recipients (as occurs in Denmark). Third, facilitate a widening of the distribution of wages paid by employers while preserving social equity through other polices.

Policies to Improve Productivity

To achieve better productivity performance, the level of competitive intensity must be increased. This involves greater openness to global competition, domestic (country-by-country) regulatory reform, and completing the process of privatization and liberalization.

Undertake a comprehensive review of regulations and industrial policies with the goals of increasing competitive intensity and removing barriers to productivity increase. Regulation is a fact of life, whether it involves ensuring transparency to protect the interests of shareholders, or whether it involves implementing health and safety regulation to protect workers and consumers, or whether it involves using a central bank to protect the financial system. However, regulation has become counterproductive in Europe, because it has been taken over by vested interests—regulatory capture. It is not possible here to examine each industry in each country and list all the specific regulations that are hurting productivity. But five examples are provided to illustrate different facets of the regulatory problem and the ways in which regulatory reform should be undertaken. Independent competition agencies in each country (like Britain's Office of Fair Trading) should be charged with identifying barriers in all industries. This is not currently part of the mandate of the EU competition authority, nor should it be. Since competitive problems inevitably will be country-specific, such assessments are best carried out at the member-state level.

■ *Land use policies must be reformed.* Economies cannot change and restructure unless there is flexibility of land use. Restrictive land use policies have discouraged new competitors from entering local markets in retailing, housing construction, hotels, and other industries. These restrictive land use policies thus discourage new companies and new job creation. Zoning is important and can be used appropriately to preserve historical values and the environment. In practice, however, zoning authorities have been captured by local interests, and zoning regulations have been used to protect incumbent companies. Zoning laws and the authorities that enforce them should be reformed so that incentives are better balanced—for example, by ensuring that local entities deciding zoning issues benefit from the new business taxes. The economic development benefits to the society as a whole must weigh more heavily in land use decisions, and these benefits should be reflected in the incentives faced by decision makers.

■ *European governments should end the practice of using overt or implicit subsidies to keep low-productivity incumbents operating.* In Britain, despite then–Prime Minister Margaret Thatcher's free-market rhetoric, large subsidies were paid to sustain low-productivity auto plants. The French government routinely provides financial support to failing companies. In Germany, subsidized funding is provided to many industries, especially manufacturing, construction, and coal. Although EU regulations ostensibly ended these subsidies, they continue. Allowing *companies* to fail is an important part of encouraging *economies* to succeed.

- *European governments should avoid policies currently being proposed to develop European champions* (related to previous point). The proposed policies are unnecessary because multinational companies headquartered in Europe are already doing well in the global economy. Michelin, Royal Dutch/Shell Group, Olivetti Tecnost SpA, Unilever, STMicroelectronics, Siemens AG, Benetton Group SpA, SAP AG, BMW Group, British and French hotel chains, and many other examples indicate that Europe already has companies with a global presence. Proposals to develop European champions are simply an excuse to continue subsidies to weak companies or to protect local companies from takeovers that could raise their efficiency, scale, and productivity.

- *Narrow, industry-specific regulations that limit competition are common and should be eliminated.* These regulations often have a long-established history and stay under the radar screen of competition policy. For example, German localities regulate the water used in beer production—in the name of purity and the environment. In reality, this regulation protects small local brewers from large multinational brewers that would otherwise take over the market. This is a small industry, but "trivial" policies like these, when replicated over and over, become an important barrier to change.

- *Administrative procedures and regulations should be reformed to encourage new business formation and expansion.* The Organization for Economic Cooperation and Development (OECD) has identified a set of regulatory barriers that discourage the formation and expansion of new firms and productivity increases in existing firms (Nicoletti and Scarpetta 2003). We strongly support their view that the permissions and paperwork required to operate new businesses or change existing ones should be streamlined and many restrictive provisions eliminated. The OECD has shown a positive correlation between low regulatory barriers of this type and productivity performance. A recent World Bank/International Monetary Fund study supports the same idea, showing how entry regulations hamper new firm formation and slow productivity increase (Klapper, Laeven, and Rajan 2004).

Open European manufacturing to global competition. There is a mistaken view in Europe that the manufacturing sector today is fully competitive, but this is not the case. Eliminating trade barriers *within* Europe increased competitive intensity in the 1990s, resulted in a convergence of prices among European countries, and contributed to improved productivity. For example, the French auto industry restructured and sharply increased its productivity as it faced full competition with the German industry. But Europe should go further and eliminate its remaining tariff and nontariff barriers with the rest of the world.

The need to increase competitive intensity in manufacturing is clearly demonstrated by three forms of evidence: (1) Industry case studies have documented the impact of trade barriers on manufacturing productivity in specific industries (see chapter 2). (2) A study of OECD-wide manufactured-goods prices showed that prices are at least 20 percent higher in Europe than those that would prevail with fully open trade.[8] (3) An Institute for International Economics study by French economist Patrick Messerlin (2001) documents the existence of widespread tariff and nontariff trade barriers in the European Union. For example, why is there a 10 percent tariff on imported automobiles when Europe is a major exporter in this industry? Messerlin estimates that eliminating existing and identifiable trade barriers in manufacturing, services, and agriculture would add 6 to 7 percent to EU GDP.

The European Union should act on these findings. At present, both EU and US trade authorities have become so caught up with jockeying for position in trade negotiations that they have forgotten that increased openness of their own markets would benefit their economies.

Complete the task of service-sector liberalization and privatization since it has produced positive results so far. The European Union made a commitment to privatize state-owned monopolies and open up Europe-wide competition in services and manufacturing. That policy has resulted in great successes. The road freight industry is becoming pan-European and increasing productivity through greater utilization of its truck fleet and by facilitating long-haul routes throughout Europe. The mobile phone industry in France was introduced as a private, competitive industry (in contrast to the fixed-line system under France Telecom), with sufficient consolidation to allow operation at efficient scale. Labor productivity in the French mobile phone industry in 2000 was twice that of the US industry. The efforts to increase competitive pressure in all service sectors, and in services of general economic interest[9] in particular, must continue despite arguments that preserving cultural traditions necessitates restrictive policies.

The financial-services industry is particularly important, not only because of its size, but also because it plays an important role in allocating capital. Despite EU efforts to develop a pan-European industry, separate national banking systems are currently preserved by member-state regulations. Unsurprisingly, comfortable oligopolies are common in this sec-

---

8. See chapter 2 for a discussion of the work by Bradford and Lawrence (2004). Corroborating evidence for their conclusion that manufactured-goods prices are high in Europe can be found in the OECD (2001c) study of the new economy. For example, the OECD reports that computer hardware prices are about 20 percent higher in Europe than in the United States.

9. This refers to economic services, the provision of which can be considered in the general economic interest, for example, postal and telephone services.

tor. Now that the euro and the ECB are firmly established, there is no reason to restrict bank takeovers or prevent the creation of a EU-wide financial-services industry subject to common eurowide regulation.[10] To date, the cost of establishing new retail branch networks creates a prohibitive barrier to entry in this industry. Therefore, it is important to allow or even facilitate mergers and acquisitions in order to develop a competitive European banking industry.

The European Union must move rapidly toward the creation of a unified European standard of professional qualifications. The inability of professional technical personnel to practice outside their national borders is a major barrier to service-sector competition overall.

Improve the market for corporate control by eliminating barriers to mergers and acquisitions. On balance, product-market competition and labor-market flexibility are the most potent tools to encourage companies to innovate, restructure, and improve their productivity. But an active market for corporate control can provide a valuable additional mechanism for increasing competitive intensity. In principle, EU rules encourage the development of a market for corporate control, but in practice many governments have opposed this development and used various tactics to discourage it. German policy is particularly a problem in this area, notably its pivotal role in blocking the original European Commission Takeover Directive in its attempt to protect, among others, Volkswagen from possible takeover. Proposals in France to create national and European champions also suggest limiting takeovers by multinationals from non-European and even other regional countries.

Policies to Increase Work Incentives and Labor-Market Flexibility

One of the reasons that it is difficult politically to actually implement many of the policies described above—even though in several cases they have been among the goals of the European Union for some time—is that restructuring and productivity increase will generate layoffs that could temporarily increase unemployment. In this book, we will argue that rapid productivity growth is good for employment over the long run, but it may involve employment costs in the short run. It is essential, therefore, that policies to encourage employment be a priority for European reform.

In fact, labor-market reform has been a priority of ongoing reform efforts, and important positive steps have been taken in several European economies. Indeed, we argue in chapter 5 that three smaller European

---

10. Anyone familiar with the inefficiencies arising from the still largely state-regulated and paper check–based US retail banking system will recognize the dangers of maintaining multiple jurisdictions within the same monetary zone.

economies have succeeded in raising employment and lowering unemployment through major programs of reform since the 1980s. Our proposals for labor-market reform in some instances simply support the steps that have already been taken. But some of our proposals go beyond any previous reform plans—at least in the major continental European countries.

The key theme of reform is that the labor market must facilitate and encourage change and job mobility while preserving, as far as possible, the traditional income protections offered in European economies. It is not easy to combine these two attributes, and important trade-offs have to be faced. But, we argue, Europe could achieve a much better point on its equity and efficiency trade-off than the one it is currently on.

Current legal and regulatory barriers to hiring and firing should be sharply reduced. Companies should be required to provide compensation for laid-off workers, but only at a moderate and predictable level. European companies are unable to restructure their companies to remain competitive because of internal redeployment and layoff restrictions. Small and large companies alike are reluctant to hire because if the business expansion fails they cannot lay off the extra workers they have employed. In many European economies, layoffs and redeployments are subject to review by regulatory authorities or by the courts. Restrictive rules in many EU economies are not consistent with a flexible labor market and are not consistent with the need to adapt to the forces driving markets everywhere.

Companies should be held liable for fair and reasonable separation payments for workers who have been with the same company for an extended period of time. However, this compensation should not be large enough to discourage structural adjustment. Although many economists have supported the policy described above for some time, policymakers in France, Germany, and Italy have so far shown little willingness to embrace this vital policy change.

The duration of automatic benefits given to the unemployed or nonemployed should be sharply cut back. But these cutbacks should be combined with programs to facilitate the return to work.   It has been firmly established by economic research that giving unemployment insurance (UI) benefits for an indefinite period encourages long-term unemployment. Several countries in Europe have set or are proposing time limits on the receipt of UI benefits. For example, such limits are part of Germany's Chancellor Gerhard Schröder's Agenda 2010 reform plan, as well as the recent overhaul of France's UNEDIC unemployment insurance plan. But it is not enough to simply cut the duration of benefits. Such a change must be accompanied by one of two additional approaches, or some combination of the two.

- *Close monitoring of individual workers.* Denmark successfully implemented this approach. Labor-market agencies monitor the actions of the unemployed. Benefit recipients are required to develop action plans for a return to work, and they are offered retraining for new jobs. The unemployed are expected to relocate in order to accept a job that opens up in a different place. They are also required to participate in work crews that perform fairly menial tasks, such as cleanup, if they cannot be placed in a regular job. The sanction for not following these requirements is an immediate loss of benefits. Although very expensive, this program has successfully increased employment in Denmark. The Danish model is effective and is part of the European tradition of helping workers find new jobs and ensuring they have the needed skills—a "third-way" solution. It is rather heavy-handed (as it needs to be for effectiveness), and it may be difficult to administer in large, diverse economies.

- *Wage insurance.*[11] Under this plan, workers who lose their jobs would receive automatic UI benefits for only a short period. But they would then be offered a wage supplement if they returned to work at a job that paid a lower wage than their previous job. For example, for two years, a displaced worker accepts a job paying 30 percent less than his or her old job; the worker would then receive a wage supplement equal to 15 percent of the previous wage—enough to close half of the wage loss. The specific parameters of the program could vary, but the crucial argument is that it is better to pay people to work than to pay them to not work. Such a program could also be much cheaper than the cost of indefinite UI benefits.

- *Combine elements of both approaches.* A program that offered wage insurance combined with access to job placement and training services could provide the best of both approaches.

The financial incentive to work must be improved. The previous bullet point described one policy lever to achieve this goal—limiting the duration of UI benefits. But there are other policies that must be adjusted as well.

- *The eligibility and duration of benefits for alternative transfer programs must be controlled.* The Netherlands and Sweden followed policies that were somewhat similar to those in Denmark, and they also succeeded in

---

11. Robert Lawrence and Lori Kletzer of the Institute for International Economies, with Robert Litan of the Brookings Institution, have been involved in the development of such a program for the United States. See Lawrence and Litan (1986) and Kletzer and Litan (2001). Germany has added a small wage insurance plan to its recent labor reform program. This, is an encouraging development, but the plan is very limited at present.

raising employment. However, the availability of early retirement benefits (see further discussion to follow) as well as sickness and disability benefits provided alternative financial support for those not working. Maintaining a humane system for the sick and disabled while avoiding program abuse or overuse is very difficult. Both the Netherlands and Sweden have recognized the problem they face and have tightened eligibility restrictions, but they still face some obstacles. There is a distinct danger that as Germany cuts the duration of its UI benefits, it will end up with increases in the number of persons on alternative income-support programs.[12] As with changes in the UI system, welfare reform should be accompanied by measures to help people get back to work (see next point).

- *Work incentives should be increased by cutting tax rates on low- and middle-wage workers.* In many European economies (and in the United States) low- and middle-wage workers face very high marginal-tax rates[13] that materially affect their decisions to participate in the labor force. Payroll taxes are generally the biggest problem, and since workers do not pay the taxes directly it is often and incorrectly assumed that they do not affect the decision to enter the workforce. In France, Germany, and Italy the "tax wedge," reflecting the difference between what employers pay and what workers receive, is around 50 percent for the median worker. Marginal-tax rates can be cut by a general reduction in payroll tax rates (which will necessarily involve cutting the benefits they finance), or such taxes can be made more progressive (as has been done in France). Another option is to offer offsetting financial payments to low-wage workers (negative taxes such as the Working Families Tax Credit in Britain or the Earned Income Tax Credit in the United States). Any of these approaches can be effective—and have been effective when undertaken.

The wage-setting process should be reformed to allow a wider distribution of before-tax wage rates. It is not enough to provide individuals with incentives to work. There also have to be incentives for employers to hire. Wages in many European economies are set to benefit the fortunate "insiders" who have jobs and seniority, while excluding the "outsiders" who remain unemployed or out of the labor force. Wages are set by unions whose bargaining power is enhanced by the regulatory and legal restrictions that reinforce the monopoly power of the incumbent workers

---

12. The proposal in the German Agenda 2010 to reorganize the Federal Employment Service (renamed the Federal Labor Agency) and combine unemployment and social-welfare benefits for eligible unemployed into the new "Basic Income for Job Seekers" (*Grundsicherung für Arbeitsuchende*) indicates an attempt to address such concerns.

13. A high marginal-tax rate means that workers keep only a small fraction of any increase in income they achieve by taking a job or working longer hours.

and firms. Minimum-wage rates set legally or by agreement are set at levels that make it difficult to achieve the wider wage distribution that would facilitate job creation. Union contract wages are often extended to almost all workers in an industry, reducing the flexibility of the labor market. In the past, many employers preferred the labor-market stability that centralized wage setting brought, but increased competitive pressure necessitates an increased ability to adapt locally to market developments, including wages. The insider-outsider structure of the labor market has been studied for many years, but policymakers in most economies have not been willing to take on the issue. There are two complementary approaches that could be followed to reform wage setting.

- *The rules that encourage or facilitate nationwide bargaining could be modified to encourage wages that are set by local considerations.* Employers that are not party to a major contract negotiation should be free to work out their own deals with their employees and not be constrained by a national contract. Such a step would introduce much greater competition to the labor market itself. Minimum-wage rates should be kept at moderate levels.

- *The steps that were described earlier to increase product-market competition should be implemented. These steps would not only raise productivity, they would also increase wage and labor-market flexibility.* In order to drive product-market competition down to the labor market, it is essential to avoid subsidizing companies that are in danger of bankruptcy. Businesses in Europe argue that they cannot face full global competition, because they are restricted by wage setting and layoffs. This argument should be rejected. Rather, force businesses to take on competition, and they will make the necessary changes on the labor side.

Ideally both of these strategies should be followed. The ability of policymakers to take on entrenched labor-market institutions depends on the strength of their political base and their willingness to face at least temporary unpopularity, manifested by public demonstrations and strikes.

Note that an increase in the before-tax wage distribution does not imply that family incomes must be grossly unequal. A progressive tax system, combined with social support for health care, will mitigate the effect of greater wage inequality. Of course there are limits on the extent to which this can be achieved without eroding incentives, but as we have described above, *some tax provisions can increase equality even as they increase work incentives*—such as wage subsidies, earned income tax credits, or wage insurance. To reiterate an earlier point, the issue of overall equality in a society depends not only on the distribution of wages but also on the availability of jobs. If the wage distribution becomes less equal, but more people can get jobs, then overall inequality will likely have been reduced in the society.

Pension and healthcare reform are essential in order to avoid further erosion of work incentives. By 2030 it is predicted that there will be one worker for each retiree in Italy and about 1.3 workers for each retiree in Germany. Given the pension and healthcare burdens this will involve, and the taxes needed to finance these burdens, there is a danger that work incentives will be sharply reduced even from today's levels.[14] There is wide diversity among European economies as to the severity of their pension problems, so generalizations are difficult, but two principles apply to many economies.

- *The age for normal retirement should be increased.* People are living longer and that means that, on average, there is an increase in the number of years during which they could be active participants in the labor market. However, rather than extending the period of employment, the age of retirement has declined in Europe. This trend should be reversed by raising the age at which full pension benefits are received. Access to various early retirement plans, which lowers the effective age of withdrawal from the labor market, should be restricted to people physically unable to continue working. Government-supported early retirement plans should not be available to the general public without a significant financial penalty relative to a full pension at the statutory retirement age.

- *Growth in the level of government-provided pension benefits should be reduced and fully funded private pension plans encouraged.* Using a gradual process, the real level of state-funded pension payments should be reduced. Unless pension levels are controlled in many European countries they will impose an unfair burden on future taxpayers as the number of retirees increases.[15] It is good policy for government to provide a minimum level of pension support because many individuals, especially those with low levels of income and education, will not save voluntarily for retirement. But beyond that basic level, people should be expected to save for themselves. Government can facilitate private pension plans by ensuring that saving vehicles offering good risk and return combinations are readily available. For much of the postwar period, private financial assets held by European savers (mostly in the form of low-interest savings accounts) earned a negative real rate of return (McKinsey Global Institute 1994).

---

14. The United States faces a similar challenge. Its social security retirement problem is serious but soluble. However, if Medicare costs per enrollee were to continue to rise at the same rate as in the past 30 years, they would reach 18 percent of GDP by 2050 according to the Congressional Budget Office. See chapter 2 for a discussion of these issues and sources of data.

15. Not all European economies face the same challenge. The Netherlands has a solvent well-funded pension plan.

- *When restructuring overstaffed companies the emphasis should be on finding new jobs for displaced workers. Strict limits should be placed on subsidized early retirement programs.* We noted earlier that the French auto industry had restructured and raised productivity. The gain to society from this was limited, however, because many of the displaced workers were put on early retirement. The Renault plant in Vilvoorde, Belgium was closed, releasing about 4,000 workers, of which about 1,000 took early retirement. These workers were as young as 48. Policies to encourage reemployment have already been described.

- *Continue with the steps already introduced to limit the growth of health costs.* In many ways the European economies are better positioned than the United States to deal with the exploding healthcare costs of the baby boom generation because they already work actively to control prices. In addition, steps have been introduced to increase copayments and require individuals to bear the cost of nonessential treatments. These should be continued and extended.

  Healthcare payment provisions ought to impact retirement decisions. Individuals, as they decide whether or not to retire, should take into account the funds they will need to pay their share of healthcare costs after retirement.

- *The cost of health care could be reduced by placing the right economic incentives on providers—doctors and hospitals.* One disadvantage of having heavily regulated and controlled healthcare systems is that healthcare provider incentives are often not aligned with efficient service provision.[16] For example, doctors and hospitals in Germany have an incentive to keep patients too long. Healthcare providers within individual countries generally believe that treatment protocols are determined by best medical practice and not by financial incentives. This is incorrect. Protocols vary widely by country in ways that reflect economic factors, so that improving incentives can reduce costs without significant adverse effects on health outcomes. In fact, sometimes outcomes are actually improved.[17]

Pension and healthcare reforms are already part of Europe's ongoing reform agenda. Under tremendous budget pressure, many countries have made cutbacks, and most politicians are aware of the impending problems from the retiring baby boom generation. Given the unpopularity of

---

16. In a more market-oriented system such as the US system, there are different inefficiencies, such as heavy administrative costs.

17. Chapter 5 discusses this issue further. Remaining bedridden for an extended period can slow recovery from illness. In addition, hospitals are dangerous places where infections are passed among patients. Releasing patients from hospitals sooner could improve their health.

these reforms, however, and the short time horizon of many politicians, it may be hard to keep the reform effort moving forward in these areas. To acquiesce to short-term political pressures would be a costly mistake, because the problems will only get worse with time.

Policies to Improve Macroeconomic Conditions

Even the most successful program of structural reform in Europe will not generate growth if the macroeconomic conditions are not right. Weakness in aggregate demand can ruin any economic party. The SGP, which was intended to provide a framework for long-term fiscal stability, now seems to be in shambles. France and Germany have said they will not abide by, at least, the letter of the SGP rules. The European Council has refrained from imposing sanctions, and its decision has been upheld by the European Court of Justice. Problems with the SGP suggest that it is in need of reform, but thus far suggested reforms have been ignored.

The ECB is in one important respect a great success. The euro has been launched and after falling against the dollar for some time, it has turned around and is now seen as a solid and established currency. By another metric, however, the ECB has not done so well. Economic growth in the euro area has been weak over the past three years, especially in Germany, its largest economy. The ECB has not moved aggressively enough to stimulate demand, even though inflation has been low, the world economy was weak, and the euro leveled off and then strengthened. In addition, the ECB has not adequately explained its goals and actions to the world at large, resulting in a confused public image. Perhaps this noncommunication is deliberate given that the bank has clearly violated the goals it stated when it was set up.

The discussion of macroeconomic policies is contained in a single chapter in this book—chapter 6—and consists largely of a critique and discussion of the SGP and the ECB. Three policy conclusions about these institutions are worth presenting here.

- The SGP is in urgent need of reform, and the European Council should drive the reform process, preferably as part of the ongoing progression toward a Constitutional Treaty. *The European Commission has proposed reforms, which should be used as the basis for changes in SGP rules. The SGP's enforcement mechanisms should also be strengthened by including progressive penalties for violators, which will signal its commitment to enforcement. However, we also recommend greater short-term flexibility in budget targets to accommodate cyclical downturns.*

- Both European and world economic performance would have been helped by more aggressive ECB countercyclical policies since 2000.

Presumably, the ECB's past efforts were focused on establishing itself as both a credible fighter of inflation and defender of the strength of the euro. Given its success, *in the future the ECB can afford to move more quickly and forcefully to counteract economic weakness in the euro area.* We are confident the ECB will act quickly to counter inflationary pressures if they appear.

■ Since the countries joining the euro have given up independent monetary policies, they need alternative forms of adjustment to weather economic shocks that affect only one or a few of the economies. We noted above that fiscal policy provides one such adjustment mechanism, but this is not enough. If the price level in one country gets too high, then there is likely to be prolonged employment and demand weakness in that country before it brings down its price level relative to the rest of the euro area. Adjustments in relative price levels within the euro area would be easier if the overall rate of inflation were not too low. *Either (best option) the ECB should raise its inflation target (currently less than, but close to, 2 percent), or it should (next best option) demonstrate its willingness to tolerate above-target inflation for a period of time to allow member economies to adjust their relative price levels downward as needed.*

Lower-Priority or Counterproductive Policies

There are areas of overlap between the reform proposals given above and the ideas developed in the Lisbon agenda that emerged from the European Council meeting in 2000. This book offers evidence to support the implementation of these reforms and suggests variations on and additions to the Lisbon proposals. Another important issue for reform is prioritization. The Lisbon agenda and subsequent Council statements have proposed policy reforms to stimulate European economic growth that we conclude are not high priority and may actually be counterproductive.

■ *Broader tax reform to lower tax rates on high-income taxpayers is a desirable goal but not a top priority for Europe.* If undertaken, however, it should be based on improving incentives rather than providing political payoffs to supporters. In general, we did not find that high taxes on the rich were a key barrier to economic or employment growth in Europe. Britain has a relatively low tax rate on high incomes, but it is the country that suffers the most from a shortage of skillful managerial and technical personnel—except in the financial sector—among the major European economies.

In most countries it is possible to undertake revenue-neutral tax reform that eliminates shelters, exemptions, and loopholes in addition to lowering tax rates for all taxpayers. This is the standard approach of broadening the base of taxable income while lowering tax rates, and several countries have adopted such measures—the United States in 1986, for example. This type of tax reform would benefit Europe as long as it does not become the centerpiece of policy and distract from overall reform efforts. Beyond revenue-neutral changes, cutting the very high tax rates levied on upper-income taxpayers may become possible in Europe provided stronger growth materializes, transfer payments or other forms of government spending are reduced, and revenue constraints are eased.

The issue of tax harmonization among EU member states is frequently brought forward as a required remedy against "beggar-thy-neighbor" tax policies. In theory, some countries could offer very low tax rates and very low levels of social services to the poor. This would encourage wealthy individuals to move into their country and encourage poor people to move out and be supported by taxpayers in other countries. This danger does not seem a major one, however, as economic migration remains limited within Europe. The greater danger is that tax harmonization will force every country to move its tax rates to the very high levels of some of the economies, which would be counterproductive. Based on the starting point in most European economies, some tax competition would be a positive move.[18]

■ *Large-scale infrastructure spending is not the way to stimulate economic growth in Europe.* Infrastructure investment seems to be needed in several of the less developed economies of the European Union, including the Eastern European economies, and also Britain, which has neglected its infrastructure. However, none of the industry case studies (even in Britain) found that a lack of infrastructure was a significant barrier to best-practice performance. Increases in government spending—with corresponding tax increases—would likely have adverse effects on private-sector employment and investment. Additional stimulus to aggregate demand in Europe, as needed, should be provided by monetary policy or tax cuts.

■ *There is no good case for rapid increases in overall government spending on education and training.* As in the case of infrastructure, with the exception of some less developed economies and of Britain, we did not find the weakness of labor skills to be a barrier to economic growth in Europe. In general, skills in Europe for the bulk of the labor force are as good as or better than in any other economic region. More than likely

---

18. This should not be seen as an endorsement of policies that extend tax holidays to companies by local governments to lure investment into the area. Frequently, the size of such offers is dictated by political considerations rather than the potential gains from a given project to the local area. For examples of excessive use of incentives to lure investment, see McKinsey Global Institute (2003).

there is a case for improving the way current education expenditures are allocated and managed for all educational levels, although that is not a focus of this book.

■ *Major government spending programs intended to encourage greater use of information technology (IT) are not needed.* While we did find that Europe lagged the United States in IT use, the gap was smaller than had been thought at the 2000 Lisbon meeting. Moreover, the collapse of IT spending in the United States since 2000 has signaled the dangers of overinvestment in the sector. There may be facilitating policies that would increase access to communications and computer technologies. But in general, regulations and lack of competitive pressure are the main obstacles to greater use of and benefits from IT in the business sector. Another barrier to IT use is its high equipment cost, which is yet another example of the broader problem of high manufacturing prices noted earlier.

Summarizing the Nature of the Reform Proposals

The reforms proposed in this book are designed to increase flexibility and improve economic incentives—incentives for individuals to work and incentives for companies to operate productively, expand business, and create jobs. Improving incentives for companies generally means increasing the level of competitive intensity they face.

Striking the right balance of incentives for the business sector not only involves encouraging competition, it also involves allowing companies and industries to evolve as technologies and tastes change. It is detrimental to protect a fragmented industry where most of the participants are below minimum efficient scale and are not using the most productive business practices. It is also bad policy to offer subsidized loans to favored companies to keep them operational. As far as possible, competition should be played out on a level playing field where new companies are allowed or encouraged and where both old and new companies are allowed to fail.

Getting the incentives right, however, means recognizing that not all industries are alike. In fact, in some industries it may be difficult or impossible to rely solely on market competition. There are a few industries (or subindustries) where there are natural monopolies, and there are sectors where there is a danger that an unregulated market will create monopolies. Finding the right *degree* of regulation, and finding the *best way* to regulate, therefore, present two of the most important challenges facing any modern economy. But it can be done. It is possible to regulate monopolies in ways that create strong performance incentives. For example, productivity growth in Britain's electricity distribution system has been rapid even without competition, because regulators put strong downward pressure on prices. Productivity growth in the US telecom industry was also rapid when AT&T had a virtual monopoly. This was not because of the monopoly, it was because the opportunities for productivity increase were large and the regulatory system in place provided an incentive to AT&T to take advantage of those opportunities. In other cases the existence of antitrust policy can be helpful by discouraging predatory practices.[19]

Germany and other European economies can overregulate the market (as Japan does) in a way that limits competition and slows change. If European policymakers are serious about reform, they will have to risk hurting established companies and workers as well as possibly making structural unemployment worse in the short run in order to achieve long-term growth. With the right set of macroeconomic and reform policies that risk can be minimized.

If striking the right balance of incentives for individuals were based on a very narrow concept of market efficiency, then people would have to face the full economic consequences of their actions. In many European countries, where people can collect substantial unemployment benefits or welfare payments indefinitely and retirement benefits are largely unrelated to private savings, the link between income and individual responsibility has been severely undermined. The right incentives mean that people are given emergency assistance and covered by insurance against catastrophic loss or injury. The existence of such social protections improves the welfare—improves the market outcome—of everyone in the society in the face of economic uncertainties. But having the right incentives also means that people should face a significant economic penalty when they choose not to work, and they should shoulder some responsibility for protecting themselves against economic setbacks through private savings.

Finding the right trade-off between equity and efficiency is indeed very difficult. However, many European countries have gone too far in the provision of social insurance. This book explores the possibility that if work incentives are too low, an unstable decline in employment could occur. Benefit levels paid to those who are not working are financed primarily by taxes on those who do work. If the benefits are too generous or are provided for too large a segment of the population, then the number of willing workers will decline over time. This will raise the tax burden on those still working and reduce even more the incentive to work. The possibility of such a downward spiral of work effort may help explain the 1970s and 1980s in Europe, but more important is the concern about the future. With the number of retirees rising rapidly and the number of persons of work-

---

19. According to Crandall and Winston (2003), however, it is hard to find evidence that specific antitrust actions have actually been helpful.

ing age declining, there is a real threat that in some European countries work incentives could erode much more and threaten a gradual collapse of the labor market.

Choosing How Many Hours to Work

There is general consensus that it would be helpful to create greater employment opportunities and thereby reduce unemployment and increase labor force participation. A more controversial idea is that full-time employees should work more hours—either longer hours per week or fewer weeks of vacation. There has been a decline in hours worked per year by full-time employees in Europe, and this can be interpreted as purely a voluntary choice.

We do not believe, however, that Europeans are freely choosing the number of hours they work in a year based on the right economic incentives. First, heavy taxes and high benefit and transfer payments affect individual choices. In particular, health and retirement benefits are not closely linked to income, while the tax burden on additional income is very high—conditions that will incline individuals to work fewer hours. For example, if the government supports college students by using tax revenues, parents of those students have no incentive to work extra hours to pay for tuition. It is not clear that such choices are optimal (or even egalitarian when low- and middle-income workers are taxed to support students from wealthy families).

Second, the number of hours per week and number of weeks per year are generally not determined on an individual basis. Instead, they are negotiated in collective agreements or dictated by policy. It is unlikely that such collective or policy decisions are made in a way that yields the best outcome for the economy overall. Policymakers mistakenly believe that shortening the number of hours per worker will raise total employment. Individuals often mistakenly assume that they can work fewer hours with no loss of real income—shorter hours are presented to them as costless so why not vote in favor of a policy to cut work hours.

Third, life expectancy is steadily increasing. If faced with the true economic consequences of this increase in longevity, individuals would likely combine higher savings with an increase in the number of hours worked. So far, Europeans have not reacted this way. Rather, earlier retirement, lower labor force participation, and lower hours worked per year have been the norm. If individuals were to face the right incentives, we judge they would likely change all three dimensions of their work choices, including choosing somewhat longer hours worked per year.

Fourth, as recently as 1973 workers in the large European economies worked nearly as many hours per year as those in other developed economies such as Australia, Canada and the United States, whereas by 2003 they were working 300–400 fewer hours.[20] This suggests that differences in economic conditions and policies may have induced the divergence in outcomes, rather than a sudden shift in deep-seated European preferences.

We are certainly not recommending policies that will force people to work longer hours per week or per year. But we do recommend that people be given the option of working longer hours. We oppose mandating shorter hours for everyone, whether through policy or collective agreements. In addition, we believe that policies that distort incentives in ways that shorten work hours, relative to optimal individual choices, impose significant costs that should be weighed against their benefits.

The Literature

There is an extensive library of literature dating back over 20 years advocating European economic reform, and many of the themes presented in this book exist in this earlier literature. The 1980s literature on "Eurosclerosis" and the barriers to European growth presented many of the relevant issues for reform.[21] However, there is substantive new material in this book that goes beyond prior literature. It is based on our own analysis as well as on a range of studies since the 1980s. We have tried to present a comprehensive analysis of the economic issues facing Europe, building on facts and supported by aggregate, economywide data and detailed case studies of individual industries.[22]

There have been major developments in productivity in recent years with faster growth evident in the United States and a few other countries. Most of Europe, however, seems to have missed the revival of productivity. Understanding what drives productivity improvement—including the role of IT—is an important task and an important element in any reforms intended to increase long-run growth in Europe. This book tries to avoid economic jargon and clearly present the forces that have shaped the European economy, the principles that should support structural reform, and the priorities for reform.[23] This is an ideal time to discuss reforms, be-

---

20. Data from Groningen Growth and Development Centre and The Conference Board, Total Economy Database, February 2004. www.ggdc.net.

21. For a leading example see Lawrence and Schultze (1987), which also contains many additional references.

22. Most of the industry-level analysis comes from work by the McKinsey Global Institute. Martin Baily is a senior adviser to McKinsey & Company and participated in most of the studies described below.

23. The findings of the Sapir report (2003) contributed to our analysis and are complementary to this effort. A recent study by Bayoumi, Laxton, and Pesenti (2003) strongly supports the benefits of competition in improving economic performance. Olivier Blanchard (2004) takes a relatively optimistic view of the situation in Europe, arguing that reforms already in

cause European policymakers are being forced by the facts to face the need for reform. And based on their public statements, they are committed to developing far-reaching reform programs.

Feasibility of Reform Proposals

This analysis presents the reforms we believe Europe should follow to become more competitive and expand employment. It is an economic analysis rather than a political analysis. If this economic analysis is to be relevant and helpful to the policy debate in Europe, there should be some relation between what is proposed here and what is feasible.

There is a relationship: The policies designed to increase productivity involve expanding trade and competition within Europe and increasing global competition. They involve continued liberalization of sectors previously dominated by state-owned enterprises and the restructuring of industries that have been overprotected. Although these reforms have been part of the policy thrust of the European Union for many years, progress has been limited. Despite setbacks and obstacles, we urge policymakers to keep moving ahead with reform instead of staying motionless or even turning back.

Reform efforts in France and Germany are currently seen as politically unpopular given the losses in French and German regional elections.[24] Transforming the European economy will require committed political leaders. Governments in most European countries today enjoy strong parliamentary mandates with time to enact required reforms before a new election cycle. Policymakers should seize this opportunity and not be deterred by the results of regional or local elections or by the actions of protesters.

To be successful, policymakers must "sell" a reform program to the electorate. French and German leaders suffered election setbacks because neither articulated a clear and honest picture of what must be accomplished by reform, the reasons for change, the likely short-term effects, and the large long-run societal payoff. Instead, voters, already discontented by cyclical weakness in their economies, were simply presented with cutbacks in entitlement programs—such as pensions and unemployment insurance—that they believed were safe. The struggle to achieve economic reform will be tough, regardless, but without a clear picture of what is at stake, there is little hope of success.

---

place, combined with competitive pressure, will make Europe more flexible. For an interesting perspective on reform, also see Baldassarri and Busato (2003). Sinn (2003) looks particularly at Germany's economic ills and proposes solutions not unlike those in this book.

24. In France, President Chirac's party, the UMP, suffered losses. Similarly, in Germany, Chancellor Schröder's party, the SDP, lost in regional elections. Voters are reportedly opposed to the economic reforms these leaders have proposed or enacted.

European policymakers may also balk at the reforms proposed to increase productivity. Incumbents are very involved in maintaining control over land use to protect their position and in retaining other narrow industry-specific regulations that protect them. However, evidence provided in this book demonstrates that when competition is permitted, economies benefit with higher productivity. The evidence to support the productivity-enhancing policies outlined here can be found within Europe as well as from US experience. European policymakers should build on their own success stories.

The same argument also applies to labor-market and social policy reforms. No country has chosen its labor-market and social insurance policies optimally, but an important lesson can be drawn from Denmark, the Netherlands, and Sweden. If major policy reforms are undertaken to increase employment incentives, employment will increase. European policymakers can, therefore, build on Europe's own success stories in this area.

If implemented, the proposed labor-market reforms would represent a significant shift in European policy, since they seek to preserve adequate income protection for displaced workers and include tax reforms to increase the after-tax incomes of low-wage workers. Although these are both market- and incentive-oriented reforms, they also recognize the goal of social cohesion. The dismantling of social welfare is not required.

We have argued that the policy proposals in the book are not modeled on US policies, and we acknowledge that that US policies are far from perfect. To the best of our ability, the analysis in this book is based on economic principles. That said, the US economy has been extraordinarily successful at job creation over the long run, and productivity growth has been strong since the mid-1990s. The US economy is market oriented and provides strong incentives for individuals to work and for companies to be productive. Therefore, it would be foolish, for us as economists or for policymakers in Europe, to ignore the lessons from the US experience if they can help Europe achieve its goals.

On the feasibility of policy reform and its implementation, we would like to draw attention to the forthcoming book on Germany by our Institute colleague Adam Posen. While Posen presents his own perspective on reform priorities, his study of German policy and reform will be very complementary to this analysis.

Chapter Summaries

Chapter summaries are included as a guide to the structure of the book. As chapters 2 through 7 are summarized, there is some inevitable repetition of the themes developed in this first chapter.

Chapter 2 examines Europe's postwar success and subsequent problems. It seeks to answer the key question: If the European economic system has severe problems, how did the region grow so strongly for so long? Our answer is that European economic institutions were sufficiently suited to the period of catch-up growth after World War II but are too rigid to succeed or adapt in the current market where flexibility is more important. The European economy had great difficulty adjusting to the effect of declining productivity growth that started in the 1970s, and to the impact of trade and technology on the demand for low-skill workers.

Over most of the postwar period, GDP per hour worked has grown faster in Europe than in the United States. This period of rapid growth shows the tremendous productivity success Europe achieved as it caught up to the US level (Britain is an exception to this statement). However, when productivity slowed this created serious economic difficulties. Not only does such a growth slowdown cause persistent unemployment, it reduces tax revenue growth and thus can lead to budget problems. It lowers real wage growth and weakens profits. It makes it much more difficult to finance the retirement income of pensioners. If Europe could increase its rate of productivity growth, this would ease its transition to a full employment economy and make it much easier to avoid any threat of an unstable employment decline.

Chapter 3 considers how Europe could improve its rate of productivity growth. The key is to increase the intensity of competition in product markets, encourage business and industry restructuring, and adopt regulatory reform to facilitate these. The chapter examines the literature, including a recently completed OECD study (OECD 2003f) of economic growth, and reviews the policy implications of it. In particular, the study found that international competition and globalization spur growth. Another powerful empirical finding is that new start-up companies in the United States are very different from those in Europe. Their employment levels have increased much more. The ability of US companies to experiment in the market is seen as possibly an important reason for stronger job creation in America, while start-up growth in Europe may be hampered by strict employment protection legislation often covering all but the smallest European firms.

Since the issue of IT has been so important to the growth debate, the chapter also explores the role of IT in US and European growth. Looking at comparable business operations across the two regions shows IT use is often quite similar for both. When IT is not used as effectively in Europe as in the United States it is mostly because of the industry structure or other barriers to innovation, rather than because of an intrinsic inability to install IT. IT is one means to achieve faster growth in Europe and does provide an opportunity that Europe should exploit given how it can improve business. But technology policies are often overrated and should not be used as an excuse to avoid more fundamental structural reform.

Europe can draw important lessons from the revival of US productivity growth. The US productivity revival took place in an environment of very intense competition, with the competition coming from both national and international sources. Therefore, to take advantage of the potential for productivity growth it is essential to allow economic change to take place and for the competitive process to work its way out.

Two major studies carried out by the McKinsey Global Institute used industry case studies and looked at the levels and growth rates of productivity in France and Germany in the 1990s. These studies determined that the nature of regulation in industries had a major effect on their performance. The industries where competition is encouraged generally achieve the best productivity performance. *A good-news story for Europe is that many of the regulatory reforms undertaken so far are working.*

Chapter 4 focuses on Britain. According to the OECD, Britain today has flexibility in both product and labor markets. If our diagnosis of Europe's problems and solutions in chapters 2 and 3 is correct, Britain should have been performing better economically recently than major continental European economies.

Although in some respects Britain has done better than other large European economies over the past few years, its economy continues to suffer from a low level of productivity relative to both other major European countries and the United States.

A review of the literature on British productivity leads us to conclude that some special factors are at play in the British economy. In addition, the particular implementation of privatization and deregulation instituted under Prime Minister Margaret Thatcher (and others) in the 1980s and the early 1990s did not immediately succeed in creating truly competitive markets—the British electricity generation market is a notorious example—and this postponed potential productivity gains. Further, Britain suffers from a relatively low-skilled workforce compared to other European countries, while also not possessing the large cohort of educated managers found in the United States.

Thus there are a variety of factors contributing to continued low relative productivity in Britain. We are optimistic that faster productivity growth will occur in that economy as the benefits of past reforms play out.[25] But we see a need for continued efforts to make product markets truly competitive across the board.

Chapter 5 turns to the issue of social policy reform. The first half of the chapter focuses on some guiding principles that such reforms should follow. These include setting time limits on unemployment insurance benefits and welfare; introducing wage insurance as a substitute for current unemployment insurance; ensuring that disability programs do not become the final inactive parking lot of a large share of the population;

---

25. Just-released new data from the United Kingdom Office of National Statistics (2004) suggest Britain's productivity growth has been faster in the last few years than previously thought.

maintaining universal health insurance but limiting its scope; shifting gradually over time to a system where pension levels are tied to private saving, beyond a minimum payment; making sure that the minimum income support level provides an adequate incentive to work; and tax rebates or negative taxes to improve the income of the working poor.

The second half of chapter 5 looks in detail at the social system, labor market, and tax reforms implemented in three small European countries—the Netherlands, Sweden, and Denmark—in the last 20 years. These three countries already have implemented national social reforms that embody many of the guiding principles laid out in the first half of the chapter, and have supplemented these with extensive active labor-market programs, such as worker training. The experiences of the Netherlands, Sweden, and Denmark should therefore provide important examples for other European countries that social reforms are possible and do work in a European political environment. None of the three dismantled its programs of social insurance. Instead each found ways within its disparate national institutions to improve the incentives to work and enhance economic performance.

Yet, chapter 5 also highlights the pitfalls of social policy reforms; how the Netherlands today may have a very low unemployment rate, but on the other hand has far more disabled people than almost any other country; how Sweden's employee absentee rate from sickness seems unreasonably high and strongly related to the generosity of sickness benefits; and how Denmark faces a huge bill for its active labor-market programs—a cost that does not seem to fall much even when unemployment is low. The examples of the three small European economies show the dangers of piecemeal reform of individual parts of a welfare state. The appendix to chapter 5 lays out the positive effects of social reforms on the significant unobserved economy in Europe.

Chapter 6 examines macroeconomic policies to support growth and reform. As noted earlier, reforms that increase work incentives will not work if there are no jobs available because of a cyclical contraction. The chapter evaluates the SGP and the performance of the ECB. The SGP contains the ingredients for a good deal of mischief. Given that Europe and the rest of the world are only now coming gradually out of a downturn, forcing fiscal contraction on Europe is a bad idea. It requires that EU countries maintain budget deficits below 3 percent of GDP and imposes fines if that target is missed. In practice the SGP has not been politically enforceable and so, as it stands, the SGP is ineffective at its original and desirable goal of requiring reasonable fiscal discipline of all EU member countries. But more fortunately, it also fails in its unintended impact of forcing a fiscal policy on the region at a time when such a policy could exacerbate the business cycle.

Many economists have set out proposals for reform of the SGP and the European Commission has critiqued these and offered its own reforms. We support the Commission's proposals with some important modifications.

The chapter then turns to monetary policy and the ECB. In practice the ECB has not kept inflation below its target and has even eased policy at a time when inflation was higher than this. Also, it did not keep money supply growth close to the target level. The ECB in practice has responded to real variables and not just to inflation or money supply growth.

While no one wants to go back to the days of excessive inflation, the world economy does seem to have changed and we have discovered the perils of inflation rates that are either too low or too high. Prices at, and possibly near, deflationary levels create or exacerbate economic problems. The countries that have entered the euro have sacrificed their ability to make independent monetary policy and use the flexibility of exchange rates to respond to country-level economic shocks—adjustments that would have changed the equilibrium exchange rate prior to the euro. Fiscal policy has limited power to offset this problem and Europe has low labor mobility so that migration provides only modest relief. The adjustment of national price and wage levels will have to substitute for the adjustment of exchange rates. This will be much easier to do if it does not require substantial downward adjustments of nominal wages and prices. The ECB should recognize the benefits of modest positive rates of inflation.

Chapter 7 looks at the reform efforts now under way to increase competitive intensity in Europe and make labor markets more flexible. The chapter starts with a description and assessment of competition policy at the EU level. The Commission has responsibility only for companies engaged in cross-border activities, leaving the regulation of many service industries, and even much of manufacturing, still at the national level. Moreover, the Commission does not control many of the regulations that affect competition in practice, such as land use. The conclusion, therefore, is that although there is considerable value in having an EU competition policy, the broad reform agenda in Europe—encompassing social policies and product-market regulations—must be carried out at the national or member-state level. That is where the power resides that can bring about the required change.

Throughout the book there has been discussion of what reform policies should be followed and the extent to which the large economies are on track to carry them out. A summary of recommendations for Britain, France, Germany, and Italy is provided in chapter 7.

The chapter concludes with a discussion of whether reform should be undertaken in one big push or incrementally. The economic case for a big push on reform is clear. Restructuring companies to raise productivity does not improve overall economic performance if alternative jobs are not available, or if workers have no incentive to accept them.

Figure 1.1 EU-15 employment growth, 1992–2003, and 2010 Lisbon goals, annual change

thousands of new jobs

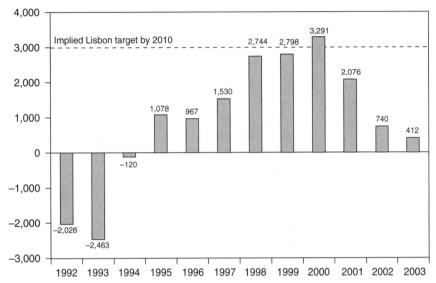

Note: Required job growth to reach Lisbon target by 2010: 21.5 million new jobs, or 3.07 million per year.

Source: Eurostat (2004a).

Concluding Remarks

It is clear that progress has been made, but much more is needed. European reforms are not being implemented at the rate that is needed to achieve the Lisbon goals—in fact, the intermediate Lisbon 2005 targets in the area of employment will be missed (European Commission 2004a, 4). Figure 1.1 shows that only in a single year at the peak of the boom in 2000 did the European Union in the past achieve the pace of employment growth that will be required to reach the 2010 goals—namely, 21.5 million additional jobs. But the question remains: Is the reform process on the right track? With some qualifications, the answer is yes. There are now examples of countries within Europe that have instituted social policy reforms and have seen employment rise and productivity increase in response. But there remains much more to do despite the signs of backlash against reform. If this book contributes in any way to sustaining the forward movement of economic reform in Europe, it will have accomplished its purpose.

2

Europe's Postwar Success and Subsequent Problems

It is not the strongest of the species that survive, nor the most intelligent, but the one most responsive to change.

—Charles Darwin

To understand what reforms should be made in Europe and why they are needed it is important to understand both Europe's huge success after the end of World War II and why this success then faltered. War and economic instability devastated Europe for most of the first half of the 20th century. Western Europe has since become peaceful and prosperous, and most Europeans like the current economic system and institutions. Given the long years of economic success, resistance by the populace to major economic reforms is natural. But unless the resistance is overcome, Europe will face continued and possibly worsening economic problems.

This chapter reviews the sources of the rapid economic growth that Europe achieved through 1973 and explains how Europe developed economic policies and institutions that worked well in rebuilding damaged economies and realizing the potential growth opportunities coming from the catch-up to global best-practice business operations.

When Europe was hit by a series of structural changes or shocks, the economic system and institutions that had worked so well for so long no longer supported continued growth. In the face of these structural shocks, constraints that did not impede growth in the 1950s and 1960s became binding.

First, the opportunity for catch-up growth was either reduced or exhausted as productivity and business practices in Europe caught up to global best practices. The *easy* opportunities for rapid growth were tapped dry.[1] Second, there was a sharp slowdown in the pace of growth at the

---

1. Some opportunities remained but were harder to capitalize on.

productivity frontier. Although the US economy is not the best-practice standard in all industries, its slowdown in productivity after 1973 was indicative of the fact that the leading edge of productivity was moving more slowly.[2] The combination of these two structural changes was a double blow to European economies. Europe's private sector lost its ability to substantially increase productivity each year. Hence, the private sector's ability to pay substantially higher real wages each year *while sustaining employment levels* was also lost.[3]

The worldwide surge in inflation was the third structural shock that occurred in the 1970s. Although partly linked to slower productivity growth, inflation also surged because of increased wage push, excessive money growth earlier in the decade, and rapid increases in commodity prices of such items as food and oil.[4] This inflation surge was subsequently reversed—helped by a large drop in oil prices in the 1980s—but its effect may have endured far longer. It triggered a period of stagflation and rising unemployment. Although inflation reversed, unemployment seems to have become stuck at a higher level. There are features of the European economic system that can cause a ratchet effect in unemployment.

The final, but very important, structural change affecting Europe began in the 1980s. Expanding trade with low-wage countries and technological progress reduced the relative demand for low-skilled workers. If market forces set wage rates in Europe, as largely was the case in the United States, this shift would have increased the wage gap between high- and low-wage workers. Instead, institutionally set wage rates for low-skilled jobs were kept above market levels, causing low-skilled job loss.

Any economic system would have difficulty adjusting to these structural shifts, and the 1970s and 1980s were difficult times for all the industrial countries. Many European economies found it particularly difficult to make the adjustments needed to limit or reverse the slowdown in productivity growth and to avoid an erosion of the employment base. In this chapter and chapter 3 we will look at the reasons why.

As part of this discussion, a simple model is developed that shows that when wage rates are not set by market forces and when social insurance programs are too generous or poorly designed, then an unstable employment dynamic may develop. A vicious cycle can develop in which a decline in labor supply triggers a rise in taxes on labor that causes a further decline

---

2. For a discussion of the slowdown and further references see Baily and Chakrabarti (1988). One important effect of the post-1973 slowdown in the United States was that productivity growth in service industries collapsed. The recovery of productivity growth after 1995 seems to have reversed that service-sector decline.

3. The data on productivity will be presented shortly. Productivity growth did not cease in Europe, but it slowed sharply.

4. The inflation problems of the 1970s actually started in the 1960s with an upward push on wages. See Nordhaus (1972).

in labor supply. This model may be useful in understanding Europe's employment pattern over the past 30 years, but it may be even more useful in describing the danger going forward. The increased proportion of the population that is elderly and receiving pension and healthcare benefits could lead to an unstable downward spiral in labor supply in the future.

What Drove Rapid Growth in Postwar Europe?

In the postwar period, Europe staged a remarkable recovery and rapid catch-up to the United States. From 1950 to 1973 real GDP per capita in the United States rose by 2.45 percent a year—a strong performance. But France grew much faster over this period, increasing its level of GDP per capita from 54 percent of the US level to 77 percent. The corresponding figures for West Germany are 49 percent to 87 percent, and 40 percent to 70 percent for Italy. West Germany's postwar recovery was particularly remarkable, given the massive destruction from the war and its division into two separate nations as the Cold War emerged. Britain started in 1950 with a much higher income level than the rest of Europe, at 73 percent of the US level. Through 1973, Britain's GDP per capita grew at almost the same rate as in the United States so it remained at 71 percent and therefore did not achieve any catch-up to the United States over this period.[5]

Clearly, the major European economies took advantage of postwar opportunities to achieve this high level of success. Moreover, they achieved this success despite operating with institutional rigidities (which were in place well before 1973) that have been blamed for later economic weakness, so there is an important question of why these problems did not stop the rapid growth and convergence from taking place.

The convergence of GDP per capita from 1950 to 1973 was not driven by a faster rate of growth of labor input in Europe than in the United States. Table 2.1 shows hours worked per capita for France, West Germany, Italy, Britain, and the United States in the two endpoint years. The figures are indexed to the United States, which equals 100 in each year. In France and West Germany labor input per capita declined a little relative to the United States. In Italy and Britain it rose a little. But in no country was the overall GDP per capita growth differential explained by changes in labor input per capita. (That statement is not true for later time periods.) It follows that the convergence in GDP per capita between continental Europe and the United States over this period was driven by much faster labor productivity growth in Europe (except for Britain).

---

5. All data from University of Groningen and the Conference Board (2004). In the 19th century per capita income in Britain was higher than that in the United States, so growth in Britain had been slower for an extended period prior to World War II. By holding its own in the postwar period, Britain actually improved over its previous growth experience.

Table 2.1   Annual hours worked per person employed, relative to the United States, 1950 and 1973 (United States = 100)

	France	West Germany	Italy	Britain	United States
1950	106.5	112.0	87.3	105.1	100
1973	95.9	105.0	95.4	108.9	100

Source: University of Groningen and the Conference Board (2004).

Edward Denison (1967), who used real national income per employee as his productivity measure, carried out the classic study of productivity growth in postwar Europe and the reasons for the differences in growth rates between the US and European economies. However, his analysis covered the 1950 to 1962 period and is therefore considered "out-of-date" by many economists. Although we will review more recent analyses of the same issues shortly, we feel that Denison's work is still worth a quick review. His work stands out because it provides detailed sources of growth and found ways to quantify the contributions during an earlier time period. But perhaps most importantly, it gets the basic story right.

Table 2.2 is drawn from Denison (1967) and shows the contributions to the growth of national income per employee from a variety of sources for France, West Germany, Italy, Britain, and the United States. The top line indicates the overall productivity growth rate and the subsequent lines show the contributions to that total. The sources of growth are broken into two subgroups, first those that affect total factor input and, second, those that contribute to growth in output per unit of input (now referred to as multifactor productivity, or MFP).[6]

Denison concludes that most of the increase in national income per employee within each country does not come from input growth—rather it comes from growth in output per unit of input. The differences in growth rates among the countries are not explained by differences in input growth rates either. According to Denison, Europe did not achieve a productivity growth advantage over this period by raising labor quality or adding more capital per worker than did the United States.

Turning next to the sources of increase in output per unit of input (MFP), Denison argues that the outward movement of the technology frontier allows all of the economies to grow, and he attributes this same source of growth to all of the economies. Increases in MFP from advances in the technology frontier account for three-quarters of a percentage point a year for all of the countries. Denison appropriately uses the term "advances in knowledge" rather than technological change to describe this source of growth. One reason the frontier of best practice moves out over

---

6. It has also been referred to as total factor productivity (TFP). Today, most use the term MFP as we do throughout the book.

Table 2.2 Sources of growth in real national income per person employed, 1950–62

Source of growth	France	West Germany	Italy	Britain	United States
National income per person employed	**4.80**	**5.15**	**5.36**	**1.63**	**2.15**
Total factor input	**1.13**	**.72**	**1.07**	**.45**	**.79**
Labor	.37	−.12	.54	.10	.22
Hours of work	−.02	−.27	.05	−.15	−.17
Age-sex composition	.10	.04	.09	−.04	−.10
Education	.29	.11	.40	.29	.49
Capital	.76	.93	.57	.37	.60
Dwellings	.02	.12	.05	.02	.21
International assets	.02	−.08	−.03	−.06	.04
Nonresidential structures and equipment	.53	.66	.45	.35	.29
Inventories	.19	.23	.10	.06	.06
Land	.00	−.09	−.04	−.02	−.03
Output per unit of input	**3.67**	**4.43**	**4.29**	**1.18**	**1.36**
Advances in knowledge	.76	.75	.76	.75	.75
Changes in the lag in the application of knowledge, general efficiency, and errors and omissions					
Reduction in age of capital	.00	.04	.00	.00	n.a.
Other	.74	.79	.88	.04	n.a.
Improved allocation of resources					
Contraction of agricultural inputs	.65	.76	1.04	.06	.25
Contraction of nonagricultural self-employment	.23	.14	.22	.04	.04
Reduction of international trade barriers	.07	.10	.16	.02	.00
Economies of scale					
Growth of national market measured in US prices	.44	.62	.55	.22	.30
Income elasticities	.49	.90	.60	.09	n.a.
Independent growth of local markets	.07	.07	.07	.05	.06
Irregularities in pressure of demand	−.01	n.a.	.01	−.09	−.04
Construction deflation procedure	.23	n.a.	n.a.	n.a.	n.a.
Balancing of the capital stock	n.a.	.26	n.a.	n.a.	n.a.

n.a. = not applicable

Source: Denison (1967, tables 21.1 to 21.19).

time is that new science or engineering-based production methods are introduced. But another important reason is that business innovations result in improved practices as well as new products and services.

Continental Europe experienced faster growth because it had further to catch up than the United States. Europe had the opportunity to grow faster than the United States because it started out far behind, having been so adversely affected by the destruction of World War II.

One important way in which catch-up occurs is that the gap between average productivity and best-practice productivity is much greater for countries in early stages of development. The European economies increased their productivity levels by adopting technologies and business methods that were already in use in the United States. Denison (1967) discovers that this practice substantially contributed to growth differentials, adding about 0.8 percentage points a year to European growth compared to the United States (almost zero in Britain).[7]

Catch-up also occurs when workers move from agriculture into industry and commerce. Typically there is very low labor productivity in agriculture at early or intermediate stages of economic development. When combined with capital investments and the transfer of technology, workers coming from agriculture can be employed in much higher-productivity sectors of the economy. Workers shifting from other low-productivity self-employment can similarly work in high-productivity sectors. The European countries, with the exception of Britain, all achieved substantial growth from these sources—close to or above one percentage point a year. In comparison, the United States grew only about a quarter of a percent a year from this source.

According to Denison (1967), fast-developing economies also have an advantage from economies of scale. He breaks this into two parts. The first is the conventional notion that as economies develop they can expand the scale of production of existing goods and services. Larger steel mills or electricity-generating plants are more productive than smaller ones (this statement would not hold in the same way today). In addition, Denison notes a virtuous circle of economic growth. As income grows rapidly, consumption also grows rapidly as people purchase more expensive, higher-value-added products and services. In the past, very few consumers purchased these niche items so they were produced at small scale and low productivity. However, as these products and services move into the mainstream, they can be produced at larger scale, often using technologies already widely used in the United States. Rapidly rising incomes and expenditures provided an opportunity to take advantage of economies of scale that were already available technologically but could not be justified when demand and incomes were low. This second source of productivity growth is measured in a way that takes the United States as a baseline. By definition, then, the United States gets a zero relative contribution

---

7. It is highly plausible that the European economies were able to apply existing US technologies and business methods during this period—indeed a whole industry of business and technology consulting developed to effect such a transfer. Note that Denison uses "errors and omissions" in his accounting to describe differences in productivity growth rates that could not be explained by specific measurable sources.

from this source.[8] Thus, this form of economies of scale is an important partial explanation of why Europe grew faster than the United States in 1950–62. Overall economies of scale add nearly a percentage point to growth in France over the period, well over a percentage point in Germany and Italy, and about 0.3 percentage point a year in Britain and the United States.[9]

Alternative approaches to growth analysis would likely yield somewhat different findings from those in Denison's (1967) framework. For example, Dale Jorgenson's analysis (1995) has given a larger weight to capital as a source of growth than Denison. The level of capital intensity in Europe in 1950 was very low, and there was rapid capital accumulation over the next 23 years. Denison allows for this, but may not give enough credit to this effect. The faster productivity growth in Europe was likely driven more by the faster growth in capital input than Denison allows for.[10] This could be construed as a form of catch-up as capital intensity equalizes across countries and technology is embodied in new capital goods.

Despite some possible adjustments to update Denison's analysis, the overall conclusions from his work still make good sense. Following World War II, both Europe and the United States experienced strong productivity growth. However, Europe's growth—with the exception of Britain—far outpaced that of the United States. The reasons for this growth differ-

---

8. Denison tries to explain the differences in growth rates between the United States and each European economy. The growth within any given European economy is calculated using a domestic price index that uses relative prices that are specific to the given country. This estimated growth rate is faster than the growth rate that would be calculated using US relative prices. The difference between the two growth rates is then attributed to the second economies-of-scale term and interpreted by Denison in the way described above. The overall growth rate of an economy is the weighted average of the growth rates of the different goods and services produced, with relative prices as the weights (plus some additional terms). Many of the items that grew rapidly in postwar Europe had lower relative prices in the United States and, hence, smaller weights when growth is calculated with US relative prices.

9. Other sources of growth differences are less significant. Productivity growth varies with the business cycle and Denison adjusts for this, although it makes only a trivial difference to the outcome. In France, the method used to calculate real construction gives a boost to measured growth in its economy. Denison also estimated that the recovery from wartime damage in Germany boosted growth in that economy after 1950. He describes that as "balancing the capital stock."

10. Denison uses national income as his output measure, a concept that is net of depreciation. In estimating the contribution of capital to the growth of output, he uses the share of capital income in national income. The use of income shares is standard procedure in growth accounting, but Denison is unusual in using the capital income share net of depreciation. Using a production-function framework suggests the contribution of capital should be based on the gross income share, which gives a larger weight to capital. It is worth noting, however, that when output measures include depreciation (as is the case, for example, for GDP or business-sector output) the growth rate will overstate the growth of economic well-being if the share of depreciation in output is rising. This point motivates Denison's use of national income and the net capital income share.

ential seem largely driven by various aspects of economic catch-up, which include the movement of workers off the farms, the rebuilding of production damaged or destroyed in the war, the expansion of the capital-intensive, high-productivity sector of the economy, the ability to exploit economies of scale, and the movement toward best-practice technologies and production methods.

This process seems to have continued well after the end point of the Denison study. The frontier of best-practice productivity was rising rapidly in the United States until 1973, sustaining the potential growth that Europe could achieve. GDP per hour worked—an alternative measure of broad labor productivity—showed that productivity was growing at 3.0 percent a year in the United States. But Europe still had room for additional catch-up through 1973 because the level of productivity was still substantially higher in the United States. In 1973, France was at 80 percent of the US level, West Germany 75 percent, Italy 72 percent, and Britain 65 percent.[11] Hence, the productivity growth potential remained greater in Europe than in the United States in 1973 and beyond.[12]

The European System's Advantages for Postwar Catch-Up

The rapid convergence of France, West Germany, and Italy toward the US level of productivity through 1973 could be considered unsurprising since economic growth theory predicts it. Common sense also suggests that transferring more productive technologies and business processes is easier than pushing out the frontier.

But convergence is not a foregone conclusion. Despite potential, many countries failed to converge toward the productivity frontier, and there was a widening gap between rich and poor. Britain is one prime example though there are many others. Therefore, the economic conditions must have been relatively favorable for convergence in France, West Germany, Italy, and many other European economies. Drawing on Denison's work (1967) and more recent studies, notably Temin's (2002) review and additional analysis, we conclude the European economy had the following advantages that contributed to its rapid postwar convergence:

- Europe was an industrial and commercial powerhouse before World War II. Therefore, its economic infrastructure already existed, and

---

11. The University of Groningen and the Conference Board (2004), based on 1990 purchasing power parity (PPP) exchange rates.

12. This description is too US-centric because it implies advances of the frontier were always made in the United States and then transferred to Europe. This is not the case. Many European innovations—such as specialized machine tools—were developed and then used in the United States. Furthermore, Japanese industries, such as steel, auto, and machine tools, overtook US productivity levels in the 1980s.

some of the technological knowledge, infrastructure, and managerial and worker skills were still available in its aftermath. Although the United States had become overall the most productive economy around the turn of the 20th century, Europe's economy was not far behind and, in fact, had many areas of strength and superiority. For example, France was a leader in commercial aviation before the war, and Germany was building its industrial strength and infrastructure. In contrast, the US economy in the 1930s was still struggling in the aftermath of the Great Depression.

- The continental European economies boosted productivity by shifting workers from agriculture into industry and commerce. Denison (1967) makes the point initially, and Temin (2002) stresses its importance, noting that unlike the United States and Britain, continental Europe still had a lot of workers in agriculture in 1950.[13]

- As Olson (1984) has pointed out, the war disrupted the existing network of anticompetitive coalitions and monopolies in Europe. In its aftermath, these economies were able to develop new industries and allow old industries to die.

- Social and economic policies focused primarily on recovery, catch-up, and growth.[14] Some have questioned Olson's thesis about the destruction of the prewar coalitions, arguing that many remained intact—the craft unions in Germany, for example. But even to the extent that this criticism is warranted, the imperative need for economic recovery and growth trumped the tendency of coalition groups to fight for the largest share of the pie, especially since the size of the pie was growing rapidly. Eichengreen (1995), for example, argues that Germany and other European economies were able to maintain a pact of cooperation with their workers that kept investment and exports profitable while sustaining rapid growth.[15] A range of national and international institutions supported these pacts.

---

13. In Temin's view, the availability of excess labor in agriculture "explains" how continental Europe grew faster than the United States or Britain after World War II. This idea should not be overstressed, however, because the bulk of economic catch-up in Europe was occurring in the nonfarm sector. We discuss Britain in more depth in chapter 4. The real puzzle is that Britain's productivity in the nonfarm economy was about half of the US level in 1950 and closed this gap only very slowly indeed over the next 50 years.

14. Crafts and Toniolo (1996) attribute much of the rapid growth of the postwar period to the slowdown that preceded it and the disruption of the war itself.

15. Eichengreen emphasizes that the pact with workers kept wage growth low but that argument seems uncompelling. Wage data are discussed again later in this chapter, but it is notable that manufacturing real-wage growth in Germany in 1950–73 was around 7 percent a year, and both France and Italy also had rapid real-wage growth (see figure 2.7). It is fairly easy to retain workers with a social pact when productivity and wages are growing so fast. As we argue later, the social pact unraveled when productivity growth slowed down in the 1970s.

- Taking the above point further, the economic coalitions that survived or developed in the postwar period may have contributed positively to rapid growth by providing job training for workers. For example, the German craft unions expanded their apprenticeship programs, which increased skill levels. To avoid labor-market failure, the European economies discouraged worker mobility and encouraged on-the-job training to retain workers.[16]

- Generous support for the unemployed and extensive job training programs ensured that displaced workers were able to survive economically and seek new positions.

- In response to the turbulence of the first half of the 20th century, households became risk averse, prompting them to save a large portion of their incomes (relative to the United States) and to place their savings in low-risk (and low-return) assets, notably in savings accounts at state-guaranteed banks. These banks then had a pool of low-cost funds, which they channeled into local business development. These funds helped rebuild and expand the commercial and industrial base of Europe's economy.

- Close ties between business and government facilitated the recovery and expansion of many key industries. France, in particular, used state subsidies, technology support, and favorable tax and regulatory conditions to encourage growth (see, for example, Zysman 1977).

Europe achieved a virtuous cycle for nearly 30 years after the war: It adopted global best practices, and enjoyed growing employment and rapidly rising real wages. Young people trained as apprentices readily found work in their chosen industries. There was investment in clearly needed sectors, and economic returns were adequate. The population was motivated to rebuild the economy and establish a peaceful and prosperous Europe.

Given their successful convergence, the social institutions and policies of continental Europe were well suited to postwar recovery and catch-up. However, the above list of European "advantages" for economic catch-up and postwar growth included warning signs of problems to come when conditions changed.

- Some economic coalitions reformed after the war, increasing rigidity in the economies.

---

16. In principle, this market failure applies only to "firm-specific" skills. Workers can pay firms to provide them with general training. However, in practice, this process is difficult to administer and enforce because high labor turnover discourages both firm-specific and more general training.

- Firms that had been committed to output and productivity increase became more focused on preserving employment as industries matured and output growth slowed.

- The apprenticeship programs faced trouble when new jobs were unavailable for their graduates. These programs created a rather rigid labor market.

- The closed capital market, which was based on close relations between banks and their borrowers, worked less efficiently as incumbent industries contracted and returns to investment declined.

- Innovative new technologies remained undeveloped by large companies with a large stake in existing technologies.

- Close relations between business and government led to overstaffed state-owned or state-supported monopolies or oligopolies.

- Generous unemployment benefits encouraged workers to remain jobless, particularly with the decreasing availability of attractive new jobs.

- Households became less risk averse and looked for higher-return assets outside the traditional banking systems.

The potential for trouble existed, therefore, even during the postwar period of rapid growth and economic success. Once the series of structural shocks hit, the underlying problems or fault lines were revealed.

The 1973–95 Global Growth Slowdown

There was a sharp slowdown in US and European economic growth after 1973. The immediate and obvious cause was the sharp increase in oil prices imposed by OPEC, compounded by a rapid run-up in world commodity prices, especially food prices. These "supply shocks" induced a surge of inflation followed by high interest rates and a sharp decline in global growth. A temporary slowing of productivity growth is naturally associated with a recession and the slowing of output growth, so initially there was little concern about its decline. As time passed, however, it became obvious that the long-run trend of labor productivity growth had slowed sharply in all the major industrial economies. In chapter 3 we explore some of the possible reasons why the productivity growth slowdown occurred in the United States and see what implications it has for Europe. The initial hypothesis blaming energy prices was incorrect. These prices affected the business cycle but cannot explain the shift in the productivity trend. After all, energy prices fell again without any resurgence of productivity growth.

Figure 2.1 Productivity growth pre- and post-1973

percent growth in GDP per hour worked

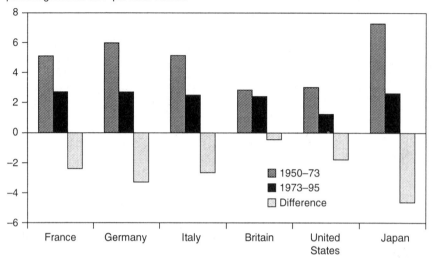

Note: Annual average cumulative growth, GDP per hour, in 1990 Geary-Khamis Multilateral Index dollars.

Source: University of Groningen and the Conference Board (2004).

The reason for the productivity growth slowdown in Europe is easier to understand if one builds on Denison's analysis (1967) of what caused faster growth prior to 1973. Since Europe was taking advantage of its opportunity for economic catch-up, it was inevitable that as its productivity level grew closer to that of the United States, its rate of increase would slow. In 1973, Europe was hit by a double blow. Its opportunity for catch-up was running out just as the pace of productivity increase on the frontier slowed sharply. (Britain was doing much less catching up and so it slowed much less.)

Figure 2.1 shows the sharp decline in productivity growth in the US and European economies as well as in Japan. The magnitude of the slowdown across the board was astounding. These wealthy countries experience a huge shift in economic fortunes and adjustment to the change was difficult in both the short term (with the surge in unemployment and inflation) and the long term. The slowdown in US productivity growth occurred rather abruptly. The growth rate dropped sharply after 1973 and stayed low until 1995. In Europe, there was also an abrupt drop in growth after 1973, but it was followed by further declines in the growth rate. However, the growth of European (and Japanese) labor productivity remained higher than in the United States *until 1996*. (Britain, which had been the productivity laggard of the group, at least kept pace with the rest of Europe and actually grew faster than the United States.)

Figure 2.2 Comparative effect of post-1973 slowdown on productivity growth and labor utilization

annual average change in GDP
per hour worked (percent)

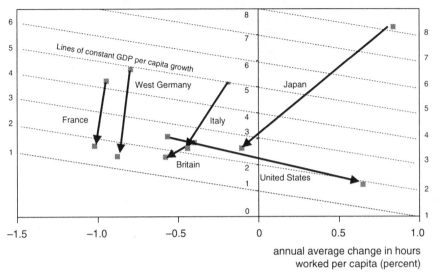

Note: 1950–73 as starting point; 1973–95 as endpoint.

Source: University of Groningen and the Conference Board (2004).

The faster productivity growth in Europe meant that catch-up continued after 1973—and even surpassed the United States. By the mid-1990s GDP per hour worked was actually higher in France and West Germany than in the United States[17]—in 1995, GDP per hour was 110 percent of the US level in France, 103 percent in Germany, and 106 percent in Italy. By contrast, productivity in Britain, at 86 percent, remained well below the US level.[18]

Figure 2.2 combines data on productivity growth (GDP per hour worked) and on labor utilization (hours worked per capita).[19] It compares the 1950 to 1973 period with the 1973 to 1995 period. The starting point of each arrow reflects the average rates of growth or decline of productivity

17. One interpretation is that France and Germany had caught up with and even surpassed the United States in technology and/or business process design, but this interpretation is not likely. Productivity data based on GDP per hour are tricky to interpret, especially when low-skilled workers drop out of the labor force.

18. Data are from the University of Groningen and the Conference Board (2004).

19. Bart van Ark of the University Groningen, Robert McGuckin of the Conference Board, and Dean Parham of the Australian Productivity Commission have all used versions of this figure.

and labor utilization for the 1950–73 period. The endpoint of the arrow does the same for the 1973–95 period. The direction and length of each arrow in the figure illustrate how productivity growth and labor utilization shifted over the two periods. The fact that all the countries experienced slower productivity growth is reflected by all the downward-pointing arrows. The degree of the vertical declines corresponds to the magnitude of the slowdowns shown in figure 2.1.

Looking at the horizontal axis, the arrow for the United States slopes to the right. There was a modest decline in the number of hours worked per capita during 1950–73. By contrast, there was a substantial growth in hours per capita in 1973–95. This was associated with the entry of the baby boom generation into the workforce and also the increasing number of women in the labor force. In contrast, the number of male workers—particularly older men—in the workforce declined slowly over this period. The substantial shift in labor-input growth, comparing the two periods, meant that the growth rate of GDP per capita declined very little in the United States. The figure also shows lines of constant GDP per capita growth, and the US arrow starts just above the 2 percent line pre-1973 and moves just below 2 percent post-1973. Without attributing cause and effect, the United States maintained a fairly stable growth in overall pecuniary living standards over these two periods because falling productivity growth was largely offset by more hours worked.

The pattern for France, West Germany, and Italy is very different. Hours per capita had been declining prior to 1973, especially in France and West Germany, and that decline continued afterward. Combining the declines in productivity growth and labor input means that GDP per capita growth fell very sharply for the core European countries and Japan. GDP per capita growth in France and West Germany dropped to about the same level as the United States post-1973, after having grown much faster prior to that year. The European pattern also holds in Britain, although the changes in growth rates were much smaller. Japan continued to experience faster GDP per capita growth than the United States over the 1973 to 1995 period taken as a whole. However, the Japanese story is more complex than the figure illustrates, since there was strong growth in the 1980s and then virtual stagnation in the 1990s.

The declines in productivity growth meant that real wages that had risen rapidly for over 20 years now either grew very slowly or even declined for segments of the population. It resulted in a surge in inflation followed by a surge in unemployment—stagflation. The US and European macroeconomic literature of the 1970s and 1980s is dominated by the problems of high inflation and high unemployment. The economies adjusted to the slowdowns in different ways given the diverse institutions and policies that were in place in each country. A central element of that adjustment is the extent to which average real wages adjusted and how that affected the trade-off between inflation and unemployment.

Figure 2.3 US wage growth pre- and post-1973, 1959–95
(nonfarm business sector)

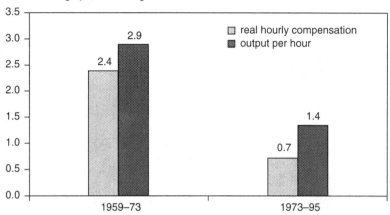

annual average percent change

Source: Bureau of Labor Statistics (2004).

The Impact of Slower Productivity Growth: The US Lesson

When productivity growth slowed after 1973, real-wage growth in the United States also slowed (figure 2.3). In fact real-wage growth slowed even more than the overall decline in productivity growth because it was particularly concentrated in goods and services that workers buy. Indeed, productivity growth in both the service and construction sector of the US economy essentially collapsed after 1973. As a result, consumption-goods prices rose more than the overall price level, hurting real-wage rates.[20]

The impact of the growth slowdown was exacerbated in the post-1973 period by the increases in commodity prices—particularly for food and energy. In the case of oil, a sharp rise in prices imposes a large consumer tax on consumers that shows up as higher profits for energy producers, including OPEC. Workers pay that tax in the reduction in their real consumption wages. Actual declines in real wages, not just slower growth, were evident in the food and energy shock period of the 1970s.[21]

---

20. See Lawrence and Slaughter (1993) and Bosworth and Perry (1994) for further discussion of this point.

21. There may be a cyclical pattern to real wages, but it is not large enough to significantly affect longer-term trends. According to Abraham and Haltiwanger (1995): "To sum up, correcting for all of the measurement problems, estimation problems, and composition problems does not lead to a finding of systematically procyclical or countercyclical real wages." Abraham and Haltiwanger do note, however, that "the cyclicality of real wages is not likely to be stable over time."

Table 2.3 US unemployment and inflation, 1950–95

Year	Average unemployment[a]	Average core inflation[b]
1950–73	4.8	2.8
1974–85	7.5	7.5
1986–95	6.2	6.2

a. Straight average of annual data.
b. Average annual percent change.

Sources: Bureau of Labor Statistics, www.bls.gov/webapps/legacy/
cpsatab9.htm; Bureau of Economic Analysis, chain price index for personal consumption expenditure, excluding food and energy, www.bea.gov/
bea/dn/nipaweb/NIPATableIndex.htm.

Therefore, a key lesson from the US experience is that the slowdown in productivity growth forced a decline in the growth of real wages—in fact, there were periods where average real wages fell. Slow growth or declines in real wages are bad enough in themselves, but their impact on the economy can be magnified if they trigger declines in employment and increases in unemployment, which is what occurred in the United States for an extended period.

Consequence of the productivity growth slowdown on the unemployment-inflation trade-off.[22] There were periods of recession and recovery after 1973, but the average levels of both inflation and unemployment were much higher than in 1950–73 (see table 2.3). We argue this was an adverse side effect of the productivity and real-wage slowdowns.[23]

The mechanism follows: It is a robust result that there is substantial inertia in wage setting, where the rate of nominal wage increase in any given year is largely predetermined by the rates of increase in wages and

22. Econometricians such as Christopher Sims (1999) and James Stock (1998) question whether there is any systematic trade-off relation between inflation and unemployment. They note that in unrestricted regressions, the unemployment rate is a poor predictor of inflation. Many observers have pointed out that outside the United States (Europe specifically), the Phillips curve relationship looks even more unstable. While recognizing the basis for the Sims-Stock viewpoint, it is still helpful to look at both inflation and unemployment together. The fact that unemployment is an unreliable forecasting variable does not invalidate the concept of an unemployment-inflation trade-off. Both inflation and unemployment may be affected strongly by other factors—unemployment is certainly not the *only* factor affecting inflation. Nevertheless, Sims and Stock raise a legitimate question. The rise in unemployment after 1973 may have been affected by structural changes within the labor market, including the rising number of young workers.

23. The idea that the changes in the trend rate of productivity growth can have a major effect on inflation and unemployment has been proposed by Alan Blinder (2000), the Council of Economic Advisers (2000), and Laurence Ball and Robert Moffitt (2001).

prices in the prior couple of years. Since labor costs are such a large fraction of total costs, wage inflation—once it develops—feeds directly into price inflation. The wage-price spiral seems to exist even though it has proven hard to demonstrate the solid economic theory behind it. Therefore, any change in trend productivity growth will immediately affect the wage-price process. Wage inflation in a given period is largely predetermined and so a decrease in productivity growth will raise the rate of increase of unit labor costs. Some part of this may translate into lower profit margins, but some part will also yield higher-price inflation. Higher price inflation then pushes up wage increases in the next cycle.

The productivity deceleration triggered inflation and an upward wage-price spiral because nominal wage increases did not parallel the slowdown of productivity growth.

The rate of change of nominal wages is sticky, but not completely rigid. The rate of nominal wage increase eventually adjusts downward to parallel slower real wage growth. In the United States it appears the adjustment occurred by the 1980s. With the drop in oil prices in 1986, the inflation spiral was reversed, and both unemployment and inflation were at moderate levels during 1986 to 1995.

This idea that a slowdown in productivity growth worsens the inflation-unemployment trade-off is supported by the US experience after 1995. When US productivity growth accelerated after 1995, unemployment fell to 4 percent with only a small increase in inflation.

In summary, the productivity growth slowdown in the United States generated stagflation for many years. Full employment with low inflation was restored only at the cost of a significant decline in real wage growth and even some absolute declines in real wages.[24] In the United States the productivity slowdown did not result in a permanent upward ratchet in the unemployment rate.

The Impact of the Productivity Growth Slowdown on the European Economy

Europe faced a slowdown in productivity growth after 1973 that was equal to or greater than the US slowdown. Unsurprisingly, this slowdown also triggered stagflation. However, unlike the United States, Europe found it much more difficult to fully adjust to slower productivity growth. Instead, after 1973 the problem of "Eurosclerosis" emerged (Giersch 1985), meaning that Europe seemed incapable of growing fast enough to restore full employment. Figure 2.4 shows the evolution of

---

24. The gyrations in oil and food prices also contributed to the episodes of US stagflation in the 1970s and 1980s.

Figure 2.4 End of economic convergence in GDP per capita, select countries, 1950–2003

index: US = 100

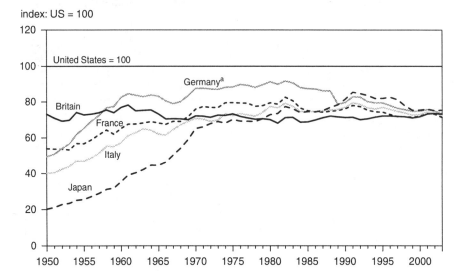

a. 1999 calculated using the Elzeko-Köves-Szule formula: 1950–88 = West Germany and 1989–2002 = reunified Germany.

Source: University of Groningen and the Conference Board (2004).

GDP per capita from 1950 to 2003 for the United States, France, Germany, Britain, Italy, and Japan. The economic convergence, which had been so pronounced in the 1950s and 1960s, continued into the 1970s for Europe and into the 1980s for Japan, but it occurred at a much slower rate than before. Moreover, the convergence process stopped and perceptible divergence began in the 1990s.

The Special Case of Germany

Germany deserves special note because reunification occurred after 1990. West Germany had reached a level of GDP per capita that was approaching the US level by 1970 (it was 88 percent of the US level that year). After that, convergence largely ceased and a mild divergence in per capita income levels emerged in the 1980s. Reunification naturally caused a drop in average per capita income level for Germany as a whole—about 10 percentage points. This pushed the combined German economy in 1989 down to 79 percent of the US level. Following reunification there was a challenge to assimilate the two parts of the country, and an opportunity for faster overall growth as capital and skills were upgraded in the East.

Significant economic resources were transferred from West to East Germany throughout the 1990s (more than €500 billion so far[25]). These resources helped East Germany catch up by improving infrastructure, providing worker training, and offering incentives for private investment. However, income support for unemployed workers also made up a significant portion of the payments to the east. All told, these resources equaled about 4 percent of West German GDP per year—a pace that continues at the same level through to the present time.

In some respects the integration of the East German economy has been a success. Labor productivity in the East has risen from 44 percent of the West German level in 1991 to 73 percent in 2000. GDP per capita has risen from 42 percent of the West German level in 1991 to 65 percent by 2000 (Burda and Hunt 2001, table 3). But the cup is simultaneously half empty and half full. Convergence between East and West Germany occurred rapidly in the early 1990s, fueling rapid growth in GDP per capita in Germany as a whole. But convergence stalled in the second half of the decade. Moreover, the burden of absorbing the East may have adversely affected the *relative* performance of the overall German economy. GDP per capita in all of Germany after 1993 grew more slowly than in the United States, France, and even much slower than Britain from 1993 to 2002.

Germany should have grown at a faster pace than other advanced economies in the 1990s because of the opportunity for the East to catch-up. One of Germany's main economic problems is insufficient job creation, as evidenced by its high unemployment. The unemployment rate in East Germany rose from 10.3 percent in 1991 to 19.0 percent in 1999 and in West Germany from 6.3 percent to 9.9 percent over the same period.[26]

Job Creation

Even though productivity growth in Europe slowed after 1973, it continued to outpace the United States until 1995. The end of the convergence in GDP per capita came from a relative decline in hours worked per capita. Figure 2.5 shows the evolution of hours worked per capita over the

---

25. In January 2004 the German Bundesrat endorsed the so-called Solidarpakt II as part of the German government's *Aufbau Ost* (Eastern Construction) program. An additional €156.5 billion will be available for reconstruction from 2005–19. See German Government, Solidarpakt wird nach 2004 weitergeführt, press release, January 21, 2004, www.bundesregierung.de/Themen-A-Z/Aufbau-Ost/Nachrichten-,611.46679/artikel/Solidarpakt-wird-nach-2004-wei.htm.

26. Germany uses a more comprehensive definition of unemployment than the United States. Adjusted to the US concept of unemployment, the overall rate for all of Germany in 1999 was 8.65 percent, according to the Bureau of Labor Statistics, whereas the German data (*Arbeitsamt*) for all of Germany was 11.7 percent. The OECD Standard Labor Force Indicators 1999 showed unemployment in all of Germany at 8.4 percent.

Figure 2.5   Total hours worked per capita,[a] select countries, 1973–2003

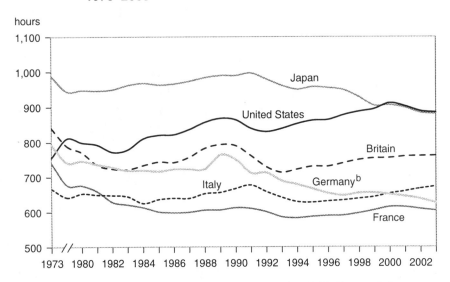

hours

a. Employment times average annual hours worked per worker divided by population.
b. 1973–88 = West Germany and 1989–2003 = reunified Germany.

Source: University of Groningen and the Conference Board (2004).

period. The figure shows that Germany, France, Britain, and the United States all had similar *levels* of labor input per capita in 1973, but there was a substantial decline over the next 25 years in the European economies while the United States had an increase. The sharp drop between 1973 and 1979 occurred as part of the cyclical slump and partial recovery of the mid-1970s.[27] For Germany the data are for West Germany until 1988 and for all of Germany thereafter. France has the lowest level of labor input per capita among this group of countries, but the trend shifted after 1993 when a gradual increase in hours worked took place. Britain experienced a less dramatic overall decline and even had a gradual increase in labor input in the 1990s. Italian employment data are somewhat unreliable because of unreported employment, but the official data show a very low level of labor input in 1973, though not much of a decline in trend after that. Japan is included only for comparison purposes. It has traditionally worked very long hours and had a higher labor input per capita than the United States. In the 1990s, however, Japan's economic problems are associated with a drop in labor input, to the point where the level was about equal to the US level in 2000.

Figure 2.6 illustrates the average employment growth of four economies in the government (public) sector and the business (private) sector during

---

27. Note that the data in figure 2.5 jump from 1973 to 1979 but are annual thereafter.

Figure 2.6 Public- and private-sector average employment growth, select countries, 1992–2001

Public-sector employment growth (percent)

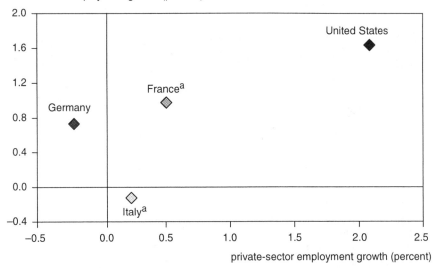

a. Data for Italy and France = 1992–99.

Note: Public sector defined as ISIC categories 75 (public administration and defense), 80 (education), and 85 (health and social work). Private sector defined as the remaining economies.

Source: OECD STAN Database (2003j).

1992 to 2001, as compiled by the OECD. The figure shows that France, Germany, and Italy all experienced either very slow growth or a decline in private-sector employment. France and Germany enjoyed their most robust employment growth in the public sector. Although public-sector employment is important, it is ultimately financed by economic activity generated in the private sector. Therefore, building a base of productive jobs in the private sector is an essential part of any successful economic growth strategy. In Europe, *the large employment losses of the 1970s and early 1980s have never been regained, particularly those in the private sector.*

As employment rates declined in Europe, unemployment rates naturally rose. Whereas unemployment rates of 2 percent or below were common in the 1960s in Europe, rates of 8 to 10 percent became the norm by the 1990s. The inflationary surges of the 1970s were overcome in Europe, just as in the United States, but the unemployment rates stayed high instead of coming back down. The traditional trade-off between unemployment and inflation seemed to shift permanently. As a statistical relationship, this (Phillips curve) trade-off for European economies became unstable to the point of nonexistence.

Reasons for the Failure to Adjust to the Slowdown

There are four possible reasons why the employment losses of the 1970s and 1980s were never regained in Europe, most notably in France and Germany. First, real wages are institutionally set and their growth rate kept high, which forces an adjustment of employment. Second, high levels of transfer payments (unemployment insurance, welfare, early retirement provisions, disability payments, etc.) discouraged labor supply and encouraged workers to remain unemployed or out of the labor force. The fact that such benefits can be collected for long periods, even indefinitely, is thought to be as important as the generosity of the payments. Third, restrictions in product markets discouraged the development of new lines of business and thus competition. Fourth, Europeans voluntarily decided they were willing to accept lower incomes in exchange for fewer hours of work.[28]

The first three reasons why employment losses have not been regained are clearly significant since they determine the incentive to work and/or access to employment in each country. The three are also interrelated: Generous transfer payments to the unemployed will discourage the supply of labor. The taxes that are levied to pay for these transfers will lower the after-tax wage of workers, which will also discourage the supply of labor (for a given level of transfer benefits). If legal or institutionally set wages are too high (above a market equilibrium), this will discourage the demand for labor. If product-market restrictions are stifling change in the economy, this will lower productivity and the demand for labor, reducing employment directly if wages are fixed. If wages are flexible, the product-market restrictions will keep wage increases down and this will discourage the supply of labor (for a given level of transfer benefit levels).

The fourth reason for continued employment losses—the preference for leisure—is hard to resolve, and we postpone a discussion of it until later in the chapter. Instead we pursue the other three hypotheses, which gave rise in the 1980s to the "wage-gap" model of high European unemployment or nonemployment.

The Wage-Gap Hypothesis

The 1980s literature on Eurosclerosis focused on the idea that rising real wages and slowing productivity had created a real wage gap in Europe,

---

28. In this discussion, we have moved back and forth between total labor input (number of jobs times hours worked per employee) and total employment. The two diverged significantly in Europe because of a substantial decline in the number of hours worked per employee. Both measures of labor input are important for different purposes. Later in this chapter, there will be a discussion of the issues that arise when labor input is reduced by decreasing hours of work rather than cutting jobs.

Figure 2.7　Real-wage compensation pre- and post-1973, select countries

real hourly compensation (percent)

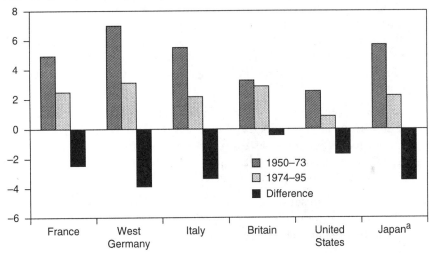

a. 1955–73.

Source: Bureau of Labor Statistics (2002, table 13).

pushing the level of wages above the level of productivity and creating structural unemployment.

Figure 2.7 shows the slowdown in real-wage growth in the sample countries after 1973. When compared to the data for the same countries in figure 2.1, it is apparent that *the slowdown in productivity growth was matched by an equal slowdown in real-wage growth.* So it looks, on the face of it, as if the wage-gap hypothesis is incorrect. Europe's institutional rigidities did not prevent real wage growth from adjusting downward by about the same amount as (or more than) the decline in labor productivity growth.[29]

As Schultze (1987) has pointed out, however, this comparison is misleading to the point where it reveals little. There is a two-way interaction between productivity and real wages.

■　Innovations that improve the technologies and business processes used in an economy[30] can also increase worker productivity and the

---

29. The wage rates shown are hourly earnings for workers in the manufacturing sector only since these can be compared across countries more reliably than broader wage measures. The price deflators used to construct the real wages are consumer price indexes, which have idiosyncrasies over time and across country. Nevertheless, the broad conclusion should be robust.

30. Innovation and business process improvement generally also involve capital investment.

demand for labor. This will increase real wages, employment, or some combination of the two. During the 1950s and 1960s both Europe and the United States benefited from this favorable dynamic.

- Real wages may be increased at a faster rate than can be accommodated by the speed of innovation and business process improvement as a result of policy interventions or because of institutional forces. In this case, companies will reduce employment causing a rise in unemployment and a reduction in hours worked relative to the size of the population.[31]

- As a result of the response of employers to rising real wages, it is likely that average labor productivity will rise at about the same pace as the rate of real wage increase, even when wages are elevated by institutional forces. Employers will adjust their employment so that productivity stays in line with real wages.[32]

- In an effort to preserve jobs, many European economies enacted layoff restrictions or penalties. This may slow job loss, but it will not halt it nor will it encourage new job creation.

- Policies and institutions can keep wage rates above the levels consistent with full employment in two ways. They can implement explicit wage-setting processes, such as high legal-wage minimums or union-set wages. Alternatively, generous income support can discourage the nonemployed from accepting low-wage jobs. Both of these forces can be at work simultaneously.

So the key question becomes whether the growth rate of real wages in Europe slowed *by enough to preserve full employment*. Unquestionably, it did not. Labor productivity in France and Germany in the 1980s and 1990s became too high relative to the level that would exist in a full-employment equilibrium. The employment growth rate exceeded productivity growth— the rate justified by the pace of innovation and capital accumulation.

How Productivity Adjusts to Higher Real Wages

The preceding discussion is based on the idea that if wages rise because of an institutional push or a decline in labor supply, then labor productivity will also be pushed up. How does this happen in practice? Standard

---

31. In practice, excess real-wage growth may not cause an absolute decline in employment, rather it may result in a slowing of employment growth relative to labor growth.

32. Firms will hire to the point where the marginal product of labor equals the real wage. In the simple case of a Cobb-Douglas production function, average and marginal labor productivity are proportional and will grow together.

Box 2.1 The timing of European welfare states

We argue throughout this book that social welfare and labor-market institutions can significantly affect national employment and productivity levels. Indeed, these institutions and policies are partly responsible for the poor employment and economic performance in the large continental European countries in recent years. Yet these same countries experienced extraordinarily strong economic performance in the period leading up to 1973. Our theory so far has been that as long as rapid catch-up was fueling economic and wage growth, the social policies were not a major constraint. They only became a problem after growth slowed in the 1970s. There is another aspect to this issue, however, which is the question of when the European welfare state was actually created. If Europe's welfare state is of more recent origin—implemented as a response to the economic and social effects of the first oil price shock in the years after 1973—the perspective changes.

Serious data problems immediately arise when an attempt is made to compare the level of and track the changes in social institutions among countries and through time dimensions since 1945. Valid cross-country comparisons of highly complex institutions are notoriously difficult and very few analyses have time-series dating back to 1945. Nonetheless, data for several important social institutions analyzed elsewhere in this book exist, and are summarized in the table below.

Social welfare and labor-market institutions, 1960–2000

	France	Germany	Italy	Sweden	United States
Government social expenditure (percent of GDP)					
1980	21.1	20.3	18.4	29.0	13.1
1998	28.8	26.0	25.1	31.0	14.6
Employment benefit replacement ratios (refers to first year of an unemployment spell averaged over three family types)					
1960–64	0.48	0.43	0.09	0.11	0.22
1973–79	0.56	0.39	0.04	0.57	0.28
1999	0.59	0.37	0.26[b]	0.74	0.29
Employment benefit duration (index 0–1, as described in source)					
1960–64	0.28	0.57	0.00	0.00	0.12
1973–79	0.19	0.61	0.00	0.04	0.19
1999	0.47	0.75	0.013[b]	0.02	0.22
Employment protection (index 0–2, as described in source)					
1960–64	0.37	0.45	1.92	0.00	0.10
1973–79	1.21	1.65	2.00	1.46	0.10
1998	1.40	1.30	1.50	1.10	0.10
Total taxes on labor (payroll tax, plus income tax plus consumption tax rate, percent)					
1960–64	55	43	57	41	34
1973–79	60	48	54	68	42
1996–2000	68	50	64	77	45
Enrollment in disability programs (20–64 years of age, stock per 1,000 population)					
1980	39.7	38.0	126.9	61.6	31.2
1999	46.8	42.4	54.9	82.1	46.8

(box continues on next page)

Box 2.1   The timing of European welfare states *(continued)*

Average retirement age (years, dynamic estimates)

Men					
1960–65	63.9[a]	65.0[e]	62.8[e]	67.7[d]	67.5
1973–78	61.8	61.7	62.5	64.2	64.2
1994–99	59.3	60.5[c]	59.3	63.3	65.1
Women					
1960–65	64.6[a]	61.9[e]	58.5[e]	63.3[d]	66.5
1973–78	63.2	60.4	63.8	64.0	65.3
1994–99	59.8	60.8[c]	58.4	61.8	64.2

a. 1962–67.
b. 1988–95.
c. 1993–98.
d. Static estimate.
e. Static estimate 1965–70.

Sources: Government social expenditure: OECD Social Expenditure database tracks government social expenditures in detail from 1980 to 1998; employment benefit replacement ratios: Nickell, Nunziata, and Ochel (2002) and Nickell (2003) track this variable from 1960 to 1999; employment benefit durations: Nickell, Nunziata, and Ochel (2002) and Nickell (2003) track this variable from 1960 to 1999; employment protection legislation; Nickell, Nunziata, and Ochel (2002) and Nickell (2003) track this variable using data from Blanchard and Wolfers (2000) from 1960 to 1998; total taxes on labor: Nickell, Nunziata, and Ochel (2002) and Nickell (2003) track this variable from 1960 to 2000; enrollment in disability programs: OECD (2002c) tracks this variable from 1980 to 1999; average retirement age: Scherer (2001) tracks this variable from 1960 to 1999.

The three main continental European economies of France, Germany, and Italy are included in the table. Sweden and the United States are also included to represent "two extremes" of a welfare state.

It is evident that social welfare payments were in place in France and Germany prior to 1973, although the programs became more generous over time. Italy had very limited unemployment benefits in the 1960s and 1970s, although this was then somewhat mitigated by the so-called "social shock absorbers."[1] Somewhat the reverse holds for employment protection provisions. Italy had very restrictive legislation throughout the covered time period, while France and Germany introduced significantly tighter regulation after 1973.

We find that there were already fairly generous welfare provisions in Europe prior to 1973, but these general provisions did not affect productivity growth until the years following a slowdown. Unemployment benefits in European countries did exist prior to 1973 but became more generous, particularly in Italy, over time. Labor protections/restrictions tightened significantly after 1973.

---

1. The most commonly used "social shock absorber" (*ammortizzatori sociali*) instrument is the Wages Guarantee Funds. Two exist: the Ordinary Fund, which was introduced in 1945, is used during temporary cyclical downturns; the Extraordinary Fund, which was created in 1968, is provided for particular firms or sectors undertaking restructuring. Both funds, on a case-by-case basis, pay a benefit to workers equal to 80 percent of the normal wage for a maximum of three consecutive months.

economics illustrates how an economy's output depends on capital input, labor input, and technology (the concept of the aggregate production function). This assumes companies choose to produce a given level of output using either a large labor force and a low level of capital or vice versa (or anywhere in between). Labor and capital can be substituted for each other and companies decide the trade-off in order to minimize production costs. This decision is often determined by the relative price of labor and capital. Holding technology constant (with a given production function), companies will reduce their labor and increase capital as the real wage increases relative to the cost of capital. This framework predicts that if real wages are pushed up for institutional reasons, this will increase average labor productivity through capital-labor substitution. Basically, higher wages lead to increased automation, which raises labor productivity at the expense of employment.

Capital-labor substitution seems to have occurred in Europe, where the ratio of capital to hours worked has been pushed up (O'Mahony and de Boer 2002). The capital market structure in Europe, particularly in Germany,[33] may have encouraged this substitution. We noted earlier that high levels of household savings were a positive contributor to Europe's successful postwar growth. Banks channeled these funds into low-cost loans to the business sector, which worked well as long as opportunity existed for output expansion. But the impact of that same capital market structure is less favorable for the economy when companies use low-cost capital to reduce their employment of artificially expensive labor.

There are several other ways in which wages can affect employment outcomes and influence productivity. For instance, there are a significant number of US jobs that are less common or even nonexistent in Europe. The retail sector in the United States, for example, employs far more workers than it does in Europe, relative to population or even GDP. The availability of low-wage labor in the United States makes it economic to keep stores open long hours and to provide additional customer service. In the United States, 8 percent of retail employees earn wage rates below the French minimum wage (McKinsey Global Institute 2002b). As wages rise, these low-productivity jobs disappear because employers no longer earn a profit (retailers that provide extra services would have to recover the costs through higher prices). After eliminating the low-productivity activities from the economy, the average productivity of the remaining em-

---

33. Broadbent, Schumacher, and Schels (2004) point out how the German banking sector, dominated by state-owned institutions (Sparkassen and Landesbanken), often has not had strictly commercial lending priorities. Aimed at encouraging investment in their local areas, and with close, if informal, relationships with local politicians serving on their boards, such German financial institutions issued very low cost state-guaranteed debt to companies, possibly aggravating the economy-level capital-labor substitution. As demanded by the European Commission, government guarantees of the debt from such financial institutions in Germany must end in 2005.

ployed workers is then higher. This scenario is familiar enough as part of the normal process of economic development, but the troubling issue for Europe is that wages have risen enough to eliminate classes of employment even as large numbers of workers remain unemployed.

There are also ways of varying the capital labor ratio apart from differences in the degree of automation. The hours that retail stores or offices operate or the number of shifts in a manufacturing plant determines the capital utilization of that facility. If wage rates or shift premiums or labor regulations make it uneconomic or impossible to increase the hours of use of a capital facility, then that will effectively increase the ratio of the capital stock to labor hours. In the case of retailing, concentrating the shopping hours to narrow periods of the day or the week increases measured productivity—salespeople spend less time with no customers to wait on. This productivity increase occurs at the expense of customer convenience, since people cannot choose to shop during evenings and weekends. In the case of a manufacturing facility, the impact of the number of shifts on labor productivity will be small, although the number of hours of operation of plants will increase the amount of capital needed to produce a given level of output (measured MFP will be reduced).

Finally, and perhaps most importantly, high-wage minimums or high transfer payments will reduce the number of low-skilled people in the workforce. If we think of productivity as a property of individuals rather than of jobs, then eliminating all the low-productivity workers from employment will raise the average productivity of those remaining.

For the economy as a whole, therefore, there is a clear link between real wage increases, employment reductions, and productivity increases, when wages are pushed up.

Cyclical and Structural Sources of Low Employment

There is a long-standing debate in economics about whether high unemployment should be seen as a result of structural problems in the labor market or as a result of weak aggregate demand. The "classical" model asserts that unemployment results from "excessive" wages that price workers out of jobs, just as a company that sets too high prices for its product will be priced out of its market. By contrast, we, like most modern macroeconomists, take the view that cyclical episodes of high unemployment are associated with swings in the overall demand for goods and services in the economy. Following a triggering event, demand falls as cautious consumers cut back on their spending and businesses cut back on investment. Companies lay off workers even though real wage rates have not increased significantly. There is a negative cycle that results in a downturn, or, in the extreme case, a depression. Similarly, cyclical recoveries generate increases in employment even though wage rates have not fallen. Demand management policies—notably monetary and fiscal—are needed to help the economy recover from a period of cyclical downturn.

The views expressed in this chapter about high unemployment and low employment levels in Europe are drawn from the classical tradition. The insufficient slowdown of real wage growth following the decline in productivity growth priced workers out of jobs (or high transfer payments have discouraged them from accepting jobs at low wages—a variant on the classical theme). How can this apparent inconsistency be resolved?

The answer depends on the time period involved. Employment fluctuates over the business cycle as a result of changes in aggregate demand. But in Europe these fluctuations have centered around a persistent trend of higher unemployment and fewer hours worked. Therefore, we focus on this persistent behavior in this analysis. The rise in structural unemployment is closely related to wages that are too high and work incentives that are too weak.

That is an oversimplification, however. There are important links between structural and cyclical unemployment. The rise in cyclical unemployment in the 1970s and 1980s, caused by insufficient aggregate demand, played a crucial role in initiating Europe's chronic high unemployment. As noted earlier, there may be a ratchet effect if workers who lose jobs in a cyclical downturn remain unemployed or leave the labor force even after the cyclical downturn is over. These unemployed workers become "outsiders" with eroding job skills who live on unemployment benefits. Hence, the existence of high unemployment no longer has any restraining effect on wage increases.

In this view, macroeconomic policymakers in Europe may bear some blame for Eurosclerosis. These policymakers could also help solve the problem by using expansionary policies, such as lower interest rates.

All the developed economies raised interest rates during the massive surges of inflation in the 1970s and early 1980s, so it is hard to blame European central banks or fiscal authorities for the early problems of stagflation. Afterward, however, an exaggerated fear of inflation, particularly by the Bundesbank, prevented more expansionary policies from being adopted once the inflation scourge was broken. Better macropolicy would have eased Europe's unemployment problems in the 1980s and might have left the region better off today.

That said, it is hard to make the case that macroeconomic policy alone could resolve the European employment problem. Such policies are not the only or even the most important reason for the persistence of low and declining employment levels in Europe over a 30-year period. Fluctuations in aggregate demand are the driving force behind short-term economic changes in the economy, but not of longer-term trends. In fact, individual economies made efforts to follow more expansionary policies, but their efforts were thwarted by rising inflation—a sign of problems on the supply side.

Regardless of the way in which the problem of low employment developed, it is imperative going forward that macroeconomic policy not be a barrier to economic recovery. Labor- and product-market reforms will be easier to undertake and more effective if the right macroeconomic policies are in effect. Chapter 6 addresses that issue directly.

Skill Differences and the Distribution of Wages

Another structural shock hit the advanced economies in the 1980s—one that intensified the negative impact of the productivity growth decline on employment among low-skilled workers in Europe.

The distribution of wages widened substantially in the US economy in the 1980s and 1990s. As figure 2.8 shows, the wage distribution in the US economy was fairly similar to that of France and Germany in 1973, but the gap widened rapidly among the countries over the next 27 years. The difference between the United States and the European countries is marked. There is some indication that the distribution of wages stopped widening in the United States in the late 1990s, but even so the wage gap between the first and ninth deciles remained much wider than before. The wage gap in France has narrowed pretty steadily while in Germany the gap fluctuated through the late 1980s and has remained rather steady since then. In Britain, the wage distribution narrowed through the late 1970s, but then started to widen, as in the United States. In 2000, however, it remains much closer to the European than to the US pattern.[34]

To a degree the differences in wage distribution may reflect differences in the distribution of worker skills within the countries. The US education system is very good at training academically gifted young people for college. Large numbers then go on to obtain two-year and four-year college degrees. However, the US system does not adequately help young people who are less academically oriented acquire skills that will allow them to earn good wages.

Europe, by contrast, has more active labor-market policies. The philosophy is to try to bring even relatively low-skilled workers up to the capability level where they can earn a good wage. The system of institutionally set wage rates is combined with job training programs intended to validate the relatively narrow distribution of wages. This is an admirable goal and the United States could well emulate some of these policies. In general, it makes sense to use active labor-market policies to increase the skill level of the workforce and to do so in a way that helps low-skilled workers improve their relative position as long as it is cost-effective.

It does not make sense to mandate a given wage distribution and then hope that the workforce can acquire the skills to validate this distribution.

---

34. Data are incomplete for Britain and Italy.

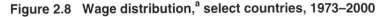

Figure 2.8 Wage distribution,[a] select countries, 1973–2000

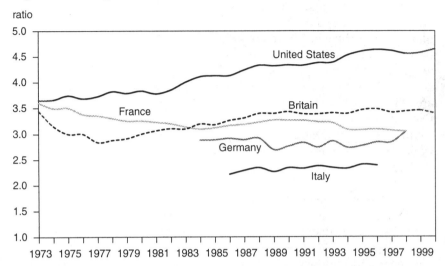

a. Ratio of the cut-off point in the first and ninth decile gross earnings for both men and women.

Source: OECD Labor Market Statistics (2003h).

Even with the best of intentions and even with expensive training programs, it may not be possible to maintain a narrow distribution of (before-tax) wages in the face of technological advances and globalization affecting Europe and the United States. The attempt to do so may make it very difficult for low-skilled workers to acquire jobs at all.

The reason for the pattern of rising inequality in the United States has been the subject of a large body of research, and the predominant view is that changes in technology have been at work.[35] There has been "skill-biased technological change" that has reduced the relative demand for low-skilled workers. The simple basis for this belief is that the relative wages of highly skilled or educated workers have risen even as the supply of such workers has increased rapidly. The relative wage shift must therefore be driven by shifts in the relative demands for low- and high-skilled workers. In particular, it is often argued that the growth of information technology has increased the value of conceptual skills in the marketplace, thereby raising the returns to skills and education. The hypothesis of skill-biased technological change has become conventional wisdom among US economists.

Skill-biased technology change is probably not the only explanation for the widening gap in wage distribution. This is something of a paradox be-

---

35. See, for instance, Haskel and Slaughter (1998); Autor, Katz, and Krueger (1997); and Berman, Bound, and Griliches (1994).

cause the 1980–95 period is supposedly one when there was substantial skill-biased technological change but little productivity growth. Harvard and IIE economist Robert Lawrence even remarked upon it: "So much bias, so little change." To reinforce the puzzle, from 1995–2000 both the pace of technological change and the adoption of IT increased, while the wage distribution stopped widening.

So while technology undoubtedly has been an important factor, there are other possible explanations for the widening gap in wage distribution. Expanding international trade may also have caused it. Under certain conditions, open international trade will push down the wages of unskilled workers in developed economies who compete with low-wage unskilled workers in developing countries. This nightmare scenario drives US and European workers' opposition to international trade.

We do not want to overemphasize this explanation. In practice the overwhelming proportion of employment in the United States and in Europe is not in industries that compete directly with low-wage workers overseas (employment in manufacturing represents only 14 percent of total US employment and only about half of manufacturing trade is with countries where wage rates are much lower). But it is likely that trade has played a role in reducing the relative demand for low-skilled workers. The production of labor-intensive products like toys and apparel has largely moved to low-wage countries such as China. Labor-intensive parts of the value chain—such as the assembly of wiring harnesses for autos—have also disappeared from developed countries. The loss of these jobs has not affected a large enough share of the overall economy to be the main determinant of low-skilled wages in developed economies, but it has made an impact.

Another important development in US wage distribution has been a change in the wage-setting environment. Wage rates in the United States are now influenced much more by market forces and less by institutional factors than was the case 20 or 30 years ago. Essentially, the United States has become less European. One obvious sign of this is the decline of unions. Unions represented 25 percent of the nonfarm workforce in 1973, and declined to only 9 percent by 2001. Even in the nonunion sector, wages were often set bureaucratically and in relation to colleagues with comparable jobs rather than on the basis of supply and demand. As competitive pressure increased throughout the economy in the 1980s and 1990s, companies looked for ways to cut costs and offered workers only what they had to pay to attract adequately qualified people. Business services such as payroll, security, and cleaning were often outsourced to companies that paid lower wages than had been paid to in-house staff. The threat to move activities offshore has been one lever US companies have used to change the institutional wage setting.[36] The increased ac-

---

36. This is now happening in Germany. Siemens used the threat of moving jobs to Hungary to force IG Metall to agree to increase the work week from 35 to 40 hours with no increase in pay.

ceptability of hiring nonunion replacement workers is another factor. President Ronald Reagan initiated this trend in the 1980s when he fired and then replaced the unionized air traffic controllers.

What are the implications for Europe? Presumably the same forces of technological change that affected the United States are influencing Europe as well, and the process of globalization is restructuring the global value chain. There has been greater protection against low-wage imports in Europe than in the United States, but the same forces of international competition are at work on that economy.[37] The low-skilled manufacturing jobs that have not already left Western Europe are leaving now as more low-wage labor becomes available in Eastern Europe.

In contrast to the United States, in Europe institutional wage setting remains the norm.[38] Also, although Europe's union membership has declined substantially just as in the United States, their power has not declined in the same way. Indeed unions negotiate wage rates that apply throughout the industry to union members and nonmembers alike. In France and West Germany 94 percent of workers were covered by collective bargaining in 1994–95, 82 percent in Italy in 1993, and 47 percent in Britain in 1994.[39] Public-sector employment is also more important in Europe than in the United States, and its wages are not determined purely by market forces.

The sectoral perspective on this issue is very important. The forces of international competition in manufacturing have been strong enough to force a great deal of restructuring in this sector in Europe. In most European economies (although not in Germany) the manufacturing employment share has declined about as much as in the United States, releasing many low-skilled workers. The problem for overall job creation is that this has not been accompanied by a rise in employment in Europe's service sector.

How much wage inequality must Europe accept if it is to maintain something close to full employment? We do not know the answer to that question, but clearly the distribution of *before-tax* wages must be wide enough that firms can attract high-skilled workers that can access jobs in the regional or even the global labor market. At the same time firms must be able to pay low enough wage rates to low-skilled workers and still earn a profit after hiring them.

In Europe the principle is still widely accepted that those who work full-time should be able to support themselves and their family on the income received from their job. The idea has a powerful emotional appeal,

---

37. See OECD (2000a) for a discussion of this issue.

38. See Nickell (1996) for a discussion of this issue.

39. Data from the OECD Labor Force Statistics (2003h). The OECD reports these percentages as workers covered by agreements as a percent of all workers in the economy. This same data source reports that 18 percent of US workers were covered by collective bargaining in 1994.

but it can create serious employment problems and is not the best way to sustain the living standards of the working poor. Rather than mandating the wages that employers must pay, it is better to implement redistributive policies to change *after-tax* family incomes. A high level of inequality of before-tax wages is compatible with a lower level of inequality in after-tax wages. *Therefore, reducing inequality in the distribution of before-tax wages should not be an important goal of economic policy in itself.*

This may oversimplify the difficulties of maintaining economic efficiency while improving the income distribution. Even the best-designed policies will end up having work-incentive effects. Regional and global competition will limit the ability of any single economy to levy high taxes on high-income individuals. In practice, there are limits to how effective redistribution can be before incentives are undermined.

That issue is taken up below, but the key message of this section is important. Europe faces the same economic trends that drove rising wage inequality in the United States as well as slower real wage growth. It has resisted the wage effects of these economic forces, but has not overcome the resulting employment effects. Institutional forces and/or policies can often control either price or quantity, but have difficulty controlling both. The goal of policy should be to reduce poverty and mitigate economic uncertainty, not to set wages or mandate a particular distribution of wages.

Taxes, Transfers, and the Willingness to Work

At several points in the above discussion we referred to institutionally set wages. We also talked about how the generous level of transfer payments to the unemployed kept low-wage jobs from being filled. These two issues are related. If there were no transfer payments made to the jobless, then they would be forced to engage in some economic activity, whether formal or informal. European economies have softened the effect of slower productivity growth and shifting demand for worker skills on wage rates. In practice, this could not have happened without substantial transfers to the nonemployed since either a political or an economic breakdown would have occurred.

Europe developed a social compact. The workforce accepts that high taxes are needed to finance the income transfers to the unemployed and retired. This social compact has functioned well enough over the past 30 years. Indeed, many Europeans strongly prefer this system to the more market-oriented US system with its greater inequality. However, this European system may not be sustainable. The system's feasibility will be explored in more detail later in this chapter, but at this point we simply want to emphasize its influence.

The European system creates a large tax wedge imposed on workers to support those that do not work. As the proportion of the population not

**Figure 2.9 Tax wedge and direct wage cost, select countries,
2003** (percent of total gross labor costs)

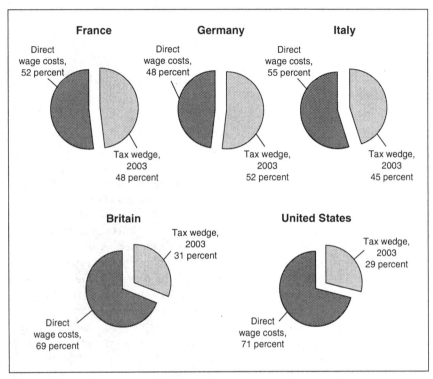

Note: Average total tax wedge includes employees' and employers' social security contributions and personal income tax minus transfer payments as percentage of gross labor costs (gross wage earnings plus employers' social security contributions). This assumes a single worker without dependents makes 100 percent of average production worker wages.

Source: OECD (2004b).

working becomes larger this further discourages employment. Also, the employer's cost of hiring a worker starts to greatly exceed the after-tax wage received by the worker. Figure 2.9 shows the tax wedges for France, Germany, Italy, Britain, and the United States in 2003. The wedge is quite substantial for all of the countries—29 percent even in the United States—but it is significantly higher in Europe at *around 50 percent in France, Germany, and Italy.* The tax wedge means that for each euro a worker earns, the employer must pay substantially more than a euro in wage costs. Table 2.4 shows the implications of these tax wedges, showing the employer cost for different levels of after-tax wage rates actually received by the employee. The numbers are quite startling. In order for workers to receive €7.50 an hour in France, Germany, or Italy, the employer would have to pay about €14 an hour.

Table 2.4   Employer wage cost for alternative hourly after-tax wage rates (euros)

Country	€5	€7.50	€10
France	9.62	14.42	19.23
Germany	10.42	15.63	20.83
Italy	9.09	13.64	18.18
Britain	7.24	10.86	14.49
United States	7.04	10.56	14.08

Source: OECD (2004b); authors' calculations.

The difference in size of the tax wedge between the United States and Britain, on the one hand, and continental Europe, on the other, is large (despite declining in recent years in Italy). But there is also a significant difference between the two regions because wage rates are set institutionally to a much greater extent in Europe. When wages are set in the market, a simple supply and demand analysis shows that any given tax wedge will be borne by both the employee (in the form of a lower after-tax wage) and by the employer (in the form of a higher before-tax wage).[40] In practice, much of the tax wedge will be borne by the employees and not the employer. In the case of market-determined wages, the tax wedge may discourage employment, but it will be driven by those dropping out of the workforce, discouraged by the insufficient incomes they receive. In the case of institutionally set wage rates, such as the legal minimum wage, any payroll taxes incurred by the employee will boost the effective minimum wage paid by the employer. It will lower employment by discouraging hiring by employers.

Low-wage rates, long hours, minimal paid vacations, and the absence of health insurance are not uncommon in the United States. These are hardly attractive features of the US labor market.[41] Europeans would not work at a minimum-wage job with neither paid vacations nor healthcare coverage. Therefore, it is not surprising that policymakers reject efforts to take away the relatively more attractive features of employment in Europe.

It is important, however, for European countries to face the consequences of the policy choices they have made. If the European Union seriously wants to increase employment by over 20 million by 2010, it must provide the right incentives to achieve this goal. The current European labor-market and social-insurance policies raise employers' cost while raising the returns

---

40. Many people believe that payroll taxes are paid entirely by employers because they write the check to the government, but that is not the case. When wages are market determined, the shares paid by the two sides depend on the elasticities of labor demand and supply.

41. The United States has its own nonemployment issues. The proportion of nonelderly adults receiving some form of disability assistance rose to around 4.5 percent of the population in 2000 (Katz 2002), and the number of persons incarcerated in the United States has risen to over 2 million.

from nonemployment, which reduces employment. The difficult task is to find alternative ways to sustain the living standards of low-skilled workers that are more consistent with maintaining the level of employment.

Europeans may have inherently different tastes for work and income than Americans. There is no right or wrong viewpoint. But, as noted in Chapter 1, the choices about leisure that have developed in Europe have occurred in an environment where work incentives have been altered substantially by the policy environment and are not optimal for the society as a whole. The short workweek and long weeks of vacation in Europe are well known. These "benefits" are generally negotiated and individuals are not given a choice. Declines in the workweek have been mandated as a measure to increase employment. It is also falsely presented to workers as a free ride without a loss of wage income. Democratic societies choose the leaders that make the policies, but few voters understand the full implications of the policies they support or oppose.

Demographic Changes: Extended Life Expectancy and Changes in Cohort Size

The previous section argued that the tax wedge between what employers pay and what workers receive is very high in Europe. One reason for this difference is the demographic changes taking place: life expectancy and the age of retirement have both shifted over time. Going forward, the demographic issue will become even more important as life expectancy continues to rise and the number of persons approaching retirement age increases. In addition, healthcare costs, which apply very disproportionately to the elderly, are rising rapidly. Therefore, standing still is not an option.

The demographic changes taking place in all the advanced economies will increase the burden of supporting the nonworking population, unless policy or other changes occur. First, life expectancy has increased and, for a given age of retirement, people are living longer in the retirement phase of their lives. Second, the age of retirement has declined, so people are retiring earlier than they used to. Third, the aging of the baby boom generation and the decline in fertility rates after that generation mean that the size of the cohort of retirees is increasing as a proportion of the population. Fourth, the cost of health care for the elderly is growing rapidly.

Life Expectancy

In 1970, the life expectancy in West Germany at age 65 was 12.0 years for males and 15.0 years for females. By 1999 these figures had increased to 15.5 years for males and 19.2 years for females. For a German 65-year-old male, the expected duration of remaining life rose by a factor of 1.29 over

Figure 2.10 Rising life expectancy after age 65, 1970 and 1999

years of life expectancy

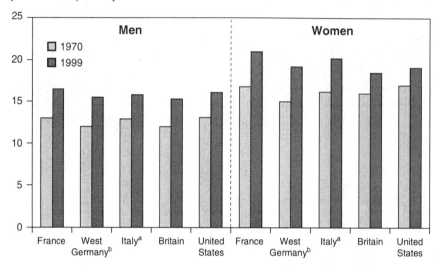

a. 1975 and 1997.
b. Data for West Germany are only for 1970.
Note: Average number of years in which a person at 65 years of age is expected to live under the mortality pattern prevalent in the country. Based on a given set of age-specific death rates in life tables.
Source: OECD Health Data (2002e).

this period—a substantial increase. The proportional increase in life expectancy for German females is about the same. Figure 2.10 shows the data and comparable figures for France, Italy Britain, and the United States. All of the countries show large increases in life expectancy at age 65. There are a variety of reasons for increased longevity, including improved nutrition and, significantly, improvements in health care. For example, there have been rapid declines in deaths from stroke and heart disease in all of these countries. Life expectancy also continues to increase, and possibly even accelerate, with advances in biotechnology.[42]

Longevity provides a net benefit to humanity, but it also creates an economic problem: people need a higher level of lifetime income to maintain a given level of consumption over a longer span of years. The economic challenge may be even more severe if you take into consideration the number of years that someone may need 24-hour care or extensive medical care to remain alive. Harvard Medical School cardiologist Dr. Eugene Braunwald seems to confirm this challenge when, referring to the drop in deaths from heart attack, he says: "These people aren't cured. They are

42. See the discussion of this issue in Aaron and Schwartz (2004).

Table 2.5 Average retirement age, select countries, 1965–99

	1965–70	1970–75	1975–80	1980–85	1985–90	1990–94	1995–99
Men							
France	65.4	63.5	62.3	59.7	59.6	59.1	59.3
West Germany	65.0	62.8	61.7	62.2	62.0	60.1	60.5
Italy	62.8	62.3	62.2	60.8	60.2	57.9	59.3
Britain	n.a.	n.a.	n.a.	62.5	62.5	61.2	62.0
United States	67.4	64.2	64.4	63.7	64.2	63.6	65.1
Women							
France	68.1	63.8	63.6	60.6	60.1	60.4	59.8
West Germany	61.9	62.7	60.4	59.9	61.6	60.1	60.8
Italy	58.5	59.7	64.3	59.5	58.8	57.2	58.4
Britain	n.a.	n.a.	n.a.	60.2	61.8	61.2	61.2
United States	67.4	64.3	62.3	64.2	65.7	64.5	64.2

n.a. = not available

Notes: Dynamic estimates are as described in source. West Germany and Italy 1965–70 and 1970–75 data static estimates as described in source; Britain 1980–85 static estimates as described in source.

Source: Scherer (2001).

maintained alive. We have converted heart disease from an acute illness to a chronic disease."[43]

Retirement Age

Table 2.5 shows how retirement ages have changed over the past 35 years. In West Germany, males on average retired at age 65.0 in the period 1965–70, a figure that had fallen to 60.5 by 1995–99.[44] This pattern of decline in retirement age is also evident in France and Italy and to some degree in the United States. It is noteworthy, however, that the pattern of decline stopped in the 1990s. The big declines in retirement age in Europe were from the late 1960s until the late 1980s. The data for Britain are incomplete and show no clear trend in retirement age. In the 1995–99 period, the retirement ages in Britain for both men and women are higher than in continental Europe, but less than in the United States.

The retirement patterns for women are somewhat different from those for men, with a sharp decline in the retirement age in France, but no decline in Germany, Italy, and Britain.

---

43. See "Gains on Heart Disease Leave More Survivors, and Questions," *New York Times*, January 19, 2003, www.nytimes.com/2003/01/19/health/19HEAR.html.

44. OECD made these "dynamic" estimates. The methodology for their calculation and the rationale for using them are discussed in the source given in the table. Taking a simple average retirement age can be misleading when there are trend increases or decreases in labor force participation by different cohorts of the population.

Figure 2.11 Rising life expectancy at effective retirement age, select countries, 1970 and 1999

years of life expectancy

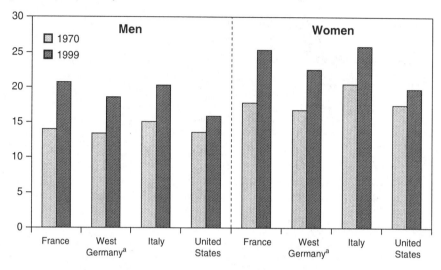

a. Data for West Germany are only for 1970.
Source: OECD (2002f).

Figure 2.11 combines the increase in longevity and the declines in re-tirement age to show the changes in life expectancy at effective retirement age. In France, for example, males could be expected to live 14.0 years after retirement in 1970, a figure that had risen to 20.7 years by 1999. The expected length of retirement increased over this period by a factor of 1.48, almost a 50 percent increase. The increases are a bit smaller in Ger-many and Italy, but still large. The increase in the United States is much smaller at 17 percent. The figures for women are similar to those for men. *These figures indicate that the impact of early retirement and increased longevity have increased the cost of retirement pensions by 30 to 50 percent in Europe over the past 30 years, abstracting from changes in the level of pension benefits.*

Rising Proportion of Elderly

The data presented so far are historical. The biggest demographic chal-lenge is ahead, however, given the rapidly increasing proportion of el-derly in the population. The effects described so far are water under the bridge. The most serious problem lies ahead. Figure 2.12 shows the pro-jected increase in the ratio of retirees to employees from 2000 to 2030 for France, Germany, Italy, Britain, and the United States. Three alternative

Figure 2.12 Number of employees for each retiree,[a] select countries, 2000 and 2030

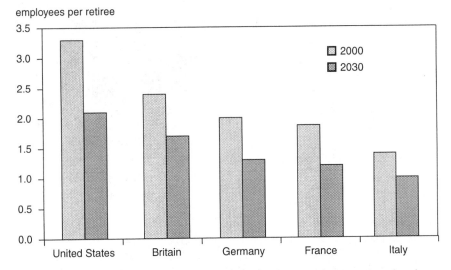

employees per retiree

a. Retirees defined as the number of people aged 55 and above who are not employed.
Source: OECD (2001d) for the United States, Britain, Italy, and Germany. Eurostat (2004a) for baseline scenario for France.

scenarios are shown in OECD (2001d) based on scenario analysis, with the different scenarios based on varying assumptions about future employment and retirement patterns. Taking scenario 2 as the baseline case, we see the ratio of retirees to employees in Italy will rise from 71.1 percent in 2000 (already very high indeed) to 103.8 percent by 2030. Thus in Italy in 2030, the central projection is that there will be just over one retiree for every person working. The data for Italy are open to some question, however, since there is some question of how well employment is measured there.[45] The picture for Germany is also pretty striking. The ratio of retirees to employees is expected to rise from 51.1 percent to 76.1 percent, dropping the ratio of employees to retirees from 2.0 in 2000 to 1.3 in 2030. The ratio in France will drop from 1.9 to 1.2 in 2030.

Looking at the United States, the demographic shift is *proportionally* similar to that in Germany. The ratio of retirees to employees rises from 30.7 percent to 47.1 percent, dropping the number of employees for each retiree from 3.3 to 2.1. The United States had a very pronounced baby boom pop-

---

45. Italy's underground economy is thought to be very large. Of course, if recorded employees are the only ones paying taxes, then the figures shown in figure 2.12 may be the right ones to think about. See the appendix in chapter 5 for an elaboration.

ulation surge and will face significant problems in adjusting to this new demographic. Unlike Europe, however, the demographic shift begins from a very different beginning point, with a ratio of employees to retirees of 3.3 in 2000, compared to 2.0 in Germany. In Britain, the demographic shift going forward is as great as in the United States and Germany, while the beginning point for Britain is intermediate between Germany and the United States.

Health Care

Eurostat (2004a) estimates that the number of people 65 or over in the European Union will reach almost 103 million in 2050, compared with 61 million in 2000, nearly a 60 percent increase. In the same period, the working-age population between 15 and 64 years of age is projected to decline from 141 million in 2000 to 118 million in 2050. This means the ratio of the population over 65 to that between 15 and 64 years of age will double from 43 percent in 2000 to 87 percent in 2050.

Of the total in 2050, the number of people over 80 is expected to increase from 14 million in 2000 to 38 million in 2050, a 171 percent increase. The ratio of persons over 80 to persons 15 to 64 years of age will rise from about 10 percent to 32 percent.

We have commented already on the impact of this demographic change on pension obligations, but the impact on healthcare costs is just as impressive. Figure 2.13 shows how healthcare spending varies with age in a number of European countries and the very sharp increases in spending that occur with increasing age are striking. Persons over 80 consume about 3 times as much in healthcare costs as persons 15 to 64 years of age. Persons 65 to 80 years of age consume about 2 times as much.

Healthcare costs will rise not only because there will be a larger number of retirees but also because of the increasing age of the retirees themselves. Good estimates of the future growth of total healthcare costs for the elderly are not readily available for Europe. But clearly, the spending increases generated by this demographic change are likely to be supplemented further through the development of new but costly technologies. As noted earlier, this technological progress is a net benefit to the society but will add to the tax burden on workers as they support the larger elderly population.

Conclusion

The rise in the number of retirees with an extended life expectancy, younger retirement age, and the rising proportion of elderly has already added to the large tax burden faced by employers and the workforce. Going forward, the cost of supporting retirees will increase dramatically unless offsetting changes are made.

**Figure 2.13 Age profiles for public per capita health expenditure,
select countries[a]**

average expenditure per capita
as a share of GDP per capita

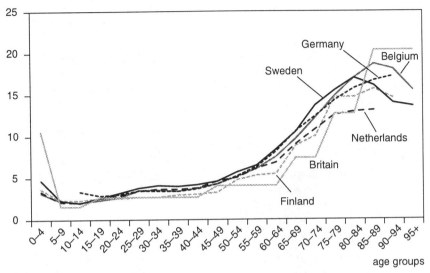

a. Data for Germany, Belgium, Sweden, Finland, and the Netherlands from 2000.

Note: Where the age profile is flat at the tail end of the profile this indicates that a breakdown across age groups was not available at the highest ages. The British age profile has several flat segments as the British breakdown across age groups differs somewhat from that of the other countries.

Source: European Commission (2001b).

The Possibility of an Unstable Labor Market: A Warning Parable

Three related reasons have been identified in this chapter for causing low levels of employment and reduced working hours: average real wages paid by employers are too high to sustain full employment; wage distribution is too narrow to sustain labor demand among low-skilled workers; and levels of benefit payments to the nonemployed are high enough to discourage them from taking low-wage jobs. This section explores the third of these reasons and describes conditions under which high benefit levels might trigger an unstable decline in employment. It is based on a simple model and not on direct evidence that the actual labor market in any of the European economies is unstable. Thus, it provides a warning parable about what needs to be done to avoid possible instability.

A key aspect of the labor market's stability is the work incentive for individuals—the relation between income earned as an employee and the level of benefits provided to those nonemployed. Benefit levels that are too high relative to after-tax wages will eventually drive too many people out of the workforce and tax those that work so heavily that the incentive to work is undermined. In this section a model that captures this possibility is explored.[46]

The model is set out in equation form in appendix 2.1, but the main ideas and findings will be described in this section. Readers who are strongly averse to formal economic analysis or supply and demand diagrams should skip this section of the chapter.

Labor Supply

The level of labor supply (measured as hours worked per capita) is assumed to depend on four variables:

1. the real after-tax wage,
2. the benefit level paid to those who do not work,
3. the labor supply in one period depends upon the labor supply in the previous period. (This means the supply of labor is assumed to adjust gradually to changes in work incentives.), and
4. a demographic variable reflecting the age distribution of the population.

With respect to the first two determinants of labor supply, wages and benefits, a strong simplifying assumption is made—namely that *labor supply depends positively on the ratio of the after-tax wage to the level of benefits received by those who are not employed.* Essentially, a larger work incentive raises labor supply. This ratio is called the *work-incentive ratio* and reflects the trade-off people make when they decide to work or not work.

This assumption oversimplifies the issue in some important respects. In particular, it is possible that labor supply might change if both the after-tax wage and the benefit level were to change, even though their ratio stayed the same. Labor supply is different from the supply of ordinary commodities because there are income and substitution effects at work. A higher wage does encourage people to work more because each extra hour worked yields a higher return (the substitution effect). But on the other hand, a higher wage means people have higher incomes and can afford to take more leisure time (the income effect). It is certainly possible and even likely that in a very high-productivity, high-wage economy, people would choose to reduce their time at work. This view is excluded from this model in order to focus on the implications of the main alternative explanation of

---

46. The model developed by Olivier Blanchard and Lawrence Summers (1987) has some similarity to, but is not the same as, the one used here.

the decline in work hours—the consequences of a too-low work-incentive ratio. Perhaps the most compelling reason to think this last explanation is important is that most of the jobless in Europe are the lower-skilled and less affluent persons in the economy—not primarily the idle rich.

With respect to the third determinant of labor supply, the model captures the fact that it will not change abruptly in response to changes in work incentives. For example, if benefits paid to the nonemployed are increased beyond a certain point, this will not cause a sudden drop in labor supply. Rather the labor supply would gradually decline over time. Capturing the gradual adjustment is important because the impact of policy changes on the labor market can be masked by lags. It has been noted that Europe had generous benefit levels for some time before low employment became a problem. In part that is because wage growth was faster and employment opportunities were greater prior to 1973, but in part there may have been a long time before the full effects of labor-market policies were realized.

The model makes a specific simplifying assumption about how labor adjusts over time. It assumes that *the rate of change of labor supply over time depends on the work-incentive ratio.* In particular, if there is a strong incentive to work (a high work-incentive ratio) then this encourages people to look for jobs and labor supply increases over time (the rate of change of labor supply is positive). If, however, people see only a small economic advantage from working then the number of people seeking work will decrease (the rate of change of labor supply is negative). This specification therefore implies that there is a critical value for the work-incentive ratio. *Labor supply declines when the work-incentive ratio falls below a critical value.* Labor supply increases when the work-incentive ratio rises above the critical value. When the work-incentive ratio is at the critical level, then labor supply remains unchanged (is stationary relative to the population).

The relationship of labor supply to demographics will be developed further once the basics of the model have been explored, but clearly they will play a role. For example, the bigger the fraction of the population that is 65 or older, the smaller will be the supply of labor (fewer hours per capita) for a given value of the work-incentive ratio.

Labor Demand

Labor demand depends negatively on the real before-tax wage. Therefore, as hiring costs rise employers will reduce their demand for labor. Labor demand depends positively on multifactor productivity. Therefore, improved business processes or technology are assumed to increase the profitability of production and have a positive impact on overall labor demand (a productivity increase shifts out the demand for labor for any given wage). This result is standard in economic models at the aggregate or whole economy level. As we discuss in chapter 3, productivity increases can lower employment in specific firms and even industries. But for the economy as a whole, a higher level of productivity lowers unit labor costs and makes employment more profitable at a given wage.

A Balanced Budget Condition

It is assumed that taxes on labor income must pay for benefits to the jobless. This budget-constraint condition is important to the model and serves as a good starting point. Different assumptions could be made, and we explore these alternatives after the results of the basic model have been presented. In practice, most of the tax money that finances unemployment, health insurance, disability, and retirement benefits comes from taxes on labor—specifically payroll taxes.

A Stable Case

A stable labor market is illustrated by figure 2.14. The economy is assumed at time t to be at employment level L_t (point A). The level of the after-tax wage is shown at point C, while the before-tax wage is shown at point D. The difference between the two is the tax wedge. Total payroll tax revenue is defined as "tax receipts in period t." The benefit level per person is shown in the figure by the distance AB, but the total amount of benefits paid out to the nonemployed at time t is not shown in the figure. By assumption the payroll tax revenue (HDCJ) is just enough to finance total benefits to the nonemployed.

The economy changes over time because the employment level L_t and the after-tax wage at that employment point lie on the short-run labor supply schedule, but not on the long-run supply schedule. By assumption, the work-incentive ratio is below its critical value and labor supply is declining over time. The impact of this change is also shown on figure 2.14. The number of hours worked declines to L_{t+1} in the next period. As a result of this employment decline, the number of nonemployed increases and the total benefits paid out also increase. This increase in benefit payments is the shaded area marked in the figure to the left of AB and marked explicitly. Because there are fewer hours worked and more benefits paid out (the benefit paid per person stays the same but there are more benefit recipients), the tax wedge increases from DC to EF.[47]

The drop in employment has increased the before-tax wage as the economy moves (up to the left) along the labor demand schedule. In this stable case, the rise in the before-tax wage is enough to result in an increase

47. By construction in the figure, the total payroll tax revenue at time $t+1$, area GEFI, is greater than the area HDCJ by just enough to pay for the increased benefits required for the additional persons not working.

**Figure 2.14 A stable labor market: As employment falls, the
work-incentive ratio rises until it reaches its
critical level**

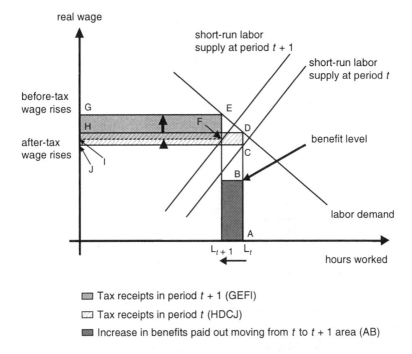

■ Tax receipts in period t + 1 (GEFI)
☐ Tax receipts in period t (HDCJ)
■ Increase in benefits paid out moving from t to t + 1 area (AB)

in the after-tax wage also, even though the tax wedge has increased. With
the benefit level fixed, this means the work-incentive ratio has increased
over time. As the work-incentive level rises, it reaches the critical value
and the decline in labor supply ceases. The economy has reached a stable
equilibrium.

This stable case is the one that is generally assumed to apply to economies that pay benefits to the nonemployed. There is a distortion to labor
supply decisions and a reduction of work effort, but the offsetting advantage to the society is that there is greater income security to those who do
not work from the availability of guaranteed benefits. Many may regard
such benefits as worthwhile and the distortion of individual decisions as
the price paid for greater security. In fact, many Europeans say they are
willing to make this trade-off—providing a higher guaranteed income in
return for lower employment and lower GDP per capita.

An Unstable Case

Figure 2.15 illustrates the possibility of a labor market with an unstable
employment decline. Just as in the previous case, the economy is assumed
at time t to be at an employment level L_t (point A). As before the work-

Figure 2.15 An unstable labor market: As employment falls, the work-incentive ratio falls

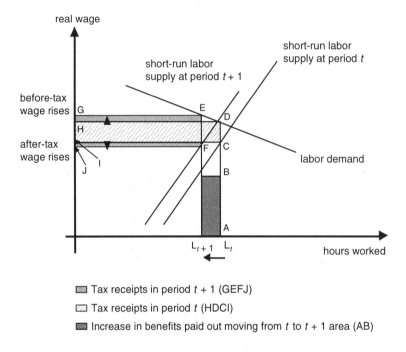

Tax receipts in period $t + 1$ (GEFJ)

Tax receipts in period t (HDCI)

Increase in benefits paid out moving from t to $t + 1$ area (AB)

incentive ratio is assumed to be below its critical value. Employment is at a point on the short-run labor supply schedule but not the long-run schedule, and labor supply is declining. After a period of time (at $t+1$) the economy has moved to the employment level L_{t+1}. As in the previous case, the before-tax wage has increased with the decline in employment (from D to E), but now the after-tax wage has actually declined (from I to J) because the increase in the tax rate is greater than the increase in the before-tax wage rate. Hence, the work-incentive ratio has fallen.[48] Employment will keep declining until a policy shift—such as a reduction in benefit levels (or even a shift in labor supply or demand conditions not captured in this model)—arrests it.

How does instability arise? As employment falls, real wages rise, which helps increase the work-incentive ratio.[49] But in addition, more and more

48. By construction in the figure, the total payroll tax revenue at time $t+1$, equal to GEFJ, is greater than the area HDCI by just enough to pay for the increased benefits required for the additional persons not working.

49. We have asserted several times in this book that one reason for Europe's high average labor productivity is low employment. Some people disagree, arguing instead that productivity is insignificantly affected by employment reductions and that average labor productivity is high in Europe for other reasons. Maybe so, but if that argument is correct, then the key factor stabilizing employment in the model pretty much disappears.

people collect benefits and the tax rate for workers increases—lowering the work-incentive ratio. The stability of the process depends on which of these forces is larger. The difference in the two figures is that the labor demand schedule is flatter (more elastic) in figure 2.15. A given fall in employment has induced a smaller rise in the before-tax real wage. Economic modeling can never give definitive answers to complex empirical situations, but, as the appendix shows, it is surprisingly easy to find examples of instability, where the work-incentive ratio will keep falling if it is set initially below its critical value.

To clarify: Europe is not currently caught in an unstoppable employment decline. The decline in the work-incentive ratio can always be halted or reversed by policy changes. Payroll taxes were in fact reduced in many European economies in the 1990s. One way to create a more stable situation would be to finance a greater fraction of benefits with value-added taxes rather than payroll taxes. Then benefit recipients would share the cost of their own benefits by paying taxes on their own consumption purchases. This limits the erosion in the work-incentive ratio.[50] This simplified model has ignored many of the ways in which policymakers in practice encourage people to work rather than collect benefits. For example, policy may mandate that the unemployed accept any available jobs.

But while the model should not be overinterpreted, neither should its lesson be ignored. The model is a warning parable. It points to the danger of creating a vicious cycle in any situation where generous social welfare benefits are supported by taxes on wages. It may explain why efforts to increase employment in Europe by increasing work incentives in the 1980s did not work as well as expected. If a continuing decline in employment was under way at the time, the restraints on social-welfare benefits may only have been enough to slow or flatten out the employment decline but not enough to generate a reversal.

The Impact of Changing Demographics

The framework of the model allows an evaluation of other structural changes. For example, a change in the population demographic will affect labor supply. The increasing percentage of elderly in an economy will lower the supply of labor relative to population for any given work-incentive ratio. With a larger fraction of the population retired and receiving tax-financed benefits, higher tax rates will be imposed on workers, thereby lowering the work-incentive ratio for any given level of real

---

50. Value-added taxes do still lower real wages, but they fall more or less equally on both wage and benefits receipts, so they do not materially affect the work-incentive ratio.

benefits. The demographic changes coming over the next decades therefore carry the danger that they will push the work-incentive ratio below its critical value and start a dynamic of employment decline.

Although policymakers do not think in terms of economic models like the one described here, the serious concerns currently being voiced about pensions and their possible cuts are described very much in the terms used in this model. In Italy, where estimates show that one retiree will be supported by only one worker, and in France, where pension benefits are very high, the danger is real.

Increases in Productivity

Rapid productivity growth reduces the possibility of unstable employment declines and could offset the impact of changing demographics. There was an important buried assumption in the model as it was described. Labor supply was defined as hours of work supplied relative to the population. But the labor demand schedule was drawn as a stable schedule in figures 2.14 and 2.15. This assumption is valid only if labor demand is moving out over time at a rate fast enough to accommodate the rise in population. Since population growth in Europe is very slow, that is a pretty easy hurdle to reach, and in practice the demand for labor is likely to move out faster than this, as a result of trend productivity and technological improvement. Therefore, there is room to accommodate gradual increases in before-tax wages without reducing employment. Productivity growth can work to increase the work-incentive ratio over time, or it can offset the tendency for the work-incentive ratio to decline as the number of retirees increases. An important caveat to that point, however, is that if benefit levels are increased in line with wage increases then the work-incentive ratio stays the same.

Even though productivity improvements accrue by only small percentage point steps each year—going from a one percent rate of increase to, say, a two percent rate would be a major achievement—productivity growth is potentially the key to returning Europe to full employment. Based on the model, it would allow real wages and the incentive to work to rise without reducing labor demand. In the actual economy it would be even more important. The decline in productivity growth was a key trigger to the rise in inflation and unemployment in the 1970s that started the negative economic cycle. An increase in productivity growth would go in the opposite direction, raising GDP growth, lowering inflation and allowing more expansionary policies, and improving profitability and investment. These effects were all seen in the United States starting in the mid-1990s. Moreover, faster productivity growth works wonders for fiscal problems, potentially turning deficits into surpluses. This could open the door to lower taxes on wages and further improvements in work incentives.

Figure 2.16 Comparative effect of productivity growth and labor utilization pre- and post-1995, select countries

annual average percent change in GDP
per hour worked

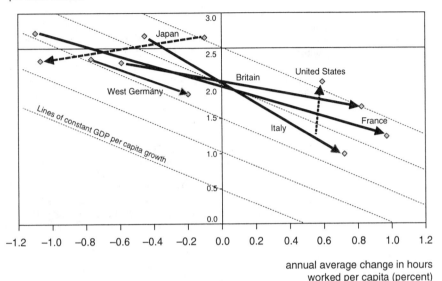

annual average change in hours
worked per capita (percent)

Note: 1973–95 = starting point, 1995–2000 = end point.

Source: University of Groningen and the Conference Board (2004).

Economic Performance since 1995

So far, the analysis of Europe's economic difficulties has largely been based on what occurred during the 20-plus years from 1973 to 1995. But circumstances have changed since 1995, and we need to look at how the most recent period affects the story. In particular, there was a strong boom in the industrial economies through 2000, followed by a slowdown that continued through early 2004.

Earlier in this chapter figure 2.2 showed how output-per-hour growth had declined in the major industrial economies after 1973, and that hours worked per capita had declined in most of them also, with the United States as the main exception to the decline in hours. Figure 2.16 is structured similarly to figure 2.2, with the starting point of each arrow giving the combination of output-per-hour growth and hours-per-capita growth (or decline) that prevailed over the period 1973 to 1995 in each country. The endpoint of the arrow then shows how these same variables performed over the 1995 to 2000 period.[51]

---

51. The data reflect recent revisions, including new estimates of the US population.

The figure shows that the employment situation (hours worked per capita) increased greatly in France, Italy, and Britain, with France going from the fastest rate of hours decline in the pre-1995 period to the fastest rate of increase in the post-1995 period. Germany also moved to the right, but remained in negative territory. (Japan showed a sharp decline in hours worked per capita.) The fact that Europe was able to share in the 1990s boom and raise employment is a sign that macroeconomic conditions are important, and suggests that efforts to increase labor-market incentives and flexibility may have been paying off. Employment growth in the United States over this period continued to be high, but since the economy had reached a point not far from full employment by 1995, the employment increase was only slightly faster than the growth of population.

Box 2.2 *(continued)*

A study by Jorgenson (2003)[1] has also applied US high-tech deflators to other countries and found bigger differences from the standard productivity measures than reported by the OECD. Jorgenson suggests that IT investment in Europe provided a significant source of productivity improvement in the 1990s. Jorgenson's study used faster rates of "hedonic" price decline than O'Mahony and van Ark and he also added consumer durables, which raises his measure of real GDP growth in Europe and Japan.

In terms of the implications for this study we draw the following two conclusions. First, based primarily on the work by the OECD as well as by O'Mahony and van Ark, we conclude that the standard growth data at the aggregate level portray a relatively accurate picture about the United States and Europe. The United States experienced slower productivity growth than Europe for many years, but its growth started to improve sharply after 1995, in contrast to Europe, where it seems to have slowed, at least in the large continental economies. If the period of rapid US productivity growth had ended in 2000, one could perhaps make the case that the new economy of the late 1990s was a temporary blip that was partly the result of the computer deflators. However, since rapid US productivity growth has continued and even strengthened since 2000, this suggests that a new trend of faster growth has occurred. This US resurgence may provide useful lessons for Europe. (Moreover, the rapid productivity growth since 2000 has not been driven by a surge of production in the high-tech sector—indeed the opposite.) Second, we want to reiterate that this study is not about resolving a horse race between US and European growth. Rather, it is intended to help transform the European economy. If there are ways in which Europe can boost its productivity growth rate (and we believe there are), these will help resolve its labor-market problems and improve its standard of living, regardless of how the United States performs.

In chapter 3 we discuss ways of raising productivity in Europe using extensive use of case study analysis. The analysis applies a common measurement approach across countries.

---

1. See also Jorgenson's Web site at Harvard, which reports revised results as of March 15, 2004. http://post.economics.harvard.edu/faculty/jorgenson/papers/handbook. extract03152004.pdf.

The productivity picture after 1995 differs from that shown in figure 2.2. Whereas all the industrial economies experienced a decline in growth after 1973, there was a divergence of experience after 1995. The productivity slowdown *worsened further* in the large European economies and in Japan. In contrast, productivity growth improved in the United States.[52]

To a degree, the slowing of labor productivity growth in Europe in the late 1990s can be seen as a natural consequence of increasing employment, particularly in Britain, France, and Italy. More low-skilled workers were brought into the workforce. However, this factor alone was not enough to

---

52. The United States was not unique in this regard. Other economies, such as Ireland and Australia, not shown in the figure also had productivity accelerations in the late 1990s.

trigger a slowdown in productivity. That certainly seems to be true in Germany, which did not experience the same strong employment growth of Britain and France. In addition, the US experience suggests it is possible to achieve solid productivity growth even when employment is expanding. Even though the rate of employment increase in the United States was not as fast as in France and Italy, the fact is that US employers were often desperate for workers and hired people with low levels of education and work experience. Even so, US employers managed to increase output per hour fairly rapidly.

Figure 2.16 does not include data from the years since 2000. The information is omitted because preliminary data are often revised, so it is hard to be sure what the most recent figures are really saying. It is also omitted in part because there are cyclical movements that affect different regions at different times, which makes interpretation difficult: GDP growth since 2000 has been much weaker in all developed countries. The US economy went into recession in 2001 (earlier than Europe) and seems to be recovering strongly as of mid 2004. Europe's growth held up better in 2001, but France, Germany, and Italy have experienced GDP declines in the first half of 2003 with recovery still rather sluggish. (Britain has had some cyclical weakness also but has done relatively well from a cyclical viewpoint.)

Picking out productivity growth trends from preliminary data that include cyclical shifts is particularly hard, but the indications from the United States are that the faster rate of growth that was achieved after 1995 has been sustained since 2000. It is also possible that a further acceleration has occurred. In contrast, European productivity growth, which was slow from 1995 to 2000, seems to have slowed even more since then. Productivity is usually weak in downturns but the Center for European Policy Studies (2002) argues that productivity growth is getting weaker even after adjusting for the cycle. It is too early in the recovery to be sure, but the fact that the latest figures show such weak productivity growth in Europe is not a good sign.[53] (Productivity growth has been fairly weak in Britain also.)

The Diagnosis

The economic problem in Europe is a combination of low employment and a slowdown of productivity growth. The core economies in Europe could not adjust to the sharp slowdown in productivity that began in 1973. The impact of the productivity slowdown has been exacerbated by

---

53. The European Central Bank (2004) just released a study showing slow growth in labor productivity for the nonfarm business sector of the euro area economy—only 1.2 percent a year, 1996–2003.

a decline in the relative demand for low-skilled workers, caused by some combination of biased technological change and globalization.

The loss of employment that started as cyclical became structural over time. In part this was because average real wage growth, even though it slowed, was still faster than the rate consistent with a return to full employment. In addition, the level of income support provided to those not working was sufficient to discourage job seeking, especially by the less skilled.

The low level of employment in Europe is the result of too little demand for labor—because employer wage costs are too high—and too little supply of labor—because unemployment benefits are either too generous or structured in a way that reduces employment incentives.

Europe developed a vicious cycle where a decline in employment triggered a rise in workforce taxes to support the nonemployed, which in turn lowered work incentive. When this ratio gets too low, employment starts to decline and the cycle continues. Policymakers finally cut back benefit levels for the jobless to halt this decline, but not before employment had already fallen drastically.

Since the problem is low employment and slow productivity growth, clearly the solution is to seek policies to improve both problem areas. The path to faster productivity growth is the topic of the next two chapters.

Appendix 2.1
A Model of Employment and Productivity

Labor Demand

Labor demand is determined from the real wage and a production function:

$$Q = A\overline{K}^{\alpha}L_t^{1-\alpha}$$

Q is output, A is a constant, K is the fixed capital stock, L_t is hours worked in period t. Labor demand is then determined by equality between the real wage, W_t, and the marginal product of labor.

$$W_t = (1-\alpha)A\overline{K}^{\alpha}L_t^{-\alpha}$$

$$L_t^D = BW_t^{-\frac{1}{\alpha}} \tag{1}$$

Equation (1) gives the labor demand schedule, where B is a constant.

Labor Supply (hours worked per capita L_t^S with population assumed constant)

$$L_t^S = D(W_i(1-T_t), b_t, DEMOG_t, L_{t-1}) \tag{2}$$

where L_t^S is labor supply in time t, T_t is the tax rate on wage income, b_t is the benefit level paid to those who do not work, $DEMOG_t$ reflects the age distribution of the population, and L_{t-1} is employment in the previous period.

$$D_1 > 0, D_2 < 0, D_4 > 0$$

If there is a demographic shift, so that a greater proportion is elderly, for example, then labor supply falls, ceteris paribus.

Supply and Demand Equilibrium

For given values of T_t, b_t, and L_{t-1} there is a conventional supply and demand equilibrium, which is a short-run equilibrium. There is a gap between the real wage paid, W_t, and the wage received, $W_t(1-T_t)$. If $L_t^S < L_{t-1}^S$, then the labor supply moves to the left. As employment declines, the before-tax real wage rises. If the labor tax rate, T_t, were held constant, then a long-run equilibrium would ultimately be established. In the long-run equilibrium, employment remains constant.

The discussion so far, however, has ignored the issue that could create instability as described in the text. As employment falls the total cost of benefits paid to persons without jobs will rise. That aspect is now added to the model.

Benefit Determination: The Work-Incentive Ratio

$$\phi_t = \frac{W_t(1-T_t)}{b_t} \tag{3}$$

The benefit level, b_t, is assumed to be set over time by policy. The "work-incentive ratio," ϕ_t, is then defined as the ratio of income received from working to income received by not working.

Budget Constraint

In the calculation of the model in the text, benefits paid to persons without employment are supported solely from taxes on labor income so that:

$$b_t N_t = T_t W_t L_t$$

Where N_t is the number of people not working. The population is fixed by assumption at P. So:

$$b_t(P - L_t) = T_t W_t L_t \tag{4}$$

A Special Case of Labor Supply

Take the demographic variable as a constant for the present and assume the following form for labor supply, shifting to a continuous time frame.

$$\frac{dL_t^s}{dt} = f\left(\frac{W_t(1-T_t)}{b_t}\right) = f(\phi_t) \tag{5}$$

It is assumed further that $f(\phi_t) \leq 0$, if

$$\frac{W_t(1-T_t)}{b_t} = \phi_t \leq \bar{\phi}$$

It is assumed that the work-incentive ratio must be at or above a critical level $\bar{\phi}$ in order to prevent labor supply from declining. The model will not address in detail what happens if ϕ is above $\bar{\phi}$. Presumably employment increases, but there will be a limit to this as full employment approaches. There could also be shifts in the labor supply relation, $f(\phi_t)$, as employment falls lower and lower, but that too will not be explored. This model is an exercise to see what happens in a region around an initial employment level.

Tracing Out the Effect of a High Benefit Level

In this model, there are three equations that determine L_t, W_t, and T_t once the government has set the path for transfer benefits, b_t.

Setting the Work-Incentive Ratio Constant. One way in which instability in employment will occur was not described in the text of the chapter. If b_t is set at a level over time that keeps pace with changes in the after-tax wage rate—keeps the work-incentive ratio constant—and at a high enough level that $\phi < \bar{\phi}$, then employment will keep declining until $f(\phi_t)$ changes or the system breaks down. The possibility that benefit levels could be set in this way is not an extreme assumption. It would be the case if there were a decision to preserve the distribution of income and to maintain a minimum income level based on relative income.

The Case where the Real Benefit Level Is Held Constant. Unfortunately, the model can develop an unstable case even if the real benefit level is held constant over time. Suppose b_t is set initially so that $\phi_t < \bar{\phi}$ and then b is held constant over time. There is still a potentially unstable dynamic because as employment falls, the number of persons receiving benefits rises and this increases the tax burden and discourages employment further. But offsetting this effect is the fact that before-tax wages rise. How does this play out? The answer depends on whether ϕ rises or falls. With b fixed we have:

$$sign\frac{d\phi_t}{dt} = sign\left[(1-T_t)\frac{dW_t}{dt} - W_t\frac{dT_t}{dt}\right] \tag{6}$$

Then from labor demand:

$$\frac{dL_t}{dt} = -\frac{1}{\alpha}BW_t^{-\left(\frac{1+\alpha}{\alpha}\right)}\frac{dW_t}{dt} \tag{7}$$

And from the budget constraint:

$$[-b-T_tW_t]\frac{dL_t}{dT_t} - T_tL_t\frac{dW_t}{dT_t} = W_tL_t\frac{dT_t}{dt} \tag{8}$$

Using the value of L implied by the employment demand equation, simplifying and using $\alpha = 1/3$ gives:

$$sign\frac{d\phi_t}{dt} = sign\frac{dW_t}{dt}\left[1 - 3\left(\frac{b}{W_t} + T_t\right)\right] \tag{9}$$

Since the before-tax wage is rising, the sign depends on the parenthesis. With any likely combination of tax rate and ratio of benefit level to the wage, this expression implies that ϕ would fall over time. This means that setting a benefit level that is too high will not only reduce employment in the short run, but may trigger an unstable decline in employment over the longer term. The attempt to fix a benefit level that is too high leads to a gradual increase in the tax rate that triggers further employment declines and an even higher tax rate. The real wage does not rise fast enough to off-set this process.

A key reason for this instability is the assumed Cobb-Douglas produc-tion function that implies a very elastic demand for labor. Rather small in-creases in the equilibrium real wage (which help stabilize the system) re-sult from large declines in employment (that destabilize the system). In the specific example, a 10 percent employment decline goes with a 3.3 percent wage increase (a 3.3 percent increase in the marginal product of labor).

It is certainly possible that the true labor demand elasticity would be different—although note that it is the long-run elasticity that is relevant here. If the elasticity of labor demand is unity, equation (9) changes to:

$$sign\frac{d\phi_t}{dt} = sign\frac{dW_t}{dt}\left[1 - \left(\frac{b}{W_t} + T_t\right)\right] \tag{10}$$

Even in this case, stability is not assured. A combination of a benefit to wage ratio plus tax rate that is greater than or equal to unity will still give a continuing decline in labor supply and employment. Obviously this model is very simple, but it does raise the possibility of an unstable de-cline of employment over some range.[54]

Variations on the Model

Capital Taxation. One possible variation on the model would be to allow some part of the benefit cost to be borne by capital taxation. That would reduce the impact of paying benefits on the work-incentive ratio. How-ever, it is not clear that stability would be enhanced once the full effects

---

54. Note also that the size of the labor demand elasticity is tied to the extent to which pro-ductivity increases in an economy when wages are pushed up by institutional forces. In this chapter a reason given for high labor productivity in Europe is that low-wage jobs are elim-inated. Some people have been skeptical of this argument. If they are correct, then this sug-gests a large labor demand elasticity and increases the likelihood of labor-market instability.

were included. Paying benefits to the nonemployed reduces labor supply and this pushes up the real wage paid by employers and reduces the return on capital. So even without explicit taxation on capital, there is a reduction in capital income as a result of the drop in employment. In fact if capital were mobile (at the limit it must earn the same risk-adjusted return everywhere), the amount of capital would decline as employment fell. In this case, the labor demand relation would become more elastic than the one used here (where the amount of capital is taken as given). Any attempt to tax capital to pay for benefits, over and above the impact of rising wages, would be met with a reduction in the amount of capital and the incidence of the capital taxation would fall largely on labor in the end.

Value-Added Taxation. Perhaps a more relevant alternative is that value-added taxes would be used to pay for benefits. This means in practice that the tax burden falls both on wage income and on benefit income. A rise in value-added taxation, to a first approximation, would reduce both the numerator and the denominator of the work-incentive ratio. This would help stability in the model, as noted above in the text of the chapter, compared to the case where benefits are paid only from payroll taxes. There is a more general point here. The adverse effects of benefits on employment in this model are the result of the particular structure of taxes and benefits assumed. If welfare and unemployment support can be restructured to have fewer adverse incentives then the negative cycle of decline outlined in this model can be avoided.

Demographic Change. As the proportion of the population that is elderly increases, this will reduce the supply of labor relative to the size of the population at any given work-incentive ratio. It will not in itself change the critical value of the work-incentive ratio, which will depend on the preferences of the potentially economically active population. However, the larger the proportion of elderly in the population receiving retirement benefits that are paid for with payroll taxes, the lower will be the work-incentive ratio. A rising burden of support for retirees increases the danger of pushing the work-incentive ratio below its critical value.

Productivity Increases. Improvements in MFP are captured in the model by increases in the A term in the production function, and these in turn will increase the term B in the labor demand relation. If $\alpha = 1/3$, then each one percentage point of MFP increase will lead to a three percentage point increase in the demand for labor at a given wage. Over time, this will result in somewhat higher wages (before- and after-tax wages) and higher employment. This result of course assumes that aggregate demand will rise fast enough to absorb the resulting increase in aggregate supply. If capital were to expand also in response to the MFP increase, then the employment effects would be larger.

3

What Drives Productivity Growth and How to Improve It in Europe

While it is possible to change without improving, it is impossible to improve without changing.

—Anonymous

Economic growth is the result of increases in hours of work combined with increases in output per hour, or labor productivity. As described in chapter 2, there may be a synergy between these two elements of growth. Productivity increases can fuel employment growth by some combination of making employers more willing to hire workers, making workers more willing to work, and allowing governments to reduce the labor tax burden without facing budget deficits.

This chapter considers how Europe could improve its rate of productivity growth. The key is to increase the intensity of competition in product markets, encourage business and industry restructuring, and adopt regulatory reforms that facilitate these. Both product and labor markets are important in this respect, but this chapter focuses on the product-market side. We make the case that European product markets are not as open and competitive as they need to be and point to ways in which this can change.

First, we review the findings of a major Organization for Economic Cooperation and Development (OECD 2003f) study, *The Sources of Economic Growth in OECD Countries*, that looked directly at steps to improve productivity. It drew policy implications for all OECD countries, but many focused particularly on Europe. The OECD study found that trade openness has a very positive influence on productivity. Therefore, we include box 3.1 to describe important recent work on price comparisons among manufactured goods. Bradford and Lawrence (2004) suggest that manufacturing industries in Europe are not fully open to competition when based on in-

Box 3.1 Prices of manufactured goods: Evidence that Europe still has trade barriers

Because the single market in Europe is opening up it is sometimes assumed that there is strong competitive intensity in manufactured goods in the region. Research by Scott Bradford and Robert Lawrence (2004) for the Institute for International Economics suggests otherwise. Every three years the OECD collects final-goods price data across countries as part of their program to construct purchasing power parity (PPP) exchange rates. As far as possible, the OECD compares the prices of the same or comparable goods across economies.

In order to compare producer prices, Bradford and Lawrence stripped out the impact of taxes and distribution margins to estimate the factory gate prices for a detailed list of manufactured goods.[1] As a way of presenting their findings, they then found the lowest price for each good anywhere among the countries and set this price equal to unity—the "world" low price of that good. Then each country's prices for individual manufactured goods were expressed as a ratio to the world low price, comparing like good to like good. The result is a set of indexed manufactured-goods prices for each country that consists of values equal to or above unity for all the goods. *The extent to which the prices for a given country exceed unity—on average—then is a measure of the extent to which its manufacturing price level is above the lowest world prices.* Since some goods are obviously more important than others, a weighted average of the prices for each country was calculated. The weight or relative importance given to each good depended on its importance in total expenditure. The weighted average price index for a given country is then a measure of the extent to which its manufacturing sector has limited competition from the lowest prices in the world.

The results of the calculation, which are striking, are shown in the table on the next page. US prices, on average, were 16 to 24 percent above the world's lowest prices during the 1990s. In other words, the US manufacturing sector is not completely open; it maintains prices around 20 percent above the world's lowest prices. Notably, however, its prices are the lowest among the countries studied in the 1990s. The European economies are much less open. For Germany the gap to the world's lowest prices ranges from 98 percent to 48 percent, and the other European economies' gaps are

---

1. The Bradford and Lawrence data included agricultural goods, but these do not change the averages significantly.

(box continues next page)

---

ternational price comparisons. *Therefore, there seems to be great potential for increasing competitive intensity in Europe even in manufacturing.*

Next, we examine the US economy, where productivity growth accelerated after 1995. Understanding the reasons for this acceleration could provide important lessons for Europe. In particular, we study how information technology (IT) was one driver of US productivity growth.

Next, we review a set of industry case studies of France and Germany. These case studies identified specific barriers to productivity growth and stressed the importance of a high degree of competitive intensity in driving innovation. The case studies identify restrictions that limit competition in Europe, but they also highlight examples where barriers to growth have been removed and productivity has improved rapidly. These show

Box 3.1 *(continued)*

similar. Japan's prices, on average, were even higher than Germany's. By this measure, Australia and Canada are noticeably more open than Europe.

Bradford and Lawrence's earlier work covered fewer comparison years and therefore could have been sensitive to exchange rate movements. But that is not the case here. The US dollar has been both strong and weak against European currencies over the 1990s and yet the same basic result holds. There are fluctuations across the 1990s, but, strikingly, there is no clear tendency for the European price premium to get smaller. Despite a single market, Europe did not open up to the lowest-price competition worldwide in a consistent way through the 1990s—although there is some sign of improvement in this respect in Germany, Italy, and the Netherlands in 1999.

The Bradford and Lawrence results are based on final-goods prices so it is not certain that manufactured intermediate goods are included in the calculations. These results may apply only to a subset of all manufacturing in a given economy. For large economies like Germany this is unlikely to be a serious problem. However, it could account for the surprisingly large price relatives for small economies such as Belgium and the Netherlands that produce a great amount of exported intermediate goods.

Producer prices in sample countries relative to world's lowest prices

Country	1990	1993	1996	1999
Belgium	1.66	1.82	2.04	1.70
Germany	1.61	1.75	1.98	1.48
Italy	1.57	1.85	1.62	1.34
Netherlands	1.62	1.80	1.90	1.65
Britain	1.60	1.72	1.68	1.78
Australia	1.50	1.45	1.47	1.33
Canada	1.62	1.47	1.32	1.25
Japan	1.96	1.96	2.28	1.93
United States	1.19	1.16	1.24	1.24

Note: Data are expenditure-weighted average ratios of imputed producer prices to the lowest price in the sample.

Source: Bradford and Lawrence (2004).

that when product-market reforms are adopted in Europe, they have been successful.

Policy Implications of the OECD Growth Analysis

The OECD has been at the center of economic and policy analysis relevant to improving Europe's economic performance. Although the OECD studies all member countries it gives particular focus to the issues that arise in Europe since a majority of members are from the region. The OECD recently completed an extensive project focusing primarily on economic growth in the 1990s (although the 1980s is often used for comparison).

The study (OECD 2003f) draws from a wide range of economics literature for its substantive new analysis.

The OECD report starts with a general review of facts. Widening disparities in rates of GDP per capita growth occurred in the 1990s. Some disparity is a result of continued catch-up of low-income countries in the sample. For the most part, however, widening disparities were the result of high growth rates in some already affluent countries such as the United States, Canada, Australia, the Netherlands, and Norway, combined with low growth rates in much of continental Europe (OECD 2003f, 31). The OECD study also notes that disparities in growth have arisen greatly from differences in labor utilization, with low-growth countries experiencing slow growth or declines in employment and hours worked. Furthermore, weakness in labor utilization was not offset by faster productivity growth. The study also finds that "labor upskilling"—a shift to a more experienced or better-educated workforce—contributed to some fraction of overall growth, but notes that in the slow-growth countries "this was partially due to the fact that the low-skilled were kept out of work." In general terms, therefore, the story told earlier in this book is reinforced by the parallel findings in the OECD growth study, with its broader sample of countries.

The study next analyzes the sources of economic growth, basing it on aggregate data and cross-country regression analysis. The report also pays particular attention to how policies affect outcomes. The causal variables it reviewed apparently explain much of the observed growth differences over time and across countries. For example, it discovered that investment in both physical and human capital is important to growth; sound macro policies yield higher growth; and the level of government involvement in the economy may hinder growth (particularly if it becomes too large, although the pattern varied). Some government spending was conducive to growth, while high levels of direct taxation (taxes on wages and profits) discouraged growth. Business-sector research and development (R&D) activities yielded high social returns, and hence contributed to growth, but there was no evidence in this analysis of any positive effect from government R&D. The study found some evidence that financial markets are important to growth, by encouraging investment and channeling resources toward the most rewarding growth opportunities (OECD 2003f, 89–90).

An interesting result from the aggregate regression analysis is that "exposure to international trade" is an important determinant of output per working-age person. The analysis finds that an increase of 10 percentage points in trade exposure (an adjusted average of exports and imports as percentages of GDP)[1] raises output per person by 4 percentage points

1. The variable is described as a "weighted average of export intensity and import penetration. In the empirical analysis this measure was adjusted for country size (log(Trade exp)adj). It was achieved by regressing the crude trade exposure variable on population size and taking the estimated residuals from this exercise as the adjusted trade exposure" (OECD 2003f, box 2.3, 78).

(OECD 2003g, table 1). This result is remarkable because of its magnitude—the report states that between the 1980s and 1990s trade exposure on average increased by about 10 percentage points. This result, if taken at face value, strongly supports the view that increased globalization improves economic performance. It suggests that Europe should aggressively remove remaining barriers to trade, both within its region and with the rest of the world, for its own sake.

The OECD study does not highlight the conclusion about trade in its main report, perhaps because it is difficult to interpret. The issue is whether trade leads to stronger growth or whether stronger growth leads to more trade. Since trade is so concentrated in manufacturing, which is only a modest fraction of GDP, the implied effect on the industry would have to be four or five times as large as the effect on GDP—a result that may be hard to swallow. Nevertheless, the fact that this result appears in the regression analysis so strongly is reassuring to those who believe trade and other forms of globalization are important factors in improving productivity. After all it is easier to think of scaling back an effect that looks too big than trying to rationalize why an effect considered to be important does not show up in the regression.

In the OECD study, some of the limitations that apply to the coefficient on trade exposure in their regressions also apply to other aggregate findings. There is always the possibility that correlations at the aggregate level are not reaching the underlying causal structure. For example, rapid growth in a country will require fairly high levels of capital investment and will benefit from an ample supply of educated workers. But it is just as plausible that a high rate of, say, capital investment is more the result of rapid growth than the underlying cause. An increase in business opportunities in an economy will spur both growth and investment.

Acknowledging the limitations of aggregate regression analyses, the OECD study then turns to a more micro focus, looking both at growth by industry and at company dynamics. The industry analysis determines what fraction of productivity growth within the OECD countries is the result of shifts among industries. Historically this has been important, as workers move from low-productivity jobs in agriculture into much higher-productivity jobs in industry and services. As we saw in chapter 2, Denison's analysis (1967) argued that this shift accounted for an important part of the rapid growth in Europe and Japan after World War II. In the 1990s, however, industry shifts had less importance in France, Germany, Italy, Britain, the United States, or Japan. Most of the disparity in overall growth rates is accounted for by differences in productivity performance within industries. The industry analysis also revealed that productivity growth differences across countries *within* manufacturing industries were not large. However, the larger US high-tech sector gave it an advantage in productivity growth in the manufacturing sector as a whole.

The data in this OECD study end in 1998 and are not focused on a US-Europe comparison. But the findings are consistent with those in van Ark, Inklaar, and McGuckin (2002), who compare the United States to individual European economies and find that the productivity growth gap that emerged after 1995 was associated with faster growth in US service industries together with the larger contribution of high-tech production.

The OECD regression analysis of industry productivity starts by estimating multifactor productivity (MFP) growth for each industry in each membership country between 1984 and 1998—a huge data exercise. MFP growth in a given industry/country/year then depends on the productivity leader's rate of MFP growth (a measure of how fast the frontier is moving out); the MFP gap from the productivity leader (a measure of the potential for catch-up); and a set of policy variables. Tests check the effect of industry and country dummy variables and additional regressions are run to assess the role of R&D, corporate structure, and industrial relations systems.

The conclusions—particularly the policy implications that emerge—from this effort are as follows. The most important conclusion is that "stringent regulatory settings in the product market, as well as strict employment legislation, have a negative bearing on productivity at the industry—and, therefore, macro—levels" (OECD 2003f, 121).[2] This broad finding is qualified, however, by the argument that the effects of regulation[3] depend on the nature or position of an industry. In particular, product-market regulation has a larger impact on productivity the further an industry is from the productivity frontier. This finding makes sense since the structural changes needed to reach the frontier will be larger in those cases and presumably more sensitive to barriers to change created by regulation.

The impact of labor-market regulation also varies. Hiring and firing restrictions have a negative effect on productivity performance when they are not offset by lower wages or by internal training. Thus, the adverse effect of labor-market rigidity is mitigated, according to these findings, if workers are willing to pay for it through lower wages, or if firms respond to it by providing additional worker training.

The OECD study also finds some support for the view that R&D contributes to growth, but the effects depend on "market structures and in-

---

2. See also Nicoletti and Scarpetta (2003).

3. Although not part of the OECD study, the World Bank (2003) carried out some related work on the impact of business regulation on productivity. Using a broader base of countries, the World Bank compiled a set of regulatory indicators based on ease of starting a business. The index considered hiring and firing, contract enforcement, obtaining credit, and closing a business. Their results indicate a rather clear relation between the level of labor productivity and the ease of starting a business. These results are driven in part by developing economies, but still they support the view that the wrong kind of regulation can have a very negative impact on productivity performance.

dustry regimes" (OECD 2003f, 121) and therefore seem inconclusive. This dataset does not provide clear guidance on R&D's role or importance to growth. There is one intuitive result that is linked to innovation, however. The OECD study finds that a German-style company structure does well in making incremental innovations in industries with a stable dominant technology (one thinks of the success of German capital-goods producers). In contrast, a more relaxed structure without institutionalized labor relations is more innovative with rapidly evolving technologies (one thinks of IT and Silicon Valley).

This finding may explain, in part, the problems with job creation in Europe. Innovation in large firms with established technologies will often result in productivity growth that reduces employment. This is the picture in industries such as steel and automobiles. Innovation in new firms or new establishments is more likely to involve new products and services.

The study's final step is to incorporate findings from a large volume of new work based on data from individual firms or establishments. Data at this level have revealed a very large degree of heterogeneity among firms in productivity growth rates and levels. This is consistent with a "creative destruction" view of the economy in which new firms enter, weak firms exit, and incumbent firms struggle for market share and profits. There is also, of course, the problem that data errors introduce spurious differences across firms or over time. It is easy to see the heterogeneity, but discerning clear patterns in the data is much harder. The OECD and the academics involved in the study worked at length to clean the data and capture their insights. The study examined Finland, France, West Germany, Italy, the Netherlands, Portugal, Britain, and the United States, and the productivity growth calculations were based on two five-year intervals, 1987–92 and 1992–97. The results for manufacturing are more extensive than those for the service sector.

For these OECD countries, the first insight is that the bulk of labor productivity growth comes from improvements within firms rather than from reallocation of output or inputs among firms. The entry and exit of firms into the market is important, however, accounting for 20 to 40 percent of total growth. For most of the countries examined the entry of new firms adds to productivity growth, but the United States offers a different experience. Entrants in the US market start with productivity levels well below the average and grow from there. The positive contribution to productivity growth in the United States comes from the exit of low-productivity firms. Inevitably, the contribution of entry to growth is greater over longer periods of time.

The findings for MFP are a bit different. Productivity growth within a firm is a smaller part of the total growth, and the impact of entry, exit, and reallocation are larger. Tentatively, therefore, the conclusion is that incumbent firms, which are generally larger, are able to invest and raise labor productivity while new firms bring more innovative technology or new business processes.

An important and very surprising finding is that entry and exit rates for the United States and the European countries are not too different. Despite the similarity in average turnover rates across countries, the regression analysis does tease out a negative effect of both product- and labor-market regulation on entry rates of firms. Controlling for other determinants of entry and exit, the impact of regulation does show up in the data.

There is a compelling argument that rigidities in Europe discourage the entry of new firms and restrict the exit of old firms. If this is correct, it is very surprising that it does not show up as lower overall entry and exit rates in Europe, relative to the United States, either in manufacturing or in the broader business sector. How can this puzzle be resolved? One likely answer is that rigidities in Europe *delay* adjustment and the exit of firms, but over time they cannot override the market forces that force uneconomic firms to leave. In fact if the discussion in chapter 2 is correct and real wages are stuck at too high a level in Europe, then the economic pressure on firms to exit, over this period, was even higher than in the United States.

Regardless, there is a vital lesson that emerges from the firm-level analysis for European policymakers. First, current policies to preserve employment by discouraging the exit of firms are not working. The rate of firms exiting the market is just as high in Europe as in the United States. Second, the argument is made that Europe lacks entrepreneurial talent or ability, which is the reason its growth is so sluggish. The very high rate of firm entry in Europe does not support that view.

There is another important finding that concerns the success of those firms that do enter an industry. The most dramatic difference between the United States and Europe that shows up in the OECD's firm-level analysis is the extent to which entering firms increase jobs over time. This finding has received a good deal of attention and understandably so. Figure 3.1, using data from Bartelsman, Scarpetta, and Schivardi (2003), illustrates net employment gains for new firms in selected countries. It shows that entering firms in the United States have dramatically increased their employment after two, four, or seven years relative to their initial size. US entrants overall are smaller in initial size, have an above-average probability of survival, and grow employment much more than entrants in the other countries. The weakness of employment growth among entrants in Europe may be a sign of weaker entrepreneurial performance. However, it may also reflect barriers to hiring and expansion in Europe.[4]

---

4. Brandt (2004), using a newer and "cleaner" European firm-level dataset, finds a somewhat higher two-year employment growth among European firms from 1998 to 2000 than did Bartelsman, Scarpetta, and Schivardi (2003) and thus indicates a smaller US advantage

Figure 3.1 Net employment gains among surviving firms at different lifetimes[a]

Total economy

net gains as a ratio of initial employment

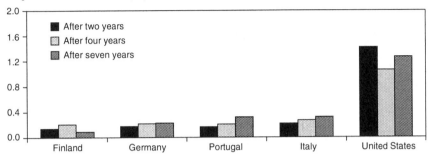

Total manufacturing

net gains as a ratio of initial employment

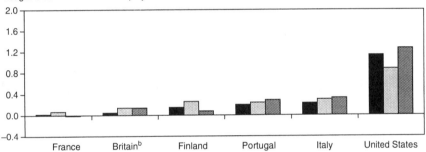

Business service sector

net gains as a ratio of initial employment

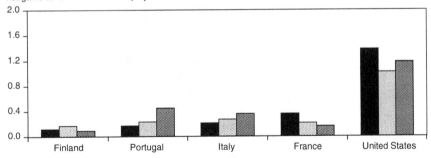

a. The survival rate at duration (j) is calculated as the probability that a firm from a population of entrants has a lifetime in excess of (j) years. Figures refer to average survival rates estimated for different cohorts of firms that entered the market from the late 1980s to the 1990s.

b. After six years for Britain. Data for Britain refer to cohorts of firms that entered the market in the 1985–90 period.

Note: Key same for all 3 figures.

Source: Bartelsman, Scarpetta, and Schivardi (2003).

In summary, the firm-level analysis does provide some intriguing insights, if not yet complete answers. The study stresses, correctly, the high degree of churning (entry and exit) in all countries. The importance of the creative destruction process and market experimentation is clear. Compared to Europe, entering firms in the United States are smaller and of lower relative productivity. If successful, however, new firms in the United States grow employment much more rapidly than entrants in the other countries.

In the policy arena the firm-level analysis supports the idea that excessively stringent regulation in both product and labor markets will hinder growth. It shows that even though many European countries have barriers to prevent economic change, the change happens anyway. Instead, these barriers may slow the pace of innovation and the creation of employment opportunities among those firms entering the market.

The OECD growth study provides a valuable perspective on drivers of growth in the industrial economies it examined. It makes it clear that not all European economies had the same growth experience in the 1990s. Some showed growth and productivity accelerations after 1995 just as the United States did. Some non-European economies also performed very strongly over this period—Australia, for example. But the United States is worth a separate look, not only because it is such a large economy but also because it has the advantage of a large body of detailed data and economic studies to draw from.

Understanding What Drives Productivity Improvements Based on US Experience

According to the Bureau of Labor Statistics,[5] labor productivity growth in the nonfarm business sector of the United States grew by 2.4 percent at an annual rate from the fourth quarter of 1995 to the first quarter of 2001 (the National Bureau of Economic Research [NBER] has dated March 2001 as the peak of the expansion). However, even stronger productivity growth, on average, has prevailed from the first quarter of 2001 through the fourth quarter of 2003, despite the economic weakness for much of that time. Output per hour grew at an annual rate of 4.4 percent. Preliminary productivity data are notoriously fickle, and in recent years downward revisions have followed initial reports of startling increases, so it is wise not to overinterpret the latest numbers. Nevertheless, barring unusually large

---

in this area. However, she notes that this difference might stem from the fact that her new data were collected during a cyclical boom period only. Despite this and other differences, Brandt concludes that the finding that new entrants in the United States have higher employment growth is likely to be a robust one.

5. BLS data are drawn from the BLS Web site at www.bls.gov (accessed February 2004).

Figure 3.2   US labor productivity (nonfarm business, output per hour), March 1973–December 2003

Index 1992 = 100

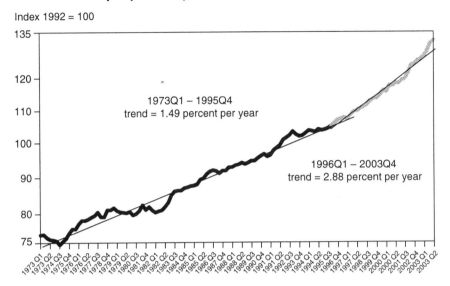

Q1 = March of year
Q2 = December of same year
Q3 = September of next year
Q4 = June of second year

Source: Bureau of Labor Statistics.

revisions, it does appear as if the trend of labor productivity growth in the nonfarm business sector in the United States has ranged between 2.5 and 3 percent a year since 1995, compared with a trend of around 1.5 percent from 1973 to 1995 (see figure 3.2). The speed of productivity growth since 1995 is not an unprecedented phenomenon in US experience. Labor productivity increased by nearly 2.7 percent a year from 1947 through 1973, so the current trend seems to be a return to a pace closer to the postwar trend of productivity growth.

This section examines the latest evidence about the causes of productivity growth in the United States and its acceleration. Particular emphasis is given to understanding the importance of IT to growth, relative to other sources. To anticipate the answer: IT is undoubtedly an important enabling technology that has allowed many companies to increase productivity growth; however, it is important not to exaggerate its importance to productivity or to assume that increases in IT capital will automatically raise productivity.

IT can enable important business innovations, which are the basic source of productivity increase. But adding IT without those innovations is generally worth little. The sources of many business innovations are not directly linked to IT. Other technological changes are equally important as is product and process redesign. Furthermore, diffusion of innovation is as essential to productivity growth as the creation of brand new inventions. Innovations and their widespread adoption are both fostered by a high level of competitive intensity.

Can Growth Accounting Track US Productivity Trends and Reveal the Role of IT?

Economists have stressed IT capital as the key source of the productivity acceleration because the results obtained from applying the "growth accounting" framework to the 1995–2000 time period. So it is important to look at what this framework says and how much weight can be placed on its findings.

The growth-accounting approach examines a period of years to see how well input growth can explain output and productivity growth. Although the precise timing of shifts in the trend rate of productivity growth is not known with certainty, a frequent practice in the productivity literature is to evaluate the sources of growth prior to 1973, 1973–95, and 1995–2000.[6] Growth accounting uses the framework of a neoclassical production function to estimate the contributions to nonfarm business output per hour coming from increases in capital per hour worked, labor quality, and MFP, with the MFP estimated as a residual.

Table 3.1 gives estimates made by the Bureau of Labor Statistics (BLS) covering the periods 1948–73 and 1973–95. The findings are remarkable. They indicate that the contributions of capital services and labor quality to labor productivity growth changed little or not at all in the periods before and after 1973. Therefore, the sharp slowdown in labor productivity growth that occurred after 1973 does not seem to be explained by a drop in the pace of capital accumulation. Instead, it comes from an equal decline in the unexplained residual item of MFP growth.

---

6. Statistical tests show a decline in the trend rate of labor productivity growth in the early 1970s (in nonfarm business although not in manufacturing) and an increase (in both sectors) in the early 1990s. However, there is uncertainty around the exact timing of the trend shifts (see Roberts 2001 and Hansen 2001). Many statistical tests use the Hodrick-Prescott filter, but this is not an ideal approach. The algorithm for this filter looks at future data when deciding when and by how much the trend has shifted. Since slope discontinuities are penalized, the method tends to anticipate a trend change before it actually happens—a questionable procedure. The common alternative of reviewing the data and picking different trend periods also has pitfalls. There is a tendency to date the change in the trend at a quarter with a particularly large disturbance. This same problem also arises in more formal statistical methods that search for the best fit of a piecewise linear trend. Dating trend changes at times of business-cycle peaks and dips has the virtue of being objective to the researcher, but productivity trends do not always match business cycles.

Table 3.1 Productivity growth accounting pre- and post-1973 in nonfarm business (percent per year)

	1948–73	1973–95	Difference
Output per hour[a]	2.9	1.4	−1.5
Contributions from:			
Capital	0.8	0.7	−0.1
Information technology	0.1	0.4	0.3
Other	0.7	0.3	−0.4
Labor quality	0.2	0.2	0.0
Multifactor productivity (MFP)	1.9	0.4	−1.5
MFP from research and development	0.2	0.2	0.0

a. Contributions do not add exactly to the total (output per hour) because growth rates compound multiplicatively and the numbers are rounded.

Source: Bureau of Labor Statistics (2001).

But although the overall contribution of capital services to growth in output per hour barely changed, the composition of these capital services shifted substantially. As table 3.1 shows, IT capital accumulation became more important while all other types of capital lost importance. In this period economists were puzzled as to why productivity growth was so slow despite widespread use of IT. This was the time of the famous paradox highlighted by Robert Solow, which said that computers were everywhere except in the productivity statistics. The growth accounting framework, therefore, did not provide a satisfactory explanation of the 1970s growth slowdown, nor did the rapidly increasing investment in IT seem to show up in faster labor productivity in the 1980s.

Did the growth accounting framework better capture the increase in productivity growth after 1995? Table 3.2 shows three estimates of the decomposition of the increase of productivity growth after 1995. Although updates of these numbers are now available, we have used the 2000 end point because recent data—as noted earlier—are subject to greater error and to cyclical effects. Each estimate in the table calculates the growth accounting decomposition of the level and sources of growth for 1995–2000 and then subtracts the level and sources of growth for 1973–95. The first column updates the results of Oliner and Sichel (2000),[7] the second column updates the estimates reported in the *Economic Report of the President* (Council of Economic Advisers 2001),[8] and the third is from Jorgenson, Mun, and Stiroh (2001).

According to the results in the first and third columns, IT is primarily responsible for the acceleration in labor productivity growth after 1995. The rapid accumulation of IT capital provided a large boost to labor productivity—more than offsetting the slowdown in other capital contribu-

---

7. The figures in table 3.2 were supplied by Daniel Sichel.

8. Revised figures were provided by Steven N. Braun at the Council of Economic Advisers.

Table 3.2 Accounting for the post-1995 productivity speed-up
(percent per year)

	Oliner-Sichel[a]	*Economic Report*[b]	Jorgenson-Mun-Stiroh[c]
Output per hour[d]	1.15	1.39	0.92
Contributions from:			
Capital services	0.34	0.44	0.52
IT capital	0.59	0.59	0.44
Other capital	−0.25	−0.15	0.08
Labor quality	0.04	0.04	−0.11
Multifactor productivity (MFP)	0.77	0.91	0.51
Computer-sector MFP	0.47	0.18	0.27
Other MFP	0.30	0.72	0.24

a. Updated figures (nonfarm business) provided by Daniel Sichel.
b. Updated (nonfarm business) by the authors using data provided by Steven N. Braun.
c. Business sector plus consumer durables and owner-occupied housing.
d. Contributions do not add exactly to the total because growth rates are compounded multiplicatively.

Note: Difference in growth (1995–2000 minus 1973–95).

Sources: Oliner and Sichel (2000); CEA (2001); and Jorgenson, Mun, and Stiroh (2001).

tions. There was also a boost from faster IT MFP within the information technology sector. Of course, this still means that a change in output per hour is assigned to an MFP residual effect, but this case is much less mysterious than the traditional MFP residual. It is well known that the computer and semiconductor industries increased the rate of introduction of new generations of chips as a result of an increased pace of technological advance and intense competitive pressure. Both studies also find an increase in other MFP, which suggests a modest boost in innovation outside the IT-producing sector.[9]

The estimates used in the 2001 *Economic Report* give a picture that is partly the same and partly different. In this analysis, the combined impact of increased IT capital accumulation and increased IT MFP is also large. But this approach finds a larger overall acceleration of productivity growth and a smaller estimate of the direct impact of the IT sector. As a

---

9. Neither study made any adjustments for the business cycle. Productivity tends to grow rapidly in booms and grow slowly in downturns, so the economic boom of the late 1990s may have pushed up productivity growth. Therefore, the faster pace of other MFP may have simply been a short-term business-cycle effect. Under that scenario the acceleration in productivity growth after 1995 is "explained"—or at least easily described: After adjusting for cyclical effects, faster labor productivity growth was solely the result of faster MFP in the IT sector. The rapid growth of labor productivity since the end of the boom has modified ideas about the business cycle's role in the late 1990s. The adjustment equations that attributed a big part of the 1990s productivity boom to cyclical effects no longer yield the same conclusion when the most recent data are added in. More intuitively, an important question about the post-1995 productivity acceleration was whether it would simply vanish once the boom ended. Clearly it has not. See Gordon (2002).

result, about half of the overall acceleration in labor productivity comes from the residual term of increased MFP growth in non-IT sectors of the economy. These estimates suggest that the faster productivity growth after 1995 included a partial reversal of the unexplained collapse of MFP growth that occurred after 1973.[10] This unexplained surge in other MFP after 1995 may or may not be independent of IT advances.

The different approaches used by the three studies in table 3.2 are important, but less important than their similarities. Regardless of which set of estimates are used, the growth accounting framework applied to the pre- and post-1995 periods strongly suggests that IT played a very large role in the acceleration of labor productivity. Is that a valid conclusion? There are several reasons for concern that this general approach might provide a misleading explanation of the productivity resurgence of the late 1990s.

The BLS methodology for estimating the rise in IT investment has raised questions. The amount spent on computer investment certainly rose in the 1990s (nominal investment), but it was real (price-adjusted) investment that really took off. The capability of computers and related equipment rose dramatically, and this surge was captured by rapid declines in the quality-adjusted price index for computers.

The central question is then whether or not these measured price declines accurately captured the use value of the purchased IT equipment. There are two methods used to determine the extent of price changes for computers. One method is to "match models." In this approach, the price of a computer of given capability (CPU speed, memory size, and so on) is compared to another with the same or very similar capabilities in a prior period. Typically the price of the computer of a given capability is lower in the second period, giving a measure of price decline. The alternative approach is applied when there are no good matches over time. A statistical regression is used to determine how different attributes of a computer are valued in the market—for example, what is the cost differential for a computer with faster CPU speed. This so-called hedonic approach creates, using statistical methods, an effective match of computer models over time even when the development of new generations of computers precludes a literal match.[11]

---

10. The 2001 *Economic Report* suggests the business cycle did not cause faster productivity growth because the level of productivity was already about 2 percent above trend by 1995. Recent estimates from the same cyclical adjustment model, developed by Steven N. Braun, now indicate that actual productivity growth in 1995–2000 was slightly slower than the structural trend, because of the sharp drop in the rate of growth during 2000.

11. There are technical issues raised about the hedonic approach. The theory behind the approach assumes the industry that produces computers is perfectly competitive. This is not necessarily true, given the very large fixed costs of developing new chips and other components. Nevertheless, alternative approaches that use a more realistic market structure still show very rapid rates of computer price decline. See Pakes (2002).

On the face of it, this two-prong approach provides the reliable and well-known result that quality-adjusted computer prices have fallen very fast indeed. But how valid are they as indicators of how effectively computers are used in practice? Skeptics point out that current personal computers have greater functionality than those of five years ago, but the basic office tasks of word processing and spreadsheet analysis have not changed significantly. Furthermore, a banking industry case study found that despite placing high-powered new computers on the desks of bank tellers in the 1990s, there was little evidence that the tellers used them more productively (MGI 2001).

Supporters counter this skepticism by stating that the price indexes reflect what customers are willing to pay to add more and newer computers to their production processes. If faster CPU speed commands a price premium in the marketplace, then business customers must believe the extra speed is worth its contribution to their productivity. The benefit of hindsight is that we can find examples where IT investment did not pay off, but that is true of all types of investment. The growth accounting analysis simply assumes IT capital had a productivity payoff that is the same as any other capital, with some uses yielding above-average payoff and some below average.

More detailed data analysis is needed to resolve this debate (we will look at industry and case study evidence shortly), but, at the conceptual level, the important issue is whether or not there are systematic reasons why the payoff to IT capital might not have been as large as is implicitly assumed in the growth accounting estimates. One obvious possibility is that businesses got carried away with enthusiasm for IT and overinvested. We turn to that point below. But first there is an alternative possibility that is linked directly to measurement. Do the network characteristics of IT make it a different kind of capital—making it hard to measure the effective use value of new generations of IT investment?

In most business uses of IT the value of a computer depends heavily on whether it is similar to or very different from all the other computers used in the same company. To a degree, it is also based on how similar it is to computers in general use in the economy. When bank executives in the 1990s upgraded the computers of their tellers, was this because of an irrational or mistaken belief that the tellers would be able to profit from the faster computers? Or was it largely because the existing IT systems had become obsolete and worn, and there was a companywide decision to follow a replacement cycle on a uniform basis? Low-power replacement computers were not an option, even if they had been available on the market. Why? Because hardware replacement cycles are often accompanied by software replacement, and company uniformity demands it for daily operations. In the case of IT replacement cycles, the technological capability of the installed computer systems may be largely dictated by the needs of the prevailing software standards and the high-end IT users—not by the needs of tellers or other less computer-savvy employees. The entire convoy must move at the same speed, which is often determined by the fastest, not the slowest, ships.

Older computer models or computers with low CPU speed or memory capacity command very low prices in the market, because they are not compatible with the latest software and networked office systems. Hence, computer buyers often find themselves on a treadmill where they are "forced" to purchase a new computer in order to run current software for the same basic office tasks.

Therefore, IT's network character makes it hard to infer from market-price data what effect the surge in IT investment had on productivity in the late 1990s. This leaves a great deal of uncertainty about how much growth causality can be determined from the growth accounting framework.

The second issue has already been alluded to. The coincident timing of the surge in productivity and IT investment in the late 1990s is the main reason for thinking the latter caused the former. But correlation does not determine the direction of causality or even whether a causal relation exists. And that is particularly true when we are talking, basically, about one observation. Instead of asserting that a surge in information technology caused the productivity surge, the reverse causality is also possible. With strong demand and strong productivity, profitability was high. The stock market was also experiencing a massive boom, so there was plenty of corporate cash flow and cheap financing available for investment. Great rewards were promised from IT investment, and the Y2K problem made computer upgrades an imperative in many companies. Chief information officers had the upper hand in struggles with chief financial officers. Thus, to a degree, the broader economic boom of the late 1990s and groupthink approach to investment caused the explosion of IT investment.

There is a third important issue relevant to assessing the contribution of IT to productivity growth. As already noted, productivity growth has been very rapid over the past three years—possibly even more rapid than during the late 1990s. But this period has coincided with a bust in technology spending. The rate of growth of IT capital stock has slowed sharply. So the simple correlation between productivity acceleration and rapid growth of IT capital has now broken down. During 2001–03 there seems to have been productivity growth everywhere except in the IT investment—the opposite situation from the Solow paradox of the 1980s.[12]

---

12. There is a historical parallel here. The slowdown of productivity growth in the early 1970s coincided with a sharp rise in oil and energy prices. Many economists drew a connection and said that the rise in energy prices had caused the productivity growth slowdown. There was even a convincing story to go with this hypothesis. Labor productivity growth, it was argued, is generated by the substitution of machine power for muscle power. But machines use energy, so that when energy became much more expensive, this process slowed

The data are uncertain and some of the time periods are very short, but *the simple inference from reviewing the growth accounting framework over the past 15 years or so is that the link between trends in productivity growth and IT investment is weak.* There was the period of the Solow paradox in the 1980s when computer investment was picking up but productivity growth was not. Then we had the five-year period 1996–2000, when IT investment and productivity moved in sync. But since then we have had a three-year period when IT investment and the productivity trend seem to have parted company again.

At the risk of arguing both sides of every issue, it is important to bring in yet another viewpoint on this issue. Economists who take the view that IT is really the key driver of productivity in the modern economy provide another explanation for what has happened over the past 15 years. IT capital alone does not allow companies to raise productivity. What it does is create the opportunity for companies to make changes in the way they conduct business, to innovate, and to change their business processes. They argue that these business process innovations take time to occur. That is why productivity growth did not do much in the 1980s, because companies had not yet figured out how to really take advantage of their increasing IT investments. This also explains why productivity growth continued apace after 2000, because companies were taking advantage of the IT capital that they had already put in place.

This explanation is plausible and surely has a lot of truth to it; it is an idea we will return to later. But accepting this story comes with a price—namely, it reveals that the growth accounting framework is too simple because there are lags that are not captured. There is also intangible capital accumulation associated with business process innovation that is not captured in the data used in the framework.[13]

In order to go beyond aggregate growth accounting numbers and supplement our understanding of the causes of productivity acceleration, we turn to industry data and case studies.

Industry Data and Case Studies: How Much More Do They Explain?

Table 3.3 shows estimates of labor productivity growth by industry from 1989–95, from 1996–2000, the difference between these two periods, and then the growth rate from 2000 to 2001 based on updated data from

---

down and labor productivity growth slowed down. There were skeptics about this hypothesis and they were vindicated when energy prices fell sharply in the mid-1980s and productivity growth did not accelerate. The simple correlation between energy prices and productivity growth broke down over time.

13. For further discussion of these issues, see Gordon (2003b).

Table 3.3 Labor productivity growth by industry, 1989–2001
(GDP originating per person engaged in production, average annual percent changes, selected periods)

Industry	1989–95	1995–2000	Difference	2000–01
Mining	4.72	−0.48	−5.20	−1.51
Construction	−0.13	0.05	0.18	−1.40
Manufacturing	3.14	4.43	1.29	−1.61
Durables	4.30	7.10	2.80	−0.37
Nondurables	1.61	0.94	−0.67	−3.38
Transportation	2.44	1.79	−0.65	−4.32
Trucking and warehousing	1.89	0.77	−1.12	−4.15
Air	4.54	2.11	−2.44	−6.82
Other	1.62	2.75	1.13	−2.28
Communication	4.86	2.59	−2.27	9.97
Electric/gas/sanitary	2.36	2.00	−0.36	−9.80
Wholesale trade	2.85	7.48	4.63	4.27
Retail trade	0.91	5.19	4.28	4.32
FIRE	1.64	3.44	1.80	2.51
Finance	2.96	7.65	4.70	6.13
Insurance	−0.27	1.29	1.57	−1.88
Real estate	1.59	2.67	1.08	2.05
Services	−0.79	0.13	0.92	0.52
Personal	−1.39	0.70	2.09	0.81
Business	0.81	0.40	−0.42	3.37
Health	−2.13	0.01	2.14	−0.04
Other	−0.61	0.06	0.66	−0.62
ICT-intensive half	2.44	4.12	1.69	2.13
Non-ICT-intensive half	−0.01	1.42	1.42	−0.76

ICT = information and communication technology

Source: Bureau of Economic Analysis data, NIPA tables and GDP by industry revised, October 28, 2002.

October 2002. Each industry's output reflects its value-added and labor input as measured by the number of persons working, including full-time equivalent employees (FTEs) and the self-employed (the number of FTEs). Table 3.3 shows a wide range of rates of growth and decline, and some of this variation surely reflects noise in the data. But the overall picture suggests there was a broad acceleration of productivity growth across a range of industries including durable manufacturing and service industries.[14]

---

14. Some earlier data had indicated little or no acceleration of labor productivity in service industries after 1995—including major purchasers of IT capital. However, the picture subsequently changed when new data on industry output was released, which incorporated new price deflators for many service industries.

The resurgence of productivity was especially strong in a few industries.[15] For example, there was a surge in productivity in wholesale and retail trade and in the finance sector. The surge in retail is particularly important because it is such a large sector. Although not shown in table 3.3, a more detailed industry breakdown reveals that much of the productivity acceleration in finance is driven by a small niche—security and commodity brokers—where measures of productivity are questionable. But depository institutions (banks) now show a solid acceleration of labor productivity of 1.22 percent a year, in contrast to earlier estimates. Within durable-goods manufacturing, a more detailed breakdown shows that a large portion of the gain was due to computers and semiconductors.

Nordhaus (2001) showed that in looking at the sources of productivity gains, both within-industry effects and mix effects can be important in particular cases. For example, the telecommunications industry contributed to overall productivity acceleration even though it did not accelerate its own productivity growth. It did so because the telecommunications industry already has an above-average level of labor productivity, so when the industry expanded its share of aggregate employment, it pulled up the average level of labor productivity. Overall, however, the productivity acceleration is the result of accelerations occurring within industries, not because of major shifts among industries (Nordhaus 2001).

What about the link from IT capital to productivity in the industry data? Table 3.3 reports, in the last two rows, the results of a simple exercise. The industries were divided into those that were more IT-intensive and those that were less so, measured by information technology capital in 1995 relative to value added. The IT-intensive group had much faster productivity growth throughout and larger productivity acceleration.

Stiroh (2002) explores the links from IT capital to productivity acceleration by industry using gross output per FTE as his labor productivity measure (table 3.3 reports value added per FTE), and his strongest results come from defining the intensity of information technology based on how large the share of information technology capital is in total capital for each industry in 1995. If that proportion is high, Stiroh argues, it "identifies industries expending tangible investment on information technology and reallocating assets toward high-tech assets" (2002, 10). He finds that industries that are above the median in their IT intensity, by his measure, have much larger increases in labor productivity after 1995. His findings are robust to the exclusion of outliers and certain other tests. However, one area that produces weaker results is when IT intensity in 1995 is calculated as IT services per full-time equivalent employee.

---

15. Using gross output per FTE rather than the value added per FTE shown in table 3.3 reinforces the conclusion that the productivity recovery was broad-based across industries.

Stiroh's findings give new support to the connection from IT capital to productivity growth and acceleration, but a study by Triplett and Bosworth (2002) points away from this view. They focused on service industries and evaluated the extent to which the industries that had experienced a surge in labor productivity growth had also had a surge in IT capital accumulation. They found no such correlation. According to Triplett and Bosworth, it was a surge in the residual MFP growth that accounted for most of the acceleration of labor productivity in service industries.

Industry Case Studies

One way to drill down further to the sources of productivity increase and the role of IT is to do case studies of individual industries. There have been two studies released by the McKinsey Global Institute (MGI) (2001, 2002a) that have utilized this approach. The first study was a series of eight industry case studies, looking in detail at what happened to US productivity in the 1990s and what caused its acceleration. The second study was more specifically focused on IT and on the ways that it does or does not improve productivity, without particular regard to explaining the productivity acceleration.

In the first MGI report, case studies of eight industries were included. Six of these industries had contributed disproportionately to productivity acceleration: wholesale and retail trade, computers and semiconductors, telecommunications, and securities. Retail banking and hotels were included as two industries that had invested heavily in IT but had experienced no surge in productivity (McKinsey constructed its own banking productivity measure and did not use the measure given in table 3.1).

Based on these case studies, the report concluded that competitive pressure was the main driver of productivity acceleration, because it forced improvements in business operations. In the retail trade case, they found that Wal-Mart played a pivotal role, because its large size and high productivity put competitive pressure on other retailers. In the semiconductor industry, Intel came under competitive pressure from AMD, which resulted in an accelerated decline in the price of microprocessors but translated into productivity acceleration in this industry. Conversely, the study found that hotels and retail banks faced less competitive pressure and were able to earn profits without pushing as hard to improve efficiency.

The case studies also make clear that productivity improvements come from a variety of sources, not just from IT. Improvements in retail productivity came about through organizational improvements, the advantages of large-scale "big box" stores, and by a shift to higher-value goods associated with the growth in the number of high-income consumers.

The case studies reveal the complex relationship between IT and productivity.[16] In some cases, investments in IT yielded little payoff. As noted earlier, for instance, banks invested heavily in powerful computers that were negligible for the tasks that most bank employees were performing.[17] Generally "customer-relations management" systems that were intended to track customer use patterns and generate new sources of customer revenue did not succeed. In other cases, IT contributed substantially to productivity. The telecommunications industry is a direct application of IT, and the explosive growth of the mobile-phone sector was made possible by technological advances. The Internet allowed much higher productivity in the securities industry, and IT is used heavily in the wholesale and retail sectors. Wal-Mart, for example, has relied on IT to operate its efficient supply chain—indeed, Wal-Mart operates the largest commercial database in the world. In still other cases, IT systems developed prior to 1995 were vital facilitators of productivity improvements after 1995.

The second MGI study (2002a) further investigated the ways in which IT affected productivity at the industry level. It confirmed that IT contributes to productivity growth only when it is accompanied by business-process innovation. Large amounts of IT hardware and software were sold in the 1990s based on their dazzling technological promise. If companies had not applied the technology to improve operating processes or create new value-added goods or services, then the investment was a failure.

This conclusion helps us understand why the link between IT and productivity growth was hard to unscramble from the industry data. Some companies and industries were successful in making business innovations, and the IT provided an important tool. Other companies invested in the IT, but failed to make the required business process innovations.

The MGI study also found that the way IT contributes to productivity varies significantly across industries. Even though much of the IT investment in banks did not pay off, there were examples of particular investments in this industry that did succeed. For example, voice response units (VRUs)—automated devices that handle customer inquiries—allowed banks to field a 21 percent annual rate of increase in customer inquiries (1994–98) with only a 13 percent rate of increase of personnel. Many of us dislike these devices and would prefer a real per-

---

16. The 2001 study calculated IT contribution to growth differently from standard methodology. Most economists (Jorgenson, Mun, and Stiroh 2001; Oliner and Sichel 2000) have included the entire acceleration of productivity in the IT-producing sector as part of the contribution of IT to the overall acceleration. However, the 2001 MGI study attributed only the amount that IT itself contributed to the productivity acceleration within its own sector.

17. Although not stressed in the MGI study, it is also reported that bank consolidations meant inconsistent IT platforms had to be reconciled—a costly task with limited payoff, at least in the short run.

son, but would be outraged if we were asked to pay the true cost of receiving that service. Since such calls are not paid for directly, productivity measures did not capture the output created by responding to 2.3 billion such calls in 1998.

In the semiconductor industry, design capabilities have not kept pace with Moore's law, so that design has been the bottleneck to better chips, rather than the ability to put more transistors on a given chip. In the 1990s, new EDA (electronic design automation) tools allowed companies to reduce "real" design time—that is, the amount of design time per gate.[18] In 1995, a complex chip design took 15 months, had a team of 60, and included 6 million gates per new design. By 2001, the design time had increased to 24 months and the team size to 180, but the average gate count per design had risen to 94 million.

There were differences in how IT was used even within a given industry. For example, in retail, mass-market discount stores such as Wal-Mart were able to improve their distribution logistics and improve their operational effectiveness. Stores like Sears that offer low-price promotional specials were able to more effectively monitor their sales trends and schedule labor to take advantage of them. The specialty apparel chains, such as Gap and The Limited, used "vendor-management systems" to shorten the time to market and improve sourcing. The study found that companies with effective IT performance measurement tools in place were the companies that obtained the greatest productivity improvement. The study also found that successful companies developed their use of IT in a sequential pattern and built their capabilities at each step.

These conclusions are helpful as a cautionary tale for economists who think a simple model or parable will illustrate how IT affects the economy. There is no one simple way to characterize IT's effect on the economy because it depends on the specific conditions and business methods of a particular industry, or even of a subsector of an industry. In a sense, IT is not what actually improves productivity at all. It is the improvement in business processes—facilitated by IT—that accomplishes this. The results are also helpful in understanding the long lag time that seems to have occurred between the development of computers and the appearance of productivity gains. The effective uses of computers have to be customized to specific activities. Companies and even an industry itself may have to evolve in order for the full benefits of IT to be realized. Additionally, the right performance measures have to be found.

---

18. In a semiconductor, the basic building block is a transistor. A group of transistors put together is called a gate. There are three types of gates: AND, OR, and NAND. They are used to create logical functions. For example, the rider in a microcontroller in an elevator would use the OR gate to program a command to open its doors. The function would read: "if the button is pressed to floor 11, OR if a person in floor 11 presses the button, open the door of the elevator at floor 11."

A Summary Explanation for the Post-1995 Improvement in US Productivity Growth

There is no consensus among US economists about what caused the improvement in productivity growth. The following is an attempt to bring together the different strands of evidence into a reasonable summary view—one that is also consistent with the productivity slowdown after 1973.

The innovations made during the 1930s and in World War II were exploited during postwar recovery. The rapid productivity growth of the 1950s and 1960s in the United States reflected the economy's ability to translate these innovations into improved performance, and the large US market provided a level of competition that encouraged this growth.[19] The macroeconomic environment was stable (a sharp change from the 1930s). There were regulated monopolies in the utilities and telecommunications industries, but the companies were privately held and the nature of regulation encouraged productivity increase. The consolidation of previously fragmented industries allowed productivity gains from increases in scale in the industrial sector, but also in services where, for example, there was a shift from traditional grocery stores to supermarkets.

Once the easier ways to raise performance had already been exhausted, a productivity lull occurred. In many industries stable oligopolies developed, and the full force of global competition was not yet felt. The rise in oil prices triggered a period of greater macroeconomic instability, including steep recessions in 1975 and in the early 1980s. Such economic downturns can stimulate productivity improvement in some companies as they downsize and restructure, but the economy as a whole only benefits if the resources released in this process find productive new uses. That did not seem to happen in the 1970s and 1980s. A period with oil shocks and stagflation is not one that favors risk taking and the development of new products and services.

Despite the economic difficulties, there was an ongoing push of economic change and innovation during the 1970s and 1980s. The IT revolution was moving forward, even though the benefits were not showing up in measured productivity. The makings of a stronger competitive environment were also under way with the deregulation movement and the expansion of global competition. In the 1990s, a new flow of productivity-enhancing innovations emerged in a very favorable macroeconomic environment and in a strongly competitive microeconomic environment, and this allowed a return to faster productivity growth. The 1990s economy experienced heightened competition in an increasingly deregulated environment with strong international competition. In particular, US service industries, which often compete on a global scale, sought out new tech-

---

19. See Baily and Gordon (1988) for an analysis of alternative reasons for the post-1973 productivity slowdown.

nologies to improve their productivity. Business innovation in IT is driven by the demand for improved technologies in the industries that can take advantage of it. Silicon Valley was the creation of a group of extraordinary IT innovators, but was possible only because the markets were demanding new products and services.

High competitive intensity in a market raises productivity growth for four reasons. First, it will increase static efficiency and drive out slack (sometimes called X-inefficiency), and this will raise productivity growth for a period of time. Second, research on individual firms and establishments reveals that productivity growth over extended periods is driven by the expansion of high-productivity enterprises and the contraction or closure of low-productivity enterprises, a process that is sustained by competition. For example, recent research based on census data of US retailing establishments revealed the following: "Our results show that virtually all of the productivity growth in the US retail trade sector over the 1990s is accounted for by more productive entering establishments displacing less productive exiting establishments. Interestingly, much of the between establishment reallocation is a within, rather than between firm phenomenon" (Foster, Haltiwanger, and Krizan 2001). Third, in many industries competition encourages the adoption of innovation within establishments as companies are forced to change in order to survive. The fourth reason, which is related to the three above, is that competitive intensity forces companies to establish incentive programs that encourage productivity improvements throughout their operations.

Another reason the 1990s was a particularly favorable time is that rapid advances in computing power, software, and communications capabilities formed a set of powerful complementary innovations. When complementary innovations occur, the effects can be much greater than the sum of each innovation separately. These complementary innovations made IT user-friendly and enabled it to be applied by a much broader group of persons and for a much wider group of activities.

There is no solid reason for the rather *abrupt* shift in the productivity growth trend after 1995, but it seems clear that economic conditions in the 1990s favored improved productivity performance. The most important source of sustained productivity increase is business process innovation, and this accelerated in the 1990s for reasons that seem linked to the high level of competitive intensity that developed in the US economy.

That conclusion provides a lead into the next section, where the focus shifts back to Europe. Detailed industry case studies from France and Germany are examined to identify barriers to productivity improvement in these economies. The industry cases also reveal a number of examples where regulatory reform and increased competition have yielded a strong payoff in faster productivity growth. Europe does not have to look only to the United States for examples of how increased competitive pressure strengthens productivity. It can look at its own examples.

Case Study Evidence on the Importance of Regulation and Competition in Europe

In 1997 the MGI completed a study of the levels of productivity in France and Germany, adding the United States in order to make comparisons among the three countries. In 2002 a second productivity analysis was carried out, motivated in large part by the acceleration of productivity growth that had occurred in the United States and the slowing in France and Germany. The project did look at productivity levels, but its focus was on productivity growth over the 1990s (MGI 1997 and 2002b).[20] The role of IT in growth in France and Germany was an important concern of the second project and the findings in that regard are discussed in the next section.

The approach in both studies was to use industry case studies. The first report tackled automotive, housing construction, telecom, retail banking, retail trade, and software. The second looked at telecom, retail banking, automotive, road freight, retail trade, and electricity and gas utilities and the results from this second study of growth will be the ones discussed here.

The pattern of productivity performance that emerges is as follows. First, there remains a significant gap in the level of labor productivity in France and Germany relative to the United States in most of the industries studied. The weighted average of the productivity levels of the industries studied was, for both France and Germany, 20 percent below the productivity of the benchmark industries (the US industry was the benchmark except for Japanese autos). The only industries where the labor productivity levels were higher than in the United States were food retail in France and mobile telephony in both France and Germany. This conclusion suggests there is a substantial potential for productivity increase in the private business sectors in these two countries.

Second, over the decade of the 1990s as a whole, productivity grew more rapidly in the United States in about half of the industries and more slowly in the other half. More of the industries in France were growing faster (French industries were often catching up), while more of the industries in Germany were growing slower (German industries were often falling behind). The French productivity lead in food retail was getting

---

20. In order to avoid the reunification problem in Germany, "the 1990s" generally refers to the period 1992–2000. Largely because of the short time period of available data, not to mention the difficulty of analyzing second derivatives, the study did not make a comparison of growth pre- and post-1995 in Europe. Both studies were carried out by teams of business consultants from the Paris and Germany offices of McKinsey & Company. Bill Lewis directed the 1997 study and Diana Farrell the 2002 study in collaboration with the Paris and Germany office managers. The working teams in both studies were from France and Germany. There were academic advisers for both studies, the first chaired by Robert Solow and the second by Olivier Blanchard. Martin Baily participated in both studies.

Figure 3.3 French and German productivity performance relative to the United States, 1992–2000

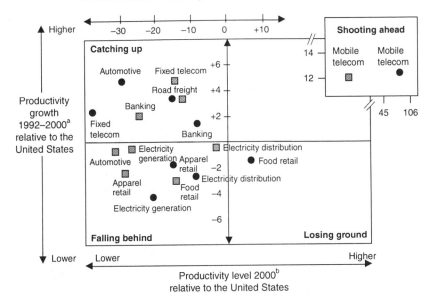

● France
▨ Germany

a. Automotive and utilities 1992–1999; banking 1994–2000; retail 1993–2000.
b. 1999 for automotive and utilities.

Source: MGI (2002b).

smaller over time. Productivity in mobile telephony in France and Germany not only had a productivity lead but also was growing much faster than the US industry.

These conclusions are illustrated by figure 3.3, in which individual industries are positioned on the vertical axis depending on how fast they grew in the 1990s and on the horizontal axis depending on their relative level of productivity.

These industry results are consistent with aggregate data in that the growth of GDP per hour in France and Germany is similar to that in the United States for the decade of the 1990s as a whole. They differ from the aggregate data in finding a lower level of labor productivity in France and Germany than in the United States. Previous studies at MGI as well as other authors have also concluded that a productivity gap exists at the industry and sector level (van Ark, Inklaar, and McGuckin 2002). Evidence from a sample of industries is never conclusive, but since the pattern shows up in different studies, this makes it more likely to be correct. The obvious explanation is that the PPP exchange rate estimates made at the

OECD (using Eurostat data for EU countries) somehow build in the assumption of low relative productivity in the United States for sectors such as government services, health care, and education that are large in overall GDP but are not covered in the private industry case studies. Another possibility is that the case studies used industry-specific PPP exchange rates developed by the McKinsey teams, or physical output measures. These can give productivity measures different from those implied by the OECD's PPP prices.[21]

The next step is to understand this productivity pattern, why there are productivity-level differences among the three industries, what drove the growth, and why some of the industries were falling behind. The comparisons between France and Germany can be as illuminating as those with the United States. The first broad answer is that restrictive or badly designed regulation held back productivity performance in many cases. Regulation can hurt productivity performance by limiting competitive intensity in an industry and discouraging industry restructuring and innovation.

The second reason for productivity performance differences was shown by several cases where scale or network effects are important. In these industries, the intensity of utilization had a major impact on productivity and US industries often operated at a higher scale or had a higher rate of utilization capacity. There is an interaction between these first two causes of productivity performance differences—regulation can affect utilization by restricting industry consolidation. But it is also the case that the United States, having higher income overall, tends to use the industries where scale is important more intensively than does Europe (the United States sends a lot more electricity per capita down its power grid than Europe, for example).

As noted earlier, however, there are important positive stories in France and Germany associated with deregulation, privatization, and the increased competition coming from a single market. In the case studies, deregulation and privatization were often reasons for rapid productivity growth in a sector and often accounted for the sectors that were rapidly catching up to the US level of productivity.

The first example where poor regulation reduces the level and growth of productivity is automotive. Until recently, there were volume restric-

---

21. The OECD must rely on individual-country statistical agencies to collect the price data. In the United States, these data are supplied by BLS, but there is no specific appropriation for this task and no price survey that is tailored for this purpose. In carrying out industry comparisons across a range of countries, the McKinsey teams have often concluded that the individual, micro PPPs from the OECD are surprising and at variance with the firm's knowledge of global pricing behavior. One hopes that more aggregate PPPs benefit from an averaging or "law of large numbers" effect that reduces the overall error. But it does raise a concern about the aggregate comparisons.

tions on non-European imports into the European Union. In Germany there was an "understanding" that kept the share of Japanese autos in Germany at 16 percent in 1993 and explicit limits that kept the share in France at 5 percent. The European companies were also able to enforce exclusive dealer relations that made it more costly for foreign autos to enter. In addition, the European Union has a 10 percent tariff on autos.

Over the 1990s, competitive intensity did strengthen within Europe as a single market emerged in this sector. The German industry had a substantial advantage in product quality and productivity relative to its competitors in France at the start of the decade and introduced several successful new products in the 1990s. Since it lacked intense pressure to improve its productivity, however, and since it faced substantial adjustment costs if it downsized its labor force, the German industry made only modest progress in improving its manufacturing productivity. In France, by contrast, Renault was largely privatized and faced a battle for its very existence. In response it was forced to make massive restructuring efforts and increase its productivity. Making large layoffs is costly in France but the French government, recognizing that the industry had to restructure or die, was willing to allow the layoffs to take place and absorbed some of the costs by subsidizing early retirement for older workers. As a result, productivity grew much more rapidly in the French industry than in Germany and the level of productivity overtook the German level by 2000.[22]

As a comparison, the US industry faced its own intense competitive struggle as the highly productive Japanese industry expanded its market share in autos. GM, Ford, and Chrysler responded by closing the least productive plants, making productivity improvements in the remainder, and successfully expanding the market for SUVs, pickups, and minivans. The high markups on these vehicles show up as high measured productivity.[23] Transplants from Japan operate at high productivity levels in the United States and increased their productivity strongly in the 1990s. So the combined industry (Big Three plus transplants) in the United States also achieved rapid productivity growth and its level remained above that in France and Germany in 2000.

---

22. This good-news story for France is qualified by the fact that the workers released as the industry downsized were placed in early retirement programs. They did not, for the most part, move to new jobs. See chapter 5 for a discussion of labor-market policies.

23. Regulation also shaped the US industry. Fuel economy standards are set differently for SUVs and pickups, allowing the Big Three to sell large vehicles to consumers where they had a competitive advantage over the Japanese nameplates. Gas prices were low for much of the decade. Depending on one's view of the policy issue, one can argue that regulating fuel economy standards was a distortion that depressed productivity in the US industry until the companies found a way of evading the regulation. Or one can argue that productivity is overstated in the US industry because the impact of high gas consumption on the environment or US energy dependence is ignored.

Privatization and the increased competitive intensity resulting from the European Union are working in this industry to raise productivity. The French industry, which had resisted restructuring, was forced to improve its productivity under competitive pressure. The German industry, including the subsidiaries of US companies in Germany, is now faced with the same pressure, as the industry in France has become more competitive and the Japanese transplants in Europe expand their supply. The prospects for employment in this industry, particularly in France and Germany, are not strong, however. Some new plants are being built, such as the Toyota plant in France, but existing plants face employment reductions and new investment is seeking lower labor costs in other parts of Europe, notably Eastern Europe.

Mobile telecom is a case industry where regulation in the United States has resulted in lower productivity, in both level and growth. In an effort to promote competition, the US regulators sold spectrum to many different companies who set up competing networks and a variety of incompatible standards. In 2000 in the United States there were 50 mobile companies with fewer than 200,000 subscribers and the average size of mobile telephone companies was 561,000. In France there are competing service providers, but their number has been limited, so each one uses its network much more effectively. The average number of subscribers is 900,000 to 1 million. Labor productivity in France is about twice the US level. Labor productivity in Germany is higher than in the United States, but much lower than in France, because Deutsche Telekom was allowed to dominate the market. In the United States there were too many competitors, while in Germany one company was allowed to dominate the market.

This is a new industry where there was no incumbent workforce and where private companies were used from the start and used competitively, especially in France. The industry illustrates the subtlety of achieving the right competitive environment. Having too few companies results in an oligopoly or monopoly that will raise prices and fail to increase productivity. But a fragmented industry fails to achieve economies of scale. It is likely that over time there will be consolidation in the US industry and the right number of competitors will emerge. Going for a competitive industry was not a foolish strategy, if flawed in its execution in the United States. Regulating this industry correctly is a moving target.

In fixed-line telephony, the United States retains a productivity advantage. This is particularly the case relative to France where France Telecom has been slow to reduce its workforce despite being privatized. Germany has been more effective in raising competitive intensity and encouraging innovation in the fixed-line segment. An important reason for the productivity-level differences, however, is the fact that the United States makes vastly more calls per subscriber. This is in part due to differences in income levels and different pricing strategies, but it may also reflect cultural differences and different business practices.[24] Internet use in the United States was also much higher than in France and Germany as of 2000.

In comparing France and Germany, again there is a clear case that regulation and institutional rigidities are at work in explaining differential performance. France Telecom has not been faced with strong competition and has a workforce that is able to resist restructuring and the elimination of excess employment.

In retail banking, the industries in France and Germany made substantial productivity gains in the 1990s but still lag behind the US level in productivity. The US industry does not have world best-practice productivity because of its own legacy of regulation. Restrictions on interstate banking created a fragmented and somewhat inefficient industry. It has also been slow to shift to electronic funds transfer, and instead kept a paper-based check system that is labor intensive. Despite these factors limiting productivity, the US industry has become very competitive and uses labor much more flexibly, particularly compared with Germany. German banks have been unable to take full advantage of back-office automation and other innovations because they cannot lay off unneeded workers. The German industry is also very fragmented and small Landesbanken are given access to favorable mortgage guarantees that protect them from competition from more productive larger banks. Labor productivity in retail banking in Germany is 36 percent lower than in the United States. It is also much lower than in France, where the French industry is more consolidated than in Germany, and both back-office and retail branch operations are more efficiently run. France uses paper checks much more than does Germany, which gives it a productivity disadvantage that is more than offset by greater efficiency.

The current regulatory environments in the three countries, and the legacy effects of past regulation, account for much of the gap to best practice productivity in all three economies. In particular, because of the importance of banking to overall economic stability, and the banking problems of the 1930s, bank regulatory systems developed that discouraged all-out competition. Over time, it has become apparent that good regulation can combine a sound financial system with efficiency-enhancing competition. Competition got started earlier in the United States, when money market accounts were permitted in the 1970s. The increased intensity of competition even overcame some of the regulatory barriers as small banks outsourced activities such as check clearing in order to take advantage of economies of scale. German banks are an example where the lack of intense product-market competition combined with labor-market rigidity have hampered productivity improvements.

---

24. Most US customers face zero marginal cost for local calls. However, the disparity in the number of phone calls extends to long distance calls. The United States permits businesses to make marketing calls to consumers that account for a significant fraction of total phone traffic.

The road freight sector is one where there was rapid productivity growth in both France and Germany in the 1990s, around 5 percent a year, enough to reduce if not close the gap to the United States, although the level of productivity remained below the US level at the end of the decade. One of the most important reasons for the productivity improvement in Europe is that deregulation in the European Union, including the abolition of tariffs and the relaxation of market access rules, allowed freight companies to be more competitive and cover a wider geographic area. The competition forced companies to make operational improvements and encouraged consolidation in the industry. Companies benefited from economies of scale in terms of increased capacity utilization, although the full benefits of the opening of the single market are yet to be realized. In addition, there was an easing of truck size restrictions and speed restrictions. The remaining productivity gap to the United States was attributable to higher utilization rates in the United States, linked to better use of IT. Also, deregulation occurred earlier in the United States, so consolidation and operational improvements have gone further in the United States. The United States has longer haul lengths than Europe (output is measured by ton-kilometers).

The case study of retail trade focused on food retail and specialized apparel. In food retail, labor productivity was 7 percent higher in France than in the United States in 2000, resulting from a 19 percent advantage in modern food retail formats (supermarkets and "hypermarkets"). This is a situation where the industries in both France and the United States are competitive with high operating efficiency both in US stores and in French stores such as Carrefour. Regulation in this industry is actually raising labor productivity in France. There are tight zoning restrictions that limit the number of locations where hypermarkets can be built. There is 50 percent less retail space in modern food retail stores per unit of sales in France compared to the United States. There are limits on opening hours in French retail, and very high minimum wages. The combined effect of this regulatory environment is that throughput per square meter and per employee is very high in France. Retailers in the United States stay open longer hours when relatively few people are in the stores (130 hours per week compared to 72 in France). Staying open more hours is not economic in France because of the high wage rates even when there is no regulation preventing it. Retail food stores in the United States also offer customer services, such as grocery bagging, that are not economic to provide in France, given the wage structure. Eight percent of employment in the US industry is at wage rates below the French minimum wage.

Food retail is a case where the impact of wages on productivity and employment is quite visible. The difference between France and the United States comes partly from capital labor substitution (fewer stores that are used more intensively). In addition, there is a reduction in the service level in France as low-productivity activities are eliminated in response to high wage rates. Partially offsetting the productivity advantage in modern food retailing formats is the fact that traditional stores make up a larger fraction of total food retail employment in France—40 percent of the total, as compared to 8 percent in the United States. The greater share of traditional stores in France is also a consequence of the zoning laws that limit the number of hypermarkets.

Although the level of productivity was higher in France in food retail, the growth rate was slower, 0.2 percent a year, compared to 1.6 percent in the United States. The growth in the United States was driven by innovative business processes, notably those in supply chain management and the use of IT. Wal-Mart became the largest food retailer in the United States over this period.

Competitive intensity in food retailing in Germany is lower than in France or the United States as zoning regulations and labor laws limit the ability of the industry to evolve. A much smaller proportion of food retail throughput is sold at large-scale supermarkets and hypermarkets, which have the highest productivity levels and which can make best use of IT and integrated supply management systems. The amount of retail space per unit of sales is high in Germany, concentrated in smaller supermarkets, so that sales per employee and sales per square meter are lower than in France. Labor productivity in Germany in food retail is 86 percent of the US level (with France at 107 overall). The lower productivity in modern formats accounts for this gap.

In specialty apparel retailing, such as Abercrombie and Fitch or the Gap, competitive pressure is high in the United States because these retailers are under constant threat not only from each other but also from discounters like Costco, Wal-Mart, and Target. In France, the hypermarkets do put competitive pressure on the specialty retailers, but this sector of retailing is less developed because land use restrictions have limited the growth of shopping malls. There are more traditional stores remaining in France, where labor productivity in France is 85 percent of the US level in specialty retailing. In Germany, the competitive pressure is lower still because there are fewer hypermarkets and discounters because incumbent retailers use their influence with zoning authorities to make sure desirable locations for new stores are not given to potential best-practice entrants. Labor productivity is 71 percent of the US level. Productivity in the United States also has an advantage because the United States has higher income levels and so more high value-added items are sold in specialty apparel stores.

The electricity and gas utility industries are gradually being transformed in Europe, and indeed in the United States also, as a result of privatization and/or competition. In electricity generation, labor productivity growth in Germany was 5.2 percent a year 1992–99 compared with 1.3 percent in France and 5.5 percent in the United States. Growth was even faster in Britain at 7.0 percent a year. The pattern of multifactor productivity, taking account of capital and fuel inputs, was slower, but had a similar pattern across countries (MFP was not computed for Britain). The level of MFP in France was 87 percent of the US level and in Germany was 90 percent.

The higher level of productivity in generation in the United States was related to capacity utilization. The margin of spare capacity in generation was reduced as the industry transitioned to deregulation. Historically, better use of capacity has been a strength of the US industry, but in some states in the 1990s the margin dropped too low, causing brownouts or blackouts. Electricity demand is more variable in the United States because of the peak air conditioning season. At least for California, the problems encountered with deregulation are well known, even if the causes and cures of the problems are subject to disagreement.

The strong growth of productivity in Germany and in Britain over the 1990s was driven by market liberalization. Britain privatized the industry in the early 1990s, while Germany opened up the wholesale and retail electricity markets at the end of the 1990s. The impact of this opening up in Germany was felt well before the event, however, as generators prepared for the new competitive environment starting in the mid-1990s. They greatly improved their operating efficiency and eliminated excess labor. The productivity of plants in East Germany was substantially improved.

France, by contrast, did not open its generation market and the plants are state owned. The industry did not have an incentive to eliminate excess employment or to increase the standardization of processes, which would have improved efficiency. The level of labor productivity in France is very high and MFP is pretty high because of the extensive use of nuclear technology in France, so its productivity potential is actually quite a bit higher than that in either Germany or the United States. Concerns about safety in Germany and the United States (exaggerated perhaps) have resulted in regulatory barriers to the use of nuclear technology.

Electricity distribution is a natural monopoly and has been regulated in all the countries throughout the 1990s. The United States has a substantial productivity advantage, as noted earlier, coming largely from the high volume of electricity distributed to each customer. In part this is because electricity is much cheaper in the United States, but in addition, higher incomes and air conditioning give rise to different demand patterns. What is most interesting in the analysis of this industry, however, is that the way in which this sector is regulated, including changes in the 1990s, shows up in higher or lower productivity. Britain started with very low productivity but has privatized the industry and forced price declines through several rounds of regulation (see also chapter 4). The result has been very large increases in productivity. France, by contrast, did not regulate aggressively for productivity by, for instance, requiring equal network access for new third-party entries at regulated prices and growth has been much less. *Aggressive productivity-forcing price regulation can have a large payoff in, for instance, natural monopoly sectors, where it is not feasible to just use competition as a forcing device.* (See box 3.2.)

Box 3.2 National regulatory barriers limit competition within the European Union—but the European Commission is fighting back

The creation of a single market was an idea that was central when the European Union (and its predecessor, the EC) was created. The Treaty Establishing the European Union (Article 14(2)) described the internal market as "an area without internal frontiers in which the free movement of goods, persons, services and capital is ensured. . . ."

In practice, however, the countries of the union have kept in place national regulations that limit the intensity of competition and partially thwart the original intent of the founders of the common market—a point that has been made in this chapter using industry case examples. This box, which includes information that became available to us as this book was being prepared for publication, documents some additional barriers beyond those described earlier. But it also notes efforts now being made by the European Commission to overturn these restrictive rules and regulations.

The first three examples are relevant to this latter point and are based on cases where the European Commission is taking individual countries to the European Court of Justice (ECJ).

■ In April 2003, the European Commission took Italy to the ECJ because its national highway code regulations on agricultural trailers require that fixtures for coupling trailers to tractors must comply with national technical rules. As a result, most trailers manufactured outside Italy are not accepted, constituting (in the opinion of the Commission) an obstacle to the free movement of goods.[1]

■ Simultaneously, the Commission brought charges against the Netherlands at the ECJ for its requirement of non-Dutch private security services companies to (for a fee) obtain a prior Dutch authorization. As this authorization does not take into account the obligations companies have already fulfilled in their own member state, nor recognizes non-Dutch professional qualifications, it (in the opinion of the Commission) constitutes an unjustified limitation on the freedom to provide services.[2]

■ In December 2003, the Commission, as a first step prior to referring the case to the ECJ, requested that Germany modify its legislation on supplying hospitals with medicines. Currently German hospitals are required to obtain supplies from local pharmacies, subject to control by a local pharmacist. Germany's opinion that the legislation is needed to ensure the safety of pharmaceutical products and thus to human health seems an obvious example of regulatory capture that grossly distorts the market in favor of local suppliers.[3]

Next, there are five examples where, in principle, regulations have been harmonized across the EU but where individual countries have not implemented this harmonization in practice, providing a barrier to EU-wide trade. While it is mandatory for member states without delay to implement nationally European Commission Directives (these will have been negotiated with member states prior to adoption), implementation sometimes occurs only late, or in a way that is not on a sound legal basis.

■ Safety procedures to prevent workers from falling are mandatory under EU law for working heights above 2.5 meters. A Dutch machine tool company producing personal fall arrestor devices, certified in the Netherlands, is excluded from the British construction market, because British standards in this sector require what is termed a "fall prevention cushion."

(box continues next page)

Box 3.2 *(continued)*

- Harmonized EU regulation exists in the markets for locks and security systems. However, a Norwegian exporter of such items reports that these are overruled by national requirements for fire protection. For instance, Germany has fire protection regulation making mandatory control and testing by German fire inspectors.

- A Spanish producer of upholstered furniture in principle is covered by mutual recognition rules that should allow it to export its furniture to Britain. In practice British fire protection rules for the foam and textiles used in the furniture impose additional testing and costs of production.

- A Dutch food producer encounters barriers from the lack a common interpretation of what constitutes "a sauce." What in some countries is "a sauce" is in other countries "vegetables based on solids." Predictably, this complicates testing and marketing in export markets.

- A Spanish meat manufacturer describes how British authorities do not accept Spanish sanitary certifications, and demands that the company at its expense use a private British company to annually carry out the "European Food Safety Inspection Service."

The latter five examples are from a recent survey by the Union of Industrial and Employers' Confederations of Europe (UNICE) of 200 European businesses (2/3 small and medium-sized enterprises with fewer than 250 employees) that export products covered by harmonized EU regulation to other European countries (EU and EEA members[4]). The survey found that more than half of the companies (115) continue to encounter mandatory, national export-market requirements, necessitating product changes, almost half (92) meet extra national export-market testing and certification requirements, while 15 percent (34) meet other supplementary national requirements, such as compulsory extra documentation (UNICE 2004). While there may be some bias in the answers to the survey, its results do indicate the substantial scope of the problem.

Recognizing problems like these, which are particularly widespread in the service sector, the European Commission states in its latest report on the implementation of the Internal Market from 2004 that "there is no genuine Internal Market for services yet; 53.6 percent of the European Economy is still not integrated" (European Commission 2004e,10). Progress has been made in financial services with the Financial Services Action Plan, although it is too early to gauge its effect, as it is still largely unimplemented. More discouragingly, harmonized legislation in areas such as regulation of sales promotion, clearing and settlement of securities, and particularly the recognition of professional qualifications remain nonexistent. Until such legislation is in place, implemented, and enforced, the single Internal Market does not exist.

As an indicator of the extent to which national governments have implemented their directives, the European Commission publishes a regular "scoreboard" of member state performance. In the most recent form (2004f), only a third of member states (Britain, Spain, Finland, Sweden, and Denmark) fulfill the target of a nonimplementation ratio of only 1.5 percent, and it is noticeable that the three big continental European economies— Germany, France, and Italy, all have more than twice that percentage of outstanding directives (European Commission 2004f). In response to a failure to implement directives, the European Commission will typically ask member states to bring an infringement to an end, and may subsequently refer the case to the European Court of Justice for punitive sentencing. According to the latest "scoreboard," France and Italy have the largest num-

(box continues next page)

ber of infringement cases against them—two to three times as many as does Britain, an economy of roughly the same size (European Commission 2004f, figure 8).

The European Commission's procedure to force member state compliance is frequently very time consuming. Should the case involve the ECJ, litigation time is invariably measured in years. This may in itself be sufficient to deter especially smaller companies from entering markets in other member states. Aware of this issue, in July 2002 the European Commission started its SOLVIT system, which allows EU citizens and businesses to bring cases of misapplication of Internal Market rules directly to the attention of an offending member state's administrators and thus bypass the requirement for Commission involvement. The target process time is ten weeks—very fast in cases involving the administrative bureaucracy of a foreign country. While these are early days, preliminary data indicate that this system solves almost three quarters of complaints to the satisfaction of the plaintiff in an average of only 64 days (European Commission 2003a, 2004f, 15), and thus could become a powerful tool to promote market integration in the future.

1. European Commission Press Release IP/03/581, April 28, 2003.
2. European Commission Press Release IP/03/581, April 28, 2003.
3. European Commission Press Release IP/03/1755, December 17, 2003.
4. European Economic Area countries, which participate in the Internal Market without being members of the EU. These are Iceland, Norway, and Liechtenstein.

Lessons for Europe about Procompetitive, Productivity-Enhancing Regulation

All industries are subject to laws and regulations and depend upon them to function. Property rights are enforced and even new and freewheeling industries like high tech make use of patent protection. Companies sue each other regularly under the antitrust statutes. And zoning laws are essential—how would you like a noisy factory next door to your house? The debate should be about how much regulation is optimal, how to regulate in ways that achieve social goals most efficiently, and how to use regulations or laws to make markets work better.

The conclusions of the case studies of industries in France, Germany, and the United States give clear evidence that regulation matters for productivity and employment. When regulations are used to restrict competition or to prevent industries from consolidating and evolving toward more productive formats, there is a significant productivity price to pay. And the good news is that when sound regulatory reform is carried out, it shows up in higher productivity growth. Based upon the case study evidence, France and Germany could raise their productivity growth rates and hence levels.

The bad news is that restructuring often involves the loss of existing jobs. Job losses are usually costly to the workers that suffer them, but this does not mean those losses should be repressed. Instead there should be assistance given to those who lose jobs to help them financially in the short term while they find new jobs, an issue taken up in chapter 5. Attempts to slow or stop industry restructuring do not work in the end and may even lead to larger not smaller employment declines. Long-run job security is not provided when a company is forced to maintain excess employment. A failure to restructure weakens companies and makes them less able to compete in the long run. The ultimate adjustment of employment may be greater and more costly.

The main industry among the case studies where restructuring need not involve a net loss of jobs in the industry is retailing, where jobs could probably be gained in France or kept in Germany if more flexible land use allowed the growth of specialty retailing and if wage levels were market determined. The United States uses shopping malls to do this, and these are very popular with consumers. But there are other alternatives, more consistent with Europe's desire to preserve the existing downtown areas, that could be chosen instead, such as the development of urban shopping districts.

The lessons for product-market regulation and deregulation from the case studies can be summarized as follows.

- *Procompetitive product-market reform has been tried in Europe and it is working.* As examples, the auto industry in France and utilities in Germany have responded to deregulation and competitive pressure and raised productivity.

- *There are still many sectors where reform is needed.* Many industries remain productivity laggards and the direction of movement is not always positive. Examples include the utilities in France and the banks in Germany, both of which maintain overemployment and do not achieve best-practice operational performance.

- *It is essential to identify the ways in which regulation provides a barrier to competition and productivity improvement in each industry.* The barriers are often quite specific to a particular industry. It is important to identify the barriers to change and performance improvement and then do something about them. Barriers are often justified by a variety of more or less plausible rationalizations: "In our country people do not want to shop in the evenings," for example, or "our consumers do not want to buy trashy products from discount stores." Instead of coming up with rationalizations, it is better to give consumers the opportunity to shop in the evening and give low-income families the opportunity to buy low-price clothing for their children. They can choose for themselves rather than having choices made for them by regulators or politicians.

- *Implicit as well as explicit barriers can be important.* Many barriers to the entry of new competitors are hidden quietly in the way laws and regulations are administered in practice. Providing low-cost financing to an incumbent auto producer can slow down the process of restructuring, for example. Another example is that regulation of the water used in beer manufacture discourages the consolidation of the German beer industry.

■ *Land-use policies create a large barrier to the creation of new businesses and new jobs.* Zoning laws are of course essential, but they should be eased to allow more development. Policies to encourage more flexibility of land use can encourage development without reducing green space.

■ One way of shifting land use policies is to *make sure that the entity that is controlling land use is closely connected or the same as the entity that receives the property tax and a portion of the other tax revenue that results from economic development.* If local authorities receive most of their revenue from a central government, they will have only a modest incentive to favor new land use and job creation. If economic development requires expensive new infrastructure, this can create a strong incentive for local authorities to refuse permission for economic development.

■ *Capital-market pressure can be a valuable addition to product-market competition in forcing productivity increases.* This was a conclusion from the France-Germany study. It was not the most important factor in any one industry, and the results are hard to document because it was not generally possible to talk about specific company performance in the results. But looking across the results, the productivity laggards were often companies that were not facing strong shareholder pressure. To improve performance takeovers should be facilitated, not forbidden. And companies that have lost competitive advantage should be allowed to cease operations and not be propped up by bailout loans.

■ *Labor-market reform must accompany product-market reform.* Product-market reform leads to the restructuring of firms and industries and likely will result in layoffs. Without labor-market reform and greater wage flexibility these will lead to lower employment and higher unemployment. The benefits from restructuring an industry to raise productivity will accrue to the whole economy only if either output expands in that industry enough to maintain employment levels or labor is redeployed into other activities.

The Role of IT in Productivity in Europe: Is an IT Policy Needed?

In setting their goals in 2000, the EU Council clearly believed that IT was a key element in improving economic growth and even employment. Part of the statement of goals says that Europe should become "the most competitive and dynamic knowledge-based economy in the world. . . ." To achieve this, it argues, requires "preparing the transition to a knowledge-based economy and society by better policies for the information society and R&D. . . ."[25] In the discussion in previous sections, based on the OECD study of the sources of economic growth or in the McKinsey case studies, there was little emphasis given to technology or technology policy. It is time now to consider the role of IT and whether there are technology policies that could add significantly to European growth.

In 2000, it appeared there was a clear story to tell about productivity growth in Europe compared to the United States. The United States in the 1990s had learned to make use of advances in IT and increased its own productivity growth. Europe had not invested as heavily in IT and had not increased its productivity growth. In order to improve their economic performance, European countries had to learn to take advantage of the new technologies.

The discussion of the productivity revival in the United States has shown that the first link in that chain, while not broken, shows more complexity and uncertainty than had been thought. The United States did benefit from new technologies, certainly in the industries producing the hardware and in industries using IT hardware and software. But the United States may have overinvested in the IT-using industries or not invested wisely. We saw that there was not a clear relation between the industries whose productivity accelerated after 1995 and the industries whose IT investments increased.

The idea that the root cause of Europe's slow productivity growth in recent years is the result of a failure to use enough IT or to use IT effectively is one that has been developed in several studies. It is worth reviewing the nature of the evidence that emerged from these studies. Even though we disagree with their final assessment, they were serious and careful studies and it is important to see what they had to say. In deciding what Europe should do to improve its economic performance it is important to determine whether increasing the usage of IT and improving the way IT is used will substantially help performance.

---

25. In Lisbon in 2000 EU leaders also launched the *e*Europe Action Plan, aimed at "bringing Europe online." Benchmark targets were set up in areas such as access to the Internet, price of Internet usage, e-commerce, and online public services. This Action Plan was subsequently renewed in 2002 with the *e*Europe 2005 Action Plan. See the European Commission *e*Europe Web site at www.europa.eu.int/information_society/eeurope/2002/action_plan/mid-term_review/index_en.htm for an overview of the plan's current content. The Action Plans are predominantly a passive monitoring exercise of numerous IT-related benchmarks and, while these do have linkages to other EU initiatives, do not entail significant independent expenditures or legislative action. The *e*Europe Action Plans hence cannot be said to constitute an *EU IT policy*. Other broader goals of the Lisbon agenda, such as the goal to raise R&D expenditure to 3 percent of GDP, are also not specific *EU IT policies*.

The Role of IT in European Economic Growth

The OECD economic growth project described earlier took place over an extended period. Prior to the main report (OECD 2003f) that was reviewed earlier in this chapter, there was an earlier study entitled *The New Economy: Beyond the Hype* (OECD 2001c), which makes a careful assessment of the role of IT in growth (the OECD terminology is to refer to information and communications technology, or ICT). The report acknowledges that there was a great deal of hype around the new economy, which resulted in an overstatement of what the technology had done or could do. But in the end, it says: "Nevertheless, the evidence suggests that something new is taking place in the structure of OECD economies. Furthermore, it is this transformation that might account for the high growth recorded in several OECD countries. A surge in hardware and software investment is one consideration, while ICT appears to have brought 'soft' economic benefits too, like valuable networks between suppliers and more choice for consumers, notably thanks to the Internet. Crucially, ICT seems to have facilitated productivity-enhancing changes in the firm, in both new and traditional industries, but only when accompanied with greater skills and changes in the organization of work" (OECD 2001c, 10).[26]

This conclusion is measured and actually not that different from the conclusion we reached earlier in this chapter in assessing the evidence on the United States. The report argues that productivity growth differences among the OECD countries are accounted for by a variety of factors, of which IT is only one, and that IT raises productivity only when it is accompanied by business system innovation.

Bart van Ark, Robert Inklaar, and Robert McGuckin (2002) make a forceful argument that Europe's failure to achieve stronger productivity growth in the 1990s was, to a substantial degree, the result of its failure to take advantage of IT in key service industries, such as retail and wholesale trade. Table 3.4 is taken from their paper and shows the pattern of productivity growth for the United States and the European Union from 1990 to 1995 and from 1995 to 2000 broken down by the industries that produce IT and those that use IT. The big difference in performance lies in the IT-using service industries. In further analysis, the authors carry out the same calculations for each of the EU countries separately and the same basic pattern seen in table 3.1 applies individually to France, Germany, Italy, and Britain, the countries that have been the focus of this book.

As van Ark, Inklaar, and McGuckin (2002) point out themselves, however, these industry findings do not show that IT alone is the reason for the productivity growth differences. There could be other factors that

---

26. There was also a follow-up study by the OECD, *The Economic Impact of ICT* (OECD 2004f), which concluded that ICT continued to be an important source of productivity increase, despite the slump in ICT spending.

Table 3.4 Labor productivity growth (value added per person employed), 1990–2000 (by industry group, average annual percent change)

	European Union		United States	
	1990–95	1995–2000	1990–95	1995–2000
Total economy	1.9	1.4	1.1	2.5
ICT-producing industries	6.7	8.7	8.1	10.1
Manufacturing	11.1	13.8	15.1	23.7
Services	4.4	6.5	3.1	1.8
ICT-using industries[a]	1.7	1.6	1.5	4.7
Manufacturing	3.1	2.1	−0.3	1.2
Services	1.1	1.4	1.9	5.4
Non-ICT industries	1.6	0.7	0.2	0.5
Manufacturing	3.8	1.5	3.0	1.4
Services	0.6	0.2	−0.4	0.4
Other	2.7	1.9	0.7	0.6

ICT = information and communication technology

a. Excluding ICT-producing industries.

Source: van Ark, Inklaar, and McGuckin (2002, table 6).

were at work and one way to see this is to look more broadly at the pattern of speedups and slowdowns. The focus of attention has been on the relatively rapid growth in the United States in the post-1995 period, but one could also ask why the United States grew so much more slowly than the European Union in the first half of the 1990s. The industries that do not use IT intensively, based on the van Ark, Inklaar, and McGuckin assessment, achieved fairly rapid productivity growth in the European Union (much faster than in the United States) before 1995, and then much slower growth after 1995. In part, the explanation of the puzzle of slow growth in Europe in the late 1990s depends on changes that took place in the industries that were not intensive users of IT.[27] The bottom-line conclusion the authors draw from their study is similar to that of this book,

---

27. There are also some measurement questions. The data on IT investment and use by industry are not very good in Europe. In the van Ark et al. study, industries are assigned to the different categories based on the IT intensity of the same industry in the United States, not on how much IT is used in Europe. And when deciding whether a particular US industry is IT intensive or not IT intensive, the basis for the decision is the share of IT capital in total capital. Alternative assignments could be considered, such as IT capital per worker, or IT capital per unit of output. The answers might be different. For example, retail trade is a large industry that had a large acceleration of productivity in the United States after 1995. Based on IT capital per worker hour, it is not that intensive in IT use. Based on share of IT capital in total capital it is classified as IT intensive and that helps drive the results of this study. The procedures used in this study are very sensible, but other approaches might give somewhat different perspectives.

that IT is important but not by any means the only driver of productivity or productivity differences across economies.

Two IMF economists, Markus Haacker and James Morsink (2002), go a bit further and make a spirited case for IT as the key source of productivity growth based on regression analysis. They use growth accounting to compute a residual estimate of multifactor productivity (MFP) growth for 20 OECD countries. This procedure, you may recall from the prior discussion, assumes a substantial contribution of IT capital to the growth of output. The authors then take this MFP residual and ask whether the acceleration or deceleration of MFP after 1995 in each country is related to IT expenditure or IT production in the country. They find that it is, using a variety of different specifications. Somewhat surprisingly, they conclude that *expenditure* on IT hardware has a more significant impact on productivity growth than does the *production* of IT hardware.[28]

These results are interesting and suggestive. The question mark about them is the extent to which investment in IT hardware was a cause or a consequence of rapid economic growth. The authors of the study acknowledge the potential problem of reverse causality and it is an easy criticism to level at many statistical studies of economic data—we questioned the exogeneity of the independent variables in the OECD study also. The problem is of particular concern in this case, though, because IT hardware has become part of the backbone of any modern economy and the faster the overall economic growth, the faster will be the pace of investment in IT hardware. There is a strong possibility that rapid GDP growth leads to rapid IT hardware investment, rather than vice versa. This is not just a business-cycle issue. It will arise for longer time periods also.

It is important to question the results of aggregate studies, but this does not mean their results should be discarded completely. These analyses are valuable and interesting and the results surely reflect the fact that indeed the use of IT does play a role in understanding Europe's productivity performance. The question of determining exactly how much remains open, however. Moreover, this approach to understanding the impact of IT leaves open the issue of how IT is affecting growth and what barriers may exist to its use in a country or sector or company that is making less use of IT than in best-practice industries or companies—a point we suspect the authors would agree with.

The additional way to add information to the debate about the importance of IT to growth in Europe is to reexamine the industry case studies and see how companies are actually using or failing to use IT effectively. The MGI studies did ask specifically how IT had affected productivity in the case industries so we will summarize their findings in this area.

---

28. Surprising because we know almost as a matter of arithmetic that since IT-producing sectors had very rapid MFP growth in the 1990s, the larger the share of these industries in GDP, the faster will be the growth of MFP.

The study found clear examples where IT played a critical role in generating productivity growth. For example, in mobile telecom the industry was essentially created by developments in technology, while in retail banking new technologies allowed back-office automation, created the opportunity for a shift to electronic payments and for online banking. The team concluded that technology developments were the source of about half of the gains in productivity in retail banking in France and Germany in the 1990s.

There were examples where industries in France and Germany had failed to take full advantage of the productivity-increasing advances in technology. In retail banking the improvements in back-office automation did not produce the reductions in employment in Germany that could have been achieved, because of the difficulty of laying off workers. In retail, the advanced supply chain management systems used in the United States had not been put in place in Europe to the same degree. These systems allow collaborative supplier relations when used with key IT applications such as point-of-sale data on individual products, data warehouses, forecasting tools, and development of a common IT platform for information sharing. In road freight, IT-based network optimization tools were not implemented in France and Germany to the same extent as in the United States.

There were also examples going in the other direction, however, where a US industry had not achieved the productivity gains from IT that had been reached in France or Germany. Mobile telecom, as we have seen, was an area where suboptimal scale in the United States reduced productivity. In retail banking, paper checks account for a very large fraction of the payment transactions in the United States, thereby reducing the use of electronic funds transfers and reducing productivity in payments, compared to its potential.

While its primary focus was on the case studies, the McKinsey team also evaluated the aggregate data on IT spending in France and Germany. They concluded that the gap in IT spending to the United States was not as great as had been suggested in some studies because in-house IT development is larger in France and Germany than in the United States. In 2000, they estimate that internal IT spending was 1.4 percent of GDP in the United States, compared with 1.8 percent in Germany and 1.7 percent in France. Overall IT spending by users in 2000 was 7 percent lower in Germany than in the United States and 18 percent lower in France (this discussion refers only to spending by users of IT, not producers of it).

On balance, the conclusion from the case studies is that IT is indeed used somewhat more intensively in the United States than in Europe.[29] So the findings do provide some support for the studies cited. That support

29. See also Inklaar, O'Mahony, and Timmer (2003) for industry-level detail of higher US usage of IT.

is limited because the overall study shows clearly that the driver of productivity growth in these industries in France and Germany is not just IT and often is not primarily IT. In many cases, in fact, IT is not a central reason for the productivity increase. Furthermore, much of the difference in IT use comes from the fact that some industries in Europe are less consolidated than in the United States and have more traditional operating formats. The team often found that when comparing similar operations across countries—auto plants or large financial institutions—then IT is used in very similar ways in the two regions.

The Lisbon Accord said that the radical transformation of the European economy that the EU leaders wished for would take the form of a shift to an information economy. And indeed the European economy, like that in the United States, is becoming an information economy to a greater and greater extent each year. But it is a mistake to think that the main focus of growth policy should be on finding ways to push IT onto companies or individuals. With the possible exception of the study by the IMF authors, none of the evidence discussed above leads to the conclusion that Europe should embark on a deliberate policy effort to increase the use of IT in companies. Given the collapse of IT spending in the United States, we doubt the European Council would have placed the same emphasis on the information economy if it were to rewrite the Lisbon Accord today.

To the extent that more IT is needed, the biggest impetus to this in Europe would come naturally from the overall reform of the economy. As industries consolidate and modern production facilities and retail formats replace more traditional formats, European companies seem capable of determining when IT investment will pay off.

Of the policy suggestions about IT use developed in the OECD's *New Economy* study (OECD 2001c, figure 11.1, 28), two stand out as being appropriate responses to a desire to enhance the benefits of IT.

- According to the OECD's price comparisons, the United States had by far the lowest price for IT equipment in the 1990s. The price of office and data-processing machinery (averaging 1993 and 1999 prices) exceeds the US level by nearly 30 percent in Britain, by over 30 percent in France, by close to 40 percent in Italy, and by about 45 percent in Germany. The purchase price of the equipment is only one element in total IT costs, so equalizing hardware prices will not change overall IT costs in proportion. Nevertheless, there is no reason for these price differences, since the same companies are selling hardware in both regions. And the high prices must discourage IT use to some degree. EU countries should take an easy step on the way to a more competitive economy by eliminating the barriers to competition that create these price differentials in the market for IT hardware. Removing restrictions on imports or Internet sales would likely be all that was needed.

- Education is not a focus of this book, but the evidence of rising wage inequality and the increase in the return to education suggests that there is a substantial payoff to education that may be linked to the shift to an information economy. Making sure students acquire the skills needed for IT use is a necessary condition for expanded use of the technology. It is encouraging to note that *e*-education to improve IT skills for students and teachers—and in fact all Europeans—features prominently in the *e*Europe Action Plans mentioned above.[30]

---

30. The opening statement for the *e*-education part of the Action Plans is "Every European citizen should be equipped with the skills needed to live and work in the information society. *e*Europe proposes to connect all schools to the Internet, to adapt school curricula and to train teachers to use digital technologies." See European Commission Web site at www.europa.eu.int/information_society/eeurope/2002/action_plan/eeducation/index_en.htm.

The Productivity Puzzle in Britain

He who rejects change is the architect of decay. The only human institution which rejects progress is the cemetery.

—Harold Wilson, British Labour Prime Minister (1964–70, 1974–76)

Previous chapters have made the case for economic reform in Europe as a key instrument of improving economic growth, and we have argued that both product-market and labor-market reforms are important. According to some estimates (notably the rankings prepared by the OECD and discussed later in this chapter), the British economy has both liberal and flexible product and labor markets. On that basis, we should expect the performance of the British economy to be among the best in Europe.

In practice, recent British economic performance has not been bad, indeed real GDP grew at close to 3 percent a year on average from the fourth quarter of 1992 through the fourth quarter of 2000, and the British economy has come through the global slowdown after 2000 relatively well (figure 4.1). This compares to the situation for much of the postwar period, when the British economy was more rigid and economic growth was much slower than in continental Europe. The level of GDP per capita, the British economy is now comparable to France and Germany.

The biggest puzzle of the British economy is that the level of productivity remains substantially lower there than in France, Germany, and the United States—a gap of about 20 percent in 2001.[1] Britain has achieved a level of per capita income comparable to that in France and Germany by greater utilization of labor. Labor productivity growth was not bad over the period 1980 to 1995, as measured by GDP per hour worked, but was not fast enough to significantly close the gap with the other economies. Moreover, the rate of productivity growth seems to have slowed since then.

---

1. This gap is based on GDP per hour worked. Comparisons of business-sector output per worker find a larger gap. See Griffith, Harrison, Haskel, and Sako (2003).

Figure 4.1 Britain's real GDP growth, 1992–2002

percent of real GDP growth

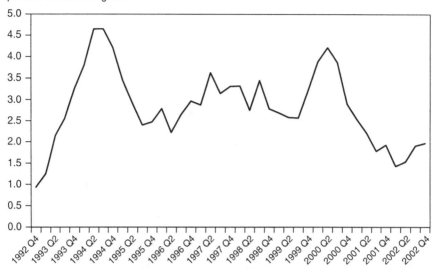

Note: Quarterly real GDP growth compared to same period previous year. Seasonally adjusted at chained volume measures.

Source: UK Office of National Statistics (2003).

Understanding the reasons for the low level of productivity in Britain is important in itself, but it also has implications for the earlier discussion about how to improve productivity growth in the rest of Europe. If the British economy really has flexible and competitive markets, then this paradox challenges the conclusions of chapter 3.

We will argue that resolving this paradox relies on several factors. First, productivity in the British economy was held back by several problems that are separate from market competition and flexibility. One such issue is the relatively low-skilled workforce. Second, a time lag seems to be at work. Many of the economic reforms and policy changes that have occurred in Britain have not yet achieved their goal of closing the productivity gap. If true, productivity growth should increase more rapidly going forward. Third, even though significant economic reforms were implemented in Britain, some were incomplete or were not accompanied by a regulatory environment that really encouraged greater competition. Indeed, in some areas, reform efforts were quite inadequate.

Finally, it was noted earlier in this book that average labor productivity in France and Germany is inflated by the exclusion of low-skilled workers from employment. By the same argument, when comparing Britain to France and Germany, the higher levels of British employment are likely to carry a productivity penalty. Although this last point can explain only a portion of the productivity gap to continental Europe and none of the gap to the United States, it is worth noting.

This chapter will provide a summary view of the productivity issues in Britain. Since the time-lag hypothesis is an important one, this summary starts with a short historical context as a background to understanding the current productivity puzzle.

Economic Performance in the Postwar Period

Although British unemployment, like unemployment in many other European economies, remained low in the 1950s and 1960s, there were other signs of economic difficulties.[2] In particular, productivity growth and overall economic growth were much slower than in the rest of Europe, as we noted in chapter 2. Britain's slow economic growth actually preceded the post–World War II period. Although the first country to industrialize, Britain fell behind the United States in per capita income in the 19th century and then experienced severe economic problems and very high unemployment throughout the interwar years.[3] In 1945, Britain therefore faced the major economic challenge to rebuild and modernize its economy and resume its place as one of the high-income, high-productivity economies. The country did succeed in rebuilding after the war and restoring a full-employment economy, but it failed to meet its full growth performance potential. In fact, Britain became known as "the sick man of Europe."

Among the many reasons for this poor relative performance, the fact that Britain had fought two world wars and experienced chronic high unemployment in the interwar period influenced economic policy priorities and social attitudes. As part of the winning alliance of both world wars, Britons saw the postwar period as a time to reap the returns of victory and preserve traditional jobs and institutions[4]—not a time to embark on an intense global struggle for economic success. The development of the welfare state became a priority of economic policy, and major industries were nationalized rather than being allowed to contract or restructure to be more competitive.

In the British labor market, an attitude prevailed that emphasized fighting over shares of a given economic pie rather than expanding the size of the pie. In contrast, although World War II inflicted terrible losses on the

---

2. The classic study of postwar Britain is by J. C. R. Dow (1964).

3. Britain was hardly the only country to experience economic problems in the interwar years. It missed out on the extended period of prosperity that the United States achieved from 1918 to 1929 and then was caught up in the Great Depression of the 1930s.

4. The British "government sought a cooperative 'social contract' with the trade unions, in which wage restraint was accepted in return for welfarism, a commitment to full employment and noninterference in industrial relations" (Bean and Crafts 1996, 141).

losing countries—Germany, Italy, and Japan (and even France, which had been occupied)—Olson (1984) has stressed the economic advantages for these countries in losing the war, in terms of disrupting existing special interests and forcing a focus on rebuilding, restructuring, and recovery.

When the slowdown in productivity growth occurred worldwide after 1973, Britain was somewhat insulated. Since the country had never achieved rapid growth after the war, it had never reached the productivity frontier and therefore did not face a substantial slowdown. In other respects, however, Britain did share the tough economic conditions of the 1970s and the high inflation associated with oil price shocks and other disruptions affecting the other advanced economies.

Discontent over prolonged poor economic performance and the sharp relative decline of the British economy compared to Europe eventually caused major change in political fortunes and, hence, in economic policy. The Labour Party lost support in the 1970s partly because of its inability to stand up to intractable unions that escalated strike activity. Margaret Thatcher, who had become the leader of the Conservative party in 1975, became prime minister in 1979. The Social Democratic Party split from Labor in 1981 and together with the preexisting Liberal Party further fragmented the opposition, allowing Prime Minister Thatcher to sustain a majority in the Parliament and remain in power until 1990.[5] The Conservative party under John Major held on to power further until 1997.

Unlike traditional Conservative party leaders, Thatcher was an ideological free marketer, whose mission was to overturn the rigid British economy that had developed for much of the 20th century and break the power of the labor unions. She also wanted to cut back the welfare state that had grown up after the war, reduce taxes as a way of improving economic incentives, and privatize the state-owned industries that had been nationalized by postwar Labour Party governments. Thatcher was a reformer who embraced many of the economic principles that have been praised in this book. In practice, however, her economic policies were a mixture of good and bad.[6] She favored market solutions and privatization, which was usually a move in the right direction for improving productivity. However, these free-market policies did not always result in a high level of competition—an essential element if market forces are to drive higher productivity. In fact, in some industries there are tricky regulatory issues that cannot just be left to the market—situations in which Thatcher was unwilling to face up to the implications of market failures.

In order to reform the British economy, Thatcher had to maintain support among Conservative Party MPs (members of Parliament), whose base of support included a number of special-interest groups uninterested

---

5. The Social Democrats and the Liberals united in 1988 as the Liberal Democrats.

6. For a critical view of the Thatcher policies, see Buiter and Miller (1983).

in creating a fiercely competitive economy. We will document later, from case study evidence, some of the ways in which both barriers to competitive intensity and subsidies to failing companies were kept in place. But even before that, we have seen in chapter 3 that manufactured-goods prices in Britain in the 1990s were as far above the lowest world prices as those of the other countries in Europe. Thatcher's reforms apparently did not render the British economy fully open to international competition.

Another important issue is macroeconomic policies. Britain faced a serious inflation problem in the 1970s. Thatcher embraced monetarism and the use of rigid money supply targets as the solution to inflation. Paul Volcker did the same when he took over as Federal Reserve chairman in 1979, but he quietly abandoned the use of money supply targets in 1982 when the US economy was plunging into decline. Thatcher and her advisers were not as flexible. In Britain between 1981 and 1995, the unemployment rate exceeded 10 percent for 9 years out of 15 and was below 8 percent in only 1 year.[7] In the United States, by contrast, the unemployment rate exceeded 10 percent only very briefly and was below 6 percent by the end of the 1980s.[8] The macroeconomic instability and stagnation of the 1980s in Britain discouraged investment and left millions of long-term unemployed with limited work experience. *Thus, the poor macroeconomic environment slowed the British economy's ability to achieve strong growth after reforms.*

Despite these setbacks, Thatcher substantially transformed the labor market and shifted away from nationalized industries. The labor unions' power to set wages and control work practices was greatly diminished. With union power reduced, an independent Bank of England committed to flexible inflation targeting has achieved a combination of low unemployment and low inflation since 1997.[9] On the product-market side, one can argue that the rush to privatize was necessary to lock in the shift away from government ownership. Even though the privatized companies remained inefficient and monopolistic for some time, competition increased gradually in such industries as telecom and electricity generation (in the case of the railways, however, privatization has been a failure).

The New Labor Party has been in office since 1997 under Prime Minister Tony Blair but is very different from the old Labour Party. Although there has been a lot of talk and some action to improve social services like

---

7. The figures are from the US Bureau of Labor Statistics and are comparable to US unemployment definitions.

8. It should be noted that despite the fact that Thatcher was no particular fiscal hawk, British government spending was generally less expansionary than that of the United States during the Reagan years in the 1980s. According to the IMF *World Economic Outlook* database from April 2004, the average British general government balance in percent of GDP from 1980–89 was 2.3 percent, whereas the US similar average balance was 4.4 percent.

9. The Bank of England was granted independence from the UK Treasury by the new Labour government in 1997.

the National Health Service (NHS), most of the fundamental economic changes Thatcher initiated have remained.

In summary, Thatcher was a blunderbuss who first shot away some of the long-standing rigidities in the British economy but was unable to follow through with consistent volleys by not supporting competitive markets and by misunderstanding the real needs of the market.

Resolving the Productivity Puzzle: Capital, Skills, and Other Factors

While reviewing the economics literature we encountered several explanations for the productivity puzzle, and we address some of these issues in this section.

- The level of the capital stock is low in Britain.

- British companies may not be using enough information technology (IT) or using it effectively.

- The British economy is not seen as very innovative. The level of research and development (R&D) is low, and British universities have not developed links with business to the extent that US universities have. Porter and Ketels (2003) have suggested, in particular, that Britain lacks the university-centered technology clusters needed for rapid economic growth.

- The quality of the British workforce may be lower than in other advanced economies. This argument takes various forms: British students perform poorly on standardized tests of literacy and numeracy and many of them lack the job skills that businesses need; A relatively small fraction of the British population has received advanced education; British managers may be inferior to managers from the United States or continental Europe; and British workers are difficult to manage, either because of unions or the legacy of many years of conflicts between workers and managers over work practices.

- Britain is still relatively highly regulated in some sectors such as retail distribution.

We will explore these issues in turn, but some important caveats should be kept in mind. First, even if some of these reasons for lower productivity are valid, they may not be root causes of the problem but instead symptoms of deeper causes. Second, while it is possible to look quantitatively at the education level of the workforce and at the results of standardized tests, the nebulous questions of worker attitudes and managerial capability are harder to pin down. In general, it seems best to rely on explanations of this type only as a last resort.

We start with results from the growth accounting framework, which provides a base analysis of the importance of capital and education/skills to the productivity gap, two of the issues raised above. Growth accounting has been applied to comparative data to assess the relative contributions of different factors to the productivity gap between Britain and other major economies. We noted in chapter 3 how growth accounting is used and some of the problems with this approach, but it is helpful to see what the studies say.

Using Growth Accounting to Decompose the Productivity Gap

A study by O'Mahony and de Boer (2002) compares Britain to France, Germany, and the United States, and the results are illustrated in figures 4.2 and 4.3. The figures take the labor productivity gap in either the market economy (figure 4.2) or the whole economy (figure 4.3) between Britain and each of the other three other economies and sets that equal to 100 for each bilateral comparison. Growth accounting is then used to determine the proportion of each gap accounted for by differences in labor quality (skill), capital intensity, and multifactor productivity (MFP).[10]

Taken at face value these 1999 results show that for the market economy, Britain's labor productivity gaps to France and Germany were mainly due to differences in capital intensity followed by differences in labor quality. For Germany there is also an MFP advantage relative to Britain. In contrast, the gap to the United States in the market economy is mostly attributed to MFP differences, though capital intensity also plays a role. In addition, the United States has a small skill disadvantage relative to Britain.

With the exception of France, a different picture emerges for the productivity gaps for the whole economy. For Germany, MFP is no longer a factor, and the overall productivity gap is accounted for mostly by capital intensity and some skills. In the comparison to the United States, the gap is accounted for roughly fifty-fifty by MFP and capital intensity. The sources of the labor productivity gaps with France look very similar in both the market and total economy.

Some general conclusions can be drawn from these rather diverse results. First, capital intensity is lower in Britain than in the other three countries. Second, France and Germany maintain a productivity advantage because of higher skill levels in the workforce, whereas the United States has higher MFP. Germany too may have higher MFP in its market economy.

---

10. Note that the MFP differences are basically the residual gap and unexplained by the other two factors.

Figure 4.2 Labor productivity gap: Contribution of capital intensity, skills, and MFP to the market economy, select countries, 1999

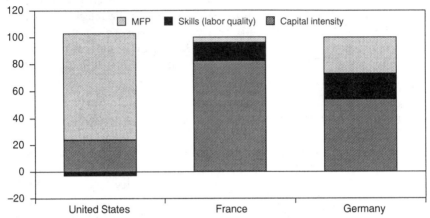

percent of contribution

MFP = multifactor productivity

Note: Labor productivity gap = 100.

Source: O'Mahony and de Boer (2002, table 8).

Results like these have given rise to a fairly widely held view of the productivity problem in Britain. Britain has failed to make adequate investment in both physical capital and human capital, which explains why it lags behind continental Europe. Compared to Britain, the United States also has high capital intensity. However, like Britain, the United States has weaknesses on the skill side, which is balanced by better management and business systems that result in higher MFP.[11] Based on these aggregate comparisons, we look in more detail at the issue of capital intensity and skills in Britain.

Capital Intensity

Various explanations have been suggested for Britain's historically low capital intensity compared to its peers: a low rate of national saving; failure to take advantage of economic opportunities; a history of macroeconomic volatility that has reduced investment; and a largely equity-based financial market that favors a short-term outlook.

---

11. In part France and Germany enjoy the "skill advantage" because these economies eliminate many low-productivity jobs and exclude many low-skilled workers from employment.

Figure 4.3 Labor productivity gap: Contribution of capital intensity, skills, and MFP to the total economy, select countries, 1999

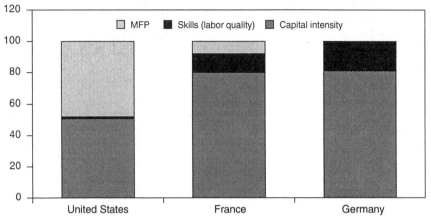

percent of contribution

MFP = multifactor productivity

Note: Labor productivity gap = 100.

Source: O'Mahony and de Boer (2002, table 8).

Not all of these explanations make sense. Britain has had a sophisticated and international capital market for many years, with substantial inflows and outflows of capital. If there were good investment opportunities available in Britain, domestic companies could have taken advantage of them, rather than investing heavily overseas. Instead, Britain is the largest holder of foreign direct investment (FDI) in the United States—presumably because British companies judged the returns to be higher.

Given the aggregate findings, it is apparent that British companies do not have the level of capital equipment necessary to become "best practice." The following example illustrates both this point and the fact that just adding capital will not necessarily solve the problem.

In 1994, BMW purchased Rover for £800 million from British Aerospace.[12] Subsequently, BMW invested nearly £4.5 billion in the automobile company, which also included the Land Rover and Mini brands. Nevertheless, BMW had difficulty improving the quality of the vehicles—particularly of the Rover brand—to generate adequate sales, and they faced significant financial losses. In 2000 BMW discarded most of the assets, transferring Rover to its former management team in a management buyout for the "princely sum" of £10 and the Land Rover brand to Ford Motor

---

12. British Aerospace acquired Rover from the British government in 1988.

Co. for £1.8 billion. BMW CEO Bernd Pischetsrieder, the original architect of the Rover purchase, was fired, and BMW retained only the Mini brand.

The new and completely redesigned Mini has achieved some success, particularly in the United States, after its launch in 2002. Nonetheless, the small volume of Minis that BMW will sell cannot recoup the previous losses it incurred. Hence, while BMW has proven that successful cars such as the Mini can be manufactured efficiently and competitively in Britain, this required billions of pounds in product development and capital investment.[13] Although an increase in capital investment did raise labor productivity in the end, it is clear that BMW received an inadequate return on that investment. BMW's experience in the British auto industry can be contrasted with that of the Japanese, which is more fully described in the case study given later in this chapter. The Japanese built new plants and brought their whole production system with them; they did not try to improve old plants.[14]

More generally, while additional capital is a necessary ingredient in many industries to bring productivity up to world-class levels, the fundamental question is why Britain's rates of return from investment are not more attractive, for both British companies and foreign multinationals seeking FDI opportunities. If market conditions and the resulting rates of return to capital were more attractive, the lack of capital problem would solve itself.

One reason sometimes given for the low capital intensity in Britain, compared with Germany, is that Britain has an equity-based capital market (where companies are expected to show high profit growth even in the short run). By contrast, Germany has used high domestic-saving rates to channel funds to national companies through local banks with very strong ties to area businesses. The high domestic saving then resulted in high domestic investment. Although this may provide a partial explanation of higher capital intensity in Germany, it is less clear that an equity-based system is really the problem. As noted earlier, the German system worked well during the postwar years of rebuilding and expansion, but it is less successful now.[15] Moreover, it is not clear that equity-based systems consider only the short term. For example, there is evidence that the equity market values R&D investment.[16] One can even argue that shareholders in the US equity market in the 1990s were actually placing too great a value on companies with neither short-term earnings nor prospects of positive

---

13. For additional information on BMW's purchase of Rover, see Brady and Lorenz (2000).

14. Honda, which previously owned 20 percent of Rover, supplied engines and engineering expertise to the company until it was sold to BMW in 1994.

15. See Broadbent, Schumacher, and Schels (2004) for a critique of the German capital allocation model.

16. For examples, see Hall (1998) and Hall, Jaffe, and Trajtenberg (2000).

Table 4.1 Growth in capital investment, 1979–99 (percent)

Years	Britain	United States	France	Germany[a]
1979–99	2.78	0.77	2.48	2.71
1979–89	2.74	0.50	3.20	2.42
1989–99	2.81	1.04	1.75	2.99
1989–95	3.62	0.80	2.50	3.45
1995–99	1.60	1.40	0.62	2.30

a. Derived by using growth rates for West Germany for 1979–89 and unified Germany from 1989 to 1999.

Source: O'Mahony and de Boer (2002, table 4).

future earnings for many years into the future. Thus, the US equity market perhaps had too long a time horizon or too rosy a view of the long run. Presumably investors thought there would be profits some time.

In short, the low capital intensity in Britain may be a proximate cause of the productivity gap with continental Europe and the United States, but it is surely not the root cause. Rather, capital investment has not in the past earned a high enough return to justify closing the capital intensity gap with other countries, as illustrated by the BMW example. The case studies discussed later in the chapter also shed light on the issue.

Even though capital intensity is relatively low in Britain, capital investment has increased significantly in the last decade and was particularly strong in the early 1990s (table 4.1).[17] Increases in capital investment indicate that some of the reasons for low returns may have diminished as the British economy was liberalized and that productivity growth will also pick up going forward.

Innovation and R&D

Product and process innovation is the key to productivity growth. In chapter 3 competitive pressure was emphasized as the most important driver of innovation, and the nature of productivity-enhancing innovation is often organizational rather than technical.

However, in a range of manufacturing industries technology can drive innovation and productivity, and R&D is an important sign of innovative effort. R&D's importance to productivity is necessary given the need for industries to possess the technological sophistication to take advantage of worldwide advances, even if they have not developed the technology themselves. A study of a group of Organization for Economic Cooperation

---

17. In fact, capital intensity actually grew faster in Britain than in the United States, France, and Germany from 1979–95.

Table 4.2 Average research and development (R&D) expenditures as shares of output, 1973–98

	Britain	United States	France	West Germany
Total economy (percent)				
1973–79	1.36	1.54	1.06	1.42
1980–84	1.45	1.83	1.19	1.75
1985–89	1.49	2.04	1.35	2.04
1990–98	1.35	1.98	1.45	1.77
Manufacturing (percent)				
1973–79	4.61	6.34	3.95	3.77
1980–84	6.13	8.31	4.85	5.17
1985–89	5.73	9.28	5.73	6.16
1990–96	5.94	8.39	6.61	6.37
Relative R&D stocks/output, 1996				
Total economy	100	138	100	126
Manufacturing	100	142	106	109

Source: Crafts and O'Mahony (2001, table 4).

and Development (OECD) countries by Griffith et al. (2000) further supports this view. The study finds that R&D increases productivity directly through more innovation and indirectly via increased technology transfers.

Britain lags France, Germany, and the United States in R&D spending in relation to GDP (table 4.2). In addition, R&D in Britain is concentrated in only a few industries: the pharmaceutical, biotechnology, aerospace, and defense sectors. This contrasts with total R&D worldwide, which is largely concentrated in IT hardware, automotive, pharmaceuticals, and electronics sectors (DTI 2002a).

Does Britain's lack of R&D spending suggest technological inferiority is a reason for the productivity gap? Not necessarily since too much emphasis should not be placed on R&D. The bulk of the British economy—and other advanced economies—is in the service sector where very little formal R&D occurs. In fact, these sectors often use technology but can generally buy existing technology on world markets.

As we will see later in this chapter, there are indeed signs that the British economy lacks innovative initiative. But as was the case with physical capital, the low level of R&D seems more a symptom than a basic cause of the productivity gap. Policies that increase competitive intensity are likely to increase R&D spending and innovation as firms become more efficient in response to increased competitive pressure.

One policy reform that could help the technology sector is to increase basic R&D funding at universities and encourage links between academia and private companies to speed the flow of ideas into commercialization. Although already under way in some schools such as Cambridge University, the funding could be spread more widely. The United States provides numerous examples of how university funding can increase innovation in high-tech sectors.

IT Capital Investment

Studies have examined the role of IT capital in Britain's productivity growth to determine whether business has invested adequately in IT and whether the investments have been used effectively. Oulton (2001) looks at four types of IT—computers, software, telecommunications equipment, and semiconductors—in an attempt to estimate the contribution of this type of capital to growth in Britain. Based on standard data it seemed that Britain's IT investment level was pretty low.[18] But Oulton adjusts Britain's official numbers for software investment upward by a factor of three on the basis that official statistics are substantially understating the figures.[19] In addition, he uses US producer price indexes (PPI) for IT (after adjusting for exchange rate changes) because the US indexes capture the rapid growth in computer quality over time whereas the British deflators do not. Accepting Oulton's adjusted figures, total British investment in IT was more than 3 percent of GDP in 1998, which is as large as total US IT investment (figure 4.4).[20] The stock of IT capital in Britain is lower than in the United States, but the growth in investment is very similar. OECD comparisons of IT investment also suggest that Britain has invested comparably to France and Germany in this form of capital. Therefore, a lack of IT capital is not an important source for Britain's productivity gap.

Studies by Basu et al. (2003) and by van Ark, Inklaar, and McGuckin (2002) break down the total economy into industry groupings based on

---

18. In the past, the higher cost for computer equipment and peripherals in Britain may be one reason the country lagged behind the United States in IT investment. However, these prices are declining rapidly. Brand (2001) provides a comparison of the British producer price index (PPI) for desktop and laptop PCs and US PPI for desktops and workstations. Note, though, that IT prices remain high for British consumers.

19. Oulton (2001) justifies the adjustment on the basis that British software investment in the 1990s was approximately 39 percent of computer investment compared to 140 percent for the United States using official figures—numbers that Oulton does not consider feasible. Oulton also does not find it feasible that the proportion of sales of the computer services industry defined as investment in Britain was 18 percent in 1996 compared to 60 percent in the United States. Furthermore, applying the US methods for estimating "own account" software and a reexamination of the survey data reinforces the need to triple the official software numbers. Finally, Oulton measures capital services differently than the UK Office of National Statistics, where cumulative investment is used to estimate the capital stock for each asset and depreciation is taken to be geometric at Bureau of Economic Analysis (BEA) rates. The assets are then weighted together based on rental prices rather than asset prices to obtain the total capital stock.

20. Oulton estimates software investment to be 1.56 percent of GDP in 1998, which is very close to the 1.7 percent estimate provided by Ahmad (2003). Ahmad's figures were based on OECD Task Force recommendations for estimating software in the national accounts.

Figure 4.4   Adjusted total IT investment in Britain and the United States, 1974–98 (current prices)

percent of GDP

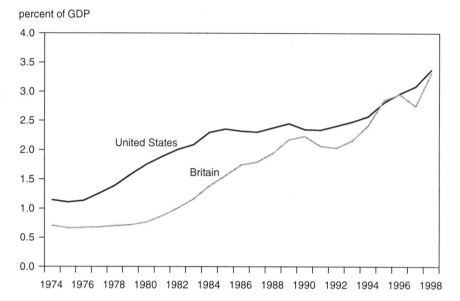

IT = information technology

Source: Oulton (2001, chart 1).

their use of IT. We discussed the van Ark, Inklaar, and McGuckin study in chapter 3. It suggests that industries using IT in Europe were not as successful in taking advantage of new technological advances as were US companies in the same industries. For Britain, van Ark, Inklaar, and McGuckin found that slower productivity growth after 1995 was concentrated in industries that were not major IT users.

The Basu et al. study (2003) focuses on comparing the effect of IT in the United States and Britain. The main hypothesis is that a lag time exists between purchasing IT capital and its subsequent positive productivity. The lag occurs because companies must accumulate know-how or other forms of intangible capital along with the IT investment. Basu et al. argue that productivity growth will actually be held down during periods of rapid IT capital accumulation because companies devote resources to developing the intangible capital needed to take advantage of their investment rather than just producing output.[21]

The authors' key empirical result, based on industry-level productivity estimates over time, is that US MFP growth is positively related to past IT

---

21. Basu et al. acknowledge that the lag-time hypothesis is present in earlier literature. See also chapter 3 for more information.

investment but negatively related to contemporaneous IT investment.[22] Therefore, they conclude that *IT investment has a strong positive but delayed impact on productivity*, with a lag of about five years. Basu et al. apply this idea to Britain and argue that the rapid IT investment in the late 1990s actually slowed productivity growth in the same period. They are correspondingly optimistic that future growth will be faster. They are very cautious in their ultimate conclusions, however, because the statistical regression analysis that showed the delayed effect of IT in the United States failed to yield comparable results in the British data.

Although some merit should be given to the Basu et al. argument, some caution is needed as well. As they acknowledge, their empirical results are not strong enough to take a lot of weight. For instance, the authors turned US standard growth accounting on its head by suggesting that the rapid rate of IT capital investment in the late 1990s actually lowered productivity growth.

We believe that the evidence about the lag time between IT investment and productivity does provide some support for the view that the productivity convergence in Britain will occur. But in line with the discussion in chapter 3, it is important not to overstate the extent to which IT is the cause of slow or fast productivity growth. The evidence described in this section is valuable but not conclusive.

Labor Skill and Education: Skill Shortages Affect the Productivity Gap

One interpretation of the growth accounting results given earlier is that Germany and the United States followed different paths to high productivity. Germany relies on a workforce with a large segment of workers with intermediate (vocational) skills (and high capital intensity), a large manufacturing sector, and the production of high-quality, high-value-added products. Although the bulk of the US workforce is low skilled, the United States also has strong universities as well as a strong managerial and entrepreneurial component to balance its workforce. The high variance of skill levels in the United States is reflected in the wide distribution of wages.[23]

Britain's economy falls between two stools. Lacking trained and innovative managers, Britain does not have the ability of US companies to be

---

22. Since their dependent variable is MFP growth, Basu et al. have included the normal positive effect of contemporaneous IT capital investment on labor productivity growth. Their regression results then suggest that standard growth accounting substantially overstates the effect of IT capital on labor productivity growth.

23. Unlike Britain, the United States has an extensive community college system that primarily teaches vocational skills with training programs in such fields as electricity, auto mechanics, and computer technology. In 2000, nearly 6 million students were enrolled in these two-year colleges in the United States. Davis and Wessel (1998) argue that community colleges have increased worker skills and allowed people to find employment or obtain better jobs.

Figure 4.5 Skill levels of workforce, select countries, 1999

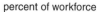

percent of workforce

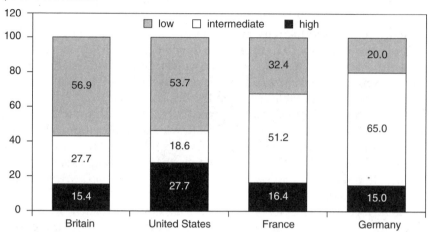

Note: High = degree level or above
   Intermediate = vocational qualifications above general schooling but
      below degree
   Low = general schooling only

Source: O'Mahony and de Boer (2002, table 5).

productive with low-skilled workers (the Wal-Mart or McDonald's model). The country also does not have the highly skilled labor—created with vocational training—to produce high-value-added products like German luxury autos or specialized machine tools.

In evaluating this idea, there clearly is evidence that the skill and education level of the British workforce is low. Figure 4.5 illustrates the pattern described above, with Britain having fewer intermediate-skill workers than France and Germany and fewer high-skilled workers than the United States. According to the Sector Skills Development Agency (SSDA) (2003, 7), "over a third of the working-age population in Britain have no trade, professional or advanced qualifications" and "nearly 7 million adults are functionally illiterate." Many children in Britain drop out of school at age 16 (the legal minimum), and Britain has one of the lowest participation rates in education among OECD countries for those 17 years of age (SSDA 2003, 7).

The SSDA also reports that "at least a third of organizations [in England] that experience skill shortages or skill gaps report negative effects on organization performance" (2003, 6). In 2001, 8 percent of all establishments in England had skills shortages and 25 percent of companies with vacancies found it hard to fill positions due to the lack of appropriately skilled workers. A study by Campbell et al. (2001) for the UK Department of Education and Skills concluded that skill deficiencies in certain occupational categories have a more pronounced negative effect in the range of problems they cause and the number of organizations they affect, particularly for those in management, skilled trades, and professional occupations.

The UK Employers Skill Survey of 2002 (Hillage et al. 2002) also measured skill gaps. The survey asked respondents (employers in the sample) to assess whether their employees were fully proficient at their job and, if not, to what extent they were not proficient. In the survey a firm has a skill gap if some employees are not considered fully proficient. The main components of proficiency according to the survey respondents are quality and efficiency of performance. The survey results suggest that about 23 percent of firms had internal skill gaps in 2002—an increase from the 16 percent reported in 2001. The skill gaps occurred most frequently among sales and customer-service staff, with only 16 percent of respondents considering over half or more of their staff proficient at their job.

Management skills in Britain are considered by many to be below US standards. One reason put forward is that many British firms do not operate on the best-practice frontier and therefore many managers learn the job in a second-best environment (Nickell 2002). Moreover, Britain has a lower share of formally educated managers and tends only slowly to adopt modern management techniques. For example, according to Mason and Finegold (1997) graduate engineers are responsible for gradual innovations and improvements in the work of less-skilled employees in US manufacturing factories that increases productivity, whereas Britain has a relative shortage of graduate supervisors in the manufacturing sector.

A statistical study by Haskel and Pereira (2002) used matched employer-employee data on individual British establishments to examine what proportion of the variation in labor productivity across establishments is due to differences in skills. Their findings suggest businesses that hire more highly skilled workers (above median human capital) have higher productivity than businesses hiring less-skilled workers. The positive effect of hiring more highly skilled workers in terms of productivity gains was found to be economically significant, although it explains only a small proportion of the variation in productivity across establishments.

Case Study Evidence on the Importance—or Unimportance—of Skills and Education

Further evidence of education's role in productivity is provided by the case studies described in chapter 3. The McKinsey Global Institute (MGI) has explored reasons for productivity differences across a wide range of countries and industries—the studies of France and Germany were described earlier in chapter 3, but the results from other countries are also informative. For instance, the MGI teams did not find that differences in *production-worker* capabilities were a major reason for productivity differences across countries. Brazil, in particular, was a surprising study. In Brazil the general consensus is that low education and the low-skilled workforce are a key reason for low productivity. In construction, for example, the workers lack the basic literacy skills to read plans, which apparently creates an important barrier to high productivity. However, the same MGI team from Brazil visited a construction site in Texas and found it is *five times as productive* despite the fact that most of the workers were Mexican immigrants who could not speak English and also lacked basic literacy skills. The difference seemed to stem from larger-scale projects, better work planning, more use of prefabricated materials, and better-designed buildings (making them easier to build). Thus, if the low level of production-worker skills among Brazilian construction workers is not the main barrier to higher productivity in that industry, then one wonders if there might not be ways to use British workers much more productively, despite their skill deficiencies.

Other evidence comes from the Japanese auto industry. Japanese companies entering or expanding US operations carefully screen and select a small number of workers. The companies test for dexterity, ability at spatial relationships, numeracy, and—most importantly—attitude. They want workers who will show up on time, work hard, be trained, and be infrequently absent. These skills may be correlated with school performance but, with the exception of numeracy, are not based directly on what children learn in school. Many companies report a preference for hiring workers from farm families even though their education may not be of the best quality, thus making the case that people raised on farms learn to work hard.

Companies may not emphasize education-based skills because they can design business processes and train workers to maximize their potential. For example, we are told that British store clerks cannot correctly make change for someone purchasing three items. In contrast, checkout clerks at a German grocery chain are trained extensively to accurately make change and may even be required to memorize the prices of all items in the store. But how big a problem is the lack of arithmetic skill? Modern retail stores have scanners and automatic change machines, so whatever the deficiencies of the British workers, these should not block the road to higher retail productivity. In fact scanners have the additional advantage that they allow for efficient inventory management, so even the German stores invest in the technology. In a food retail study (MGI 1998), productivity in Britain was actually very high and was constrained mostly by the small size of the stores, not by labor force skills.

Not all the evidence from company or industry studies points in the same direction, however. The work of Bartel, Ichniowski, and Shaw (2002) on steel and other industries has pointed out ways in which skill require-ments have changed over time, particularly because of increased IT use. In the past, for example, steelworkers worked on the factory floor monitoring and adjusting machines mechanically. Today, steelworkers work with computers away from the factory floor and make changes electronically. Autor, Levy, and Murnane (2001) find that computers reduce the demand for workers who perform routine manual activities and increase the relative demand for workers who can perform tasks using information to make decisions. These studies support a broader literature that links rising returns to education with the increase in IT use in companies. The increased demand for skilled workers (the existence of skill-biased technological change) may strengthen the case for education.[24]

Moreover, even if companies do not demand that workers have strong educational qualifications, they generally train workers with the specific skills they will need to perform their jobs. Rural workers in Mexico are given six to twelve months of training when they join an auto plant. The Japanese plants in the United States and in Britain also train their workers continuously while they are employed.

On-the-job training is an important issue. British companies complain that their trained workers are often hired away by smaller companies who can offer higher wages since training costs are unnecessary. This "externality" from training is well known in the literature, and it implies that too little training will be offered. In the British case studies discussed in more detail later, the auto industry illustrates how the low-skilled production workers posed a problem for the Japanese transplants in Britain.

In contrast, Germany provides an apprenticeship program, which locks workers into the company that has trained them. Although the externality inflicted by worker poaching is avoided, the program imposes substantial costs. It fosters the labor-market rigidity that Germany must overcome. During the postwar period when the demand for skilled workers in established companies was growing, the system worked well to provide the high-quality workforce that was needed. In the current economic environment where greater mobility is needed, however, the apprenticeship programs have become a barrier to change. With employment declining in manufacturing industries and the need for overall labor-market flexibility, it would be hard to justify setting up a German-style apprenticeship system in Britain today.

---

24. The increased demand for skills could simply mean employers find it more important to hire workers with high intrinsic ability. Moreover, some studies find that the return on education is much higher for graduates of elite schools than for those from other schools. Elite schools may provide a better education—or a degree from a school such as Harvard may indicate superior skills.

Overall Assessment of Education and Skill as Reasons for Britain's Low Productivity

In economics, there is robust empirical evidence that years of education are strongly correlated with earnings, even after controlling for other observable characteristics of individuals (Ashenfelter, Harmon, and Oosterbeek 1999; Card 1999). For a given family background and IQ score, for example, persons with a higher level of education will earn more than those with a lower level of education. A natural concern about this result is that higher-ability individuals will generally choose to acquire more education, so the causality may run in the other direction. Through a variety of creative statistical techniques, however, labor economists have concluded that this possibility of reverse causality does not eliminate the result that more education implies higher earnings.[25]

Despite the studies noted above supporting the theory that more education and training equal higher wages, support for the productivity value of the education itself is much more mixed. The basis for linking earnings to productivity is the argument that employers would not pay higher wages to more educated or skilled workers unless they were more productive. However, the value of increased education to overall economic growth may not be as great as this implies, if education is valued primarily as a signaling tool to employers (diplomas may have a substantial value in the marketplace even when the education itself has only a modest effect on a worker's productivity).

Empirical work that could estimate the direct contribution of education to overall economic growth or to productivity growth has produced very mixed results. There is no question that wealthy societies tend to have a better-trained and -educated workforce than poor ones, but the direction of causality in this relation and the exact importance of education and training to economic success are hard to pin down.

Educational quality should be improved for many good reasons. Not only does education broaden one's knowledge and perspective as a citizen in a global world, there are also positive benefits to economic growth. Furthermore, the current labor market may well require more advanced literacy and numeracy skills than past jobs required. In fact, there is evidence that US workers who can use computers fare better in the labor market than those who cannot (Autor, Katz, and Krueger 1997).

So on balance, it is likely that part of the productivity gap between Britain and Germany may be the result of a more skilled workforce in Germany. And some part of the gap with the United States is because in the United States a larger number of people go on to obtain higher education.

---

25. The identical-twin studies are one such example. A twin with the same genetic and environmental conditions as its sibling will achieve higher earnings if he or she acquires more years of schooling (Krueger and Ashenfelter 1994).

The growth accounting calculation suggested that 19 percent of the productivity gap between Britain and Germany was the result of skill differences. Even if this is correct, it means that worker skills account for only a modest part of the total productivity problem in Britain.

Because of concerns about the quality of education, spending on education in Britain has been rising. In 1999 the share of the English population holding qualifications equivalent to NVQ4 or NVQ5[26] was 26 percent, up from 17 percent in 1991. The share of those employed qualified up to NVQ3 has also increased, whereas the share of the employed population with no qualifications has declined significantly from 25 percent in 1991 to 13 percent in 1999 (Campbell et al. 2001). Therefore, if skill levels are a reason for the productivity gap today, this gap should diminish going forward.

Productivity Differences Associated with Nationality of Ownership and with Being Part of a Multinational Company

An interesting line of productivity research used in the United States has been applied to British data with some new results. We discuss these findings in this section because they are both useful and suggestive about the reasons for the British productivity gap. Although the new findings do not definitively find the root cause of the gap, they add to the overall perspective on the performance of British companies.

Many studies have found that foreign-owned firms operating in Britain have substantially higher productivity than their British equivalents (Davies and Lyons 1991, Oulton 2001, Griffith and Simpson 2003). But why are British firms less productive? A number of obvious explanations immediately come to mind, including one mentioned earlier: British managers are less skilled than their counterparts. Less obvious explanations, however, may include the fact that foreign-owned companies may be more capital intensive.

A recent study by Criscuolo and Martin (2002) of companies operating in Britain has added a new dimension to earlier findings. Using newly available (pooled cross-section, time-series) data covering 1996–2000, they compare the productivity performance of foreign-owned and British manufacturing firms separated for the first time into multinational and domestic manufacturers.[27] Looking at the raw data, Criscuolo and Martin discovered that the labor productivity of plants owned by British multi-

---

26. NVQ4 is defined as a first degree, teaching or nursing qualification or higher diploma. NVQ5 refers to master's degree or above.

27. Their work parallels the US studies by Doms and Jensen (1998a, 1998b).

nationals was £36,900 compared with £28,000 for plants owned by purely domestic British companies—a productivity advantage of 32 percent. The productivity of plants operated in Britain by foreign-owned multinationals is higher than that of plants operated by British multinationals, but the gap is not as large as that found in previous studies when all British-owned companies are grouped together. Plants operating in Britain owned by foreign non-US multinationals have a labor productivity of £43,100 (an advantage of 17 percent over British multinationals), while US multinationals had productivity of £46,600 (a 26 percent advantage).

In order to control for other factors, Criscuolo and Martin conduct a regression analysis. After controlling for industry they find that if a plant in Britain is part of a multinational company it has a 28 percent advantage over domestic companies. If that plant is also part of a foreign-owned, non-US multinational then there is an additional 4.7 percent productivity advantage (i.e., these plants are 32.7 percent more productive than domestic plants). A plant that is part of a US multinational has an additional advantage of 14.7 percent (these plants are 42.7 percent more productive than domestic plants and 10 percent more productive than plants owned by non-US foreign companies).

When the authors add additional controls to their analysis, notably the age of the company and size (number of employees), then the productivity gap associated with being part of a multinational is reduced to 16 percent (but it is still statistically significant). The additional advantages of being owned by a non-US foreign-owned multinational or a US multinational are not substantially different.

Criscuolo and Martin then see whether or not their results carry over into differences in MFP by using gross output per employee as their labor productivity measure and controlling explicitly for the capital-labor ratio and the level of material inputs per employee. The productivity advantage of being part of a multinational company drops sharply in these results—to 4.7 percent, still statistically significant. So the productivity advantage of being part of a multinational seen in the prior results seems to be associated with the fact that the multinationals have more capital and/or use material inputs more effectively. The productivity advantage that foreign non-US-owned plants have over British plants largely disappears—it falls to an insignificant 1 percent. The productivity advantage of US-owned plants compared to British multinationals is 4.5 percent, which is not a huge gap, but one that is statistically significant.

Summarizing these results, domestic British plants on average have much lower labor productivity than plants operated by multinationals, regardless of the nationality of the owners. Plants owned by US parent companies have the highest productivity, while foreign-owned non-US plants are somewhat more productive than the plants owned by British multinationals.

The gaps in labor productivity carry over to some extent into differences in MFP. Being part of a multinational company still confers a modest MFP benefit, but being owned by a US parent company confers an additional advantage. In the MFP estimates, there is little productivity difference between British-owned and foreign non-US-owned plants. Of course it should not be surprising that the gaps in labor productivity are larger than those in MFP. Important advantages of being a multinational are the lower cost of capital, better supply chains, and the ability to source components at lower cost.

The idea that low capital intensity is a productivity issue in Britain can be inferred from Criscuolo and Martin's results, but the fact that British multinationals seem to use lower capital intensity than other multinationals indicates that these companies are choosing not to invest, rather than being unable to invest. This conclusion is reinforced by the fact that British multinationals invest heavily overseas, including in the United States.

Because they were able to track plants over time, the authors also made the important discovery that plants operated by US multinationals were generally highly productive at the time they were taken over. Managers at US companies therefore are better at buying productive plants.

Can these results help explain Britain's relatively poor labor productivity performance in the manufacturing sector relative to its peers?[28] One could claim that Britain had relatively few multinational companies compared to other countries. That is not the case, however. The concentration of foreign manufacturing affiliates was relatively high in Britain, accounting for 20.4 percent of total British manufacturing employment in 1999. Although France had an even higher share of foreign affiliates at 28.5 percent, US foreign manufacturing affiliates accounted for only 15.1 percent of total manufacturing employment and Germany had an even smaller share at 6.2 percent. Moreover, to the extent that the US productivity advantage comes from acquiring the most productive plants, the productivity impact of encouraging takeovers by US companies would be limited.

One possibility consistent with the Criscuolo and Martin findings is that domestic British companies are not exposed to the kind of competitive pressure that multinationals face; therefore, they do not develop best-practice operations. Regulation or a specific market niche could be mechanisms to protect these domestic companies.

There is also the residual possibility that highly skilled managers are unavailable in Britain. The multinational companies may hire the best managers or transfer their own managers to Britain. Although it is possible that managers are of intrinsically lower quality in Britain, it is more likely that British managers with high intrinsic ability are inexperienced

---

28. In 1999, labor productivity in the British manufacturing sector (excluding food) was $32 per hour compared with $40 per hour in Germany, $49 per hour in France, and $49 per hour in the United States.

in operating a well-run company. If true, weak productivity may become self-perpetuating or at least slow to reverse even if regulations are eased or competition heats up.[29]

Case Study Evidence of Barriers to Productivity in Britain

In October 1998 the MGI released a study using data from the mid-1990s that examined six industries—automotive, food processing, food retailing, hotels, telecommunications, and software—to determine the extent to which British labor productivity lagged behind the US and continental European levels and, if applicable, why the lag occurred. As mentioned earlier, the MGI study of France and Germany also included Britain as a comparison country in its analysis of electricity generation and distribution. The specific results are summarized below.

Automotive

The automotive industry in Britain developed as a mixture of local companies such as Austin and Morris competing against transplants from the US industry, primarily Ford and GM Vauxhall although Chrysler was also present in the market for a short period. As in many markets, the industry underwent a series of restructurings, and smaller or weaker companies were taken over or shut down. In the 1980s the British government negotiated with the Japanese to allow their companies to enter the market. The first Japanese company in Britain was a large Nissan plant in Sunderland. Today, Toyota and Honda also operate in Britain.

In 1996 the labor productivity of vehicle assembly (the original equipment manufacturers, or OEMs) in Britain was 40 percent of the best-practice Japanese industry and well below the US industry.[30] Figure 4.6 shows how the level of labor productivity was distributed among the main auto assembly plants in Britain in 1996. Confidentiality restrictions prohibit identifying specific plants, but the three large Japanese transplants are acknowledged. As the figure shows, the Japanese transplants were able to achieve high labor productivity levels—ranging from 75 to 100 percent of the average Japanese performance. One large Japanese transplant actually equaled the Japanese average. In contrast, the older, established British plants had dramatically lower productivity, with one

---

29. These issues were recently discussed by Dominic Casserly, in a lecture in London organized by the MGI and the London School of Economics, March 15, 2004.

30. The British study excluded light trucks and SUVs, an area where the US industry has relatively high productivity because of high value-added production. If only cars are included in the study, the US industry had 71 percent of the Japanese labor productivity in 1996. Therefore, these numbers differ from those in the France-Germany study discussed in chapter 3.

Figure 4.6 Level of labor productivity among main OEMs[a] in Britain, 1996

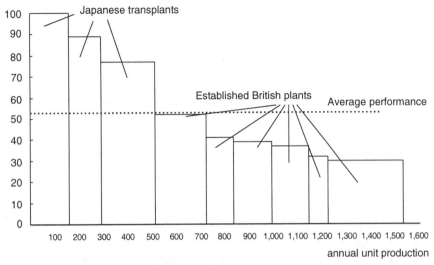

OEMs = original equipment manufacturers
a. Represent 90 percent of British production.
b. Level of Japanese auto companies, operations located in Japan.
Source: EIU data, company accounts, DRI data, MGI (1998).

very large plant below 30 percent of the level of the best-practice Japanese industry in 1996.[31]

The auto parts industry in Britain had similar levels of relative labor productivity, with the sector as a whole achieving 45 percent of the Japanese average. The British industry did appear to improve its parts industry in the 1990s with labor productivity growing at 9 percent a year from 1993–95 compared to slow productivity growth in Japan and the United States. Although the parts industry in Britain was highly fragmented, there was no correlation between plant size and productivity level.

Based on comparisons of plant-by-plant performance in the assembly sector, a major reason for Japan's higher productivity was its detailed assembly line operation, which made it much more efficient (lean manufacturing). Japan's success also depended on specific operational differences, including the use of teams and multitasking, continuous improvement programs, employee suggestions, and statistical measures to aid improvement. Another important factor is that the Japanese cars are designed to be

---

31. Note that the comparison is with the Japanese industry average since they have the best-practice standard. The highest productivity plants in Japan are well above this average.

simpler and easier to assemble. Employees also affected productivity. As noted earlier, Japanese transplants carefully screened their workforce, testing for attitudes and numeracy skills as well as providing extensive training for employees. This investment paid off with higher motivation levels and lower absentee rates than in traditional plants. The transplants also did better at matching capacity to demand and in managing their relations to parts suppliers.

Compared with Japan, Britain's capital intensity was also lower in the traditional assembly plants and in the parts sector, which contributed to the productivity difference. The lower relative cost of labor in Britain motivated the use of somewhat lower capital intensity, relative to the United States, Germany, and Japan. In 1995, labor costs among British autoworkers were 78 percent of those in Japan and just over 50 percent of those in Germany.

The key issue for the automotive industry, then, is why the traditional British producers did not improve their performance as the level of competitive intensity increased with production by Japanese transplants and increased imports from other European producers. A number of reasons come to mind. First, it takes time for any new entrant to establish a significant market share, including developing products best suited locally. For example, Japanese auto companies took many years to gain significant market shares in both the United States and Europe. Thus, it took time before the extent of the foreign-owned companies' threat was appreciated.

Second, the British industry maintained production by exporting to the rest of Europe by relying on lower labor costs. Third, although the European auto market became much more integrated in the 1990s, the Japanese companies were subject to quantitative restrictions by many EU countries—notably France, Germany, and Italy. The restrictions prevented the Japanese transplants in Britain from expanding production by exporting to the rest of Europe, which would have increased the average level of productivity in the British industry.

Fourth, the traditional auto producers in Britain had great difficulty modernizing their operations. Both unionized production workers and the existing cadre of managers were highly resistant to change.[32] Threatening to close a plant or ordering massive layoffs may be required to force major changes, but sometimes such measures are too late at that point. Fifth, all auto companies in Britain report that the quality of graduate engineers in the industry is low.

Sixth, massive state aid was provided to prop up the weak auto plants in Britain. From 1973 to 1988, £3.4 billion were given to the Rover company alone. Even after the European Union tried to restrict further state aid, loopholes allowed state aid to plants in "development" areas. Britain

---

32. Resistance to change is not a problem unique to Britain, it is also a serious problem in the US and German industries.

alone did not continue in this policy direction—there is large-scale over-capacity in Europe.[33]

Britain's auto industry is an important example of why labor productivity in manufacturing is low even though international trade exposure has apparently become much higher over time. The good news is that the exposure to best-practice competition is now working. British policymakers encouraged best-practice Japanese companies to enter the market, bringing the same successful production methods used in their own country and the United States. Traditional British suppliers are now restructuring, and some plants have been sold to US or German companies. However, plants where workers and managers resisted change are being downsized or closed.

The bad news is that the process of increasing British productivity is very slow because the forces resisting change were strong. In fact, change was slowed significantly by state support for low-productivity plants. Lack of skills and education also affected the rate of change.[34]

At the engineering level, the US and German auto industries were able to raise productivity in some of Britain's traditional plants by designing higher-value-added vehicles and avoiding some of the drastic production changes that would have been necessary to remain competitive.[35] Since engineering and design skills are available on a global basis, the lack of these skills may not be an insurmountable problem. Nevertheless, having skilled engineers in close proximity to production facilities is an advantage in the automotive industry, and therefore a potential disadvantage for the British industry.

Food Processing

The food processing industry, which is the largest manufacturing sector and one where competition is less intense, was examined in the second MGI manufacturing case study. Since tastes in food differ quite strongly across local and regional markets, processed food is produced domestically in most countries to a greater extent than other manufactured goods.

---

33. It is notable that the Thatcher government did not halt state aid. Prime Minister Thatcher could thus be "strategically ambiguous" in her commitment to reducing government involvement in the economy: Most of the state aid to Rover (then British Leyland) was disbursed in 1983—just prior to a national election in Britain.

34. State aid included using local training colleges to augment production-worker skills.

35. This is not intended as a statement about what constitutes good business strategy over the long run. In the United States, the Big Three auto manufacturers are now facing increased competition in the SUV and pickup market. And the luxury German producers have reportedly "overengineered" their latest models, so their US reliability ratings are now very low (see Consumer Reports 2003, auto ranking reported in USA Today, November 3, 2003, www.usatoday.com/money/autos/2003-03-11-cr-picks_x.htm, accessed May 24, 2004).

There has been substantial foreign direct investment in this industry, however, allowing for the entry of best-practice methods—at least in principle.

Labor productivity in Britain was 74 percent of the US level in 1994 at a time when the German industry productivity was 94 percent of the US level. Capital intensity is relatively low in the food processing industry, especially relative to Germany. Multifactor productivity in Britain was about the same as in Germany and 81 percent of the US level.

Food processing encompasses a wide range of subindustries, and labor productivity varies quite a bit among them. Nevertheless, differences in the mix of subindustries accounted for minimal differences in overall productivity in Britain, Germany, and the United States. Rather, the gap occurs within each subindustry. Therefore, two subindustries—biscuits (and bakery) and dairy—were chosen for detailed analysis.

Labor productivity in the British biscuit industry lags the United States by 36 percent and is about the same as the German industry. Capital intensity is very low in Britain so the MFP gap to the United States is 15 percent while MFP is higher than in Germany. Britain manufactures many more products than the United States (2.6 times the number of stock-keeping units, or SKUs), which causes the 15 percent gap in productivity. The greater number of products reduces the ability to automate production in Britain, the "run time" for any product, the resources devoted to process improvement in any particular product, and the scale of production.

Then why are British manufacturers not consolidating some of the brands in order to take advantage of the higher productivity and lower cost that would follow? The MGI research team's immediate answer is relative market size. They find that Britain's food industry is dominated by large retailers who demand product proliferation despite a small overall market. In contrast, large US food processors such as Nabisco have established national brands with name recognition in the larger US market. New products are introduced only after successful test marketing and only when a large enough market is available to justify production at minimum efficient scale.

That answer is not reasonable from an economic point of view, since there must be a reason for the retailers' demands. Given the importance of shelf space—retailers often apply pressure to reduce, not increase, the number of SKUs—retailers are obviously responding to British consumers' preference for a range of biscuits.

The biscuit case study illustrates an important principle: In manufacturing industries where consumers have strong preferences for local products, overall competitive intensity of the industry is reduced and global best practices do not emerge. From a policy point of view, there is little to be done. This may simply be a situation where the larger scale of the US economy confers some advantage. More generally, free trade does not always produce a fully competitive domestic industry, particularly in the short run. If adult consumers purchase the same products from childhood (an important issue in food processing) then new product entry may be slowed and local producers will survive, even if their productivity is lower than best practice.

The dairy industry is somewhat similar to the biscuit example. Product proliferation resulting in small-scale operations causes lower labor productivity, with some combination of consumer tastes and retailer pressure again at work. Britain's labor productivity is 84 percent of the US level, while Germany's labor productivity is far higher (132 percent of the United States)—driven largely by very capital-intensive production methods. The US industry is not world best practice by a wide margin and is characterized by highly regulated local markets.

Productivity in the British dairy industry is affected adversely by EU regulation. Under the Common Agricultural Policy the flow of milk products is restricted. Fresh milk is a relatively low-value-added per worker activity and is always produced locally for freshness. Fresh milk takes up much of British milk production, and dairy processors cannot get access to additional milk product supplies to produce higher-value-added dairy products. The output of the dairy industry in Britain is 60 percent fresh milk compared with 47 percent in the United States and 28 percent in Germany.

Food Retailing

Britain not only has a high level of competitive intensity in food retailing but its major retailers are quite efficient. Nevertheless, their labor productivity is at 88 percent of the US level and even lower compared with France at 118 percent of the US level. Britain's planning restrictions have slowed the introduction of large retail stores that allow higher productivity.[36] France also has strict planning restrictions, but exceptions have allowed large hypermarkets to develop, which account for the bulk of food sales.[37]

An MFP calculation, using square meters of retail space as the measure of capital, suggested productivity is as high in Britain as in France and higher than in the United States. US MFP is lower because stores stay open longer than British and French stores, which lowers measured labor productivity.

Britain made a trade-off between encouraging maximum labor productivity in retailing and attempting to preserve local, small retailers. How-

36. Wal-Mart has become the largest food retailer in the United States since the mid-1990s, and its distribution system may be the most efficient in the world. Wal-Mart's efficiency pressure on competitors was a major driver of faster productivity growth in retail in the United States since the time of the data reported here. Wal-Mart has also entered the British market by acquiring Asda. However, this is one of the smaller players in Britain and has small supermarkets.

37. For stores selling both food and merchandise, like hypermarkets in France, the MGI team separated the value added and the hours associated with the food retailing in their productivity estimates.

ever, consumer demand for large supermarkets is gradually overwhelming this policy decision, and the small grocery stores are disappearing despite efforts to save them.

Hotels

Labor productivity in the British hotel industry is very low at 55 percent of the US level—compared with France, which is at 88 percent of the US level. Modern, productive hotels have a number of advantages. They are designed to allow rapid servicing of rooms—maids can use service carts and follow standard procedures for each room, which allows quick turnaround and customer satisfaction. Hotel layouts are also well structured to be efficient in terms of size and location (e.g., storage areas, kitchen placement, etc.). Large hotels are more productive than small ones because of scale economies of operation, and franchise hotels have access to both computerized reservation systems (raising occupancy levels) and bulk suppliers.

The United States and France have a much higher proportion of modern, productive hotels than Britain. First, planning restrictions in Britain make it very difficult to build new hotels or even modernize old ones. Second, both business and vacation use of hotels is very low, and the market has not grown rapidly. Third, an inefficient construction industry makes it costly to build new hotels. The fact that hotels are relatively expensive in Britain is of course an endogenous reason why demand growth has been weak. But beyond the price effect, the lack of business travel reflects the concentration of the business activity in London or in cities a short train ride or drive from London.

Based on both the food retailing and the hotel case, it is clear that planning restrictions are holding back Britain's productivity. Although we do not support the unrestricted takeover of land that seems to characterize US development, there are ways to achieve the goals of a highly productive industry sector while preserving open land and historical values. For example, the historical façade of a hotel can be saved while gutting and remodeling the interior, which is not currently possible in Britain. A French company that operates hotels in both France and Britain provides a telling example of each country's barriers. Operating in France is a nightmare because of complex labor laws that require the company to retain a permanent team of lawyers to avoid ongoing problems.[38] Operating in Britain is a nightmare because the company cannot move a door or

---

38. High labor costs lower employment and raise labor productivity in French hotels. For example, low-price hotels in France have automated check-in and check-out procedures and very few employees.

change a doorknob in any hotel classified as historic.[39] It is also noteworthy that British-based companies operate large-scale hotel networks in the United States. They apparently moved to the US market after giving up on profitable expansion in Britain—yet another example of why capital intensity is lower.

Telecommunications

The study of the British telecommunications industry is rather dated, because it does not reflect the effect of the mobile phone network. However, the analysis of the wire-line industry is still a helpful case study since it examines the Thatcher-inspired privatization of the old post office–run telephone system. As of 1995 labor productivity in the telecommunications industry in Britain was comparable to other European industries, and MFP was higher than the rest of Europe. Comparison with the US system was less favorable with labor productivity 49 percent of the US level and MFP at 62 percent.

The higher US productivity levels in fixed-line telecommunications are familiar from many comparisons with European industries. The United States has a higher volume of phone calls and consequent network usage, which partly stems from more aggressive marketing and pricing. Sweden is similar to the United States in terms of productivity performance as well as marketing and pricing strategy. Furthermore, phone usage seems to reflect household income and taste differences as well as business practice differences.[40]

British Telecom (BT) was established as a private company in 1984 and faced a single competitor, Mercury. A strict price-cap regime forced BT to reduce the price of a basket of telephone services, and any increase in access charges (the fixed cost of having a phone line) were also regulated. Although these regulations were helpful in forcing efficiency and productivity gains, they lacked full flexibility and discouraged the two companies from lowering the cost per call, which would have encouraged greater use of the system. Other aspects of the regulatory system effectively maintained the BT monopoly so that by 1992 the company still controlled 93 percent of the market.

After 1992 open competition made it easier for new companies to enter the market, and in 1995 price restrictions were lifted. In 1996 BT's market

---

39. An abandoned Victorian hospital in London provides another example of preservation laws run amok in Britain. The century-old building remained idle and decaying for years, because it could not be remodeled for alternative uses. Arguably, bulldozing the building would have been optimal for both aesthetic and economic grounds.

40. Marketing calls are illegal in most European countries.

share had fallen to 84 percent, which indicated that open competition was slowly working and reiterated the fact that developing full-scale competition with equal partners is not an easy task. Since the mid-1990s, however, mobile telecommunications has exploded and is providing significant competition to the fixed-line providers. Although the productivity benefits of privatization and competition were very slow in coming in Britain, it is apparent that if given enough time and incorporating evolving technology, a state-owned monopoly can eventually be transformed into a more efficient industry.

Software

The British software industry in 1996, which compared somewhat more favorably with France and Germany, was much smaller and less productive than the US software industry. Productivity in software services (measured as sales per employee) in Britain, France, and Germany was estimated to be about 75 percent of the US level. At the time of the MGI study, the size of the European industries was much smaller than their counterparts in the United States (on a per capita basis). Subsequent work has suggested that in-house software development is much larger in Europe than in the United States so these size comparisons were likely misleading.

The productivity of packaged software in Britain (again using sales per employee) was 53 percent of the US level, less than France at 59 percent, and much less than Germany at 84 percent of the US level. The production of packaged software has very high fixed-development costs and low marginal costs (low cost for the production of each package). High productivity in the US packaged-software industry is driven by a small number of software vendors (such as IBM, Microsoft, Oracle, and Computer Associates) who operate at large scale and have benefited from first-mover advantages. Germany has been quite successful in this industry also, notably with SAP.

The software industry's success is based on the strong demand for leading-edge programs in other industries. For instance, in the United States in the 1950s and 1960s military demand prompted many innovative developments in software. As the industry shifted toward civilian-oriented demand, the existence of a dynamic US service sector drove the need for software and hardware. In Germany SAP developed a strong customer base among manufacturing companies. In Britain, one area of relative strength in software is in companies that serve financial institutions in the City of London.

Over time, a successful software company can expand to a global market and is no longer reliant on its domestic industries. But in the start-up phase, the existence of large dynamic domestic customers is critical to success. Therefore, policies that stimulate growth in several large sectors of the economy will generate spillover benefits to industries such as telecommunications and software. Any industry subject to high fixed costs or some other form of increasing returns to scale will benefit in its productivity from increased growth and demand from the rest of the economy.

Electric Power

Looking back, the power industry illustrates the dangers of a hasty, ill-conceived liberalization.[41] In 1989, the UK Electricity Act created four separate entities from the government-owned generation and transmission monopoly known as the Central Electricity Generating Board: two power producers (PowerGen and National Power), a transmission company (National Grid Company [NGC]), and a distribution network (consisting of 12 regional power companies). All four entities were gradually privatized.

In order to balance the national supply and demand of power in the newly privatized sector,[42] the British government established "The England and Wales Power Pool" to act as the link (clearinghouse) between producers (PowerGen and National Power, plus a limited number of independent power producers) and consumers. The "power pool" functioned via a day-ahead uniform price auction, i.e., an auction in which the price of power is set a day in advance, and all consumers pay the same price. Producers, such as PowerGen, would announce the amount of power they would be willing to supply to the grid at a given price—the higher the price, the more power a producer would generally be willing to supply. Electricity demand, based on consumer requirements, would subsequently be estimated, and the price at which the power market for the day after cleared, meaning where power supply and demand equaled each other, would be determined. All consumers would pay the price of the marginally supplied unit, with supply generated by power producers, whose "supply-bids" were at or below the market-clearing price for the day.

With PowerGen and National Power by far the dominant producers in the British electricity market (just below 70 percent of generation output in 1990), however, it quickly became apparent to government regulators that the two were able to use their market power to manipulate the power-pool price. In 1993 PowerGen and National Power were forced to auction 15 percent of their generating capacity to rectify their duopoly of the market. While the forced auction likely enhanced competition, the fact remained

---

41. This section on the development of the British power industry is not based on the 1998 MGI study.

42. Due to the large fluctuations between times of peak demand (morning and early evening hours) and "trough demand" (nighttime), and the twin facts that power is "instantaneous in character" and cannot be stored profitably (which means that grid supply must effectively equal grid demand at all times), this is a highly complex operation.

that power prices in Britain rose from 1990 to 1998 by 10 percent despite privatization, capital cost declined up to 40 percent, fuel (spot gas) prices declined by almost 50 percent, and the introduction of a daily spot market for power highlighted above.[43] Obviously such increases in energy prices adversely affect companies' profitability, investments, and, ultimately, productivity. In other words, during the 1990s, the power industry was a clear example of economic liberalization producing an unfavorable consumer outcome.

Despite the adverse effects of the misguided privatization of Britain's power industry, incentives to increase labor productivity were created. In the electricity generation sector from 1992 to 2000, the British industry attained labor productivity growth of 7 percent a year—faster growth than the United States, France, and Germany (albeit starting at a rather low level). (Unfortunately the study did not compute an estimate of the capital stock of the British industry.) Britain's rate of labor productivity growth in electricity distribution was actually even faster at 7.7 percent growth a year over the same period, which again made it the fastest in productivity growth among the studied countries. This latter result is particularly noteworthy because the distribution system was a monopoly, and its strong performance was achieved only through the privatization and liberalization of its operating procedures in response to regulatory pressure to reduce prices. Nevertheless, as of 2000 Britain's level of productivity remained lower than the other countries.

To overcome the remaining problems in the power industry, in 2001 the British government instituted the New Electricity Trading Arrangement (NETA) to replace the power pool, opening up for bilateral contracts (direct contracts between particular producers and consumers) as well as power futures exchange trading (contracts for the delivery or purchase of a given amount of power at a fixed time in the future). Both factors have greatly facilitated competition by empowering consumers and have led to significant price declines of 20 to 25 percent, depending on the time of consumption.[44]

The power industry is an interesting case study. It shows that economic liberalization can raise productivity and lower prices. However, the full benefits of economic liberalization were delayed by more than 10 years because of weaknesses in the process and the restrictive regulatory structure that was created. We believe that future benefits are likely to be substantial in the industry.

---

43. Data from Eileen Marshall, *What NETA Was Designed to Achieve*, Office of Gas and Electricity Markets (OFGEM) presentation, May 20, 2003.

44. See OFGEM Web site, NETA at a Glance, www.ofgem.co.uk.

Overall Conclusions from the Case Studies

The case studies of British industries reveal that several sources of the productivity gap described earlier are affecting the market: Privatization, liberalization, and reform appear to be working in the industries where they have been implemented though *the time lag seems unnecessarily long.* The process of reaching best-practice productivity levels is occurring over many years.

In several of the case studies, the high level of capital intensity in Germany is a factor in explaining Britain's productivity gap, which is consistent with the growth accounting results reported earlier. It is less clear whether specific policies are needed to overcome this gap. With expensive, inflexible labor and low-cost capital, it is not surprising that German companies reduce employment as much as possible and rely on automation. However, the same level of automation may not be optimal or profitable in Britain.

The lack of skilled workers—particularly in engineering and design—showed up as a problem in the automotive industry and may have slowed the expansion of transplant production in Britain. Furthermore, managers and workers alike resist change in production processes in traditional auto producers and may have also affected productivity (although whether this is worse than in other countries is debatable).

None of the case studies supported the idea that Britain's low productivity stems from a failure to develop clusters, even in the food processing industry. The most productive automotive plants were built in the north of England away from the location of traditional suppliers and assemblers, and most other service industries are scattered round the country serving local customers. However, Britain has successfully developed in industries not examined in the case studies. For example, the financial service industry already has a cluster in the City of London. In high-tech and biotechnology, Britain is in fact at the European forefront of clustering with more than 1,600 high-tech firms established around Cambridge University by 2001.[45]

The results of the case studies suggest that the British economy is not as competitive and deregulated as is sometimes claimed. The biggest barrier to industry change and greater competition came from planning restrictions (reinforced by a weak construction industry; see box 4.1). The Thatcher government and subsequent policymakers have been reluctant to deal with that problem. It is a very sensitive political issue in Britain since preservation is an important tradition. Based on MGI studies in several European economies, the general conclusion is that intelligent plan-

---

45. See *The Economist*, "Silicon Fen Strains to Grow," www.economist.com/displaystory. cfm?story_id=569685 (accessed April 12, 2001).

Box 4.1 Problems in the construction industry exacerbate problems from planning restrictions: Conclusions from a UK Treasury report

It would be too optimistic to assert that improving land use planning in Britain would solve all of the problems described in the industry case studies. A recent UK Treasury report on British housing supply (Barker 2003), which includes an in-depth study of the British construction sector, suggests a complex relationship between the construction sector and planning regulation. It is not simply a lack of available land with the required planning permits that beleaguers Britain. The UK Treasury reports that planning regulation in itself does not prevent developers from obtaining the necessary building permits to rapidly meet demand in the housing market. In fact nearly all British home builders own substantial "land banks" for which planning permission has already been obtained and which is frequently "worth" several years of development capacity to develop land for the company.

Instead of serving as an obstacle, the planning permits and the Section 106 obligations[1] significantly increase the value of builders' detailed knowledge of a local housing market. The builders' advantage creates a highly localized and fragmented construction industry, limiting companies' opportunities for introducing economies of scale as well as the ability to raise capital, which subsequently reduces their ability to undertake single big development projects. More importantly, the highly fragmented construction industry serves to promote opportunities for "localized market power" to small firms thereby reducing both real competitive intensity and the pace of innovation.

This problem is exacerbated by how companies manage the "approved land banks." In the highly volatile British housing market a "wait-and-see" behavior—where local supply is restricted—allows the home builders to gauge local price signals and mitigate their market risk. Thus, "approved land banks" are highly valued, and may soon drive profitability for a British home builder rather than its ability to provide high-quality, price-competitive housing.

In other aspects the UK Treasury study uncovers the same British productivity weaknesses described elsewhere in this chapter. Fully 80 percent of home builders and their subcontractors report difficulties in recruiting skilled laborers such as bricklayers, plasterers, and carpenters (Barker 2003, 97). Aggravating this skills shortage is the very small number of apprentices in the British construction industry—only a quarter of the relative German level and less than half the corresponding level in the Netherlands (Barker 2003, table 6.4). Subsequent quality problems seem to plague the industry with only 54 percent of new homebuyers saying they would buy a new home or another home from the same home builder.

The bottom line is that even substantial improvement in Britain's planning regulations would not be enough. The construction industry must also reform and greater competition from best-practice companies must be allowed.

---

1. This section of the 1991 Planning and Compensation Act lets local planning authorities "require specified operations or activities to be carried out in, on, under or over land" available for development.

ning could free up land for commercial and industrial use without destroying the historical and aesthetic assets of the country. Resistance to liberalized planning is often irrational, whether it takes the form of preserving aging buildings created in Britain during the industrial revolution or preserving pig farms in the Netherlands in the name of saving green space.

The lack of competition resulting from consumer preference for local products and the resulting product proliferation and inefficient scale create another interesting issue. In a study of South Korea, product proliferation in food processing appeared to be a market failure: Local companies had overinvested and failed to test-market new products while multinational food companies had been excluded from the economy. In Britain the situation is different: Big multinationals such as Nestlé, Nabisco, and Procter and Gamble all compete in the market. In fact, the large retailers are driving suppliers to achieve lower costs. The food processing industry may consolidate over time, or else consumer tastes will prevail and measured productivity will understate the value of product variety to consumers.

In many country studies regulation on agriculture has been found to negatively affect the food processing industry. The dairy industry in Britain is one such example, where restrictions created under the Common Agricultural Policy prevented the development of a segment of the food processing industry in Britain.

In Britain and other countries, initiating reform can generate faster productivity growth in scale-dependent industries, such as telecommunications and software. Britain should be doing pretty well on that score since it has had relatively strong GDP growth, especially in service industries that are big customers for other industries.

Why Does the OECD Conclude that Product Markets in Britain Are Deregulated?

As mentioned at the outset of the chapter Britain has the least regulated product markets according to the OECD product-market regulation (PMR) index (see box 4.2). The OECD summary PMR indexes are meant to capture the influence of regulations on the intensity of product-market competition. The detailed indicators refer to economic regulations concerning market access, administrative regulations, and barriers to trade and investment.[46] The OECD defines restrictions to competition as "barriers to access in markets that are inherently competitive, or as government interference with market mechanisms . . . in areas in which there are no obvious reasons why mechanisms should not be operating freely" (Nicoletti, Scarpetta, and Boylaud 2000, 8).

In chapter 3 we described how the OECD PMR indexes are indeed correlated with productivity performance across the OECD economies as a whole (Nicoletti and Scarpetta 2003). That makes sense since many of the problem areas the indexes discover—such as the difficulty or delay in starting a new business—are indeed important in several OECD econo-

---

46. The indexes deal only with formal regulations, not enforcement issues.

Box 4.2 Constructing the product-market regulation (PMR) index

Members' responses to the OECD regulatory questionnaire provide most of the basic data used for the PMR index. The questionnaire requested information on 1,300 regulatory provisions concerning economywide and industry-specific laws, regulations, and administrative procedures in 1998. The data are qualitative and quantitative, and the responses are classified according to three criteria:

- Scope: economywide (e.g., administrative burdens) and industry specific (e.g., price controls in a particular industry);

- Type of restriction: thematic domains (e.g., state control, barriers to entrepreneurial activity) that identify how regulation may restrict market mechanisms; and

- Function: economic (e.g., legal barriers to competition, barriers to trade and investment) versus administrative (e.g., reporting, information, and application burden on start-ups) regulations.

The raw data were coded into numerical values, and 17 detailed indicators were constructed. The 17 indicators were then classified into three domains: state control over business enterprises, barriers to entrepreneurship, and barriers to international trade and investment. The 17 detailed indicators are aggregated into summary indicators by regulatory area. A statistical approach based on factor analysis is used, where each component of the regulatory framework is weighted by its contribution to the overall variance in the data.

mies. However, the restrictions to competition that showed up in Britain's case studies would not have been captured by the OECD indexes given the way these are constructed (see box 4.2)—in particular the planning restrictions, the subsidies to failing companies, and the spillover from agricultural policy to food processing.

Boylaud and Nicoletti (2001) construct an index for the retail distribution sector along the same lines as the overall OECD PMR index. Regulations are sorted into three categories: restrictions on access (includes store size), restrictions dealing with operations (store hours, for example), and price regulations. In 1998, France, Japan, and Greece had the most restrictive regulations in retail distribution whereas the Czech Republic, Switzerland, and Australia were the least regulated. In contrast to the overall OECD PMR index where Britain is the least regulated country, Boylaud and Nicoletti's index found it to be the eighth (of the 21 countries in the sample) most regulated country for retail distribution.

What caused the difference? One of the main reasons is that large retail establishments—and expanding stores—require a complex and burdensome application procedure. Moreover, existing retail stores enjoy considerable product protection: Some items can be sold only in outlets under local or national monopoly, and professional bodies (such as an association of pharmacists) and/or representatives of commercial interests influence licensing agreements.

Conclusions on the Productivity Gap in Britain

Some uncertainty about the reasons for Britain's productivity gap remains. After reviewing the literature, we are somewhat surprised that the current productivity gap remains as large as it does. We determine that the main reasons for the continuing productivity gap are as follows (listed in subjectively determined order of importance):

- Many of the causes of weak productivity in Britain, including low competitive intensity, have been reduced or eliminated, but the productivity benefits have not yet occurred. The time lag is an important consideration.

- The deregulation of the product market in Britain was less complete than is suggested by the OECD PMR indicators. Significant barriers to full industry evolution and consolidation remain, especially those created by restrictive planning regulations and a low-quality, expensive construction sector. Weak companies were protected, which limited the effect of rising competition.

- The nature of the privatization and deregulation instituted under the Thatcher government lengthened the time lag before productivity benefits were realized. Privatization occurred without adequate competition and without the right procompetitive regulatory structure in place.

- Britain's workforce does seem to fall between two stools. There remains a large proportion of the workforce that has very low skill and education levels. And a large cadre of managers is inexperienced and untrained in best-practice companies.[47]

- The slow adjustment to rising competitive pressure in the traditional part of the automotive industry suggests that the legacy of conflicted labor relations is still hampering the transition to more productive operations in some sectors.

- Part of Britain's productivity gap is associated with a lower level of capital intensity, which appears to be a symptom primarily of other problems that limit the returns to investment.

- Improving basic science and engineering education and research would be helpful as part of the creation of a stronger R&D and technical base. British universities are not as closely connected to the business sector as US universities.

---

47. An article by David Turner and Dell Bradshaw in the *Financial Times*, March 18, 2004, discusses the issue of Britain's lack of managerial skills, including a proposal in the new government budget to provide financial incentives to overseas managers to transfer to Britain.

5

Reforming the Labor Market and Social Programs

Some people change their ways when they see the light; others when they feel the heat.

—Caroline Schroeder

In chapter 2 we concluded that three interrelated factors caused the structural decline in Europe's employment. First, average real wages are too high to sustain full employment. Second, low-skilled workers are discouraged from taking jobs because of an inadequate return from work. Third, employers are required to pay high-wage rates and high payroll taxes that discourage them from creating low-skilled jobs. Thus, there is a problem in the level of wages and the distribution of wages.[1]

In chapter 3 we found that one way to solve these problems is by increasing productivity with better business practices, stronger competition, and a progrowth regulatory environment. These steps will raise employment over the long run without reducing wages. But barring a productivity miracle in Europe, the road back to sustained economic growth will also require labor-market reform.[2] In fact, even if there was a productivity miracle it would probably occur with a good deal of employment restructuring that could raise unemployment in the short run.

---

1. The second and third reasons may seem contradictory. How can wages be both too high and too low? One answer is that in different countries or different types of jobs, employment may either be supply constrained or demand constrained. In addition, as noted in chapter 3, the large gap between company labor costs and worker net pay can cause the wage discrepancy.

2. Faster growth in Europe will also require an increase in aggregate demand, which will be discussed in chapter 6. This discussion, like the one in chapter 4, is about structural issues.

Reform and European Labor-Market Values

European policymakers recognize that employment incentives must be increased (European Council 2003), but some countries are still profoundly reluctant to increase incentives enough to generate an effective full-employment supply of labor. Reform programs in Europe are expected to be consistent with "European values," which includes paying a full-time employee a high enough income to support a family. Any effort to lower the wage rates paid to low-skilled workers would violate that principle. Even when low-skilled jobs are available, many are undesirable tasks. If people receive an adequate income without taking such a menial job, they will choose not to work. Increasing the work incentives implies providing only a rather limited income to those choosing not to work, which violates Europe's commitment to "social cohesion." Similarly, both low- and high-skilled workers are often willing to retire early once they reach their 50s, if pension and guaranteed health insurance are available. Supporting cutbacks or the elimination of early retirement provisions is not only difficult politically but also seen as a violation of the social cohesion principle.

Another common belief in Europe is that existing jobs should be preserved as much as possible. Workers should not be expected to move to new jobs if a transfer entails a change of residence, a long commute, or a substantial decline in wages. Although worker mobility is recognized as inevitable, it is only grudgingly accepted.[3]

When thinking about preserving social values, however, it is important to take a broad view. First, social cohesion must take into account the burden that will be placed on future generations of workers. In chapter 2 we illustrated how life expectancy at effective retirement age has risen dramatically over the last generation while the size of the younger generation is declining. Many current European pension systems, if left unreformed, will be unsustainable going forward. The value of social cohesion should be viewed across both current and future generations.[4]

Second, the value of social cohesion should be applied to those excluded from the mainstream economy—not just those within the mainstream. Workers on the *inside* of the labor market are frequently in heavily protected well-paid jobs. Those *outside* the labor market are given basic

---

3. With the introduction of the euro the lack of cross-border labor mobility has achieved additional importance, since it may enhance inflation differentials between individual countries. In several European countries the lack of labor mobility has been linked to the high transaction costs of buying and selling a house, reflecting a lack of competition in the real estate market.

4. Some public opinion polls indicate that future European generations of retirees have limited faith in the sustainability of the current system. Up to 80 percent of workers under the age of 35 in France, Germany, and Italy believe that public pension systems will be substantially reformed within the next 10 to 15 years. See Boeri (2003).

income support but are not part of the active society. In European labor markets in 2002 fully 60 percent of the (large segment of) unemployed had been without a job for more than 6 months and 44 percent for more than a year.[5] These high figures are not socially cohesive for the society as a whole. Immigrant communities are often part of the excluded segment.

Thus, it is important that European policymakers make hard choices now. After all, it will not be possible to continue to provide social insurance income support to the extent that has been achieved in the last decade or two. However, it is not necessary to eliminate social programs or create a harsh environment. Instead, social insurance programs can be restructured in ways that retain their ability to provide income insurance in the short run, while providing greater work incentives. Moreover, as noted in chapter 3, once employment increases, a virtuous cycle can be created where the tax burden created by payments to support the non-employed is reduced, and increasing workers' incomes can provide more work incentives.

Policies should be designed to facilitate job mobility instead of discouraging or preventing it. But to ease transitions, workers can be assisted in making job changes and provided with temporary income insurance rather than permanent jobless benefits.

The European labor market is currently not achieving its social goals. Segments of the population, including youth, are persistently unemployed or outside the labor force. The policies intended to preserve existing jobs are not successful either. Overall rates of job loss in Europe are high, as noted earlier in the OECD firm-level analysis. People argue that they are willing to sacrifice productivity in order to preserve jobs, but that is not what happens as a result of current social- and labor-market policies. The reverse, in fact, occurs since jobs are sacrificed and productivity is pushed up artificially.

Although the path to major labor-market reform will be arduous, there are clear indications that European views about social reform are changing, and policymakers and even voters are now more willing to tackle the problems. Some of the smaller European economies have already made reforms and the larger continental economies are being driven toward reform by current and future budgetary pressures.[6] For example, in a speech given to the Bundestag on March 14, 2003, German Chancellor

5. Data are for the European Union. There are large differences among the countries. In Austria and Denmark only about 20 percent of the total unemployed have been unemployed for more than a year, whereas in Italy the number is a devastating 60 percent. In the United States in 2002 only 21 percent of the unemployed had been without a job for more than 6 months and only 9.5 percent for more than a year. All data are from OECD Labor Market Statistics, www1.oecd.org/scripts/cde/members/lfsdataauthenticate.asp (accessed October 8, 2003).

6. Major labor-market reforms have been carried out in Britain. Britain's labor market and productivity issues are discussed separately in chapter 4.

Gerhard Schröder made the case for significant reforms.[7] He noted, "Non-wage costs have reached a level at which they have now almost become unbearable for employees. And on the employers' side, they are an impediment to creating new employment."[8]

In this chapter we look first at the principles that should be used to guide social policy reforms in ways that improve incentives while maintaining the essential elements of an economic safety net. Next, we evaluate the social policy reforms undertaken in the Netherlands, Sweden, and Denmark.

Whole treatises have been written on reform strategies for each aspect of social policy, so a detailed analysis of reforms in these programs goes far beyond the scope of this book. But the basic goal of reform is to rebalance programs so that employment incentives are improved as much as possible while ensuring that citizens are safeguarded against poverty. The next section will set out some principles for reform that draw upon the literature on this topic.

Social Policy Reforms

Health Care

Freeman (2002) has pointed out that health care likely influences workforce participation. He suggests that maintaining health insurance coverage is an important factor encouraging Americans to remain in the workforce. This is because Americans under age 65 generally receive employer-subsidized healthcare coverage through their employers but lose that benefit when they lose their jobs.

In contrast, Europeans are covered whether they work or not. Freeman supports the European system of universal coverage despite its impact on labor supply. He argues that the disincentive to work is worth the price to avoid the social cost from a lack of health insurance. After all, roughly 40 million Americans lack health insurance for some period each year, and millions more are concerned about losing their coverage. We agree with Freeman that universal health insurance to cover large medical bills or the cost of a chronic illness should be an essential part of the social safety net of any advanced economy, and it makes sense to encourage cost-effective

---

7. The discussion and the quotes are translated from an advance text of the speech. Gerhard Schröder, Policy Statement on "Courage for Peace and Courage for Change" at the German Bundestag, Berlin, March 2003, eng.bundesregierung.de/frameset/index.jsp (accessed December 8, 2003).

8. In mid-December 2003 the German Bundestag finally approved the reform package, called Agenda 2010.

preventive care. However, the impact of healthcare coverage on labor supply is more complex than Freeman indicates.

There is no question that free health care is a substantial benefit to workers. If coverage is provided regardless of employment status, it plays an important role in determining work incentives. Universal health insurance then becomes a substantial income subsidy, which has been shown to lower labor supply (the income effect reduces labor supply). Many Americans contemplating early retirement decide not to retire before 65 because they do not want to lose employer-subsidized health care before the point at which Medicare eligibility begins.

However, Freeman overstates the extent to which the US healthcare system provides a work incentive. In comparing the two regions it is worth noting that the US system provides a substantial work incentive for only some Americans. If one member of a family has health insurance, other members do not need to work to receive coverage.[9] On the employer side, providing health insurance to employees at very high premium levels (currently rising at 10 to 15 percent a year) creates a heavy payroll tax for US companies. It also makes employers reluctant to hire older workers or workers with chronic diseases (e.g., diabetes). Further, low-income families can face a substantial disincentive to work because if they fall below an income threshold they become eligible for government-provided health insurance under Medicaid. Medicaid is a more comprehensive insurance program than those offered by many employers of low-wage workers (indeed many such employers offer no health insurance at all). At the Medicaid cut-off point, many workers face a marginal tax rate of 100 percent or more in the United States (especially since other income-support programs also phase out as income rises). Finally, in most US states, hospitals are required to treat all patients that come into an emergency room. Thus, people without health insurance do have access to emergency health care, and many low-income, uninsured families rely on this free care. In short, the US healthcare system does not provide a clear-cut work incentive for many Americans and is not the main reason why employment levels are higher than in Europe.

The basic structure of universal coverage for large health expenses can be maintained in Europe while reducing the work disincentives—and the budgetary costs—the current system creates in two ways. First, the coverage that is provided on a comprehensive basis should be restricted to serious or life-threatening health problems and to cost-effective preventive care. Second, certain drugs and medical procedures for nonlife-threatening problems could be either subject to substantial copayments or not covered at all.

---

9. Most firms charge employees an additional premium for family coverage, so the additional coverage is not free.

Rationing health care is essential. Otherwise a healthcare system that pays doctors and other providers on a fee-for-service basis and grants patients unlimited access to any treatment paid for by a third party will spiral out of control in total cost. In order to ration health care, either doctors or other providers in a national system must face incentives to reduce marginal or unneeded treatments, or the market must limit insurance coverage for minor medical problems. A combination of both measures could also be used. Shifting the financial burden of minor medical treatments to individuals would be helpful as a rationing device for healthcare systems and would increase work incentives.[10]

Putting greater financial responsibility on patients has already been accepted in much of Europe. Some European countries have also initiated the practice of copayments for general medication and hospital treatment. In France, the insured person's share in the cost of medication is up to 65 percent for prescriptions against certain ailments and 100 percent for nonessential drugs. In Belgium, the insured person's share for medication, excluding serious illnesses, varies according to drug category but ranges between 25 and 80 percent. In Sweden, patients pay the full cost of medication up to $97 (900 Swedish kroner) during the first year after initial purchase and then gradually their share of the cost decreases as drug expenses rise. Denmark has a similar system to Sweden—the patient pays the first €69 (540 Danish kroner), and then gradual support is increased to 85 percent above a certain level of costs. Note that patients in Denmark always pay some proportion of the cost of medication, although total out-of-pocket expenses are capped for those with very severe or chronic problems.

For doctors' fees, the insured person in France pays a statutory 30 percent while the insured person in Italy pays up to 36 percent for each visit to or test at a medical specialist. Sweden and Finland also charge copayments for doctors' visits.[11]

In short, having patients substantially share the cost of their treatment is already well established in Europe and is reflected in the numbers shown in figure 5.1 for 2000. By extending the copayment approach throughout Europe—while preserving protection for catastrophic expenses—Europe has the potential to surpass the US system of protection, and still provides adequate work incentives.

The second way work disincentives could be reduced in Europe is to improve healthcare providers' incentives, so they are motivated to reduce the overall cost of the system. This is especially important going forward as the number of elderly increases.

---

10. The discussion in this section is based on an extensive comparison of the healthcare systems of the United States, Germany, and the United Kingdom. See Baily and Garber (1997) and MGI (1996).

11. All data are from the European Commission MISSOC Database of Social Protection in Europe, www.europa.eu.int/comm/employment_social/missoc/index_en.html (accessed May 24, 2004).

Figure 5.1   Out-of-pocket patient financing as a percent of total healthcare expenditure, select countries, 2000

percent of total healthcare expenditure

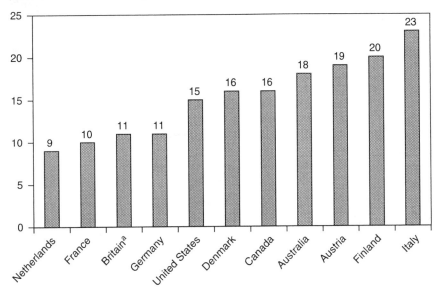

a. Data for Britain are for 1997.
Source: OECD (2003c, annex table 3.9).

US hospitals are pretty efficient in providing treatment, largely because the public reimbursement schemes, which are copied by the private insurers, encourage the facilities to treat patients quickly and release them. Thus, high healthcare costs in the United States are a result of the high prices paid for drugs, supplies, and equipment as well as the high cost of administering the US insurance system (currently $111 billion according to 2002 data[12]).

In contrast, financial incentives in Germany encourage excessive hospital stays because of the way doctors and hospitals are reimbursed. Hospitals have an incentive to keep their beds full, and doctors treat private patients in proportion to the total number of patients they have in the hospital. Germany has made improvements in the incentive structure of its healthcare system (e.g., limiting prescriptions), but more could be done to improve economic incentives and reduce the rate of increase of healthcare costs. Reducing the cost of the healthcare system would help control the

12. Testimony from Karen Davis and Barbara Cooper, "American Health Care: Why So Costly?" before the Senate Appropriations Committee, Subcommittee on Labor, Health and Human Services, Education and Related Agencies. Hearing on Health Care Access and Affordability: Cost Containment Strategies, Washington, June 11, 2003, www.cmwf.org/programs/quality/davis_senatecommitteetestimony_654.pdf (accessed January 5, 2004).

payroll taxes that pay for it and avoid squeezing the after-tax income of workers supporting the system.

The structure of health insurance is particularly important in the retirement decision, which we discuss below. As noted in chapter 2, a large fraction of healthcare costs are provided to persons who are elderly. In both Europe and the United States most of these costs are supported by payroll taxes on current workers. If retirees were required to pay for a portion of their own healthcare costs they would likely work longer and retire later. It is reasonable that workers deciding whether or not to take early retirement at, say, age 55 should think about what financial resources they would need to contribute to their own healthcare costs over the additional 25 years or more they could live.[13]

Reducing Income Risk and Facilitating Mobility

Job loss can be a painful and sometimes traumatic event for workers. Some workers are hit hard and risk becoming unemployed long term whereas others manage to move to even better jobs. Lori Kletzer's research (2001), which was based on the 1998 Displaced Worker Survey in the United States, found that among those who had new jobs, younger workers (under age 45) on average did well.[14] Younger workers actually *increased* their earnings by 5.5 percent when reemployed. Older workers did not fare as well, since they found it harder, for example, to acquire new skills and relocate. Workers aged 45 to 64 experienced earnings losses averaging 12 percent when they were reemployed. In addition, not all displaced workers had found new jobs at the time of the survey (about two years after the job loss). Kletzer's research also found that women were more likely to remain jobless than men, which may result from their inability to relocate because of their husbands' employment.

Given the uncertainty created by economic change, it is desirable that some form of unemployment insurance (UI) be provided to workers[15] who lose their jobs. UI programs in Europe operate differently in each economy with variations in the amount of time for which benefits can be collected and differences in the generosity of benefits. There are also differences in the use of "active labor-market policies" in combination with UI. For example, displaced workers may be required to attend training pro-

---

13. We have argued that catastrophic insurance should be provided to all. There are, however, difficult issues at the intersection of ethics and economics concerning the desirability of heroic and very expensive treatments that prolong the lives of very old patients by only a few days or weeks. That issue is beyond the scope of this study although, as a principle, the provision of catastrophic insurance should be limited by reasonable cost-benefit criteria.

14. The US labor market was very strong at that time with low and falling unemployment.

15. Typically, employees become eligible to collect UI benefits after working at a company for a period of time.

grams or face penalties for refusing any available job. In this section we review the issues that arise with different benefit payment structures. Later in the chapter we will see how active policies have been used in practice in specific countries.

The effect of UI on European and US unemployment has been studied empirically,[16] and the strongest finding is that the duration of UI benefits affects unemployment—particularly long-term job loss (e.g., Layard, Nickell, and Jackman 1991). The structure of benefit programs has also been examined theoretically, and it is important to note that UI serves a positive function in the economy. UI acts as an automatic stabilizer against macroeconomic fluctuations and provides greater income security in a way that the private market would not match.[17] UI can encourage people to work secure in the knowledge that they are protected from the effect of job loss. Thus, a well-designed UI program can actually contribute to increasing labor force participation.

Theory reinforces the conclusion of the empirical literature that time limits should be placed on unemployment benefits. Economic analysis suggests that UI benefits should start at a rather high level—covering almost all prior wages—and then gradually decline to provide incentive for workers to find new jobs. If this "economists' solution" is too difficult to explain or track, the alternative is to simply set time limits. Six months, give or take, may be the right time frame for UI benefits. A policy reform that placed a six-month time limit on UI would have a large effect on measured *unemployment* rates in Europe. It would have a substantial impact on *employment* rates only if it was combined with reform in welfare, pensions, and disability programs (discussed in the next section). A time limit on UI benefits would not be effective if the unemployed could simply transfer to another benefit program and receive a similar amount of money.

The generosity of UI benefits also strongly affects unemployment. In some European economies, low-wage and some high-wage workers can receive UI benefits equal to 60 or even 80 percent of their previous wage if they lose their jobs although in most countries such benefits are capped at certain payout levels. Providing such a generous benefit without requirements such as job training classes only encourages unemployment at taxpayers' expense.

Combining UI Benefits and Wage Insurance to Encourage Mobility

The above discussion has kept within the conventional bounds of UI in which benefits are paid to the unemployed and then cease once a new job

16. See Atkinson (1999) for a discussion of evidence and theory. Design of an optimal UI program is explored in Baily (1978) and Shavell and Weiss (1979).

17. Workers prone to unemployment would likely buy private insurance. The market equilibrium might well involve either no insurance or very little, very expensive insurance. As in many insurance situations there are problems of "moral hazard" and "adverse selection."

is accepted. It is possible to go beyond the conventional framework and provide wage supplements as an alternative form of insurance and to encourage displaced workers to take new jobs.

In the 1980s Lawrence and Litan (1986) proposed a program of wage insurance for workers displaced by the effect of international trade. This idea was picked up again by Kletzer and Litan (2001), who suggested a program in which workers would receive a supplement to their wages. The supplement would be a fraction of the difference between the previous wage and the new wage for a period of up to two years. Kletzer and Litan showed that the budgetary cost would be moderate if assistance were provided equal to 50 percent of the wage gap. The authors' study focused on workers who lost their jobs as a result of expanding international trade since open markets benefit economies as a whole while detrimentally affecting specific individuals. However, job displacement occurs for a variety of reasons: technologies change, low-productivity firms contract or close, and consumers buy different goods and services. This dynamism is a key factor in productivity growth, as we described in chapter 3, but it does impose a cost on those workers who lose their jobs.

Expanding the program of wage supplements or wage insurance to cover workers displaced for a broad range of reasons would facilitate job mobility, encourage productivity growth, and increase employment. Burtless and Schaefer (2003) propose to use expanded wage insurance in Germany. They point out that UI benefits in Germany in 2000 were about $20 billion, about the same amount as in the United States, despite a much smaller economy. Burtless and Schaefer propose a wage insurance program for displaced workers that would cover 50 percent of the gap between the wage in a new job and the wage in the lost job—the same as proposed by Kletzer and Litan (2001). They estimate that this would cost the German government $3 billion a year if there were no cap on the amount paid out. If the maximum annual wage insurance supplement were capped at $10,000 then the cost would fall to $1.8 billion.

Germany, as part of the recommendation of the Hartz Commission of 2003, has actually implemented a very small version of a wage insurance scheme. This is open to workers only above the age of 55, who can receive up to 50 percent of the wage differential between their new and old jobs for up to 12 months. This is an encouraging development, yet regretfully the program remains almost wholly unknown and of limited extension. Thus, while its impact cannot yet be discerned, it will likely be very limited.[18]

If wage supplements were simply added to existing benefit programs and provided to all eligible displaced workers the cost would be prohibi-

---

18. For additional information, see Howard Rosen and the Trade Directorate Trade Committee TD/TC/WP(2003)34, Structural Adjustment in Textiles and Clothing: Trade-Related Labor Adjustment Policies (2003).

tive. But if wage supplements were used as an alternative or complement to long-term UI benefits, they could actually become a money saver in Europe. As noted earlier, in some European countries workers can collect UI benefits almost indefinitely or move to another income support program once UI benefits are exhausted. Therefore, if UI programs were reformed and benefits restricted to six months reemployed workers could supplement their new income with wage insurance. Both studies propose offering 50 percent of the wage gap for two years as an appropriate amount and time period, but the figures could be adjusted on the basis of experience with the program. The wage supplement would be available as soon as a displaced worker took a job, whether that was immediately after losing a previous job or at the end of an unemployment spell. Like any benefit program, safeguards would need to be in place to ensure that people did not abuse it. For example, individuals could not simply move from job to job in order to continuously collect the wage supplement.

Financially, limiting the duration of UI benefits and providing wage supplements could be cheaper than the current UI system. The government is providing only a fraction of a worker's income while the new employer and reemployed worker are paying taxes, which lowers the net cost of the proposed program. Thus, cutting only a third out of UI benefit costs in Germany would easily pay for the program described by Burtless and Schaefer (2003).

The wage-insurance program could be abused. For example, employers might lower wage rates knowing that the government would provide a half or more of the cost to employees. Given that greater wage flexibility is desirable in Europe, this form of abuse does not seem that severe—in fact it might help move the economies toward full employment. Another possibility, however, is that employers would find a way to cycle workers into and out of jobs as a way of receiving an effective wage subsidy over the long run. Again, given the rigidities in European labor markets, it is not clear this abuse would really be that severe. Nevertheless, as noted earlier, safeguards such as monitoring both recipients and employers to prevent abuse must be in place. Unfortunately, abuse of one kind or another occurs in almost any government program—in fact, many people abuse the current UI system. Often these abuses can be reduced over time as administrators gain experience with the program. Also, one of the advantages of wage insurance is that displaced workers must be employed in order to receive the subsidy, which makes it less prone to abuse.

Wage insurance encourages rather than discourages employment. Compared to UI, it represents a different mindset. Instead of viewing a displaced worker as someone who has been irreparably harmed, it views him or her as having choices and opportunities and the ability to acquire new skills. It reinforces the fact that job mobility is inevitable and displaced workers have an obligation to actively seek new jobs.

Welfare, Pensions, and Disability Programs

Europeans want social programs to be reformed in a way that preserves social cohesion, which means that all citizens sustain a minimum standard of living. For example, Europe already provides universal access to health care, which is a big step toward supporting a minimum living standard. The next big step in preserving social cohesion is to determine the minimum level of income support a family needs to remain out of poverty. Cash welfare payments or in-kind transfers, such as shelters for the homeless and free or subsidized food, can provide this additional support.[19]

If this minimum is in fact available to all, and if work incentives are to be maintained, it follows inevitably that the minimum level of income must be lower, by a significant amount, than the take-home income of a low-skilled worker. Without a significant financial incentive, most low-skilled workers will choose not to work.[20]

The exact size of the financial incentive needed to encourage low-skilled employment is subject to empirical determination, but it seems very likely that the criterion would set a pretty low minimum income requirement, which could create greater income inequality and negatively affect a significant number of families in Europe by reducing or terminating existing support. However, the situation is not as dire as the previous sentence implies. First, a welfare payment that is higher than the minimum subsistence level can be paid to individuals less affected by work incentives such as the elderly and disabled. Second, social insurance can be provided in creative ways that preserve work incentives—providing temporary UI benefits combined with a wage insurance program, for example.

Retirement Benefits

All the industrialized economies have policies based on the presumption that persons beyond a certain age should not be required to work to support themselves and that people often fail to save when working enough to cover their future retirement.[21] A minimum base level of retirement benefits is provided to all workers and their families. Given this, the base level of retirement income should approximate the level that would be chosen optimally by workers who have worked in a low-skill job during their lifetime. This proposal means that the state assumes the responsibility for re-

---

19. The relative merits of both cash and in-kind transfers can be debated. Cash is simpler and easier to administrate, but in-kind transfers may do a better job of channeling assistance to the truly needy. This debate goes beyond the scope of this book, so we will refer simply to cash or cash-equivalent payments.

20. The problems with violating this condition were explored in chapter 2.

21. For descriptions of individual countries' pension systems see Oshio and Yashiro (1997), Blundell and Johnson (1997), Palme and Svensson (1997), Boldrin, Jimenez-Martini, and Peracchi (1997), Boeri (2003), Borsch-Supan and Berkel (2003), and Mitchell (1999).

tirement provision for low-wage workers. This is already the case in both Europe and the United States, so this principle is widely accepted.[22]

The provision of a minimum retirement income implies some erosion of both work and savings incentives. Government retirement programs in Europe and the United States are mostly financed on a "pay-as-you-go" basis—retirees are paid out of current tax revenues. Therefore, neither real savings nor accumulated assets support the liability for future retirement benefits. If a minimum retirement program were designed from scratch, there would be a strong case for building up a retirement trust fund with real assets rather than a pay-as-you-go system. Unfortunately, it would be difficult to make these changes to the current European and US systems since the baby boom generation is about to retire.[23] Preserving the base-level retirement system is preferable to having workers in poverty as they age.

In principle, it is reasonable to expect that persons with middle and higher levels of income and education will save in order to provide additional income for their own retirement (above the minimum base retirement income level provided by the state). To facilitate this, the government could either certify privately run funds or encourage employers to offer additional retirement plans and provide secure retirement funds to which people could contribute. Given the need for job mobility in a modern economy, it is essential that retirement programs be portable as workers change jobs.

The US Social Security program provides only a modest basic income that is supplemented with private pension contributions. In contrast, many European economies have set up more generous pay-as-you-go pension systems for most employees, which offer substantially more benefits than basic income but are not generally backed with real private-sector assets. For many European countries, it may already be too late to establish a system in which people must save for their retirement without government support. Current workers would understandably feel cheated if they were required to pay for current and near-term future retirees only to lose support for their own retirement.

---

22. The average retired worker receiving Social Security benefits in the United States received $895 a month in 2002. The average for a retired worker and spouse was $1,494 a month. The income provides only a basic standard of living since retirees currently must pay for outpatient prescription drugs. Data are from the *Statistical Abstract of the United States* (US Census 2003, 362).

23. Creating a pay-as-you-go pension system from scratch will inevitably provide a generational bias in favor of retirees at this time since they will immediately benefit from the new system without having paid for it. On the other hand, such early beneficiaries of a pay-as-you-go pension system will likely have provided direct support for their elders—living with them, for example, in an early form of "privatized old-age care." Nonetheless, it is important to realize that the creation of any pay-as-you-go system does create an immediate "generational liability" that will effectively have to be shared over future generations.

Figure 5.2 Total assets of private pension funds, select countries, various years

percent of GDP

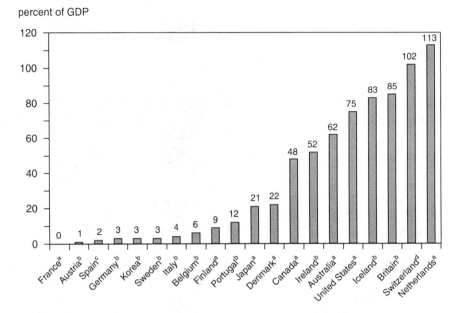

a. 2001 data.
b. 2000 data.
c. 1999 data.
d. 1998 data.

Source: OECD (2001f). Secretariat compilation from various national sources and Institutional Investors database.

Some European countries have gradually introduced private (usually supplementary) pension plans that hold sizable private assets. As shown in figure 5.2, pensions in the Netherlands seem comfortably backed by private assets while the opposite is true for the major continental European economies. Obviously this leads to wide discrepancies among European countries in terms of the fiscal sustainability of their pension systems. Any transition to a fully funded system will take a very long time to achieve. Given the demographic trends outlined in chapter 2, the way forward for countries without fully funded pension plans is difficult. Reform will require gradual downward pressure on the pensions of current and future retirees combined with increased incentives for current workers to save.[24]

---

24. Attempts in this direction were introduced in Germany in 2001, as state subsidies were introduced to encourage individuals to take out private supplementary pension plans. However, these initiatives are widely regarded as inadequate and rather unsuccessful. See, for instance, the conclusion of the government-sanctioned Rurup Commission report (2003).

One way to ease the pension problem and the looming demographic pressure in Europe is to encourage workers to retire later rather than sooner. As we saw in chapter 2, the average retirement age in Europe decreased in the 1980s. This was done in part because it was popular to offer workers the option of early retirement especially when restructuring overstaffed industries. At the policy level, there was often a mistaken belief that a limited number of jobs exist in an economy and offering early retirement would therefore increase employment among younger workers.

Because of budget pressures, government retirement programs in Europe are increasing either the statutory retirement age or the number of years (of contributions) required to obtain full pension benefits. These reforms seem to be a move in the right direction. Given the need to improve work incentives and keep payroll taxes under control, the age at which workers can collect retirement benefits should be gradually increased. However, it would be helpful to estimate how the retirement age should be varied given the increase in life expectancy. The starting point is to estimate when an average person would retire if he or she had made far-sighted decisions during his or her lifetime and saved the optimal amount.[25] The decisions on the level of savings and the retirement age are jointly determined, of course, and so that is not an easy estimate to make but it is not essential to get the answer exactly correct. But a precise age is not necessary since individuals may choose their retirement age within a state-provided pension program, which is adjusted on an actuarially fair base. For example, the US Social Security system allows workers to retire any time between the ages of 62 and 70, with the benefit level adjusted by an amount that is roughly actuarially fair. (See box 5.1.)

Welfare and Disability Programs[26]

There is strong support for providing additional income to assist single-parent families and the disabled. These two groups are important, but complex to analyze. Figuring out the right way to help them does not easily lend itself to the application of optimality principles.

---

25. A somewhat similar approach, albeit at a different unit level, was proposed by the Rurup Commission in Germany when it suggested introducing the so-called sustainability factor (*Nachhaltigkeitsfactor*) into the pension system to ensure generational fairness. The proposal would ensure that the retirement age was adjusted upward or absolute pension level downward to guarantee that the rate of pension contributions would not rise above a given level—20 percent of wages by 2020 and 22 percent by 2030—while keeping the system solvent. Detailed estimates of the potential effect of the "sustainability factor" on German retirement ages or pension levels were not been provided but will unavoidably be enormous—especially politically (Rurup Commission 2003).

26. For a helpful review of lessons Europe may learn from the US experience in welfare reform in the United States, see Blank (2002).

Figure 5.2 shows a very wide difference in the amount of real assets in OECD countries' pension systems. This difference in asset levels can obviously be ascribed, to a large extent, to disparities in pension system structures—for instance, private pension funds are unknown in France but make up the bulk of the pension system in countries such as Britain and the Netherlands. Hence, many European countries rely almost wholly on state-run pay-as-you-go pension systems, where payments to pensioners at a given point in time depend ultimately on the taxing power of the government. As pointed out in chapter 2, there are large differences in the degree of long-term sustainability of European government finances, and this could affect the certainty of government pension payments (at current levels) in the future.

Yet, the quantity of people's assets in private pension funds and the certainty of the level of public transfers in the future may not yield the full picture of the size of Europeans' "nest eggs" for retirement. This is due to the fact that just as many Europeans have income in the nonobserved economy (see appendix 5.1); many also have large savings outside regular private pension funds and—importantly—outside the reach of European tax authorities. Billions of euros in savings are kept in tax shelters, particularly in Switzerland, by a large number of Europeans; these savings are normally not counted as part of their financial wealth. There is subsequently a risk that the official picture of their prospective standards of living in retirement is somewhat direr than it should be.

Because of banking secrecy it is impossible to know with certainty the level of tax-sheltered European assets in Switzerland and other similar locations. Some estimates exist, however, and there seems to be some reason to believe that the issue is relatively larger in magnitude in the countries to the left in figure 5.2. The Bank of Italy estimates that in 2002, before the Italian tax amnesty (see below), up to €515 billion (Private Banker International, March 2002) of Italian assets might have been held abroad—this is equivalent to more than 40 percent of Italy's 2002 GDP of €1,258 billion. Similarly, German government 2000 estimates range between €300 billion and €400 billion in private holdings and up to €960 billion if corporate holdings are included—equivalent to up to 20 percent of GDP in private offshore holdings in 2000 (rising to nearly 50 percent with corporate holdings) (PBI January and July 2003).

Estimates thus indicate that such offshore European assets are indeed substantial. The sheer magnitude of the estimates indicates that offshore accounts are not kept by

(box continues next page)

Single-parent families with young children are typically led by females. It is not reasonable to expect a woman whose spouse or partner has recently departed to work full-time and look after small children on her own. Families in such a situation should be provided with an income that is above the minimum subsistence level. When welfare programs to support such families were first introduced no one thought that any major distortions of behavior would occur. Few people seriously believed that providing financial assistance to single parents would induce people to have children, have more children, or change their marital status. Today we know better. These distortions are compounded by the fact that child-support payments from the noncustodial parent are often in default.

Discussing all the pros and cons of different approaches to assisting welfare families goes beyond the scope of this book. However, we believe that part of the solution involves limiting the duration of additional in-

Box 5.1 *(continued)*

only the super-rich in Europe but by a much larger number of people. Nonetheless, as one likely needs to be at least in the upper-middle income bracket to find it worthwhile to open an offshore account, adding such holdings to a country's private pension assets will not affect the standard of living in retirement projections of the majority of Europeans—although including offshore holdings will further skew the wealth distribution.

In recent years several European governments have attempted to lure back home such offshore assets with promises of tax amnesties and "no questions asked," by letting their citizens move undeclared assets from, say, Switzerland back to their home country and only pay a fixed percentage of the amount in tax—a percentage frequently much lower than regular national capital income taxation levels. Italy from late 2001 to mid-2002 brought back from abroad between €60 billion and €80 billion under the so-called Tremonti law. This law stipulated that investors either pay a fee 2.5 percent of repatriated funds (much lower than either Italian capital gains taxes or higher brackets of personal income taxes) or put their funds into low-yielding government bonds. Germany currently has a similar scheme running until 2005Q1, under which people who have evaded tax between 1993 and 2002 can repatriate funds against a 15 to 25 percent one-off fee—this should be compared with the usual taxation up to 48 percent on such income during the period concerned (Kellner 2004). Due to the significantly higher repatriation fee involved, however, the German scheme is not expected to be nearly as successful as the Italian version.

Evidently, the politics of such amnesty schemes are problematic, in that they need to weigh the benefits of bringing back assets (in the case of Italy, the proceeds were not insubstantial for a government fighting to adhere to the deficit restrictions of the SGP) against rewarding tax evaders. Nonetheless, both Belgium and France have recently also mulled similar schemes.

Importantly, EU member states in May 2004 reached an agreement among themselves and with (notably) Switzerland and other adjacent offshore tax havens that an anonymous across-the-board 15 percent withholding tax be levied on all accounts belonging to (other) EU citizens (rising to 20 percent in 2007 and 35 percent in 2011). With 75 percent of the proceeds going to the EU member whose citizen holds the account, this agreement may present a significant new way for EU member states to raise tax revenues from their citizens' offshore accounts. Yet, on the other hand, it may also simply drive such assets even further offshore to, for instance, Asia or the Caribbean.

come support (above the minimum level) so that single parents gradually become more self-sufficient rather than permanent welfare recipients. Subsidized child care could also encourage single parents to enter the workforce. In Sweden, for example, single mothers are provided with substantial incentives to enter the workforce through subsidized child care.

A separate disability program is clearly needed since severely disabled persons cannot support themselves by working. But how does one determine disability? After all, individuals with major health problems are sometimes denied support while others feigning disability end up with undeserved assistance.[27] In some countries requesting disability support has become an alternative strategy for millions of workers who have ex-

---

27. There are a variety of musculo-skeletal and mental problems that are hard to diagnose with X-rays or other standard medical tests.

hausted UI but want to remain out of the workforce. For example, the Netherlands has successfully reduced its unemployment rate to the 4 percent range (3.7 percent in 2002 and 4.6 percent in early 2003), but its disabled population is rising—from 5.6 percent in 1998 to 6.1 percent in 2002. The number of disabled in the United States has also grown very rapidly in recent years as eligibility conditions have been eased.[28]

Disability rates differ widely by country and have varied over time within countries. Participation apparently depends on system design changes. Therefore, changes in the classification requirements and/or the procedures for determining disability can significantly influence the number of persons entering disability programs. For example, those who are disabled in a way that makes it impossible for them to continue working at their current occupation—either because of age or a physical impairment—can often become self-supporting in an alternative, less demanding position or occupation and should be expected to do so. This principle is consistent with the overall strategy of social policy programs outlined in this section, which is to encourage worker mobility.

Payroll-Tax Abatement and Negative Taxes

Work incentives are affected not only by the level of benefits paid to those who do not work but also the taxes levied on workers. Payroll taxes are one of the main sources of tax revenue in Europe. However, these same taxes reduce the incentive for low-skilled workers to accept jobs when wages are flexible and the incentive for an employer to offer a job when minimum wages are high. Several countries have attempted to alleviate this problem either by lowering the payroll tax rates on low-wage workers or by providing negative taxes to low-wage workers that partially or fully offset the payroll taxes.[29] For example, France followed the strategy of payroll tax cuts for low-wage workers, which accounted in part for the country's strong employment growth in the late 1990s. The Earned Income Tax Credit (EITC) in the United States is also an example of such a negative tax and, together with welfare reform, has encouraged many low-skilled women to enter or reenter the workforce.[30] The United Kingdom has developed a program called the "working tax credit" that is sim-

---

28. Autor and Duggan (2001) note that the share of nonelderly adults receiving benefits from the US Social Security Disability Insurance and Supplemental Security Income programs rose from 3.1 in 1984 to 5.3 percent in 2000. They trace this increase to reduced screening requirements and a rising earnings replacement rate.

29. For a discussion of how subsidies to low-wage workers might reduce the nonaccelerating inflation rate of unemployment (NAIRU), see Baily and Tobin (1977).

30. Requiring workers to pay payroll taxes and then giving a tax refund may seem—and is—a rather convoluted way of operating. The United States uses this approach to help preserve the "integrity" of the social insurance funds that the payroll taxes support—the Social Security and Medicare trust funds, for example.

ilar to the EITC in the United States, as has the Netherlands with its "labor tax credit," France with "prime à l'emploi," and Belgium with its "work tax credit" (Blanchard 2004).

Payroll tax reductions or negative income taxes are a powerful tool to encourage work while improving income distribution. Taking money away from the benefits of those that do not work and using it to add to the incomes of the employed shifts the trade-off between nonworkers and workers. Therefore, these efforts should be strongly encouraged and the scope of the programs should be increased.

The limits of such work-incentive programs are set by the need to maintain reasonable marginal tax rates at all levels of income. The US EITC program, which phases out as income rises, together with the provisions of Medicaid, food stamps, and housing allowances often create high marginal tax rates (around or even greater than 100 percent) for low-income workers, as noted earlier. It is a basic problem that either negative income taxes phase out rather quickly (pushing up marginal tax rates) or become very expensive for the budget.

There is a parallel here, however, to the earlier discussion of wage insurance. If one is deciding between welfare and a job, a wage subsidy can provide an important push into the labor market. Earlier, we argued that reducing the duration or generosity of existing UI payments could pay for a new wage-insurance program encouraging worker mobility. Similarly, reducing the duration or generosity of welfare support payments or reducing or eliminating early retirement pension benefits could pay for a wage subsidy for low-skilled workers.

As in the previous case, the key is to change people's mindset and shift social insurance programs away from payments to those who stay out of work and toward support programs for people who take jobs.

The Wage-Setting Process: Making Jobs Available

Increased work incentives can increase the number of people willing to work or the hours they work (increases labor supply), but in order to increase employment, there must be an increase in labor demand—jobs must be available for the people that want to take them. Labor demand can be increased in two ways: Either the cost of labor must come down (the amount employers pay per worker or per hour), or the demand for labor must increase at a given cost of labor.[31] This latter case could occur if productivity increased or during a cyclical recovery.

Although most of this book focuses on structural rather than cyclical issues, the economic cycle is important. Chapter 6 examines Europe's mon-

---

31. In simple economics employment can increase by moving down a given labor demand schedule or moving the schedule.

etary and fiscal policies and stresses that structural reforms can raise employment successfully only if there is sufficient aggregate demand in the economy. As this is written, it appears that Europe is making a slow recovery from a mild recession. If that recovery falters, structural reforms will not deliver on the promise of substantially higher employment. On the other hand, if structural reforms are not achieved Europe's recovery will be weaker and possibly shorter than it could be. We postpone any further discussion of cyclical questions until chapter 6.

Leaving aside recession, the main reason employment would fail to increase following an improvement in work incentives is if wage rigidity made it unprofitable for employers to hire new employees. If employer wage and benefit costs are kept above the level consistent with full employment, then underemployment will persist. Reforming social programs as suggested earlier may help to increase labor demand—for example, reducing payroll taxes on low-skilled workers or providing a negative tax could greatly alleviate this problem even without changes in before-tax wages. But only a broader degree of wage flexibility will encourage a return to full employment in Europe.

The insider-outsider view of the labor market was mentioned earlier in which wage rates and other working conditions are determined by a bargaining process between employees and their employers, with little regard to whether there are large numbers of workers who would like to work. A variation of this view involves the incentives facing different members of the insider group since some workers may be further "inside" than others. Within a company or an industry, for example, some workers have much more seniority than others. Figure 5.3 illustrates that if layoffs occur, the most recent hires lose their jobs first. Thus, if real wages are pushed up, the majority of the workers face a very low probability of losing their jobs, even if there is some job loss overall. They are laid off only if the company shuts down. Therefore, in any union vote on a wage settlement, the majority of workers have an incentive to hold out for the largest wage increase without endangering the company and their own jobs.

A centralized wage-setting process is one way of restraining wages. Some of the smaller European economies have created a cooperative situation where representatives of labor unions accept that excessive wage increases at the national level will result in job losses.[32] The centralized bargaining process occurs in a setting that recognizes the interests of the outsiders as well as the insiders. However, such a centralized wage-setting process is harder to implement in larger economies with disparate nationwide union groups. For example, in France and Italy the situation is usually aggravated as unions compete by appearing to be the most uncompromising. Moreover, there are dangers in any system in which wage

---

32. For a discussion of how wage-setting systems affect unemployment see Layard, Nickell, and Jackman (1991).

Figure 5.3 Probability of layoff following wage increase with restricted competition

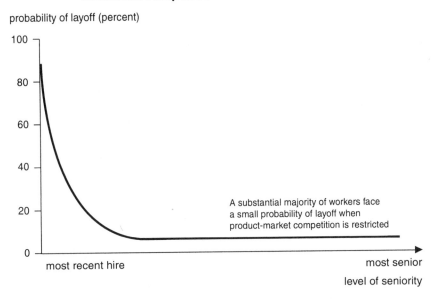

probability of layoff (percent)

A substantial majority of workers face
a small probability of layoff when
product-market competition is restricted

most recent hire

most senior

level of seniority

rates are set politically or institutionally rather than through market forces. It is very hard to facilitate job mobility and structural change in an economy where the labor market is so controlled.

A second approach to wage setting is to force a political confrontation with labor groups. Prime Minister Thatcher survived a long period of chaos and adverse economic times in order to create a more flexible workforce in Britain. Even though many of her actions were very unpopular, Thatcher stayed in power because she had the major political advantage of a divided opposition in parliament. Her party never won a majority of the votes in parliamentary elections.

US President Ronald Reagan also altered labor relations in the 1980s. When the air traffic controllers' union went on an unauthorized strike, he hired replacement workers. This move changed the US labor market by making it acceptable for corporations to hire replacement workers following a strike and by encouraging corporations to take active measures to oppose union organizing drives. The United States and Britain were both able to achieve almost full employment in the 1990s, and the labor market's flexibility may have made the critical difference particularly in Britain, where the labor groups previously had been very rigid and confrontational.

Thatcher's strategy is unlikely to be followed by the rest of Europe—in part because Britain has a different election system, which allowed policy changes to occur even though they were unpopular. Moreover, the

Thatcher-Reagan approach to flexibility comes at a cost. Unions can play a constructive role in protecting workers against mistreatment and providing a powerful, unified voice so that their interests are heard (see Freeman 1980). Often employers favor dealing with unions, since they frequently control the level of industrial unrest and strike activity.[33] However, problems arise in the labor market if unions raise wages too high, distort the wage structure, prevent needed restructuring, and protect a select group of workers (with seniority) while the majority of workers (often lower-skilled) remain unemployed.

In Europe, unions are not the sole reason for distorted wages. In France, for example, unions represent only a small fraction of the workforce, so the rigid wages and the high minimum wages can be blamed primarily on government policy. The key problem is that wages determined by union bargaining then apply to all workers throughout an industry and not just those who negotiated the settlement. The universal industry wage subsequently limits the domestic competitive pressure placed on the wage-bargaining process.

The rules extending wage bargains nationally are not applied universally now, as small firms are given greater freedom over wage setting. In reality, however, this distinction just keeps a fringe of small, low-productivity companies in business.[34]

One way to increase wage flexibility is to repeal laws and regulations that extend wage contracts negotiated by a small group of workers and employers to virtually all employees in an industry. If individual companies or even regions were able to freely negotiate their own wage contracts the overall competitiveness and flexibility of the labor market would increase substantially.

Bringing about Labor-Market Flexibility through Product-Market Competition

Another way to bring greater flexibility to the labor market is to increase the level of competition in product markets. Even if individual European economies have rules that extend their wage and employment provisions, as long as their industry competes internationally, market forces will be brought into labor-market decisions. For example, if competition opens the manufacturing market and subsidies for failing firms are removed,

---

33. Countries with strong centralized bargaining systems such as Germany or Austria are consistently ranked by the European Industrial Relations Observatory (EIRO) as having the lowest average loss of working days due to strike activity in Europe.

34. Several developing economies (Brazil is a prime example) have created an extremely unlevel playing field for business with small companies completely avoiding taxes and regulatory requirements. Thus, small companies have a cost advantage relative to larger and more productive companies. The restructuring of some industries is then slowed or stopped because the most productive companies are not able to compete.

Figure 5.4 Probability of layoff following wage increase with competition

probability of layoff (percent)

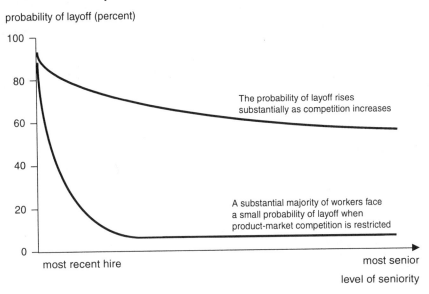

then wage concessions that are needed to preserve employment will come more quickly. The threat of bankruptcy can also prompt unions to quickly concede to lower wage increases. Figure 5.4 illustrates the idea that if the probability of layoff rises for senior workers, the willingness to accept wage concessions greatly increases—as we are seeing, as companies threaten to move to eastern Europe.

Many Europeans argue that manufactured goods already exist in a very competitive product market, but as we noted in chapter 3 that is not always true. Trade barriers in Europe are sometimes clear and sometimes both subtle and difficult to determine.[35] In the automotive industry, for example, formal and informal barriers to Japanese imports existed for years, and even now a 10 percent tariff (a pretty substantial barrier) remains. In other sectors, the trade barriers take the form of subsidies or low-cost financing, or restrictions on access to the distribution system. Eliminating existing trade barriers, within and outside the European Union, would not only help increase productivity but would also put pressure on workers and unions to demonstrate wage restraint.

As described in chapter 3, international trade can also increase competitive pressure in the labor market. If French companies can freely enter the

35. See Messerlin (2001, chapters 2 and 6) and the European Commission report (2002d). The latter deals particularly with the problems related to trade in services, and the numerous problems it laid bare played a key role in the European Commission's decision to bring barriers to trade in services to the top of the 2003–06 Internal Market agenda. See European Commission press announcement IP/03/645, May 7, 2003.

German market and vice versa, overall competitive pressure will increase. Under EU policies, these changes are taking effect, but the reality is that countries can restrict competition if they so choose.

However, international trade is not the only way to increase competitive pressure. Allowing new entrants and letting weaker firms fail would force changes in labor practices including wage setting. There are strong interactions between the labor and product markets. Many of the restrictions on product-market competition remain in place because of pressure from labor groups. A commitment to greater competitive intensity in the product market would be a major step toward a more flexible labor market. We noted earlier that some foreign competitors are struggling in Germany's retail industry. Amazon.com, the online superstore, is extremely successful, however, and putting pressure on domestic bookstores to stay open in the evenings and reduce prices.

The Paradox of Competition and Job Creation

The belief that open competition will result in job loss is the biggest reason product-market competition is restricted in European markets. Admittedly, for individual companies and workers this belief is not a false fear. But, paradoxically, the same forces that can destroy some jobs will also create others elsewhere in the economy. The job creation that occurs may be accompanied by a widening of the distribution of wages, however, which is another reason for resisting competition. But the discussion above illustrates how redistributional policies to reduce after-tax income inequality, which are part of the social policy reforms, can be used to overcome the wage gap.

Avoiding End-Game Solutions

The above discussion asserts that product-market competition will create pressure for labor-market flexibility. That argument can break down if workers can hold onto their jobs for a period of time. Some industries have very large fixed costs, and if these costs have already been incurred it may be possible for companies to compete even if their labor costs are far higher than companies in other countries (as long as they have marginal costs that are below the market price of what they produce). The companies will still have a positive profit margin, although they will not be earning a normal rate of return on their capital stock.[36] Major new investments will not be made, although smaller investment upgrades to existing capital may still be profitable.

From the narrow viewpoint of workers in such industries (the insiders) it may make sense to refuse wage reductions or changes in work rules and simply allow the company to operate until they reach retirement age.

---

36. Lawrence and Lawrence (1985) analyzed the end-game situation in the US steel industry.

Competition will not necessarily result in greater labor-market flexibility in such situations.

Many European companies seem to be operating in such a situation. They are making new investments in Eastern Europe or other low-cost locations, but not investing much in their traditional base of operations. Older US companies in such sectors as automotive and steel have labor costs (including obligations to retired workers) that make it hard for them to compete as well, and they are facing a similar situation.

European governments will have to make hard decisions. A government can continue to waste its investment by subsidizing companies with low or even negative economic returns, or it can encourage companies to confront their workers and hold out for greater flexibility. Another option is to allow some large-scale companies to go bankrupt thereby signaling that there are fatal consequences for failing a market test over the long run. The first solution is the easiest politically in the short run and has often been implemented in Europe. The second and third choices are more difficult but will pay off in the long run with better economic performance.

Overall Conclusions from Social Policy Reform

- It is not necessary to dismantle the established framework of social protections in Europe. However, this framework will require fundamental reform involving greater financial incentives on the unemployed to look for and accept jobs. The minimum level of income support provided to any individual or family must be set so that the work incentive remains strong.

- Many social insurance programs currently provide permanent or semipermanent income support. These programs should be changed so they provide only temporary support.

- Low-wage workers should be helped by negative taxes or reductions in payroll taxes, or a combination of the two.

- Labor-market policy should now assume worker mobility. Unlike past generations, members of today's workforce will undertake a variety of jobs and cannot expect to remain with the same employer or in the same location throughout their working lives.

- Given this presumption, the UI programs in Europe should be reformed. UI benefits should be paid for only a limited time, and wage supplements should be given to reemployed workers for a period of about two years as a form of wage insurance to encourage mobility.

- Ideally, wages set by either bargaining or the government should be applied only to relevant—and not all—workers in an industry. When wage rates are determined, those who have jobs (the insiders) should face the threat of market competition from outsiders who want jobs.

- Repealing the laws or regulations that extend negotiated wage contracts to the entire industry would increase the flexibility of the labor market and the degree of competition.

Given the political difficulty of imposing full flexibility on the labor market, an alternative—or complementary—approach is to increase competitive intensity in product markets. To effectively encourage competitive intensity, it may be necessary to allow some large, established landmark companies to go bankrupt and close.

Labor-Market Reforms: European Solutions That Have Raised Employment

In the first half of this chapter, we looked at some principles that could govern the design of social welfare programs, thereby improving their incentive structure while maintaining their ability to cushion families against adverse economic shocks. Although these ideas are fine in theory, is there any practical evidence that social policy reforms can increase employment? The rest of this chapter will examine the reforms that have been adopted by the Netherlands, Sweden, and Denmark. All three countries have achieved the goals of the EU Council of at least a 70 percent ratio of employment to population ratio as set at the 2000 Lisbon meeting. They each achieved this goal by modifying—but not forsaking—their social protections. The experience of the Netherlands, Sweden, and Denmark can provide insights for other European countries about reforms that have worked and areas where problems still remain.

Before proceeding, it is important to emphasize that the precise legal instruments used to achieve labor-market reforms often will vary from country to country and depend on each country's institutions, historical traditions, political sensitivities, and decision-making processes. However, this review will be organized on the basis of the economic incentives that were changed in each country and the subsequent result of these changes rather than on the specific legal or institutional details of the reforms.

The Netherlands: From Dutch Disease to Dutch Job Creation

In 1982 a deepening economic crisis caused a marked shift in economic policies in the Netherlands. Major reforms to fiscal, monetary, labor-market, and social policies were implemented with astounding, if crisis-induced, speed and laid the foundation for the impressive turnaround in

Figure 5.5   Employment/population ratio and unemployment in the Netherlands, 1980–2002 (percent of total population)

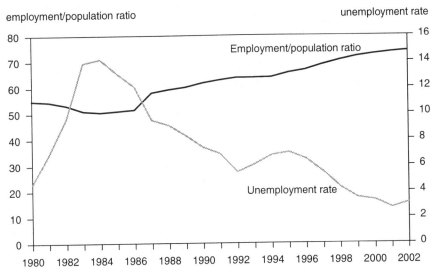

employment/population ratio   unemployment rate

Source: OECD Labor Market Indicators.

the Dutch labor market in the following years (figure 5.5). While the reforms to monetary and fiscal policies are outside the scope of this chapter, it is pertinent to briefly outline them. Reforms to monetary and fiscal policies consisted of pegging the Dutch guilder to the German deutsche mark starting in 1983 until both currencies were replaced by the euro in 1999. On the fiscal side, the growth of general government expenditure was restrained—it was reduced from 60 percent of GDP in 1982–83 to 45 percent of GDP in 2000 (Eurostat New Cronos Databases). These policies are similar to the policies currently being set for the European Union as a whole—in terms of the common currency and the Stability and Growth Pact (SGP). Thus, improvements in the Dutch labor market did not occur because it followed either an independent or a very expansionary set of monetary and fiscal policies.

Cuts in Wage Growth, Working Time, and Labor-Income Taxes

In 1982, the so-called Wassenaar Agreement was struck among the Dutch government, labor unions, and employers. Under the terms of this agreement, labor unions accepted wage restraint, cuts in social benefits, and increased labor-market flexibility in exchange for an immediate reduction in working hours and, in later years, lower taxes on labor income. Also, the automatic indexation of wages to consumer prices was eliminated, and employees with part-time work became entitled to full social security coverage.[37] In subsequent years, the same three social partners continued to cooperate (along the lines of the Wassenaar Agreement framework) in what became known as the *Dutch Polder Model*, or consensus approach.[38] For most of the 1980s and 1990s, a freeze of (and in 1984 a 3 percent cut in) the gross nominal legal minimum wage for Dutch adults above age 23 meant that the gross real legal minimum wage declined by about 20 percent from 1980 to 2000. Similarly, the average real wage growth in the Netherlands was restrained in practice, rising by only about 10 percent over the same 20 years (by much less for production workers, as discussed below). As the real minimum wage was lowered, the gap in wage distribution widened.

However, the above statements must be qualified somewhat. Collective-bargaining agreements cover 75 to 80 percent of the Dutch labor market (OECD 2003i), and the lowest wage scales in these collective agreements have risen in nominal terms so that the actual number of people on the legal minimum wage has declined over time. Full data on the wage distribution were not found, but we know that in 1997 the actual average wage of workers in the lowest wage-scale group in the Netherlands was only 7 percent above the legal minimum wage (Visser and Hemerijck 1997). For Dutch youth below the age of 23, cuts in the minimum wage were even greater than for the average—decreasing significantly for even younger workers. For example, Dutch 15-year-olds from the mid-1980s onward were entitled to only 30 percent of the adult minimum wage. In short, even though the legal wage minimum became less important over this period, the downward real wage pressure on low-skilled workers was substantial. *In fact the wage distribution in the Netherlands actually widened more from 1983 to 1999 than in the United States.*[39]

Why did the labor unions accept the wage restraints and cuts? The shortening of working hours agreed to with employers provides part of the answer. Another important part of the answer is that cuts by the Dutch government in employees' taxes and social security contributions resulted in a significant increase in disposable incomes, despite low real-gross

---

37. Six months of employment was required to start accumulating pension rights.

38. It is important to note that consensus was not a new development in Dutch society in the early 1980s—in fact numerous commentators have pointed out the emphasis on consensus throughout Dutch society and history. Nevertheless, the crisis prompted the social partners to imbue it with renewed importance through the Wassenaar Agreement. The Dutch word *polder* refers to a section of seabed converted into land by artificial docks.

39. The wage distribution is measured by the ratio of the wage at the 90 percent decile to the wage at the 10 percent decile. While the Dutch distribution widened more than in the United States, it started at a much lower level than in the United States and remained lower in 1999. Of course the Netherlands is also a smaller and more homogeneous economy than the United States. Data are from the (OECD 2003i).

wage increases.[40] The International Monetary Fund (IMF) calculated that the real gross wage of the average Dutch production worker increased by only 0.9 percent from 1983–98, while the corresponding real net wage increased by 14.8 percent.[41] Cuts in social security contributions were extended to employers in the early 1990s with a particular focus on low-wage jobs and the long-term unemployed. Hence, for workers hired at close to the minimum wage, employers' social security contributions were cut by 58 percent, which reduced effective labor costs by an average of 10.5 percent. If such a job were given to a long-term unemployed worker (out of work for more than a year), social security contributions would be completely eliminated—bringing the reduction in labor costs to almost a quarter of the total (IMF 1999, 25).

Social Insurance Reforms: Making Work Pay

Wide-ranging changes in the Dutch social security system—aimed at increasing labor supply—were simultaneously implemented with the labor-market reforms described above.[42] Prior to 1985, an unemployed person with job experience of at least 130 days in the previous year would receive a contribution-financed unemployment benefit (*Werkloosheidswet*, or WW) for 6 months worth 80 percent of the last received wage, followed by 24 months of government-financed unemployment benefits worth 75 percent of the last received wage. After 30 months, the unemployed would be indefinitely eligible for welfare.

In 1985 government-financed unemployment benefits were cut to 70 percent of the last earned wage, and in 1986 the WW was also cut to 70 percent of last earned wage. Then in 1987, the two types of unemployment benefits were combined into a single new contribution-financed type of unemployment benefit as eligibility was tightened and durations cut, especially for younger people. After 1987 all workers with at least 26 weeks of paid employment during the previous 39 weeks would be eligible for 6 months of short-term benefits (*kortdurende uitkering*) at a rate of 70 percent of the legal minimum wage. Because the legal minimum wage was frozen for long periods of the 1980s and 1990s, linking unemployment benefit levels to it constituted a reduction of the benefit level relative to average wages, which increased personal incentives to find work.[43]

There were, however, supplementary benefits available to workers with lengthy work experience. A salary-related benefit (*loongerelateerde uitker-*

---

40. Undoubtedly, the severity of the economic situation in the Netherlands in 1982 provided the crucial impetus for the labor unions' agreement.

41. See IMF (1999, figure 3.6) for detailed data.

42. This section draws on IMF data (1999, chapter 3).

43. For detailed statistics, see figure 3.5 in IMF (1999, 25).

ing) of 70 percent of the last earned wage (capped today at €59 per working day) became available for longer durations. The exact duration of unemployment assistance depended on the length of employment, but ranged from 6 months of salary-related benefit with 3 years of employment history to a maximum of 5 years of salary-related benefits with 40 years of employment history.[44] Overall, however, the reforms represented a very sharp reduction in benefits available to persons under, say, 23 years of age, and an appreciable restriction of salary-related benefit durations even for older workers, relative to the pre-1987 situation.[45] Van Ours (2003) estimates that the average unemployment benefit replacement rate in the Netherlands declined from 71 percent in 1980 to 56 percent in 2000.

In 1995 a further tightening of eligibility criteria demanded that the unemployed be willing to take any suitable job (*passende arbeid*) they are offered. Article 24(3) in the Dutch Unemployment Benefit Act states that all employment "which is within the worker's capabilities and abilities" is suitable with possible exceptions made if: the worker's qualifications are too far above those needed to fulfill the job; the pay is too low in comparison to previous employment; and the commute is too long.[46] However, the ability of workers to decline alternative employment is gradually scaled back as the period of unemployment lengthens. The longer a person remains unemployed, the fewer the demands he or she can make regarding the qualitative attributes associated with an offered job. Failure to comply with these regulations requires the Dutch social security agency to partially or completely deny benefits to the unemployed.[47]

---

44. Since the mid-1980s minor changes have been made to the formula of determining a worker's employment history and the duration of benefits. From 1995 to the present, the exact calculation of employment history has followed a two-step process. First, the individual has to review the five calendar years prior to unemployment to determine how many times wages were continuously received for at least 52 days. Second, the individual has to count the number of calendar years before this five-year period to the calendar year in which he/she turned 18. The two numbers are then added to determine the duration of benefits. For example, with four years of employment history, one is entitled to 6 months of salary-related benefits, increasing to five years with 40 years of employment record. For exact details of the gradually increasing benefit duration in the Netherlands, see the European Commission MISSOC database www.europa.eu.int/comm/employment_social/missoc/2002/nl_part10_en.htm (2004).

45. A two-year follow-up benefit (*vervolguitkering*) of 70 percent of the legal minimum wage is finally available after other types of unemployment benefits expire. For unemployed persons above age 57.5, this follow-up benefit is available until they reach age 65.

46. See European Foundation for the Improvement of Living and Working Conditions, EMIRE database, www.eurofound.eu.int/emire/NETHERLANDS/SUITABLEEMPLOYMENT-NL.html (accessed May 24, 2004).

47. Sanction is required in principle, but in reality the often close relationship between the unemployed and social security agency staff thwarts this automatic cutback. Currently up to two-thirds of benefit recipients are exempted from the job requirement—either statutorily

In 2001, through tax reform, the Dutch government introduced an EITC in an attempt to further alleviate the risk of unemployment and poverty traps[48] for benefit recipients. A general EITC for all workers was introduced, but cost concerns kept the program small in scale and it therefore had a limited effect on work incentives. For wage earners earning up to 140 percent of the minimum wage unemployment benefit, net replacement rates were brought down by approximately two percentage points, while minimum-wage workers saw reductions in net replacement rates of 2 to 4 percentage points, depending on social circumstances.[49]

The success of the structural supply-side reforms to the Dutch labor market is indicated by the impact they have had on the youth labor market. As we have seen above, many of the reforms were particularly strict for younger workers—a population in which many other eurozone countries are currently experiencing persistent unemployment problems. It is therefore encouraging that the 15- to 24-year-old segment of the Dutch labor market has undergone a similar, if even more pronounced, transformation than seen in the total Dutch labor market.

Organizational Reforms of the Social Insurance System

Starting in 1990, organizational changes were made in the way the social insurance system was administered. These reforms were designed to increase the financial responsibilities faced by firms, reduce the direct influence of employers and employees on the administration of benefits, and introduce market mechanisms into the delivery of social security services in order to align the incentives faced by benefit suppliers and job placement service providers.

New government agencies were created to regulate the collection of social insurance taxes/premiums and the payment of benefits. Previously, companies, unions, and the government had jointly administered this task.

---

or de facto. See IMF (2002a, 18). Loss of unemployment benefits in the Netherlands does not mean complete loss of income since social assistance guaranteeing sufficient resources (*algemene bijstand*) remains indefinitely available. This assistance varies according to social circumstances, with married or unmarried couples (irrespective of sex) aged 21–65 entitled to 100 percent of the net minimum wage (for example, *algemene bijstand* is subject to taxation), single parents aged 21 to 65 entitled to 70 percent, and single persons aged 21–65 entitled to 50 percent. While special assistance for exceptional needs (*bijzondere bijstand*) is available, loss of unemployment benefits in the Netherlands nonetheless implies a substantial decline in disposable income.

48. Unemployment traps refer to circumstances in which people are discouraged from exchanging social security benefits for work because the net financial gain is either small or negative. Poverty traps refer to circumstances in which people are discouraged from seeking better-paying jobs because the net financial gain is either small or negative. See OECD (2002a, 150).

49. For detailed information, see OECD (2002a, 78–80).

An important purpose of this change was to reduce the incentive inherent in the old system to move the unemployed from the contribution-based UI system to the disability system, which was mostly state funded at that time.

In 1996 firms were made legally responsible for employee sick leave payments during the first year of illness. Employer contributions to the disability plan were increased in 1998,[50] and the employer- and employee-financed unemployment benefits were increased from 8 to 26 weeks. These changes were intended to place stronger incentives for employers and union groups to police misuse of the social insurance programs and to increase their efforts to place people in new jobs.[51]

Having taken over the regulation of the social insurance programs, the government then contracted out much of its day-to-day management in 1997. Different agencies, initially set up to cover individual sectors of the economy only, were free to compete for members across sectoral borders and free to employ private companies to deliver social services such as job placement of benefit recipients. Competition introduced market forces into social service delivery, and also facilitated a targeted response by a region or sector to particular problems. For example, additional incentives could be given to private companies able to place laid-off workers from an area hit by company closings or restructuring.

Qualifications to the Dutch Labor-Market Miracle

Labor-market reforms in the Netherlands have increased the employment rate and reduced the unemployment rate. But this overall success has some qualifications.

First, the Netherlands has experienced a high and rising incidence of part-time work. Figure 5.6 illustrates that the Netherlands has approximately twice the share of part-time employment in total employment than the European Union as a whole. Part-time jobs are very common among Dutch women, associated with a near doubling of female employment (full- and part-time) from 34.4 percent in 1980 to 65.1 percent in 2002.[52] This increase to some degree represents catch-up from a traditionally low female participation rate in the Dutch workforce. The availability of part-time work is beneficial to many employees, and, according to the OECD, most part-time employment is voluntary. However, the preva-

---

50. The impact on total company wage costs was offset by decreases in other taxes and social security contributions.

51. These changes may also have discouraged employers from hiring anyone likely to become sick or disabled—known as the "adverse selection" problem in insurance provision.

52. Data drawn from OECD (2003i).

Figure 5.6 Part-time employment of total population and women, Netherlands and EU average, 1983–2002 (percent of total employment)

percent of total employment

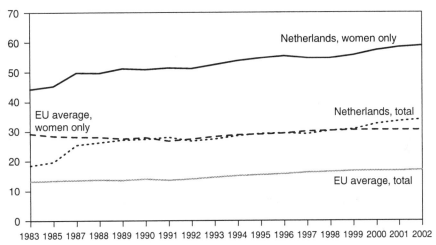

Source: OECD (2003i).

lence of part-time work may also reflect unavailability of adequate child-care facilities and the lack of incentives for full-time employment.[53]

As figure 5.7 illustrates, the dramatic increase in Dutch labor-force participation has gone hand in hand with a steep slide in average hours worked per employee in the Netherlands after 1980. The prevalence of part-time work is partly to blame for this decline, but a reduction in the full-time workweek[54] also plays a part. Today, the average workweek per employee in the Netherlands is the lowest in the OECD.[55] This has consequences for economic growth and limits the tax revenue generated by rising employment levels. The increase in employment since the early 1980s

---

53. See OECD (2002a, 149). In 2000, the right to work part-time became legal. Employees with more than 12 months of employment can ask their employers to adjust the number of contractual working hours to less than 35, unless compelling business reasons prevent it. Social partners cannot divert from these rules in collective-bargaining agreements, and rejections based upon compelling business reasons are subject to the jurisdiction of Dutch labor courts. Companies with fewer than 10 employees are exempt. See Bertelsmann Foundation (2000, 32–33).

54. The reduced full-time workweek was first initiated with the 1982 Wassenaar Agreement and continues today with the collective-bargaining agreement average of 37 hours per week.

55. See data from University of Groningen and the Conference Board (2004).

Figure 5.7 Average annual hours worked, select countries, 1979–2003

average hours worked

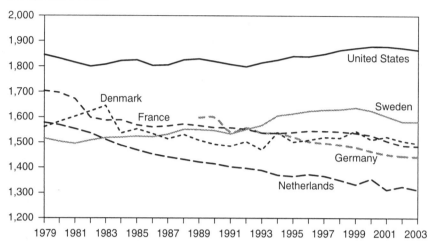

Source: University of Groningen and the Conference Board (2004).

has been achieved in part by redistributing existing work rather than by the creation of new job opportunities.

Naastepad and Kleinknecht (2002) link the relatively low Dutch labor-productivity growth in the 1980s and 1990s to the rapidly increasing Dutch employment. As we noted before, it is not necessarily bad if labor productivity in some European economies is lowered by increasing employment. But there are certainly ways in which productivity could be increased by better business operations in the Netherlands (many of the same barriers to productivity have been highlighted in Britain, France, and Germany), thereby combining higher productivity and higher employment.

Second, while many new jobs have been created, particularly in the rapidly expanding service sector, a significant number of those who lost their jobs left the workforce altogether rather than being induced to look for and find other work. These individuals entered income transfer programs other than UI—principally disability and early retirement programs. Figure 5.8 illustrates that the total share of people on social benefits in the Netherlands reached more than 25 percent in the mid-1980s, before declining slowly in the following years as a result of declining unemployment and stricter eligibility criteria for disability and social benefits. A part of the decrease in the Dutch unemployment rate is thus clearly a result of the increase in the number of persons outside the labor force. The idea that the Netherlands has been able to achieve *full employment* again is therefore questionable.

Figure 5.8 Unemployment benefit recipients in the Netherlands, 1970–2000

percent of sum of employed
and benefit recipients

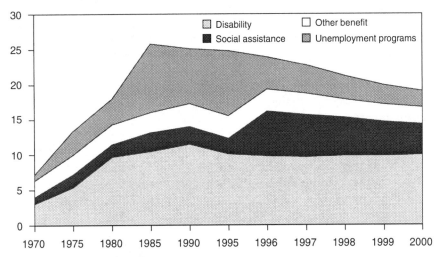

Note: Because of administrative reform in 1995, a significant number of people were moved from unemployment programs to passive social assistance in 1996.

Source: Dutch Ministry of Social Affairs and Employment, cited in OECD (2002a, 26–27).

The disability issue has shown itself to be extremely difficult to manage. In both 1985 and 1993, the Dutch government attempted to reform the disability system. In 1985, disability benefits were reduced from 80 percent to 70 percent of the last earned wage. To qualify for full disability, a person had to be at least 80 percent incapacitated. If a person was less than 80 percent incapacitated, the benefits were reduced proportionally and supplemented by unemployment benefits (the duration of these benefits expired as outlined earlier) if he/she were unable to find a job.[56] In 1993 disability benefits for new claimants were sharply reduced. The duration of full benefits (70 percent of last earned gross wage) were reduced to a maximum of 6 years for those age 58 and above and gradually declining to only 6 months for those at age 32. After these benefits expire a lower level of benefits is subsequently provided, which is calculated based on age and salary previously earned. Eligibility requirements were also tightened. The reference point for calculating disability became the ability to perform any paid job—regardless of the applicant's skill level or experience.

---

56. For additional detail, see IMF (1999, 27) and European Commission MISSOC database www.europa.eu.int/comm/employment_social/missoc/2002/nl_part5_en.htm (accessed May 25, 2004).

Third, a radical step was taken: All disability beneficiaries under the age of 50 were individually reexamined.[57] While these three steps did temporarily stem the rise in the fraction of disabled claimants, toward the end of the 1990s the fraction started to rise again, especially as more claims were accepted on psychological grounds (OECD 2002a, 85).

Van Ours (2003) uses 2001 statistical evidence to show that the share of disability recipients among women is slightly higher than among men for younger age groups (25–44 years of age), whereas the share of male recipients is twice as high as for females in some subcategories (55–64 years of age) for older workers (45–64 years of age). This finding supports the conclusion that *nondisability-related forces* heavily affect enrollment in Dutch disability programs—for example, the recent rise in female disability recipients may be linked to the easing of psychological eligibility criteria.[58]

Overall, the reforms to the disability program meant that *the share of disabled in the total labor force* stabilized. However, since the labor force increased substantially with the rise in employment, this stable share implies a large (nearly 30 percent) absolute increase in the number of disabled—from 608,000 in 1980 to 794,000 in 2000. The disability rate in the Netherlands today remains more than twice the rate found in otherwise comparable European countries, such as France or Germany.[59]

Acknowledging this, the Dutch government in 2003–04 initiated a series of further reforms to come into effect in 2006. The main aims of these are to further tighten the medical definition of full disability and restrict such to permanent cases (WAO—*Wet arbeidsongeschiktheidsregeligen*). Simultaneously, a new return-to-work scheme (WGA—*Werkhervatting Gedeeltelijk Arbeidsgeschikten*) for people not fully or permanently disabled strives to mobilize the "residual labor supply" in this group. They are to be coaxed into returning to the labor market through a combination of wage subsidies and stricter eligibility criteria. On the face of it, these proposals seem encouraging, but the devil is frequently in implementation, so their effect cannot be fully gauged as of yet.[60]

Lessons Learned

The Netherlands illustrates that determined, coordinated, and sustained government action on several fronts can, in the words of C. Maxwell Watson (IMF 1999, 2), "change the rules of the game in the labor market . . .

---

57. For additional details, see IMF (1999, 27) and European Commission MISSOC database www.europa.eu.int/comm/employment_social/missoc/2002/nl_part5_en.htm.

58. The high female disability recipiency rate for younger workers (25–44 years of age) may also be related to the rapid rise in female labor-force participation since 1982. However, the male labor-force participation rate in this age group remains higher than for females.

59. Data drawn from OECD (2002b).

60. For additional information, see OECD (2004d).

[through] chemistry, but no alchemy." As van Ours (2003, 17) puts it in his conclusion, "Labor market developments in the Netherlands were not a miracle but above all related to the restructuring of inefficient labor-market institutions." Thus, the interaction of several labor-market-related reforms proved a powerful stimulus to job creation without endangering the nucleus of the Dutch welfare state. The example of the Netherlands shows how an economy can start a positive cycle in which payroll taxes and unemployment benefits are cut, and work incentives and employment increase.

The drop in hours per employee and the growth of early retirement and disability programs are important qualifications to this finding. Dutch policymakers clearly attempted to control social programs but were unwilling to do more because of the potential political fallout. The Wassenaar Agreement was achieved with fairly peaceful labor relations.[61] Any agreement would have been more difficult without alternative social support programs for laid-off workers to move into as UI benefits were cut back. The Netherlands decided to preserve its tradition of social cooperation even though it limited the effectiveness of labor-market reforms in terms of increasing the number of hours worked in the economy.

Sweden: Reforming under Fiscal Distress

In the early 1990s Sweden suffered its steepest recession since the 1930s with real GDP declining more than 1 percent each year from 1991–93 and open unemployment more than quadrupling in 3 years to about 8 percent of the labor force in 1993 (figure 5.9)—an unprecedented level for that economy. This caused an unparalleled fiscal crisis in Sweden with the general government deficit peaking at 12 percent of GDP in 1993 and gross general government financial liabilities nearly doubling to 83 percent of GDP from 1990–94.[62] Desperate times called for desperate measures, and successive Swedish governments throughout the 1990s implemented a series of economic reforms, even through changes in the political parties in power. These reforms not only engineered a remarkable fiscal turnaround of government finances, but also laid the foundations for a robust pickup in employment. Unemployment by the end of the 1990s had halved to 4 percent, considerably lower than in other major European economies.

The great bulk of the fiscal consolidation in Sweden occurred through cuts in government expenditure after 1993. Figure 5.10 shows the decline

---

61. The European Industrial Relations Observatory (EIRO) lists the Netherlands as having the fourth lowest level of strike activity in Europe (after Slovakia, Austria, and Germany) in the late 1990s.

62. All data from OECD (2003a).

Figure 5.9 Sweden's open unemployment and participation rate in ALMPs[a] (OECD Program 910), 1986–2002

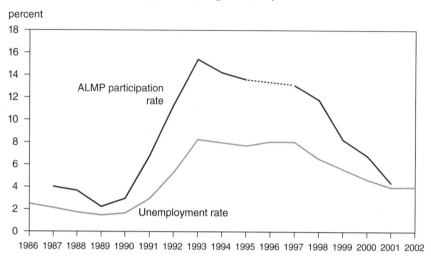

percent

ALMPs = active labor-market programs

a. Unemployment rate is percent of labor force; ALMP participation rate is percent of active labor force.

Source: OECD (2003i).

in government outlays, declining by 15 percentage points of GDP from 73 percent of GDP in 1993 to 58 percent in 2002. Of course spending at 58 percent of GDP is still very high even by European standards, with government outlays still roughly 10 percentage points above the eurozone average in 2002.[63]

Even though taxes remain very high,[64] the 1990s reforms have remarkably improved the sustainability of Swedish government finances, with the cyclically adjusted general government balance improving from –6 percent of GDP in 1991–95 to +3 percent in 2000 (and it remained positive at +0.7 percent in the latest available data from 2003) (European Commission 2004a). According to the IMF a little less than half this improvement came from a reduction in government transfers to households, while the remainder arose from cuts in government transfers to business, which had been reduced by 75 percent of their 1993 absolute value by 2000.

---

63. Similarly, the OECD (2004c) ranks Sweden first in terms of social expenditure in 1998 with total social expenditure at 30.98 percent of GDP.

64. The OECD (2003h) ranks Sweden—at 50.6 percent—as having the highest total tax revenues as a share of GDP in 2002 of all surveyed countries in its 2003 revenue statistics.

Figure 5.10 General government revenues and expenditure in Sweden and the eurozone, 1985–2002

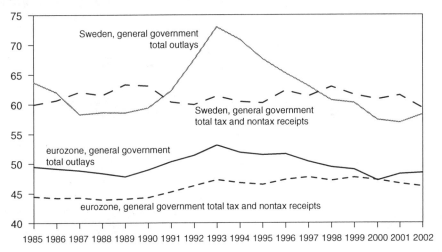

Source: OECD (2003i).

In 1997 Sweden implemented medium-term government expenditure constraints that stipulated a combination of a 2 percent of GDP government structural surplus target set three years ahead and central government expenditure ceilings. Starting in 2000 a balanced-budget requirement for local governments required a reversal of any deficits on current spending within two years. Thus, even though Sweden remains outside the eurozone, the fiscal policies it has followed are actually tougher, but more flexible, than those required by the SGP.[65]

We turn now to a description of how Sweden reduced transfers to households by up to 5 percent of GDP while improving employment. The Swedish reforms can be separated into four main areas: unemployment benefits, active labor-market programs (ALMPs), sickness and disability benefits, and comprehensive tax reform.

Unemployment Benefits: Cuts and Conditionality

There is a two-tier UI benefit program in Sweden. Most of the unemployed receive earnings-related benefits (*inkomstbortfallsförsäkring*) available to members of UI funds, which are administered by the labor unions in each sector of the economy.

---

65. See also IMF (2001a, 14–15).

Control of the UI funds serves as a powerful recruitment tool and has contributed to Sweden's very high union membership levels for both blue- and white-collar workers. It also meant that reforming the unemployment benefit system was politically very contentious in Sweden. Nevertheless, substantial changes were made to benefit levels, duration, and eligibility.

Before 1991, Swedish unemployment benefits were 90 percent of reference earnings (previous daily average earnings). In 1991, benefits were reduced to 80 percent of reference wages, before being temporarily lowered to 75 percent in 1996. A year later, the benefits were raised again to the current (and 1991–96) level of 80 percent. One study suggested that unemployment in Sweden is quite sensitive to the level of UI benefits. Carling, Holmlund, and Vejsiu (2001) estimate that the 1996 replacement rate reduction from 80 to 75 percent led to a 10 percent increase in transition out of unemployment.

The rather high replacement rates for the Swedish UI system do not apply to all workers, because benefit levels are capped. Data for benefit-cap levels in earlier years are not available, but the current cap is €73 (680 Swedish kroner) per day during the first 100 days with benefits. This cap is estimated to limit payouts for approximately 45 percent of recipients. The current cap is a significant increase compared with the €62 (580 Swedish kroner) per day level prevailing prior to July 2001 (Thakur et al. 2003, 54).

Until 2001, the duration of unemployment benefits was essentially indefinite, as eligibility spells could be extended through participation in public works or training programs (the ALMPs). The adverse effect this created for work incentives was widely noted (IMF 2001a; Calmfors, Forslund, and Hemström 2001), and in 2001 the new "Activity Guarantee" plan limited UI benefit duration to 300 days initially and extendable for another 300-day period provided that the recipient participated in one ALMP at least 70 hours per month for 6 months.

Once the unemployment-benefit eligibility is exhausted, the unemployed person needs at least 12 months of full-time employment—with membership in a UI fund—to requalify for earnings-related UI benefits. The 12-month membership rule reflects a substantial tightening in eligibility requirements prior to 1991 when only 4 months was required.

The limits and restrictions on the main UI benefit program are mitigated by the second-tier UI program, which provides a lower flat-rate basic allowance (*grundförsäkring*). This program only requires that a person be employed for at least 6 months and at least 70 hours per month. Other rules include a five-day waiting period (initiated in 1991) before payment and a nine-week penalty if a worker leaves a job without a valid reason.

The UI programs in Sweden do not simply hand out benefits without strings attached. In fact, the requirement for recipients to accept positions has been strengthened recently: Since 2001 beneficiaries have been required to cooperate with the unemployment agency to create an individual action plan (IAP),[66] which makes it clear that individuals must accept suitable job offers. The IAP also describes the possible ALMPs the unemployed will be required to participate in. Failure to comply with the IAP or take up suitable employment leads to automatic sanctions in three progressive "steps": A first-time refusal leads to an 8-week 25 percent reduction in benefits; a second refusal leads to an 8-week 50 percent reduction; and a third refusal completely halts benefits for 8 weeks.

Overall, there has been a significant tightening of the Swedish UI program over the 1990s, in terms of benefit levels, duration, and eligibility. Some reforms since 1991 have subsequently been reversed, but the net effect has been a considerable reduction in the availability of unemployment benefits.

That said, it is notable that persons who lose UI benefits do not lose income support altogether in Sweden. A low basic level of income is guaranteed through social assistance (*socialbidrag*). In 2003 this was a flat-rate basic amount of €271 (2,520 Swedish kroner) per month for singles and €492 (4,570 Swedish kroner) for couples. This basic amount can be—and is—supplemented by additional benefits for children as well as commuting by any household member, trade union membership (including the UI fund), housing, and other "needs." There are no limits on the length of time for which these additional benefits can be received.

ALMPs: A Swedish Tradition Overdone?

For many years Sweden has had extensive ALMPs. For as long as international comparable data are available[67] Sweden has been at—or near—the very top in terms of expenditure on ALMPs. Calmfors, Forslund, and Hemström (2001) describe how the original intent of these programs in the 1950s was to increase labor-skill levels and mobility, but that since the 1960s the emphasis increasingly shifted toward counteracting all types of unemployment—including cyclical unemployment. These programs became an alternative form of income support, and, indeed, there was a sharp rise in ALMP participation during the early 1990s recession (figure 5.9). In fact, most of the ALMP support during that time came in the form of subsidized employment—predominantly public employment,[68] which

---

66. These IAPs bear some resemblance to the PAP/PARE (*plan d'action personelle/plan d'aide au retour à l'emploi*) program introduced in France in 2001 and the Job-AQTIV (German acronym: A = Activate, Q = Qualify, T = Train, I = Invest, and V = Mediate) format introduced in Germany in 2002. However, the level of sanctions against the unemployed for noncompliance is greater in Sweden.

67. OECD Labor Market Indicators data go back to 1985.

68. Data drawn from OECD (2003i). The vast majority of Swedish "Youth Measures" are of similar characteristic and should—for this purpose—be included in the functional category "subsidized employment."

directly lowered the unemployment rate as measured by official statistics. However, participants in education-type ALMPs are considered unemployed in official statistics (Thakur et al. 2003, 61). Hence, the true level of unemployment in Sweden in the mid-1990s was likely significantly above the official open rate of about 8 percent shown in figure 5.9.

Calmfors, Forslund, and Hemström (2001) surveyed a range of empirical micro- and macroeconomic studies of the effect of ALMPs. They concluded that the Swedish ALMPs were not particularly efficient overall and should not be copied outright if a country's goal is ultimately to increase *private* employment. ALMPs in Sweden did succeed in lowering open unemployment, but they did so with serious "crowding-out effects" that reduced other employment. Subsequently, in 2002 Sweden's employment-to-population ratio had not yet recovered to precrisis levels, although the ratio is very high relative to other European economies. Using ALMPs in response to a sharp cyclical slowdown was problematic because the sudden surge in participation[69] made it difficult to find economically valuable activities for all participants. However, the Swedish experience does not rule out positive results from ALMPs under different macroeconomic circumstances (see the next section on Denmark for an example).

Sickness Benefits and Disability: An Enduring Swedish Addiction?

Sweden has traditionally had very generous sickness and disability benefits. In 1991 sickness-benefit replacement rates of close to 100 percent were available for an indefinite period.[70] Figure 5.11 illustrates that by the end of the 1980s expenditure on both sickness and disability cash benefits had reached 4.7 percent of GDP, and in figure 5.12 is it evident that absenteeism rose almost continuously after the introduction of sickness benefits in 1955. As awareness of the problems associated with worker absenteeism became widespread, and the fiscal situation deteriorated in 1991, the new center-right government introduced reforms in September 1991. The new rules included a one-day waiting period before benefits were provided. Also, employers now had the burden of paying benefits for the first 14 days of a person's illness or disability. Furthermore, eligibility criteria were tightened, and benefits were cut to 75 percent of wages.[71] Prior

69. Figure 5.11 shows that expenditure on ALMPs in Sweden almost doubled from 1.6 percent of GDP in 1989 to 3.0 percent of GDP in 1992.

70. See IMF (2001a, 40) for a detailed breakdown of historical sick leave compensation. Traditionally, compensation varies with the number of days one is absent and is capped at a certain fixed level. As such, only low-wage recipients will face an actual net replacement rate of 100 percent, whereas recipients with higher incomes will—due to the cap—face lower net replacement rates. See the Swedish National Social Insurance Board (*Riksförsäkringsverket*), www. rfv.se/forsak/belopp/docs/aktbel03.pdf (accessed October 29, 2003), for detailed maximum benefits in 2003.

71. Eligibility for disability for elderly unemployed persons covered by "nonmedical labor market considerations" (i.e., healthy workers "parked" on disability pensions) was also eliminated in 1991.

Figure 5.11 Select social expenditures in Sweden, 1980–98

percent of nominal GDP

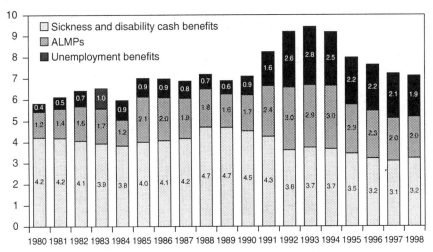

ALMPs = active labor-market programs

Source: OECD (2002b).

to this reform all employers had paid a flat amount for sickness and disability insurance regardless of the extent to which their own employees drew benefits, which limited the incentive for employers to require employees to verify sickness.

In 1995 eligibility criteria were tightened again. A physician's certificate was required after the seventh calendar day of sickness while long-term cases required a more thorough medical examination. In 1998, sickness benefits were raised to 80 percent of wages and remained at this level until July 2003, when they were again reduced, to 77.6 percent of wages. At the same time, employer-covered sick days were extended from 14 to 21. In figure 5.11 it is evident that the tightening of eligibility criteria and benefit levels did have an effect on expenditure, which fell to 3.2 percent of GDP by 1998.[72]

The most recent reforms are a direct result of the strong rebound in the number of sickness benefit recipients after 1997, which is clearly illustrated in figure 5.12. In 2003, the OECD estimates that sick leave alone kept 270,000 full-time-equivalent workers away from work for the full year. This is more than total unemployment at 259,500 in 2003 (OECD 2004e; Eurostat 2004a). The sharp increase in beneficiaries reversed the

---

72. One can expect sickness levels and the number of people on disability to be cyclical only to a limited degree, so the decline in expenditure from 1990 to 1998 can primarily be attributed to the tightening of eligibility criteria and benefit levels. Unfortunately, data do not go beyond 1998.

Figure 5.12 Sweden's sick leave, men and women, 1955–2003

annual paid days of sick leave
per insured person

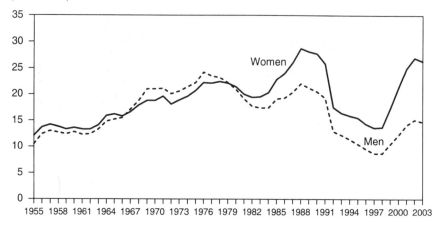

Note: Sickness benefits began in Sweden in 1955. Data are only for sickness benefits paid by National Social Insurance Board. Data do not include sickness benefits paid by employers during the first 14 days of sickness, implemented in 1992 (and extended to 21 days in July 2003). From 1998 onward, recipients of disability pensions are excluded from denominator.
Source: Swedish National Social Insurance Board, *Riksförsäkringsverket.*

decline experienced in the first half of the 1990s.[73] Several explanations for this strong procyclical rebound have been suggested. Aronsson and Walker (1997) estimate that procyclicality has been present in Swedish sickness benefit claims since the 1960s. They suggest that work-related stress and compositional effects of the workforce affect sick leave, and that the last hired are more prone to falling ill. Based on other Swedish evidence, Johansson and Palme (2003) suggest that sickness benefit claims are responsive to the incentive structure of the system. Henrekson and Persson (2004) estimates that the 5 percentage point increase in sickness benefit replacement rates in 1998 (from 75 to 80 percent) accounted for a 30 percent increase in Swedish claims.

   Since there is no limit to the duration of sickness benefits (*sjukpenning*) in Sweden, the distinction between sickness benefits and a full disability pension (*sjukbidrag/förtidspension*) is blurred. Both types of benefits expire at the age of 65 when individuals then become eligible for an old-age pen-

---

73. The rebound in sick leave after 1998 shown in figure 5.12 is staggering, since the first 14 days of sick leave paid for by the employer after 1998 are not included in the data from the Swedish National Social Insurance Board. Such a rebound inevitably questions the effect of shifting the burden of financing the initial 14 days directly to employers, since only a rise in the number of people on sick leave for prolonged periods (more than 14 days) could have caused the post-1998 increase. It seems that the effects of employer surveillance/policing of employee sickness would be extremely limited for longer periods of absence.

sion (*ålderspension*). The main difference comes in the calculation of bene-fit levels.[74] It is hard to make a clean comparison of benefit levels in the programs because of the system's complexity. There are different degrees of disability, which affect the amount and type of benefit paid. The bene-fits of the two programs are taxed differently, and disability beneficiaries receive additional allowances over and above the basic benefit level.[75] However, it would be fair to say that Sweden's sickness benefits are very generous in absolute terms and in comparison with its disability pensions.

Given the generosity and extended duration of Sweden's sickness ben-efits, this means that a number of people who would be classified as disabled in other European countries are counted as "sick" in Sweden. Therefore, the permanent level of withdrawals from the Swedish labor market through the combination of sickness benefits and disability pen-sions will likely be somewhat higher than the already high level indicated by international comparative statistics such as the OECD.

Comprehensive Tax Reform

In 1991, Sweden implemented a comprehensive tax reform. The existing system had tax rates that were extremely high on upper-income levels (very high marginal tax rates) combined with tax breaks or deductions that allowed certain forms of income to avoid taxation or be taxed at a lower rate. The main goal of the reform was to lower the highest tax brackets while eliminating tax breaks and deductions (broadening the tax base while lowering marginal tax rates). In addition, there was an effort to move toward taxing consumption and capital income, while lowering the taxes on labor income. Overall the reform was designed to be revenue neutral. A negative revenue impact of 6 percent of GDP (or more) was also expected from the cuts in income tax rates. This was to be offset one-third by new taxes on capital, one-third by broadening the base of the standard 23 percent value-added tax (VAT), one-sixth from the elimination of tax loopholes, and the remainder from revenue gains generated by higher output associated with incentive improvements.[76]

A large group of full-time employees benefited from the 24 to 27 per-centage point drop in the top income tax rate (although the top rate was

---

74. Differences in determining personal eligibility also occur, since eligibility for disability pensions generally requires a one-time assessment by a medical practitioner employed by the National Social Insurance Board, while sickness benefits may require periodic medical examinations.

75. See Swedish National Social Insurance Board (*Riksförsäkringsverket*), www.rfv.se/forsak/famba/sgi/index.htm (accessed October 30, 2003) for details regarding the calculation of sickness benefits and www.rfv.se/forsak/pension/alder/analys/index.htm (accessed Octo-ber 30, 2003) for details regarding the disability program.

76. For a detailed analysis of the Swedish tax reform, see Agell, Englund, and Sodersten (1996) and IMF (2001a).

still high at 51 percent). Subsequent estimates indicate that this drop led to an increase in labor supply of up to two percent (see Agell, Englund, and Sodersten 1998; Blomquist, Eklöf, and Newey 2001). However, ensuing estimates also indicate that the reform did not achieve revenue neutrality and, indeed, was underfunded by about 4 percentage points of GDP (Thakur et al. 2003, 16). Thus, while the tax reform plan had a direct, positive effect on the labor supply, it also aggravated the fiscal crisis in Sweden in the years following implementation in the early 1990s.

Lessons Learned

Despite the problems and issues that remain, the overall nature and effect of the Swedish labor-market and tax reforms that started in 1991 are clear: lower (but still) generous benefit levels available for shorter durations and lower marginal tax rates on labor income. These reforms have contributed to significant improvements in unemployment and a rebound in labor-force participation. Crucially, the employment increase has not been accompanied by a steep decline in average hours worked per employee, as was the case in the Netherlands (see figure 5.7).

On the negative side, Sweden also illustrates what can happen if labor-market reforms are not comprehensively implemented. The surge in sickness benefit claims after 1998 appears linked to the stricter unemployment benefit rules. As people were denied UI benefits or unwilling to meet the stiffer requirements for eligibility, they shifted to the sickness benefit program.

Denmark: Toughening the Welfare State

In 1993, unemployment in Denmark reached a historic peak of 309,000 persons (or 10.7 percent of the labor force) who included approximately a quarter of long-term unemployed.[77] This made it evident to decision makers that the existing Danish labor-market model was no longer financially viable nor delivering an acceptable outcome for the unemployed. As a result, the ruling leftist social-democratic government implemented a series of reforms in the labor market during the 1990s that successfully decreased unemployment to below US levels, while increasing an *already high* labor supply. Figure 5.13 illustrates the development of unemployment rates and employment/population ratios in Denmark, the European Union, and the United States.

---

77. Data drawn from OECD (2003i). Long-term unemployed are defined as persons unemployed for more than 12 months, which, in absolute numbers, were 77,100 in 1993.

Figure 5.13   Unemployment and employment to population rates in Denmark and the European Union, 1983–2002

unemployment rate
(percent)

employment/population ratio
(percent)

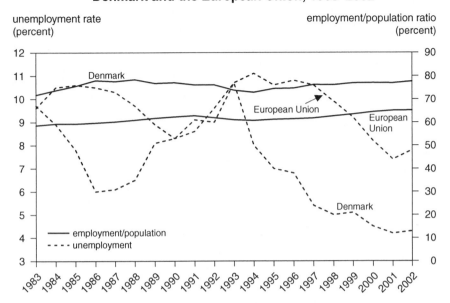

Source: OECD (2003i).

The condition of Denmark's labor market benefited from a strong cyclical recovery in 1994 with real GDP increasing 5.5 percent—up from being flat in 1993.[78] But over the period as a whole, employment growth was not driven just by demand growth. Danish real GDP growth from 1995 to 2002 was a moderate 2.4 percent a year, which is comparable to the 2.3 percent recorded for the European Union as a whole (although better than either Italy's 1.9 percent or Germany's 1.4 percent growth over the same period). The job-rich growth that occurred in Denmark reflects a substantial difference compared to the European Union as a whole, as figure 5.13 illustrates.

The Danish labor market was revamped through a series of initiatives, which were accompanied by critical periodic parliamentary reviews of these initiatives from 1994 through 1999.[79] The reforms had four main elements: decentralization and individualization; shortening the duration of unemployment benefits; the right and duty to be active while unemployed; and measures to improve youth employment.

---

78. All real GDP data from the OECD Economic Outlook (OECD 2003a).

79. The main delivery vehicles were the 1994 Labor Market Reform Package and the Annual Financial Acts (1995 through 1999). See Danish Ministry of Labour (1999, chapter 1).

Decentralization and Individualization

With the 1994 labor-market reforms, the priority of specific policy decisions was delegated to local regional labor-market boards,[80] although subject to an overall framework laid down by the Ministry of Labor. The aim was to incorporate local needs, knowledge, and expertise when allocating resources for the community. For example, local labor-market boards could select for special programs target groups of unemployed persons considered at risk of becoming long-term unemployed. Similarly, the local boards could identify sectors with shortages of skilled labor (that could create growth bottlenecks), and then take steps to overcome these shortages.

Simultaneously, individual action plans (IAPs) between the unemployed and the public employment agencies were introduced.[81] The IAPs were intended to reflect the needs of both the individual and local employers. However, to resolve possible conflicts between the two sides, the Finance Act of 1995 explicitly states that *the wishes of the unemployed in connection with the drawing up of action plans should not stand in the way of the labor needs of enterprises*[82]—in other words, the wishes of the unemployed are overruled by the needs of local labor demand.

Shortening the Duration of Unemployment Benefits

Unemployment benefit levels in Denmark are generous for low- and moderate-income workers. They are set at 90 percent of the average of the preceding 12 weeks' wages[83] but are capped at a fairly low level (currently €400 or 3115 Danish kroner/week). The UI benefit levels have not been cut with the labor-market reforms, in part because employment protection legislation in Denmark is less stringent than in the rest of Europe (figure 5.14). Company restructuring and job cuts are easy, but laid-off workers have access to generous compensation. Thus, Denmark attempts

---

80. Local labor-market boards consist of representatives from private employers and local authorities as well as workers.

81. These IAPs bear some resemblance to the PAP/PARE (*Plan d'Action Personelle/Plan d'Aide au Retour à l'Emploi*) program introduced in France in 2001 and the Job-AQTIV (German acronym: A = Activate, Q = Qualify, T = Train, I = Invest, and V = Mediate) program introduced in Germany in 2002 (mentioned earlier). However, the level of sanctions against the unemployed for noncompliance in Denmark—as in Sweden—is substantially higher.

82. Wording is from the Danish Government's Financial Act of 1995, which was reproduced in Danish Ministry of Labour (1999, 14).

83. Access to unemployment benefits is granted after membership in an unemployment insurance fund for 12 months. Benefits are financed by the state and through flat-rate contributions by salaried workers and nonwage earners to a labor-market fund. However, as employee contributions to the labor-market fund are tax exempt, in effect the vast majority of funding for unemployment benefits is provided by the state. As is the case in Sweden, labor-market funds in Denmark are administered by labor unions with similar effects on union recruitment potential and political controversy of reforms to the system.

Figure 5.14 Overall employment protection legislation indicator, 1998

index number

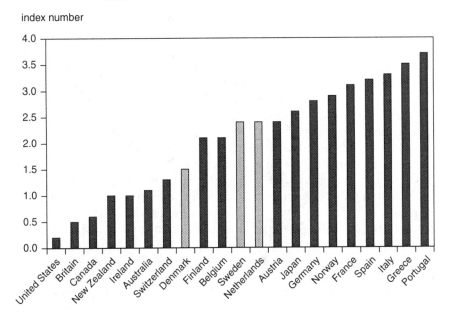

Source: OECD (2001e).

to combine income security with a flexible economy—"flexicurity." Many higher-wage workers are also covered by contracts—negotiated by white-collar unions—that provide a generous severance payment if they are laid off. Thus, both the generosity of the benefit levels and the costs of restructuring are likely greater than implied by the UI-benefit cap found in the union-run UI program and by the regulatory ease of firing.

While levels of unemployment benefits (as a percent of prior wages) have not been changed since 1994, the duration for which they are available has been cut by half to a (still generous) maximum of four years. Moreover, as of 2000, the unemployed are required to participate in training or job placement programs for the last 36 months of the four-year benefit duration period. Prior to 1994 it was possible for persons to requalify for UI benefits by participating in training or other programs, but this possibility was eliminated. By 1996 only 52 weeks of unsubsidized employment entitled an unemployed person to new unemployment benefits. The rule was changed to ensure active labor-market training would target a return to employment, rather than being just a means to continued eligibility for unemployment benefits.[84]

---

84. See OECD (2004g) for the most recent changes in legislation in Denmark and elsewhere.

The Right and Duty to Be Active while Unemployed

Although government-sponsored training programs in Sweden and in the United States have not been very successful, indications suggest the Danish programs have worked relatively well. Denmark has traditionally spent lavishly on both passive and active programs. Both businesses and unions are supporters of the programs, and potential employers even provide information regarding the skills they seek in potential employees. The programs have obtained high job placement rates for graduates.[85] The programs, which are subject to review, are credited with reducing the structural unemployment level in Denmark by 3 to 4 percentage points, as well as raising the skilled-labor supply and thereby avoiding bottlenecks and contributing to moderation in wage increases.[86]

Another important aspect of the Danish labor-market training programs is that they are not limited only to the unemployed, for whom participation is mandatory. Instead they are an integral part of an extensive program of continuing vocational training opportunities available to all Danish workers, thus ensuring knowledge of the skill requirements of the labor market.[87] Figure 5.15 illustrates that there was a near doubling of resources given to labor-market training from the mid-1990s on. The additional resources significantly expanded labor-market training programs, to the point that more than 10 percent of both unemployed and employed workers had participated in a program for at least a short period (figure 5.16). Although this labor-market approach is very expensive it does appear to have some significant positive benefits and the money has not been wasted.

The opportunities for the unemployed in Denmark to upgrade their skills are regarded as *a right of the unemployed* to improve their employability. However, it is simultaneously considered the *duty of the unemployed* to engage in ALMPs, and strict rules are in place to ensure participation. As we saw earlier, all unemployed have an IAP, which will often spell out what active training or job placement activities the unemployed will par-

---

85. Follow-up studies by the Danish Ministry of Labour indicate that from 1996–97, 46 percent of all people unemployed or activated under the ALMPs in the UI benefit system found full-time employment, and 95 percent of these had, at some point during this period, left unemployment, ALMPs, or training-leave programs. Similarly, the increase in outflows from unemployment benefits and ALMPs among long-term unemployed (more than two years of unemployment) has been significantly higher than found among short-term unemployed. See Danish Ministry of Labour (1999, chapter 2).

86. See Danish Ministry of Labour (2000, chapter 8). It must be emphasized that "participation in labor-market training" does not require long-term, full-time training, but can entail participation in short training activities.

87. In its 2002 survey of continuing vocational training Eurostat finds that Danish companies have the highest investment in training programs of all countries in the survey at 3 percent of labor costs (Eurostat 2002, cited in Employment Taskforce 2003, 51).

Figure 5.15 Passive measures and labor-market training expenditures, select countries, 1990–2000

percent of GDP

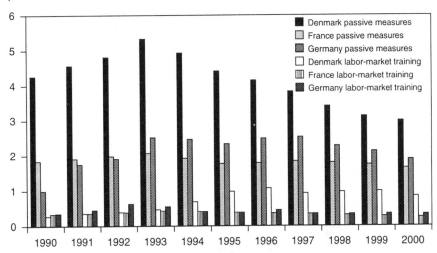

Legend:
- Denmark passive measures
- France passive measures
- Germany passive measures
- Denmark labor-market training
- France labor-market training
- Germany labor-market training

Source: OECD (2003i).

ticipate in. If an unemployed person rejects an *activation offer* (i.e., either a job or a training opportunity) during the four years of unemployment benefits, unemployment benefits are immediately and completely terminated.[88] The unemployed also have the *duty of availability to the labor market,* which means that they must be able to take up *suitable employment* with one day's notice[89] or face the complete loss of benefits. *Suitable employment* in Denmark is defined as any job that the unemployed can fulfill immediately or after a short training period within his or her field (Retsinfo 2003). Furthermore, an unemployed person must accept up to four hours of daily transportation time by public transport to get to and

---

88. The loss of unemployment benefits in Denmark does not entail complete loss of income as social benefits guaranteeing sufficient resources are indefinitely available. However, since these social benefits are fixed at a level of 60 percent of the maximum unemployment benefits (80 percent for parents), the loss of unemployment benefits may lead to an immediate 40 percent decline in income. Furthermore, maximum indefinite benefits are dependent on recipient participation in locally determined activation measures, and unjustified failure to participate automatically leads to a reduction in indefinite benefits (in proportion to absence) up to a total of a 30 percent reduction. See European Commission MISSOC database, www.europa.eu.int/comm/employment_social/missoc/2002/dk_part11_en.htm (accessed October 27, 2003).

89. "Passive availability" is also required, which means that unemployed persons participating in ALMPs must leave the program and take an available job if it cannot be filled by another unemployed person.

Figure 5.16   Active labor force enrolled in labor-market training, select countries, 1990–2000

percent of active labor force

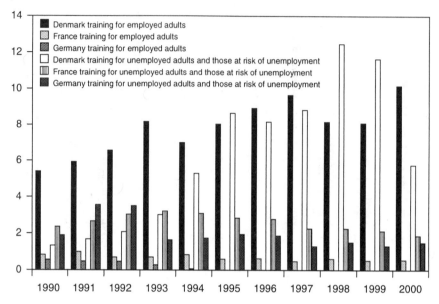

Source: OECD (2003i).

from work.[90] As such, the high level of unemployment benefits and the extensive opportunities for acquiring new skills come with significant requirements designed to return people to the workforce and to increase the flexibility of the labor market.

Measures to Improve Youth Employment

Similarly to the Netherlands, after 1996 Denmark enacted a number of policies initially targeted toward low-skilled unemployed youth and subsequently encompassing all unemployed youth. Any unemployed persons under the age of 25—apart from all the requirements listed earlier—have the right and duty to enter into ALMPs after only six months without a job. Unlike the situation for adults, the level of their unemployment benefits was cut by 50 percent. The severe cut in the unemployment benefit levels was intended to encourage the youth to quickly enroll in education or

---

90. If the unemployed person possesses an upper-secondary or tertiary education, he or she must accept a job offer irrespective of the commute. We also want to emphasize that Denmark is a very small country where all higher education is provided free of charge by the government.

Figure 5.17 Youth unemployment in Denmark, 1996–2003

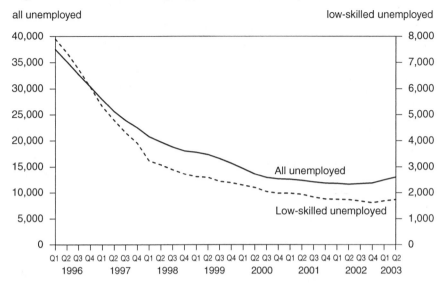

Note: Youth is defined as those 16 to 24 years of age. Unskilled defined as members of unemployment funds affiliated with the *Kvindeligt arbejderforbund Danmark* (KAD) and *Specialarbejder i danmark* (SID) unions.

Source: Danish Statistical Agency, http://www.statistikbanken.dk/.

training programs rather than remain unemployed.[91] Figure 5.17 suggests that these measures have been extraordinarily effective and have brought levels of youth unemployment in Denmark down by about two-thirds from 1996 to 2003—and even more among low-skilled youth. As a result, youth unemployment in Denmark is now among the lowest in Europe.

Qualifications to the Success of the Danish Labor-Market Reforms

The Danish labor-market model remains very expensive despite successfully lowering unemployment by the end of the 1990s. The system cost about 5 percent of GDP even with a strong economy (and low unemployment) and would presumably be much higher if unemployment were to rise for cyclical reasons.[92] Such high costs may not be justified as a social investment on pure economic grounds, and the political consensus needed to sustain the model also may not last. The high cost also makes it harder to offer the Danish model as one other countries should emulate.

---

91. With the 50 percent cut, the level of unemployment benefits became comparable to the level of state grants available to all Danish citizens enrolled in higher education.

92. On the other hand, as noted above, some of these program expenses also benefit workers by enhancing their job skills.

Figure 5.18 Disability benefit recipiency rates in the 20- to 64-year-old population, select countries, 1980–99

percent

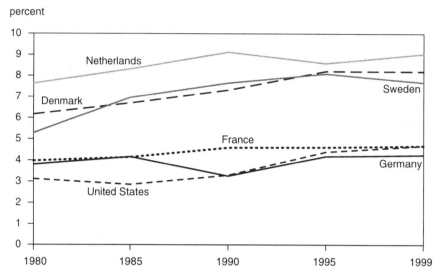

Source: OECD (2002c).

Just as in the Netherlands and Sweden, Denmark has in recent decades experienced continued increases from an already high level in the number of citizens receiving disability pensions (figure 5.18). By the late 1990s Denmark had one of the highest rates of such *working-age inactives* in the OECD. Denmark has also seen a decline in the average hours worked, putting it again among the lowest in the OECD. Therefore, Denmark has not increased total hours worked as much as employment.

Lessons Learned

Denmark shows that it is possible to maintain very high levels of unemployment benefits and still achieve a very low unemployment rate, a high employment rate, and labor-market flexibility. Their success is based upon a combination of work incentives and a very extensive and expensive program of active labor-market measures. Increased employment required that unemployment benefits and training opportunities have the necessary incentive structure in order to lure the unemployed toward regular employment. Denmark imposed severe sanctions (immediate and complete loss of benefits) even for minor noncompliance with IAPs, and also demanded strict availability requirements to ensure the unemployed person's readiness and willingness to enter the workforce with little or no advance notice. Essentially, the program placed the needs of local enterprises (labor demand) above the needs of the unemployed. It also emphasized the belief that the unemployed are not helpless—they are expected to help themselves as well.

Overall Lessons from Labor-Market Reforms

National labor markets and social security systems are complicated. It is often hard to figure out why they work the way they do and even more difficult to compare across countries. Yet, some overall lessons can be drawn from the experiences of the Netherlands, Sweden, and Denmark. First and foremost, their experiences illustrate that policy changes do make a difference, trends can be reversed, rising curves can be broken, and the unemployed can return to work. Politically hard decisions cannot be dismissed on the grounds that labor-market reforms would be ineffective in a European context.

Unemployment benefit levels and duration—especially for youth— will have to be cut in many European countries, and eligibility requirements will need to be significantly tightened. Simultaneously, payroll taxes should be lowered, particularly for low-wage jobs, since employment must not only support the worker but also be affordable for the employer. Finally, the threshold to disability pensions and other permanently inactive options for the working-aged must be raised to (or maintained at) a level that puts the benefits outside the reach of the average worker.

Yet the Dutch, Swedish, and Danish experiences also illustrate a number of other important lessons: Fairly generous unemployment benefits can still be provided, but not long term nor without stricter requirements such as adherence to an IAP with the threat of severe penalties for noncompliance. Also, active labor-market policies, if implemented with the correct incentives and incorporating local expertise, can effectively increase employment, although at substantial budget costs. Successful labor-market reforms are generally a result of simultaneous changes in multiple regulations. For example, if separate parts of a social security system are reformed independently, beneficiaries will simply move from one program to another to continue receiving benefits and to avoid changing their behavior.

In July 2003, the European Council (2003) agreed upon new *Guidelines for the Employment Policies of the Member States*. In specific guideline number 8, entitled *Make Work Pay Through Incentives to Enhance Work Attractiveness*, the European Council states that:

> Whilst preserving an adequate level of social protection, Member States will in particular review replacement rates and benefit duration; ensure effective benefit management, notably with respect to the link with effective job search, including access to activation measures to support employability, taking into account individual situations; consider the provision of in-work benefits, where appropriate; and work with the view to eliminating inactivity traps.

In particular, policies will aim at achieving by 2010 a significant reduction in high marginal effective tax rates and, where appropriate, in the tax burden on low-paid workers, reflecting national circumstances.

The implementation of such a guideline at the national level in all EU countries would result in a move toward the principles for reform set out in the first half of this chapter. Both draw attention to the problem with indefinite benefits, as well as, for low-wage workers, the problems associated with high payroll taxes and benefit levels. In fact we find the degree of overlap between our principles of social policy reform and the European Council guidelines heartening and urge progress in implementation of the latter. Implementing the guidelines would further diffuse the lessons of the Dutch, Swedish, and Danish experiences presented in this chapter. If these lessons can be applied throughout the European Union, they will substantially increase employment in the region without destroying the existing European tradition of helping those who lose their jobs.

Appendix 5.1
The Nonobserved Economy, Undeclared Work, and European Economic Reforms

To accurately measure the whole economy, GDP should encompass even the nonobserved economy (NOE). The NOE includes activities in five distinct categories:[93]

1) Underground Production, which according to the 1993 System of National Accounts (SNA) (Para 6.34) covers "certain activities that may be both productive in an economic sense and also quite legal (provided certain standards or regulations are complied with) but deliberately concealed from public authorities for the following reasons:

   a) To avoid the payment of income, value-added, or other taxes;

   b) To avoid the payment of social security contributions;

   c) To avoid having to meet certain legal standards, such as minimum wages, maximum hours, safety, or health standards; and

   d) To avoid complying with certain administrative procedures, such as completing statistical questionnaires or other administrative forms."

2) Illegal Production, which, according to the 1993 SNA (Para 3.54), if it fits "the characteristics of transactions—notably the characteristic that there is mutual agreement between the parties—are treated the same way as legal actions."

3) Informal-Sector Production, which according to the 15th International Conference of Labour Statisticians Resolution Paragraph 5(1), describes the following:

   The informal sector may be broadly characterized as consisting of units engaged in the production of goods or services with the primary objective of generating employment and incomes to the persons concerned. These units typically operate at a low level of organization, with little or no division between labor and capital as factors of production and on a small scale. Labor relations—where they exist—are based mostly on casual employment, kinship, or personal and social relations rather than contractual arrangements with formal guarantees.

4) Household Production for Own Final Use, which includes production of crops and livestock as well as production of other goods, such as own final use of cloth, home construction, imputed rents of owner-occupiers, and services of paid domestic servants.

---

93. See OECD, ILO, IMF, and CIS STAT (2002, chapter 3) for a detailed description of the NOE.

5) Production Missed Due to Deficiencies in Data Collection, which covers data deficiencies arising from enterprises' undercoverage, nonresponse, and underreporting.

The NOE—especially categories three through five, which can represent a very large part of GDP—is an issue for developing countries. On the other hand, these three categories are unlikely to significantly affect the developed European (and US) economies examined in this book.

Category two of the NOE, which focuses on illegal activities, will invariably differ across legal jurisdictions, since what is legal in one country may be illegal in another—abortion,[94] alcohol production,[95] prostitution,[96] gambling, and drug use spring to mind. Given the general similarity of criminal laws and well-developed law enforcement in the EU countries and the United States, however, these activities are unlikely to yield significant differences in their GDP estimates.[97]

Only category one, underground production, is substantially large enough to appreciably affect GDP in the EU countries and the United States. Therefore, only this category is of interest to us in the context of this book.

Underground Production in the EU Countries and the United States

It is inherently difficult to estimate the extent of underground activity when its participants are specifically trying to avoid being measured and taxed. Statisticians and economist have devised several techniques in "guesstimating" the required adjustment to GDP from underground production. The most utilized method is the so-called currency demand model, which has several forms but whose basic tenet is cash-based transactions. Thus, any changes in the cash/deposit ratio that are unexplained by other economic factors such as interest rates, changes in payment habits (often technology-induced via ATMs, for example), or income levels, are

---

94. Abortion, for instance, became legal in Italy only in 1978 and was subsequently included in household expenditures. Abortion is still illegal in Ireland, however. See OECD, ILO, IMF, and CIS STAT (2002, 39).

95. In some Islamic countries the production and consumption of alcohol is forbidden.

96. Prostitution was legalized in the Netherlands in 2000, and Dutch prostitutes currently pay 19 percent value-added tax (VAT). Similarly, since 2002 German prostitutes have been able to receive social benefits in exchange for paying taxes. The US state of Nevada has also recently legalized and taxed prostitution.

97. National estimates from the three Baltic countries as well as Poland, the Slovak Republic, and Britain for illegal value-added taxes from drugs, prostitution, fencing, smuggling, and audiovisual counterfeits all range below 1 percent of GDP. Bulgarian estimates of household expenditure on drugs range from 1.8 to 2.4 percent of household consumption. Only Bulgaria, the Czech Republic, Estonia, the Slovak Republic, and Britain make allowances for illegal activities in their GDP estimates. See UNECE (2003).

taken to indicate a change in the size of underground production.[98] However, additional assumptions regarding the size of underground activities at a given point are required—usually zero in an early base year—for the change in those activities to be computed in the model.

Other methods of computing underground production in GDP are available. In *commodity flows*, estimates of gross output and value added are approximated by markups—most commonly power usage or labor—to flows of commodities into production. *Household surveys* are also used and provide information about the location of respondents' expenditures (street stalls versus supermarkets), time of use, and occasionally respondents' assessment of how frequently they and others engage in underground production. Tax audits have also often been used.

It is important to note that the underground economy is almost wholly concentrated in particular sectors of a developed economy such as construction (home repairs), household services (cleaning and child care), retail trade, taxis, trucking, and restaurants. In other parts of developed economies—for instance, power generation, heavy industry, finance, and rail and air transportation—there is essentially no underground activity.

While many different estimates on the size of underground production in developed economies exist, of most consequence is whether or not official GDP estimates make explicit allowances for underground production. It may surprise some to know that within the European Union, the *markup* to official GDP from underground production ranges from 0 in most countries to 15 percent in Italy.

Schneider (2002) estimates the size of the underground economy in advanced economies using the currency-demand model, and figure 5A.1 illustrates his results. The European Commission in 2004 sanctioned a report on undeclared work in the enlarged European Union (Renooy, Ivarsson, Van der Wusten-Gritsai, Meijer 2004). This report lists the result of available official statistical agency work on the issue. These estimates are also shown in Figure 5A.1. Lastly, the figure shows the extent to which some countries mark up their official GDP estimates for the underground economy.[99] Schneider's estimates seem very high for some countries. Since underground activities are concentrated in only parts of the economy, it is difficult to understand how Greece or Italy could estimate a nearly 30 percent increase in total GDP. The underground share of the *susceptible sectors of the economy* would have to be unrealistically high.[100] The basic issue is that a variety of reasons may have increased cash transactions in some economies,

---

98. For surveys of the NOE and use of currency-demand models, see Schneider and Enste (1998 and 2000) and Schneider (2002). Note that currency-demand models are not restricted to "measuring" underground production but, in principal, cover the total NOE.

99. The term *shadow economy* in figure 5A.1 is the phrase used by Schneider. For the purposes of this appendix, it is synonymous *with hidden and informal economic activities* as well as *underground production* and *undeclared work*.

100. See OECD (2002g, 7) for elaboration of this point.

Figure 5A.1 Underground activities in OECD countries, 2001–02

percent of nominal GDP

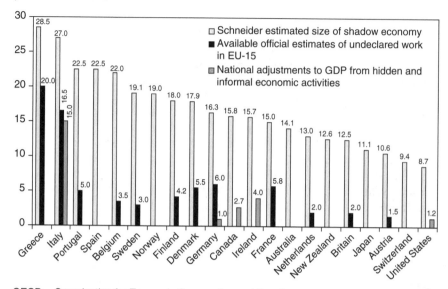

OECD = Organization for Economic Cooperation and Development

Sources: Schneider (2002), UNECE (2003), and Renooy, Ivarsson, van der Wusten-Gritsai, and Meijer (2004).

so the size of underground activities cannot always be directly linked to an increase in GDP.[101]

The much lower official estimates of undeclared work in the EU-15 seem to concur with our assessment of Schneider's estimates. However, Renooy, Ivarsson, van der Wusten-Gritsai, and Meijer (2004) lists values between 8 and 30 percent of GDP for undeclared work for the 10 new EU members, values not vastly different from Schneider's estimates for rich OECD members. The adjustments made to official GDP data in figure 5A.1 to account for underground activities are not comprehensive. The adjustments only represent the respondents to the 2001–02 UNECE survey, the *Inventory of National Practices in Estimating Hidden and Informal Economic Activities for National Accounts,* and may consequently miss some national corrections altogether. Also, the UNECE survey covers only explicit adjustments for *Hidden and Informal Economic Activities* and may therefore also not report implicit coverage of activities particular to the method of calculation of particular sectors itself.

For example, in Germany rents are calculated through the housing stock—broken down by size and other characteristics—into rent per square

---

101. In the United States, it is not certain how much currency is used in the domestic economy. US dollars are widely used around the world.

meter. Whether such income is declared for tax purposes (and thus official as opposed to underground) is immaterial to the calculation of this part of GDP (UNECE 2003, 109). It seems likely that the actual extent of underground activities is smaller than indicated in figure 5A.1, and the degree to which these are captured in official GDP estimates is greater than is shown.

Nonetheless, the countries in figure 5A.1 with high underground activity often also have high unemployment rates, which suggests that such activity may be important to the economy overall. After all, the sustained level of high unemployment in some European countries may simply mask a situation where many of the officially unemployed are in reality employed in the underground economy.

Undeclared Work in the European Union

Unsurprisingly, the European Commission has engaged in considerable effort to measure the scope of *undeclared work*[102] and has proposed national and EU policies to solve this problem (European Commission 1998; Mateman and Renooy 2001; Employment Task Force 2003; and Renooy, Ivarsson, van der Wusten-Gritsai, and Meijer 2004). Following the meeting of the European Council on July 22, 2003, the guidelines for the employment policies of the member states (European Council 2003) explicitly included the following references to undeclared work:

> Undeclared work is taken to mean any paid activities that are lawful as regards their nature but not declared to public authorities. Studies estimate the size of the informal economy on average between 7 percent and 16 percent of EU GDP. This should be turned into regular work in order to improve the overall business environment, the quality of work of those concerned, social cohesion, and the sustainability of public finance and social protection systems. Improving knowledge about the extent of undeclared work in Member States and the European Union should be encouraged.[103]

The Council also recommended implementing specific guidelines:

> Member States should develop and implement broad actions and measures to eliminate undeclared work, which combine simplification of the business environment, removing disincentives and providing appropriate incentives in the tax and benefits system, improved law enforcement, and the application of sanctions. They should undertake the necessary efforts at national and EU level to measure the extent of the problem and progress achieved at national level.[104]

The European Commission has collected a good deal of information about underground activity, and it is summarized in table 5A.1. Despite

---

102. Conceptually, *undeclared work* almost completely overlaps with the OECD concept of *underground production*, which serves to demarcate the focus of the analysis.

103. Opinions of the Employment Committee (19).

104. Specific Guidelines (9) to Transform Undeclared Work into Regular Employment.

Table 5A.1   Undeclared work in the European Union and select labor-market statistics

Country	Characteristic of the undeclared worker	Principal sector of undeclared work	Labor-force participation rate, 15- to 24-year-olds, 2001 (percent)	Labor-force participation rate, 25- to 64-year-old women, 2001 (percent)	Total tax wedge 2000[a] (percent)
Austria	One-tenth of all working-aged people have a sideline activity. The focus has been on illegal employment of foreign labor.	40 percent in building and craft, 16 percent in other trade and industrial enterprise (auto repair, machinery, etc.), 16 percent in service sector, 13 percent in entertainment business, and 15 percent in other trades and services (remedial training, hairdressing, baby-sitting)	55.0	64.8	34.6
Belgium	Semi- or low-skilled workers, male, young people	Catering, retail trade, construction, textile sector, traffic/transport, household services (private cleaning, etc.), agriculture (e.g., fruit picking)	33.6	60.0	49.3
Britain	Job holders (including self-employed), and to a lesser extent casual/seasonal workers, unemployed, benefit claimants, and illegal immigrants	Agriculture, community, social, and personal services (e.g., cleaning); construction; tourism; hotel, and catering, fashion and clothing manufacture	68.2	69.9	24.6
Denmark	Skilled and unskilled workers, students, men (twice as frequent as women). There is a geographical divide (cultural—young skilled males living outside Copenhagen)	33 percent in construction sector, 50 percent in private service sector (baby-sitting, cleaning, car repairs, gardening, etc.)	67.2	77.0	39.2
Finland	Younger skilled males	Construction, hotels/restaurants, retail trade (including car repairs), and real estate services	50.4	77.4	40.8

Country		Sectors			
France	Unemployed, illegal immigrants, self-employed, and job holders	Construction (25.5 percent), community, social and personal services (24.4 percent); retailing (20.3 percent), catering (hotel/cafe/restaurant) (14.7 percent); transport (8.4 percent), agriculture (8.4 percent), textile industry (3 percent)	29.9	70.4	40.8
Germany	Old-age pensioners, students, illegal immigrants, unemployed, self-employed, job holders	Agriculture; community, social, and personal services (e.g., cleaning, care); manufacturing and construction	51.1	67.1	43.7
Greece	Illegal/legal immigrants; old-age pensioners; women/home workers; young seasonal workers	Sectors with home working possibilities (textile), hotels/restaurants/tourism, services, household services, and transport	36.2	52.4	35.2
Ireland	Students, double workers; no illegal immigrants	Building, construction, and distribution	50.1	59.7	21.8
Italy	Students, illegal immigrants, unemployed, self-employed, job holders	Agriculture; community, social, and personal services; manufacturing; construction/building; transport; retailing	37.6	50.2	43.5
Netherlands	Students, unemployed, self-employed, and job holders	Agriculture; community, social, and personal services (e.g., cleaning, care); and construction	71.1	65.2	40.0
Portugal	Illegal immigrants, women, and unregistered workers	Construction, textile sector, and retail trade	47.1	70.3	29.0
Spain	Unemployed, and illegal immigrants	Agriculture; community, social, and personal, services, and manufacturing	46.8	54.1	34.0
Sweden	Job holders, and to a lesser extent the unemployed	Community, social, and personal services; construction; and transport	54.3	81.5	44.8

APW = average production worker
job holders = employed in a formal job
double worker = workers with multiple jobs

a. Married couples with two children, principal earner 100 percent of APW and spouse 67 percent of APW.

Sources: European Commission (1998); Mateman and Renooy (2001); OECD (2003i).

considerable detailed country differences, table 5A.1 contains some possible trends:

- In several countries (Belgium, Greece, and Italy) with very low (less than 40 percent) labor-force participation rates among youth between 15 and 24 years of age, young people and students are identified as frequently engaging in undeclared work.

- In several countries (Greece, Italy, and Spain) with very low labor-force participation (less than 55 percent) among females, economic sectors with traditionally very high levels of female employment such as household services and community as well as social and personal services are identified as sectors with high degrees of undeclared work.

- In many countries, frequently those (France, Germany, Italy, the Netherlands, and Sweden) with very high total-tax wedges (at or greater than 40 percent), existing job holders characteristically engage in undeclared work.

Keep in mind that the country differences illustrated in table 5A.1 do not rule out a connection between undeclared work and nonparticipation in the official labor force by some groups—especially youth and women in some countries. Yet, table 5A.1 also reveals that *the overwhelming part of undeclared work in Europe is conducted by persons already in employment—not by people outside the labor market* (except in some countries with large illegal immigrant populations). Thus, the belief that undeclared work, on average in Europe, reduces the importance of low labor-force participation and high unemployment rates by serving as a *substitute* for official jobs, must be dismissed in the face of these available facts. Rather, with job holders supplying most of the undeclared work in Europe, is seems likely that the decline in (official) hours worked (figure 5.7) may in fact be somewhat overstated.

The Development and Origins of Underground Production and Undeclared Work

Given the huge degree of uncertainty regarding estimates of undeclared work, time trends are also difficult to gauge. Yet, in 2001 the European Commission states explicitly that: "Nevertheless, most experts do agree that the amount of undeclared work is growing all over Europe" (Mateman and Renooy 2001).[105]

In virtually all studies of underground production and undeclared work, a positive link between increases in taxes and social security con-

---

105. See also Schneider (2002) for estimates and a survey of the literature reaching the same conclusion.

tributions and increases in the informal economy has been established (Schneider 2002, section 4). This is true for empirical studies from all parts of the European Union as well as other OECD countries. Table 5A.1 also lends credence to the link as high total-tax wedges frequently seem to drive job holders into underground production. In some sectors high labor costs prohibit hiring workers in the official economy, but make it economically feasible in the underground one.

In addition to the tax wedge, general regulatory intensity—notably in the labor market—is an important factor in increasing undeclared work, especially when it tightens restrictions on immigrants (Schneider 2002, section 4). Thus, Johnson, Kaufmann, and Shleifer (1997) estimate that a one-point increase in regulatory intensity (in a range from 1 to 5) leads to an 8.1 percent increase in a country's underground activity.

The factors included in this appendix are not an exhaustive list of the origins of undeclared work in Europe. Other country-specific issues, such as cultural acceptance of undeclared work and immigration, likely play significant roles. Nonetheless, the unambiguous finding in the literature that links high tax wedges and excessive regulation to increased underground production is an important consideration for the reforms suggested for Europe in this book.

The Effect of Suggested European Economic Reforms on Undeclared Work

The economic reforms that we suggest in this book—aimed at liberalizing product and labor markets and lowering nonwage labor costs—would have an effect on undeclared work.

Lowering payroll taxes would decrease personal incentives for individuals to supply undeclared work. Limiting poverty and employment traps would also reduce undeclared labor supply, while reducing social security contributions (particularly for low-wage jobs) would reduce the demand for undeclared work, as would general liberalization of labor-market regulation.

Increasing work incentives by cutting benefit levels and increasing job search requirements to sustain eligibility for benefits may lead some people to move into the underground economy rather than attempt to find official employment.

On balance, however, we believe that the proposed reforms will lead to better product and labor markets, which in turn will reduce the existing network of underground production and undeclared work in Europe.

6

What Europe Should Do:
Getting the Macroeconomics Right

We live in an era when rapid change breeds fear, and fear too often congeals us into a rigidity, which we mistake for stability.

—Lynn White, Jr.

Getting the macroeconomics right means getting fiscal and monetary policy right in terms of their effect on aggregate demand. As we have noted more than once in this book, structural reforms will not restore economic growth in Europe unless there is sufficient aggregate demand in the economy. The big issue in Europe's fiscal policy is the Stability and Growth Pact (SGP).[1] The big issue in monetary policy is the behavior of the European Central Bank (ECB). This chapter explores both of these issues.

The Stability and Growth Pact

The SGP is currently at the forefront of Europe's political and academic economics agenda because it required some governments to cut their deficits in 2003 (and will again in 2004)—even during a period of economic weakness. There is general agreement that constraints should be placed on member countries' fiscal policies so that excessive deficits in one or more countries do not undermine the euro or overall EU stability. But at the same time there is a real concern that the SGP could force contractionary fiscal policies on economies that are already weak. These concerns raise the

1. The SGP is a complex set of interrelated rules agreed upon in the years since the original proposals for a European monetary union were laid down in the Treaty of Maastricht in 1992. As such, coercive measures were agreed upon only in 1997, though they refer to standards laid down as early as 1992. In this book, the term SGP will be used as a broad definition—as the sum of all different EU legal instruments on fiscal policy.

question about whether or not the SGP is fundamentally flawed or simply improperly implemented. This section will first explain the different legal components and constituents of the SGP and the potential flaws of this legal design. It then goes on to illustrate how—at the time of its inception—political considerations played a decisive role in determining the SGP's implementation procedures. There is also a review of member countries' compliance to the SGP since 1999. As this is written in mid-2004 some have pronounced the SGP dead because France and Germany have said they will not comply with its provisions.

The main criticisms leveled by numerous academics and officials against the SGP are then discussed together with alternative reform proposals. The section concludes by setting out some minimum requirements for any sensible SGP-like instrument as well as a number of specific rules that should be included in it.

The Nature of the Stability Pact

The SGP was instituted under the third stage of the European Monetary Union (EMU) and consists of several legal instruments.[2] Budgetary rules are included in the EU Treaty (Treaty),[3] and these provisions of the Treaty are enforceable through the European Court of Justice (ECJ). (The Treaty in Europe is somewhat comparable to the role of the Constitution in the United States—at least until a new European Constitutional Treaty is agreed upon.)

There are also budgetary rules adopted by the European Council (Council).[4] These have the force of law within the European Union as well, but can be changed by subsequent Council votes. A resolution of the European Council established the SGP, together with provisions to prevent violations (EU Council Regulations 1966/97) and to outline coercive steps if a violation occurs (EU Council Regulations 1467/97). The European Commission also plays an important role by monitoring compliance with the SGP and making recommendations to the Council for sanctions in the event of a violation.

---

2. Legal and political distinctions must be carefully made, especially as key reference values are repeated throughout the chapter. This section is based on the European Commission description of activities under the EU framework for budgetary surveillance, www.europa. eu.int/comm/economy_finance/about/activities/sgp/main_en.htm (accessed October 28, 2003).

3. This discussion refers to the treaties of Maastricht, Amsterdam, and Nice as simply the EU Treaty. However, all article reference numbers will be to the consolidated version of the Treaty Establishing the European Community, europa.eu.int/eur-lex/en/treaties/selected/ livre2_c.html (accessed October 28, 2003).

4. The European Council refers to the gathering of member states' heads of government (and/or state) and is the highest executive authority in the European Union.

The budgetary rules in the EU Treaty require member states[5] to avoid excessive government deficits (Art. 104.1). The rules also charge the European Commission (Art. 104.2) to monitor the development of the budgetary situation and the stock of government debt in individual member countries using two criteria:

- a reference value for the ratio of the planned or actual government deficit[6] to GDP at market prices (the government deficit flow variable);

- a reference value for the ratio of government debt[7] to GDP at market prices (the government deficit stock variable)

The EU Treaty refers only to given reference values and calls for the numerical targets to be spelled out in a Protocol to the Treaty, which would later be replaced by appropriate provisions adopted by the European or ECOFIN Council. Currently the reference values are 3 percent for budget deficits and 60 percent for government debt (see below).

Exceptions to the 3 percent rule can be made if the ratio has declined substantially and continuously and reached a level that comes close to 3 percent, or if the ratio remains close to the reference value and any excess over 3 percent is exceptional and temporary. Also, the 60 percent government-debt ceiling can be sidestepped if the ratio is sufficiently diminishing and approaching 60 percent at a satisfactory pace. If a member state does not fulfill either of the two obligations,[8] the European Commission is charged with preparing a report (Art. 104.3) to the ECOFIN Council[9] and the Economic and Financial Committee.[10] In the report, the

---

5. It is important to notice that the obligations of the EU Treaty encompass all EU members and not only those members who have actually adopted the third stage of the EMU (i.e., the euro).

6. Government is defined as general government—including central, regional, and local government and social security funds, excluding commercial operations. Deficit refers to net borrowing as defined in the European System of National and Regional Accounts (ESA95).

7. Total gross debt at nominal value outstanding at the end of the year and consolidated between and within the sectors of the general government.

8. Even if a member state complies with the requirements, the European Commission can still prepare a report if it believes that the risk of an excessive deficit exists.

9. The ECOFIN Council consists of the finance ministers of member states, who hold the following number of votes respectively: Germany, France, Britain, and Italy each have 10 votes; Spain has 8 votes; Belgium, Greece, the Netherlands, and Portugal each have 5 votes; Austria and Sweden each have 4 votes; Denmark, Ireland, and Finland each have 3 notes; and Luxembourg has 2 votes. A qualified majority is defined as two-thirds (58 votes) of the total 87 votes, which means that 29 votes form a blocking minority.

10. This committee acts strictly in an advisory role to the ECOFIN Council on the subject of the European Commission's report and consists of two members from each member state, two members from the ECB, and two members from the European Commission.

Commission describes the fiscal situation in the member state, explicitly taking into account: whether the government deficit exceeds government-investment expenditure; the medium-term economic and budgetary position of the member state; and other factors deemed relevant.

The ECOFIN Council then decides, by qualified majority, whether an excessive deficit exists (Art. 104.6). If an excessive deficit is deemed to exist, the ECOFIN Council makes recommendations to the offending member state on ways to bring an end to it *within a given period.*[11] If the member state does not rectify its excessive deficit in a timely manner, the ECOFIN Council may then apply one or more of the following measures (Art. 104.11):

- require the member state to publish specified information before issuing bonds or securities;

- invite the European Investment Bank (EIB) to reconsider its lending policy toward the member state concerned;

- require the member state to make a noninterest-bearing deposit of an appropriate size with the EU Commission until the excessive deficit has been corrected; and/or

- impose fines of an appropriate size.

Finally, Article 104.14 spells out that only by a unanimous vote on a proposal from the European Commission—and after consultations with the ECB and the European Parliament—can the ECOFIN Council replace any reference values (currently 3 percent of the deficit or the 60 percent of the debt values) in this Treaty. Moreover, Article 104.14 also requires the European Council to establish the detailed rules and definitions for implementing the Treaty provisions (by qualified majority and after consultations with the European Parliament). Article 104.14 also outlines how European and ECOFIN Council resolutions for numerical targets and procedural guidelines can be used to make changes, which was crucial to the adoption of the SGP by the European Council in June 1997, since it provided political room for maneuvering in case of a future crisis.

Thus, the 3 percent and the 60 percent reference values are laid down in a Protocol to the Treaty, rather than in the Treaty itself. This clearly eases the obstacles to changing these reference values, since ratification by national parliaments and/or electorates is not required. On the other hand, the Treaty itself requires that reference values exist and that they be adhered to, and demands unanimity for them to change. Since it is virtually impossible to change the Treaty—or achieve unanimity among EU

---

11. The member state in question is excluded from votes on this and subsequent procedures.

member states for reference value changes—these values can be considered permanent for the foreseeable future.

It is, thus, noteworthy that despite the controversy surrounding the SGP, it is included almost verbatim in the Provisional Treaty Establishing a Constitution for Europe, which was published by the conference of member state representatives. Constitutional Treaty article III-76 and the attached Protocol, which contain reference values for the excessive deficit procedure, replicates the existing Treaty with only one major change: A qualified majority in the European or ECOFIN Council is now defined as the votes of 55 percent of member states representing at least 65 percent of Council member states' populations (see footnote 9 for existing rules).[12] Hence, an obvious chance to change the legal text of the SGP as part of the EU Constitutional Treaty process seems to have been deliberately missed. Alas, considering the difficulties in changing a new Constitutional Treaty, this may have been the last chance to make such a change for some time.

As stated above, the Treaty does provide the political opportunity to sidestep both the 3 percent and 60 percent reference values in special circumstances. However, any attempt to circumvent the letter of the EU Treaty—for example, by European Council decisions under Article 104.14—could be challenged in the ECJ, which is the final arbiter in cases involving the Treaty. Any legal proceeding in the European Court would, even with expedited procedures, take time to resolve and, as the European Commission would almost certainly be pitted against member states, greatly complicate either the possibility for reform, or a flexible interpretation of, the SGP.[13]

Largely at the request of Germany, the European Council in 1997 unanimously adopted three pieces of legislation designed to clarify the excessive deficit procedure described in the Treaty and ensure that any such deficits were quickly handled. The three parts are the budgetary rules of the European Council and they form the actual Stability and Growth Pact.

The two most important rules of the SGP are the following:

- Member states commit themselves to adhere to the *medium-term* (as opposed to short-term) objective of maintaining a budget that is close to balance or in surplus as part of their stability or convergence programs.

- The rules allow member states to violate the budgetary provisions of the SGP in the event of a "severe recession," which is defined as a decline of 0.75 percent or more in real GDP.

---

12. Blocking Council actions hence requires the votes of members representing more than 35 percent of the EU population. Three large countries alone cannot block actions. See ue.eu. int/igcpdf/en/o4/ea00086.en04 (accessed July 19, 2004).

13. See footnote 21 in this chapter.

According to the European Commission, the medium-term budgetary clause was added to the SGP for several reasons:[14]

- to allow member states to deal with normal cyclical fluctuations while keeping the government deficit within the 3 percent deficit limit. With the loss of exchange rate stabilizers in the EMU such automatic fiscal stabilizers were viewed with increased importance;

- to allow some member states to quickly reduce their total debt to GDP ratio, while preventing all member states from continuously adding to their total debt; and

- to ensure that member states factor in the fiscal implications of aging populations.

However, no operational definition for the medium target was given in the SGP (nor were any coercive measures of enforcement laid down). This led the European Commission to adopt a so-called minimal benchmark for assessing whether or not member states' budgets met the "medium-term close-to-balance or surplus" criterion. This minimal benchmark explicitly took only one factor into account—namely, the influence of fluctuations in economic growth on the government's budget.[15] It did not consider the differing needs of member states to reduce their total debt ratios,[16] their contingency plans for aging, or any other aspects of fiscal sustainability when assessing whether a given budget meets the "close-to-balance or surplus" criterion.

The budgetary surveillance program is to ensure that member states actually follow the budget rules. European Council Regulation No. 1966/97 presents "the rules covering the content, the submission, the examination, and the monitoring of stability programs or convergence programs"[17] as part of multilateral surveillance by the Council. Most important are the following provisions:

- Member states must present an annual stability/convergence program to the European Council and Commission covering the previous, present, and the future—with a minimum three-year projection.

---

14. These reasons are detailed in the European Commission's first report on the SGP (2000e, 61).

15. This measure of how much cushion automatic fiscal stabilizers would require to work, while keeping member states' deficits below 3 percent, is calculated by a combination of individual budget gap estimates and budgetary sensitivities to the cycle in member states (European Commission 2000a, 51).

16. That this is not the case, despite the fact that some member states still have total government debt figures above 100 percent, is an indication of how completely any debt-stock evaluation has been excluded from the SGP framework.

17. Member states that have adopted the euro present "stability programs" whereas member states that have not present "convergence programs."

- A stability/convergence program must include information regarding:
    - the medium-term objective of maintaining a budget that is close to balance or in surplus and the adjustment path toward this objective as well as the general government debt ratio;
    - the main assumptions about expected economic developments and relevant economic variables for the stability/convergence program;
    - a description of budgetary and other economic policy measures being taken and/or proposed to achieve the budgetary objective of the programs; and
    - a sensitivity analysis of the stability/convergence program to changes in main economic assumptions.
- The European Council, on the recommendation of the European Commission, examines the submitted stability/convergence programs, and if it judges that a program requires strengthening, the Council will "invite the member state to adjust its program."
- In the event of a significant divergence of a member state's budgetary position, or from its medium-term objective of the path toward it, the Council will give an early warning in order to prevent an excessive deficit.
- If subsequent monitoring finds that the budgetary position of a member state has not improved compared to its medium-term objective, or if the path toward it is persisting or deteriorating, the Council will make a recommendation to the member state to take prompt corrective action and may make this recommendation public.

The next step in the process involves coercive measures and penalties on member states that do not follow the rules—notably any violation of the 3 percent deficit rule. European Council Regulation 1467/97 Article 1 states "the provisions to speed up and clarify the excessive deficit procedure, having the objective to deter excessive general government deficits and, if they occur, to further their prompt correction." As noted earlier, the Council can impose a very stiff sanction, in the form of noninterest-bearing deposits of 0.2 to 0.5 percent of the member state's GDP—on a member state that has not implemented the corrective measures recommended by the Council. In addition, annual Council evaluations of a member state's progress toward eliminating its excessive deficits are carried out, and if the deficits have not been eliminated, further annual noninterest-bearing deposits of 0.2 to 0.5 percent of GDP may be levied. If the excessive deficit has not been corrected after two years, the deposits are converted into a fine, together with all its interest revenue, which is distributed among member states according to their respective proportion of total GNP.

There are some allowable exceptions to the excessive deficit procedure and variations in the procedures that lead up to imposing fines.

- An excessive general-government deficit is considered exceptional and temporary if it is caused by an unusual event outside the control of the member state, or if the European Commission budgetary forecasts predict the deficit will fall below the reference value at the end of the unusual event.[18]

- Up to a year can pass from the time the European Council declares that a member state has an excessive deficit before it imposes a sanction.

- Council decisions can be changed by a new unanimous decision by the European Council, which makes them significantly easier to reform than regulations included in the EU Treaty.

- There are no coercive measures attached to the objective of achieving medium-term budgetary balance or surplus. The only implicit sanction the European Council can "impose" is to make public its recommendations for a member state to rectify a deviation from its stability/convergence program.[19]

- The European Council's coercive measures against member states are related only to the annual 3 percent deficit ceiling and not to the 60 percent government debt reference value.

- The European Council annually evaluates a member state for three years before fines must be paid. (Thus, the fines might not actually be levied.)

To summarize, changing either the formal rules of the SGP or the 3 percent and 60 percent reference values is virtually impossible. However, there is substantial leeway in the system to allow a country that violates

---

18. In making this decision, the European Commission typically regards a 2 percent or more decline in GDP as a severe economic downturn. However, the European Commission must consider any observations made by the member state indicating that a fall of less than 2 percent is exceptional. In other words, the member state may be able to convince the European Commission that a decline of only 0.75 percent of real GDP is a severe downturn. As noted earlier, the implicit lowering of the threshold for a severe economic downturn from 2 percent to 0 .75 percent in the 1997 European Council Resolution on the SGP was crucial for its existence.

19. The lack of coercive measures attached to the stability/convergence program may have facilitated the ease with which France, Italy, and Germany secured repeated extensions of the deadline for their general government budgets to meet the "close-to-balance or surplus" criterion.

the rules to go unpunished, if the other countries are unwilling to enforce the system.

At the meeting of the ECOFIN Council on November 25, 2003, the political unwillingness of member states to enforce the rules of the SGP was highlighted. France and Germany, despite forecast breaches of the 3 percent deficit ceiling for three years running (2002–04), were able to avoid the initiation by the European Commission of corrective budgetary measures. The two countries had already been given an extra year, until 2005, to bring their deficits below 3 percent, provided they took steps to show how they would get back on track. However, the two countries failed to take those steps, and the European Commission asked the ECOFIN Council to allow them to initiate a sanction process (as required by the SGP). The proposed 2004 budgetary remedies consisted of cuts to the cyclically adjusted deficit in France by 1 percentage point of GDP, and 0.8 percentage point in Germany. However, the ECOFIN Council voted not to initiate the process and, without Council support, the Commission's recommended sanctions lack legal force.

While the political fallout from this apparent breakdown of the SGP is likely to be huge, with large member countries pitted against smaller member states (and the ECB),[20] it is not clear that the direct economic impact will be that big. While the European Commission could not get majority support in the ECOFIN Council for its suggested sanctions, a majority of the ECOFIN Council did support an Italian compromise proposal. According to the compromise, France must cut its cyclically adjusted deficit in 2004 by 0.8 percentage point of GDP and Germany its cyclically adjusted deficit by 0.6 percentage point, and both countries must reaffirm their promise to bring their deficits below 3 percent in 2005—economic conditions permitting. However, the ECOFIN Council's ability to enforce these promises seems improbable so their fulfillment rests solely on the political will of the French and German national governments, rather than on the rules-based approach laid down in the SGP.[21]

---

20. It is notable that many smaller countries (but now also Britain and France) must put a new European Constitutional Treaty to a referendum, and it seems likely that their electorates will respond negatively to the perception of *some being more equal than others* before EU law.

21. In mid-January 2004 the European Commission challenged the legality of the ECOFIN Council's action on November 25, 2003 to suspend coercive measures against France and Germany for nonadherence to the SGP. See *Financial Times*, "Legal Move Threatens to Reignite Europe's Conflict over Fiscal Rules," January 8, 2004, page 1, and *Financial Times* "Brussels Insists on Legal Challenge over Pact," January 13, 2004. Such a lawsuit is unprecedented in EU history, but not wholly unexpected. On July 13, 2004, the ECJ delivered a "Solomonic verdict" that allowed both the European Commission and the ECOFIN Council to claim victory. The ECJ ruled that the ECOFIN Council is solely in charge of deciding whether or not to impose sanctions on member states, i.e., it does not have to follow the recommendations of the European Commission. On the other hand, the ECJ agreed with the European Commission that the ECOFIN Council acted illegally on November 25, 2003, when it put the threat of sanctions

Fiscal Policy Leading Up to and after the SGP

The fiscal constraints embodied in the SGP originated as part of the convergence criteria for admission into the eurozone[22] and were laid down in the Maastricht Treaty in 1992. They have remained unchanged in subsequent revisions of the EU Treaty.

As can be seen in figure 6.1 significant progress was made in the 1990s by all EU members toward achieving the 3 percent deficit goal ahead of the 1997 deadline for adopting the euro. Figure 6.2 shows that the countries with the highest debt levels were stabilizing those levels and starting to reduce them. However, some EU members who wanted to join the euro area[23]—principally Italy, Belgium, Ireland, and Greece—were in substantial violation of the condition that general government debt be limited to 60 percent of GDP by 1997 when the European Council decided who could enter the euro area in 1999.[24] This obviously presented the European Council with a terrible dilemma, since it was seen as politically inconceivable to launch the euro without either Italy—the sixth largest economy in the world and a founding member of the European Union— or Belgium—the headquarters of the main EU institutions and another founding member of the European Union.

into abeyance, without being prompted to do so by the European Commission. The ruling means that no sanctions against member states will be forthcoming and that the uncertain status quo continues. Regretfully, much time at a precious time, where the SGP could have been reformed, has been lost for only a very minor procedural clarification by the ECJ. For our proposals for a revision of the SGP rules, please see below.

22. Apart from the 3 percent deficit and 60 percent debt ceilings, these criteria encompassed limits to inflation rates relative to the EU core economies as well as limits to how much a national currency could fluctuate within the European Monetary System. These criteria will be significant for new EU accession countries after May 2004. However, for purposes of this SGP discussion, only the 3 percent and 60 percent reference values are relevant.

23. Britain had opted out of parts of the Maastricht Treaty in 1992. Denmark opted out in 1993 following a referendum rejection of the Maastricht Treaty. Sweden has been unwilling to enter the third stage after joining the European Union in 1995, and its exact legal position is unclear since as a member state without explicit opt-out rights, it is in principle obliged to enter the third stage of the Maastricht Treaty. However, given Sweden's decisive rejection of the euro at the September 14, 2003 referendum, there is no chance of a near-term Swedish adoption of the euro and entry into the eurozone. Yet the European Council has not yet ruled on the issue. This impasses provides a possible indication of the status the new EU entrants from Eastern Europe will have in relation to the EMU third stage: They will be EU members, but not members of the EMU until there is domestic political will to adopt the euro, and they pass an EU political inspection that outlines their adherence to the fiscal SGP criteria.

24. Greece was unable to enter the eurozone in 1999 because of too high inflation levels relative to the other EU economies in 1997. The country subsequently adopted the euro in 2001. It is also evident from figure 6.1 that Italy achieved a remarkable fiscal improvement from a general-government deficit of 7.1 percent of GDP in 1996 to only 2.7 percent in 1997. It was widely discussed in the media and academic literature at the time that Italy was only able to achieve a deficit below 3 percent in 1997 via significant one-off accounting reallocations.

Figure 6.1   General government lending or borrowing, select EU members, 1991–2005

percent of GDP at market prices

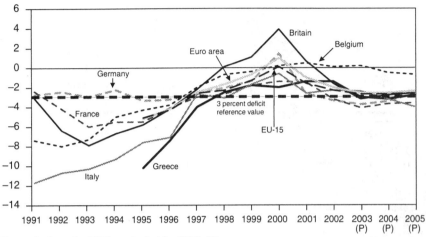

P = preliminary for 2003, projected for 2004–05.

Note: European System of Accounts 95, which includes one-off proceeds relative to the allocation of mobile phone licenses (UMTS), is as follows: In 2000: Germany € 50.8 billion, Italy €13.8 billion, and Britain £ 22.5 billion. In 2001: Belgium € 0.45 billion, Greece € 0.65 billion, and France € 1.24 billion. In 2002: France € 0.62 billion.

Source: European Commission (2004a).

As a result, the European Council decided effectively to annul the 60 percent reference value of general government debt. The general government-debt ratios of Ireland, Italy, and Belgium were ruled to be on a declining trajectory, and, hence, they were deemed eligible to join the euro area in 1999, despite the fact that the latter two's debt ratios in 1997 were both more than 120 percent of GDP. It is clear that Ireland's rapidly declining government debt ratio, down from about 100 percent of GDP at the time of adoption of the Maastricht Treaty in 1992 to just above the 60 percent threshold in 1997, provided a precedent for rapid declines in government debt-to-GDP levels. Also, the fact that the Belgian franc had maintained its de facto peg (together with the Dutch guilder) to the German mark from 1983 onward—despite the rapidly deteriorating Belgian government debt level—provided some indication that monetary stability was possible, despite high government debt levels. However, both these cases seem idiosyncratic and poor economic examples upon which to base a complete waiver of the 60 percent government debt threshold. No one can realistically expect other European economies to experience the

Figure 6.2 General government consolidated gross debt, select EU members, 1980–2005

percent of GDP at market prices

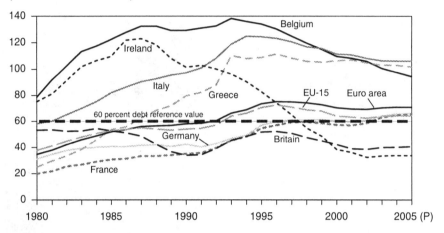

P = projected

Note: European System of Accounts as of 1996. Former definitions for earlier years, linked series.

Source: European Commission (2004a).

rapid catch-up in GDP seen in Ireland.[25] Obviously a purely political decision was made, based on the desire to include all willing European countries at the launch of the euro, to use the 3 percent deficit limit as the only binding constraint of the SGP.

Figure 6.3 shows that many EU countries did not make any further move toward budget balance once they had moved below the 3 percent threshold. Fiscal consolidation stalled at a deficit level between 1 and 2 percent of GDP, particularly among the large economies.[26] This contrasts with the improving trend in EU member-state budgeting seen in the 1990s and is significant because the SGP's intent was for countries not to quickly exceed the 3 percent limit when they encountered a period of slow economic growth. Countries were intended to operate at budget balance or surplus in normal times—leaving room for deficits in downturns without crossing the 3 percent threshold. Figure 6.4 clearly shows that by far the largest part of actual budget deficits, especially in the major continental

---

25. By not considering general debt levels, one also ignores the potentially very costly demographic changes.

26. Hallett, Lewis, and Von Hagen (2004) show forcefully how only smaller EU states have imposed fiscal discipline since 1999. They note that this is unfortunate as in smaller states "it matters the least" and suggest that big countries may think themselves "too big to fail."

Figure 6.3 Cyclically adjusted budget position of the EU member states, large EU economies, 1999–2004

percent of GDP

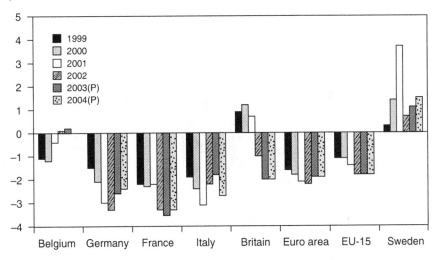

P = preliminary

Note: Under the Stability and Growth Pact, the cyclically adjusted budgetary position of member states must be close to balance or in surplus over the economic cycle. The requirement does not apply to Britain, which has officially opted out of the euro, but it does apply in theory to Sweden even though it remains outside the euro.

Source: European Commission (2004a).

European economies, is structural in nature. For example, France's structural deficit is 3.5 percent of GDP, which is larger than the 3 percent deficit threshold—virtually ensuring a breach of the SGP at any time of economic slowdown.

Problems with the SGP

Buti, Eijffinger, and Franco (2003) have outlined what they see as the main criticisms of the SGP:

- There is a reduction of budgetary flexibility that makes it difficult to use countercyclical fiscal policy. It could even impede the automatic fiscal stabilizers, since taxes fall and government spending rises in downturns even without specific policy actions. This problem is particularly important since the euro has eliminated country-specific monetary policy as a stabilization tool.

Figure 6.4 EU member states' actual and cyclical budget position, 2003

percent of GDP

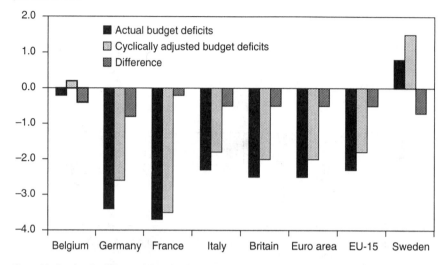

Note: Under the Stability and Growth Pact, the cyclically adjusted budgetary position of member states must be close to balance or in surplus over the economic cycle. The requirement does not apply to Britain, which has officially opted out of the euro, but it does apply in theory to Sweden.

Source: European Commission (2004a).

■ The SGP is asymmetrical, because it does not restrict a member state from increasing expenditures or cutting revenues during cyclical upturns.

■ The SGP has a lot of "bark" with firm rules and large penalties, but it may lack "bite" since the sanctions are delayed and often unenforced.[27]

■ Some countries (Britain is a current example) may wish to build or rebuild their public infrastructure. The SGP deficit ceiling is based on the assumption that capital expenditures are funded from current revenues, rather than spreading the cost over current and future generations.

■ The SGP rules are country specific with no reference to the euro area as a whole.

---

27. Of course if the rules mandate a negative outcome, then the fact that sanctions can be evaded is perhaps welcome. But repeated violations of the rules will undermine the whole goal of enforcing long-term fiscal discipline.

- The focus on the deficit ceiling encourages creative accounting and one-off measures to avoid violating the rules in the short term. The stock of public debt and pension liabilities do not enter the SGP, and, given the huge differences among SGP members in these areas, could penalize a country that has sound, long-run policies and not penalize a country where the long-run fiscal situation is not sustainable. This inequality could discourage countries from implementing long-term reforms—such as pension reform that might raise fiscal sustainability in the long run—at the cost of short-term deficits.

The SGP's design was heavily influenced by the goal of establishing a stable common currency for the European Union. The history of the 20th century is replete with examples of countries whose currencies collapsed as fiscal discipline broke down, and the use of a printing press to print money to pay the government's bills. The countries joining the EMU—Germany in particular—wanted to ensure that the stability of the euro was not undermined by the threat of debt default by a member country. Even short of actual default, the member countries wanted to make sure interest rates would not rise in all countries as a result of fiscal problems in one country.[28] The parties to the SGP wanted to discipline not only each other but, more importantly, the countries that were expected to join the euro area in the future. Hallett, Lewis, and von Hagen (2004) point out that the SGP is clearly less effective as a disciplining tool for existing member states than the threat of exclusion from the eurozone before 1997.

Reform Proposals from Economists

The reform proposals from a group of economists including Wren-Lewis (2000), Wyplosz (2002a and b), and von Hagen (2002) can be grouped into five types.

Improving Enforcement

The first proposal focuses on enforcing SGP budget rules. Part of this economist-proposed solution involves the private sector. Banks in any EU economy would be required to hold no more than 25 percent of their capital in the obligations of their national government. OECD-country government debt would be given a positive risk weighting in a bank's portfolio, rather than a zero weighting, as is the case at present. Additional

---

28. This is the origin of the explicit "no bailouts" clause in the EU Treaty. Member states wanted to avoid the moral hazard of countries "too big to fail" that could possibly weaken market discipline.

aspects of the proposals look at government institutions, and the first suggestion is to elevate the standing of treasury ministers so they may overrule spending ministers during intragovernment budget preparation and limit parliament's ability to amend budgets. Furthermore, a fiscal policy committee would be created within each country and be given the task of setting fiscal policy targets. The fiscal policy committee's aim would be to deliver long-term fiscal sustainability and flexible short-term stabilization. The proposals would go beyond national governments to suggest a supranational body with the power to assess and sanction the budgetary behavior of national governments.

These proposals would be a nonstarter politically—notably the plan to elevate finance ministers or the creation of a technocratic body at either the national or supranational level with the power to overrule democratically elected parliaments. It would also be difficult to modify the SGP framework to incorporate revised Basel debt-risk weights. However, getting the private market to play a more active role in disciplining government borrowing does have merit. The idea of moving the responsibility for fiscal discipline back to the national level—where actual decision-making power (and legitimacy) lies—also has merit. These enforcement proposals are necessary since the EU peer-pressure mechanism has failed in fiscal policy. Holding national governments accountable could potentially be combined with increased technical oversight of government fiscal reporting, so as to limit the options for "one-off accounting measures" to improve government finances.[29]

Changing the Focus to the Long Run

The second set of proposals argue that the SGP's key problem is that it does not focus on the economy's long-run fiscal situation because of its

---

29. Deciding what items are recorded as government revenue/expenditure is one way "technocratic decision making"—with potentially large effects on EU member states' fiscal policies—already occurs. A recent example is from October 2003 and February 2004, where Eurostat took two decisions on the accounting treatment in national accounts of payments to governments by corporations in the context of the transfer to the government of the company's funded or unfunded pension liabilities. As several EU member states—notably France—retain sizable publicly owned enterprises (with company-specific pension plans) scheduled for future privatization, such transactions could have a significant positive effect on public finances at the time they occur, since such companies will pay the government a lump sum to shoulder their future pension responsibilities. Perhaps conveniently the European System of Accounts 1995 (and the National System of Accounts 1993) does not recognize the increase in future government-pension liabilities as a financial instrument, and the transaction, subsequently, has no effect on the level of government debt. See European Commission News Releases Stat 120/2003, October 21, 2003, and Stat 04/26, February 26, 2004. www.europa.eu.int/comm/economy_finance/news/pressreleases_en.htm (accessed March 3, 2004).

emphasis on the 3 percent rule (Mills and Quinet 2002; Brunila 2002; IMF 2001b; Fitoussi and Creel 2002). Two different and distinct plans to introduce long-run fiscal restraint without imposing a short-term deficit target are proposed.

The first plan simply suggests placing limits on public expenditure in relation to GDP. This approach claims that expenditure limits are more controllable than deficit limits and would allow the automatic stabilizers to work on tax revenue. Controlling spending, the argument goes, will limit the size of government and thereby prevent unstable fiscal policies from developing. However, this proposal would impose a single spending rule on individual countries, whose need for public expenditures may vary widely. There is no particular reason why a country that votes democratically to increase its public spending should be prevented from doing so as long as its citizens are willing to pay the cost (of course work-incentive problems may arise, but these too are a matter for each country to decide on). Moreover, with no explicit limit on deficits, the proposal would not prevent long-term deficit spending by countries that failed to keep tax revenues in line with the level of spending.

The second way to take into account the long-run fiscal situation is the "golden rule" proposal. Under the rule, borrowing would only finance public investment. This proposal would require a dual budget process to separate consumption and investment. The proposal would spread the burden of capital projects over the generations of all taxpayers that benefit from a capital project, and it would avoid efficiency losses due to fluctuations in the tax rate over time.

Reviewing this proposal, the European Commission and Buti, Eijffinger, and Franco (2003) argue that such a rule would have to refer to net spending (for example, all depreciation should be tax financed). They also note that the private sector can provide significant parts of the infrastructure, so the need for large public bond issues is not too large and could be accommodated within the current 3 percent deficit rule. However, creative accounting is a possibility if some forms of government consumption are classified as forms of investment.

In addition to the problems highlighted by the Commission, the "golden rule" proposal also does not deal with the issue of the automatic stabilizers, which would have to be addressed by a different reform.

Addressing the Fiscal Situation of the Euro Area as a Whole

Casella (2001) has argued that the current SGP does not address the fiscal situation of the euro area as a whole. She argues that maintaining confidence in the euro requires that the euro countries as a group avoid getting into fiscal problems severe enough to trigger inflationary pressures. She argues that if only one country exceeds the 3 percent rule, then there is no significant threat to stability. However, if all countries run deficits in excess of 3 percent, financial markets and investor confidence may be affected.

One approach to dealing with the euro area as a whole is to set up a supranational entity. This entity would allocate deficit shares among member states—allowing some to overshoot, while others remain in balance—to maintain the average of no more than 3 percent. A more flexible alternative, which minimizes the role of any supranational entity, would establish a system of tradable budget-deficit permits that allow individual members to deviate from the aggregate target in case of idiosyncratic shocks, by purchasing permits from surplus countries. Based on the success of tradable pollution permits, adding a market mechanism would minimize the aggregate costs of compliance and would reward surplus countries. Reducing the role of the supranational entity would also reduce the risk of political manipulation.

The European Commission and Buti, Eijffinger, and Franco (2003) note that setting deficit goals based on the euro area or the European Union as a whole would be difficult since the Maastricht Treaty would need to be renegotiated.[30] They also argue that since the debts of different countries are not perfect substitutes, their relative values would have to be defined, which would spark political controversy. (This argument does not seem compelling since treating all euro countries equally would be an ideal starting point for this proposal.) Finally they argue that there are not enough countries to establish a competitive market in deficit permits.

Making the Target Less Arbitrary and More Consistent with the Long Run

Buiter and Grafe (2002) argue that the SGP's critical issue is that the 3 percent deficit rule and the "close-to-balance" target are arbitrary and sometimes inconsistent with an appropriate fiscal stance. Further, the goals do not take into consideration the differences of each country. Thus, Buiter and Grafe's reform proposal is based on a "permanent balance rule" under which the inflation- and real-growth–adjusted permanent government budget is kept in balance or surplus. The permanent budget balance is defined analogously to the economic concept of permanent income and is based on the difference between the long-run average future values of tax revenue and government spending. The permanent balance rule would allow catch-up countries whose growth rates are higher to sustain higher current deficit levels than slower-developing countries. The rule would also allow the automatic fiscal stabilizers to operate, as long as the long-run fiscal situation of a country was sound. Depending on the time frame used for calculating the permanent balance, the rule would force

---

30. Currently, the 3 percent deficit reference values apply to each member state and cannot, without renegotiation of the EU Treaty, be applied at the aggregate eurozone level. See Buti, Eijffinger, and Franco (2003, 19).

countries to acknowledge the fiscal impact of future pension and health-care responsibilities.

This proposal has considerable intellectual merit, but it does not completely avoid being arbitrary, since there is no compelling reason from theory why the long-run budget should necessarily be exactly in balance or surplus. Presumably a target drawn from fundamental theory would be based on an optimal growth-and-accumulation framework, and would model the way in which a government's tax and spending decisions affect and are affected by private-saving decisions. Beyond this limitation, the authors' proposal adeptly shifts the focus away from the current deficit or surplus and toward a longer-term perspective and the ability of fast-growing countries to sustain larger short-term deficits (if they so choose).

The European Commission and Buti, Eijffinger, and Franco (2003) dismiss the proposal since it requires estimating permanent values for tax and spending. However, a dismissal seems too harsh. The US Social Security Administration carries out a procedure that is essentially the same as the one Buiter and Grafe propose when it issues its 75-year projections for the fiscal soundness of the Social Security system. Although these projections can change substantially and embody difficult projections of future productivity and inflation, they have, nevertheless, proved useful in evaluating the stability of the system.

Perhaps a more telling concern about the Buiter and Grafe proposal is that it does not focus on the issue that led to the SGP being created in the first place. Some member states were concerned about possible negative financial-market responses to excessive budget deficits and the danger that through the effect of the global capital market the euro could be undermined, or that interest rates in one country would be elevated as a result of deficits in another country. The European Commission argues, along these lines, that allowing rapidly growing countries to have high deficit ceilings risks instability at times of uncertainty, because of rapidly deteriorating credit worthiness and capital flight. In principle, the global capital market should be looking at the permanent budget balance in determining credit worthiness, but in practice its view may be more short term. After all, a country that has the potential to grow rapidly in the future may not in fact achieve that rapid growth.

Basing the Target on Debt Not Deficit

Pisani-Ferry (2002) and Hallett, Lewis, and von Hagen (2004) argue that fiscal sustainability depends on the stock of debt and not on the annual deficit. Like Buiter and Grafe (2002), this argument shifts the focus away from the current deficit as a target, but bases it on medium-term rather than long-term projections. Having a debt target is one way of capturing long-run sustainability that is less rigorous but easier to measure than estimates of the long-run budget balance.

Pisani-Ferry proposes that the SGP be supplemented with a debt sustainability pact, so that countries can opt out of the SGP deficit target in the short run if they present a comprehensive medium-term (5 years is suggested) fiscal program, indicating a debt ratio target below a given level (50 percent of GDP is suggested). These fiscal accounts would include estimates of the future effect of all budgetary commitments, such as pay-as-you-go pensions. The focus of EU monitoring would thus shift to the medium-term debt ratio targets, rather than annual deficits, thereby increasing short-term flexibility.

The European Commission and Buti, Eijffinger, and Franco (2003) raise similar concerns about this plan as those leveled at the Buiter and Grafe plan. They argue that estimates of future commitments and liabilities are highly uncertain, since estimates are subject to macroeconomic, demographic, and behavioral changes as well as being prone to political manipulation of budget commitments. The Commission also believes that current deficits matter to financial markets.

The European Commission's Reform Proposal for the SGP

The European Commission offered its own reform proposal for the SGP and sent it to the European Council and the EU Parliament on November 27, 2002.[31] The proposal was to be the basis for discussion at the spring 2003 European Council Summit, although the Council did not seriously consider SGP reform. The main aim of the European Commission's proposal is to introduce more flexibility into interpreting the SGP, while ensuring stricter adherence to the SGP's goal of sound and sustainable public finances. The changes to the SGP must be achieved *within the framework of existing Treaty provisions and SGP regulations* (European Commission 2002b, 6). Recognizing that the key to adherence to the SGP lies in member-state national budget politics, the Commission requested that the European Council renew its political commitment to the SGP.

The European Commission proposal includes four main elements:

Reinforcement of Budgetary Coordination Policies

- The "close-to-balance or surplus" requirement should be explicitly defined in underlying terms throughout the economic cycle—that is, net

31. Available at http://europa.eu.int/eur-lex/en/com/cnc/2002/com2002_0668en01.pdf. Following the ECOFIN Council decision on November 25, 2003, the European Commission announced that it will publish new proposals "aimed at maintaining and stepping up effective coordination of economic policies" in the fall of 2004. Unfortunately, these are not yet available at the time of writing (European Commission President R. Prodi, speech to the European Parliament, January 21, 2004, www.europa.eu.int/rapid/start/cgi/guesten. ksh?p_action.gettxt=gt&doc=SPEECH/04/31 I 0 I RAPID&lg=EN&display= [accessed March 3, 2004]).

of transitory effects and including the effects of cyclical fluctuations on budgets.

- Member states with an underlying deficit should be required to achieve an annual budgetary consolidation of at least 0.5 percent of GDP.

Upgrading the Analysis of Economic and Budgetary Policies

- Member states shall improve the quality, transparency, timeliness, and reliability of budgetary statistics, and the European Commission shall use its own estimates to evaluate the feasibility of member states' macroeconomic assumptions.

- The European Commission will devote more attention to the quality of member states' public finances with regard to their potential for growth and employment, by focusing on the differences between tax increases and expenditure cuts, the impact of tax reforms, and the impact on consolidation of one-off budgetary measures.

- The European Commission will organize more comprehensive and frequent visits to member states and publish in-depth country studies that evaluate their economic and fiscal prospects.

More Effective Enforcement Procedures

- In accordance with the EU Treaty, inappropriate budgetary policies that move a member state's budget away from an underlying position of "close-to-balance or surplus"—including procyclical loosening of the budget in prosperous times—should be viewed as a violation of the budgetary requirements at the EU level and lead to coercive measures.

- Clarification of what constitutes a satisfactory pace of debt reduction toward the 60 percent of GDP target—accompanied with the real possibility of coercive action against offending member states—is needed.

- The European Commission, rather than the ECOFIN Council, should be given the right to issue early warnings to member states.

Better Communication Through Openness and Transparency

- The European Commission would make public its detailed assessments of member states' stability/convergence programs as well as the quarterly (rather than biannual) reports on the member states' fiscal positions.

The European Commission's proposals are less focused on the pure economics of an optimal SGP and more on how to improve the existing

SGP. Implementing this reform package would "simply" require a unanimous vote of the European Council, rather than a renegotiation of the EU Treaty or any change in national legislation. By introducing the concept of the "underlying" deficit, which is comparable to the so-called structural deficit, the proposals allow for cyclical variations in the deficit rules. Beyond this, however, the proposals strengthen the deficit rules and attempt to speed up the process of reaching "close-to-balance or surplus" budgets in all member states.[32] Adding a debt-to-GDP target would make it extremely difficult for countries with high initial debt levels, like Italy, to meet these new requirements. Ineligibility could subsequently cause countries to deny any SGP reforms since any changes must pass a unanimous vote of the European Council. As the proposal stands there is too much that is punitive relative to any increase in flexibility to make it attractive to all the members.

While it is desirable to compel member states to face up to their fiscal problems and determine ways to resolve these problems, it is not desirable to force massive fiscal adjustment—with contractionary effects—on high-debt countries at a time of global economic weakness.

Modifying the European Commission Proposals

The ideal SGP would involve policies that provide sufficient flexibility to allow individual countries to use fiscal policy aggressively in a countercyclical fashion, since country-specific monetary policies are no longer available to euro members. The ideal SGP would also place tough policy constraints on member states that might otherwise be unwilling to follow budget plans that were sustainable over the long run. Ideally, these changes would be politically feasible and require only a modest revision of the existing SGP framework. Unfortunately, it seems that no comprehensive set of policies meet all of these criteria. Therefore, the only feasible SGP reforms—given the institutional constraints—are actually the second or even third best options, relative to the ideal.

Given this, what compromises will make reform of the SGP both feasible and as effective as possible? Evidence from the United States suggests that discretionary fiscal policy is generally not very adept at stabilizing the economy (Taylor 2000).[33] However, the automatic stabilizers *are* very

---

32. The proposed reform would halt or even reverse the 2002 extensions granted to Germany, France, Italy, and Portugal. Under the current SGP ruling, the countries have until 2006 to achieve close to balance or surplus in their budgets.

33. The 2001 and 2002 tax cuts do seem to have contributed to economic recovery in the United States. They were motivated primarily by the Bush administration's desire to cut taxes and were initially proposed during the 2000 election campaign—well before the economy entered a downturn.

effective, because they do not require policymakers to predict the business cycle and time their actions in a countercyclical fashion. SGP reform, therefore, should follow the proposal of the European Commission and several of the economists by allowing for cyclical variability of the deficit.

- The deficit target should be based on the underlying or structural deficit. Although setting a rule that the structural deficit should not exceed 3 percent of GDP is arbitrary—as Buiter and Grafe point out—it is reasonable. The 3 percent reference value is high enough to allow countries to rebuild aging infrastructures and low enough to keep the debt to GDP ratio down.

- The European Commission proposal to force structural-deficit countries to make a 0.5 percent of GDP annual adjustment should be softened or removed in order to avoid requiring a country to raise taxes or cut spending in a downturn (see below for more on long-term budget issues).

We support the proposals by the European Commission and the economists that focus more attention on the long-run sustainability of the budget plans of member countries. However, we are concerned that too mechanical an application of a debt-to-GDP target ratio could force countries to maintain tax rates that are excessive. *Getting the macroeconomics right should not undermine the effort to improve work incentives.* As the US experience over the past ten years amply illustrates, the best way to deal with budget deficits and rising debt is rapid economic growth, while sustained economic weakness quickly turns surpluses into deficits.

Although the European Commission recognizes this point in its reform proposals—noting that budget policies should be evaluated with respect to their growth consequences as well as their deficit and debt consequences—they do not really follow through on it. When deciding what constitutes a satisfactory pace of debt reduction for countries that currently exceed the 60 percent target, the Commission does not take into account the possible adverse effects of remedial measures on microeconomic incentives. Italy, for example, has a very high starting value for its debt and faces a huge demographic challenge. It will be hard enough for Italy to keep its debt ratio stable, never mind bringing it down quickly to the target level. Rapid increases in payroll taxes, for example, could induce large reductions in employment.

We are less concerned than the European Commission that budget problems in one country could lead to a collapse of the common currency. The euro is now well established and could sustain shocks, even the shock of, say, Italy's departure from it. The situation of the euro today is different from when it was first introduced. For example, capital markets can distinguish between German government bonds and Italian government bonds, and they can and do introduce a risk premium in one asset and not the other. While the spillover costs of high deficits in Italy to Germany are not zero, they are also not too large.[34]

- The European Commission's plan to introduce its own budget-monitoring program to provide independent information about the short-term and long-term fiscal positions of member countries should be supported. Member states should be confronted with unbiased estimates of their true fiscal situation, as an auditing device (see also footnote 29).

- Draconian measures to quickly reduce debt ratios would be counterproductive for individual EU states and the EU economy overall. The sustainability of budget plans should be assessed over at least a 10-year horizon (preferably longer). These long-term budget plans should include meaningful and quantitative targets. Shorter time horizons for fiscal consolidation can lead to policies that exacerbate the business cycle, while simultaneously neglecting the medium- or long-term demographic challenges countries face.

Overall, we support the spirit of the European Commission's proposals, but we would modify their plan to allow even greater short-term budget flexibility. If Europe successfully carries out microreforms that enable it to grow more rapidly, short-term job disruptions will inevitably occur. It would be a tragedy if budget policy targets forced a sharp decline in aggregate demand and made it more difficult to reemploy workers who are forced out of their current jobs. In order to avoid this problem, the debt insolvency risk of individual EU countries should not be overemphasized. As we noted earlier, faster economic growth is the best way to solve budget problems. In addition, the modifications we have suggested would make it easier to pass the proposed reforms in the European Council.

More flexible SGP rules still require effective enforcement mechanisms. The sanctions for noncompliance with SGP rules must be reformed, since recent experiences have clearly found them ineffective. The European Commission's limited proposals in this area, which call for clearer definitions of when the Commission shall activate existing early warning mechanisms through existing instruments, are inadequate. Ultimate decision-making responsibilities for imposing fines on member states should remain with the elected politicians in the ECOFIN Council, but foreseen fines are so draconian that serious doubts emerge as to their actual application.[35] Also, the idea that member states should face fines that would

---

34. The Standard & Poors downgrade and Italy's debt in July 2004 did not have much effect on the other countries that joined the euro area.

35. This would cause the effectiveness of SGP rules in altering member-state behavior to wane. A quantification of risk must always consider the magnitude of the potential loss (for

aggravate already poor government finances is counterintuitive and is comparable to assisting a drowning person with a dumbbell.

Instead a number of different coercive measures of gradually increasing severity should potentially be available to both the European Commission (with limited power for milder sanctions) and the ECOFIN Council. Having an arsenal of different sanctions would greatly facilitate sound fiscal policies in prosperous times. Milder sanctions—including loss or postponement of EU structural funds or other transfers for particular projects in the country[36] or loss of the country's voting rights in some, or all, of the sectoral Council of Ministers—could be applied to countries disobeying rules prior to levying harsher penalties. These measures are more likely since they are less costly and do not require time-consuming revisions in the EU Treaty. In fact, these changes—political will providing—could be speedily enacted by the European Council itself. Furthermore, domestic pressure from groups directly affected by the sanctions could urge member governments to enact budgetary consolidation in the offending country.

Getting the Macroeconomics Right: The ECB Mandate and Its Stated Goals

The European Central Bank (ECB), which was created on January 1, 1999, has been charged with managing European monetary policy as outlined by two EU Treaty articles:[37]

- EU Treaty Article 105.1 states that the primary objective of the ESCB [ECB][38] shall be to maintain price stability. Without prejudice to the objective of price stability, the ESCB shall support the general economic policies in the Community with a view to contributing to the achievement of the objectives of the Community as laid down in Article 2.

---

example, the billions of euros in fines) and the probability that the event (for example, whether the ECOFIN Council will levy fines on offending countries) will occur. Even if the potential for levying fines is very high, the risk is limited if the probability of actually applying the fines applied is very low. Since the decision to apply fines is ultimately political in this example, it is evident that the two conditions are inversely related. Research by Adam Posen (2004) suggests that the SGP has had no discernible effect on eurozone member-state fiscal policy responses to fluctuations in GDP growth.

36. To provide incentives for compliance, project support could initially be frozen..

37. As is the case with the SGP, the EU Treaty articles concerning the ECB are included virtually unchanged in the Provisional Treaty Establishing a Constitution for Europe (Articles III-77 to III-87).

38. The European System of Central Banks (ESCB), which lists the ECB in Frankfurt first, incorporates all central banks in the eurozone.

- EU Treaty Article 2 states that the Union sets itself the following objectives: to promote throughout the Community a harmonious and balanced development of economic activities, sustainable and non-inflationary growth, respect the environment, a high degree of convergence of economic performance, a high level of employment and of social protection, the raising of the standard of living and quality of life, and economic and social cohesion and solidarity among member states.

Thus, the ECB's mandate primarily emphasizes price stability though it also places secondary emphasis on sustaining and supporting economic growth, provided this does not jeopardize price stability. The reasons for placing primacy on price stability were given in the ECB's inaugural January 1999 policy outline,[39] which lists the following four principal benefits of price stability:

1. Price stability improves the transparency of the *relative price mechanism,* thereby *avoiding distortions* and helping to ensure that the market will *allocate real resources efficiently* across use and time. A more efficient allocation will raise the productive potential of the economy. In this sense, price stability creates an environment in which the necessary structural reforms implemented by national governments to increase the flexibility and efficiency of markets can be most effective.

2. Stable prices *minimize the inflation risk premium* in long-term interest rates, thereby lowering long-term rates and helping to stimulate investment and growth.

3. If the *future price level is uncertain, real resources are diverted to hedging* against inflation or deflation, rather than being put to productive use. Credibly maintaining price stability avoids these costs and provides the environment for efficient real-investment decisions. Price stability also eliminates the real costs entailed when *inflation or deflation exacerbates the distortionary effects of the tax and welfare system* on economic behavior.

4. Maintaining price stability *avoids the large and arbitrary redistribution of wealth and incomes* that arises in inflationary as well as deflationary environments, and therefore helps to maintain social cohesion and stability.

The ECB then concludes that these arguments collectively suggest that maintaining price stability in itself contributes to the achievement of output or employment goals. The logic underlying both the Treaty and the euro system's stability-oriented monetary policy strategy is thus that out-

---

39. ECB, *Monthly Bulletin,* January 1999.

put and employment goals are best served by a monetary policy that focuses on price stability.[40] This conclusion, together with statements from ECB officials,[41] strongly suggests that the ECB sees no conflict between the goals of price stability on the one hand and employment and growth on the other.

The EU Treaty explicitly grants the ECB independence to define its own monetary policy target (Article 110), so in January 1999 the ECB adopted a quantitative definition of price stability based on "a year-on-year increase in the Harmonized Index of Consumer Prices (HICP) for the euro area of below 2 percent."[42] In order to achieve this goal, the ECB designated a reference value of 4.5 percent for the growth rate of the broad money supply aggregate, M3, together with a broad-based assessment of the outlook for future price developments and the risks to its price stability definition in the euro area. On May 8, 2003, the ECB Governing Council confirmed its original monetary policy strategy. However, the ECB then added *a lower threshold for inflation* clarification:

> At the same time, the Governing Council agreed that in the pursuit of price stability it will aim to maintain inflation rates close to 2 percent over the medium term. This clarification underlines the ECB's commitment to provide a sufficient safety margin to guard against the risks of deflation.[43]

Furthermore, the ECB explicitly states that it believes this clarification sufficient to ward off any adverse effect from "the implications of inflation differentials within the euro area"[44]—in other words, if inflation in the euro area as a whole is kept close to 2 percent, then no single country in the eurozone is expected to experience deflationary pressure. So far this precautionary measure seems to have successfully warded off deflation. In May 2003 only Germany came close to deflation with a year-on-year increase in prices of only 0.6 percent (Eurostat 2004a).[45] A monetary envi-

---

40. ECB, *Monthly Bulletin,* January 1999, 40.

41. For instance, see Duisenberg's testimony and other testimonies, Hearing before the Committee on Economic and Monetary Affairs of the European Parliament, December 2001, www.ecb.int/key/key.htm. See also Issing et al. (2001) and Truman (2003, 123–34).

42. ECB Press Release, "The ECB's Monetary Policy Strategy," May 8, 2003.

43. ECB Press Release, "The ECB's Monetary Policy Strategy," May 8, 2003. See also Truman (2003) and ECB (2003a) for a review of the ECB policy.

44. ECB Press Release, "The ECB's Monetary Policy Strategy," May 8, 2003.

45. Germany has consistently had the lowest inflation rates in the eurozone with only 0.9 in June 2003 and 0.8 in July 2003. Austria, Belgium, and Finland experienced 0.9 percent inflation in May 2003, May 2003, and October 2003 respectively, and are the only other countries in the eurozone to experience year-on-year inflation below 1 percent since the ECB's May 2003 statement.

ronment without deflation is, however, hardly sufficient to qualify as successful monetary policy.

In May 2003 the ECB announced that monetary policy decisions would henceforth be based on a two-pronged approach: economic analysis to identify short- to medium-term risks to price stability, and monetary analysis to assess medium- to long-term trends in inflation. This monetary analysis takes into account a wide range of monetary indicators, including M3. As such, retaining the quantity of money as an indicator of monetary conditions is no longer a target per se. Rather the money growth target now "mainly serves as a means of cross-checking, from a medium- to long-term perspective, the short- to medium-term indications coming from economic analysis."[46] Subsequently, the M3 reference value of 4.5 percent growth, while not completely discarded, has been given a much less prominent stature in ECB monetary policy, and its validity will no longer be annually reviewed.

External Assessments of What the ECB Has Actually Done

Meeting Its Own Targets

The ECB has been heavily criticized for its choice of goals and the monetary target it set to achieve these goals—notably the low target rate of inflation (less than but close to 2 percent growth for the HICP) and the money growth target (M3 growth of 4.5 percent), both of which were in place until May 2003. Has the ECB actually achieved its goals for price stability? Apparently not. Figure 6.5 clearly indicates that the ECB did not maintain HICP inflation below 2 percent a year prior to May 2003. In only about a third of the period from January 1999 to May 2003 (20 months of the 53 months from January 1999 to May 2003—and only for three months from May 2000 to May 2003) did the ECB succeed in reaching its own goal. During May 2003–May 2004 (data for May 2004 are preliminary at the time of writing), the HICP was between 1.6 and 2 percent for seven months, and the ECB can therefore reasonably be said to have been more successful recently. However, preliminary estimates of 2.5 percent HICP inflation for May 2004—up from 1.6 percent in February—bring these recent improvements into question (European Commission 2004a). All in all though, since actual eurozone HICP inflation has remained above the ECB target for most of the period since 1999, de facto monetary policy has been somewhat looser than stated ECB targets would suggest.[47]

---

46. ECB Press Release, "The ECB's Monetary Policy Strategy," May 8, 2003.

47. If the ECB's focus on achieving its inflation goal "in the medium term only" was the reason behind this initial—relative to its own goal—loose monetary policy, then the results of recent months can be said to have vindicated this approach. This remains true despite the recent uptick in HICP inflation, as core inflation remained subdued at 2.1 percent in the most recent month of May 2004 (European Commission 2004a).

Figure 6.5 Eurozone inflation and ECB main refinancing rate, January 1999–May 2004

percent of inflation

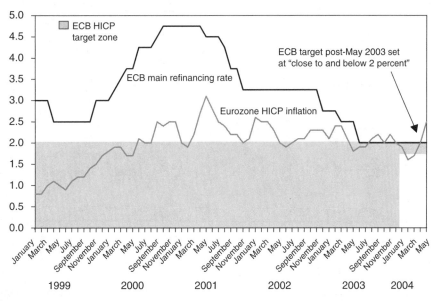

ECB = European Central Bank
HICP = Harmonized Index of Consumer Prices

Sources: ECB Online Statistics, www.ecb.int (2001, accessed May 28, 2004); European Commission (2004a, 2004d); Key Indicators for the Eurozone, May 28, 2004, update, www.europa.int/comm.economy_euroindic_eu.pdf (accessed May 29, 2004).

The ECB also failed to accomplish its second goal of an annual M3 growth rate of 4.5 percent (figure 6.6).[48] Only 45 percent of the time (24 months out of the 53 between January 1999 and May 2003) has the ECB been able to achieve M3 annual growth of ±1 percentage point of its stated reference value. As all cases outside the ±1 percentage point band were above 5.5 percent annual growth, the ECB's actual monetary policy has been significantly more accommodating than its own reference values would indicate.

In the case of inflation, which is the more important target, the case can be made that the ECB was looking forward and was able to foresee that price inflation would be moving toward the target value over time, as indeed it did from mid-2001 on. In terms of the money-growth target, how-

48. Until mid-2001 the ECB warned that its M3 calculations were biased upward, since it included nonresident holdings of money market funds, liquid money, market paper, and securities. However, all these holdings were finally removed as of October 2001, so the updated ECB data are presented in this book.

Figure 6.6 Eurozone M3 annual growth rate and ECB main refinancing rate, January 1999–May 2003

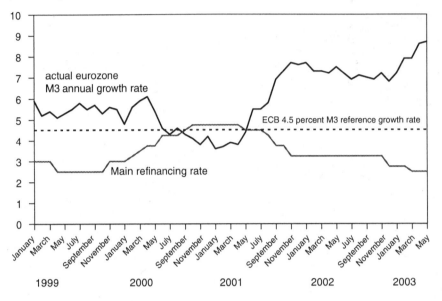

percent of growth

ECB = European Central Bank

Source: ECB Online Statistics (2000), www.ecb.int (accessed May 29, 2004).

ever, figure 6.6 shows the M3 annual growth rate well above the target rate while the ECB refinancing rate was being lowered. Hence, the May 2003 clarification of the ECB monetary policy strategy, which raised the threshold for inflation and relegated M3 growth to secondary importance, can be said to bring stated ECB monetary policy more in line with actual policy.

One view of the ECB's behavior is that it has adopted a "publicly hawkish" inflation stand, while in reality its decisions consider growth and employment as well as other real economy variables. There is a large gap, in this view, between what the ECB says and what it does. In this, the ECB would apparently be following in the footsteps of the German Bundesbank, which, between 1973 and 1999, allowed its numeric monetary targets to be frequently breached in order to accommodate both foreign-exchange movements and German economic growth considerations. Publicly, however, the German Bundesbank preserved its reputation as an unbending inflation fighter (Clarida and Gertler 1996; Clarida, Gali, and Gertler 1997).

A detailed analysis of the ECB responsiveness to real economic indicators is beyond the scope of this book (see Truman 2003 and Posen 2004). But figure 6.7 does seem consistent with the view that the ECB has been influenced by growth and employment developments in its policy deci-

Figure 6.7 ECB main refinancing rate and selected economic indicators, January 1999–December 2003

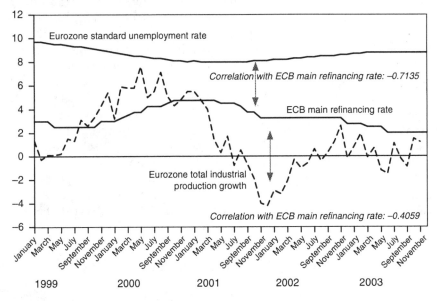

percent of growth

Note: Correlations are simple pairwise Pearson correlations, statistically significant at a 99 percent level.

Source: ECB Online Statistics, www.ecb.int (accessed May 29, 2004).

sions. Movements in the refinancing rate are correlated (with the appropriate sign) with movements in euro area unemployment and industrial production.

The CEPR Assessment

The Centre for Economic Policy Research (Begg et al. 2002a,b) analyzed ECB policy and attempted to answer the hypothetical question: What would European monetary policy in 2001 have been if the US Federal Reserve (Fed) had been setting European interest rates, based on estimates of the Fed's "reaction function" or Taylor Rule[49] for policymaking?[50] The

---

49. Originally proposed by John Taylor (see, for instance, Taylor 1993), the rule proposes that real short-term interest rates be set according to (1) where actual inflation is relative to where a central bank wants it to be, (2) where economic activity is relative to the "full employment level," and (3) what level of short-term interest rates would be consistent with full employment.

50. The CEPR actually estimated the rule that best fit the Fed response to changes in various economic variables during Chairman Alan Greenspan's tenure and then applied this descriptive device on eurozone economic news in 2001.

CEPR concludes that European interest rates in 1999 and the first half of 2000 would have been up to one percentage point higher than those actually set by the ECB, while in the latter part of 2000 and 2001 the ECB and Federal Reserve would have set roughly similar interest rates. In addition, they found that a Taylor Rule for the ECB that weights both inflation and GDP growth tracks the actual policy decisions that were made. This further indicates that the ECB considered other macroeconomic variables rather than exclusively focusing on reducing HIPC inflation to below 2 percent a year at the time.

Of course even if the ECB follows the same policy approach as the Fed, there is no guarantee that the monetary policy in Europe will be a good fit for any individual member state in the euro area. After all, although diverse, the United States has the advantage of a more closely integrated market and greater labor mobility when dealing with such heterogeneous outcomes. The ECB faces a tougher problem than the Fed in trying to set monetary policy that is appropriate for both a main economic power like Germany and the peripheral countries of Europe. Such is the cost of a single currency.

Is the ECB Following the Right Monetary Policy?

The two issues at stake are (1) the use of inflation targeting as a goal for monetary policy and (2) the appropriateness of recent ECB policy responses to the economic downturn in the eurozone. It seems clear from the above that neither the ECB nor the Bundesbank were or are "pure" inflation targeters. They looked at the real economy when making their decisions, and not just at inflation. As Truman (2003) has pointed out, however, a thoughtful inflation targeter will take the real economy into account, since understanding it will provide important guidance on the future path of inflation. But given the persistent deviation of actual inflation from the target level, it seems as if the ECB has willingly violated its stated goal of putting price stability first and foremost, and has included real economy performance as a goal, and not just as a result of price stability. The ECB has not behaved as a pure or even semipure inflation targeter, but has traded off real growth against inflation.

The Euro and the Need for a Higher Inflation Target

It is just as well that the ECB violated its own rules, since the goal of pushing overall eurowide inflation below 2 percent was a bad choice. The ECB's arguments for price stability are not well supported by empirical analysis. In fact, empirical evidence finds little support for adverse effects on real growth from inflation, provided the rate stays below 5 percent a year (see

Truman 2003, 25). We do not advocate letting inflation go as high as 5 percent under normal circumstances, but the goal of keeping inflation close to 2 percent is too stringent. Thus, the ECB should allow a rate of inflation in Europe that is a bit above its current stated goal.[51]

Akerlof, Dickens, and Perry (2000) point out that in an economy where prices and wages are sticky downward, the economy will benefit from positive overall inflation. Real wages of workers, whose market position has deteriorated, can decline without forcing the contentious downward adjustment of nominal wages that can require prolonged high unemployment or job loss. The issue is not just with relative wages. If periods of sharply rising commodity prices are accommodated with a short burst of overall inflation, broad declines in real wages, which are a necessary response to the changed supply conditions, are induced. This pattern occurred with the oil and food shocks of the 1970s, although the resulting burst of inflation was too large and too extended.

In the euro area, the argument for significant positive inflation holds even more strongly than in the United States. The euro area countries have eliminated the adjustment of their relative exchange rates, which means that idiosyncratic shocks to individual countries may require the adjustment of relative price levels. Currently, Germany is undergoing a difficult price-level adjustment, having entered the euro at a value that was above its long-run sustainable level. *It is much easier to generate a downward adjustment in the relative price level of one country if the price levels of the other countries are rising.* The adjustment can then be achieved by, say, letting Germany have a lower rate of inflation than the EU average.

What if Britain were to enter the euro area? Currently, Britain receives a substantial foreign exchange benefit because it produces its own oil. When that oil runs out, Britain will have to bring about a substantial downward adjustment of its price level in order to ensure that its manufacturing sector becomes more competitive. Even though the labor market in Britain is more flexible than in the past, this would still require an extended period of slack demand.

Having an inflation target of close to 2 percent (but not below) might not in itself be such a problem if the ECB were willing to act more aggressively on a short-term basis to deal with, for example, a very weak European or world economy, or to respond to unexpected events such as oil price or other supply shocks. Unfortunately, actual ECB policy over the past few years does not indicate such a willingness.

---

51. One may argue that the phrase *close to 2 percent* leaves significant room for a flexible interpretation—for instance, it could mean up to 2.5 percent. However, such an interpretation would certainly be counterproductive for the ECB, since it would only serve to undermine the credibility of its stated policy goals and sow confusion in financial markets. It would be wiser to publicly state that the inflation target was in fact 2.5 percent.

How Good Has the ECB Policy Been During the Recent Downturn?

The second issue in assessing the ECB is whether it has done a good job or not—regardless of whether it followed its own rules. We disagree with the CEPR assessment that the ECB did just as well as the Fed in steering the economy. Fitting Taylor Rules can lead to mischief when interpreting past monetary policy. Most of the time a reasonable Taylor Rule will track actual Fed policy, which is unsurprising given the way time-series macro-variables are related. But a Taylor Rule does not always illustrate well what policy should be out of sample or in an unusual situation. For example, Alan Blinder reports that, while vice chairman of the Federal Reserve (1994–96), he asked the staff to estimate various Taylor Rules and many of them had an excellent fit to past data and policy choices. However, the different specifications gave very different prescriptions about the desirable future path of interest rates.[52] Thus, the answer you get from a given Taylor Rule depends on the exact specification used.

This point is illustrated and strengthened in an analysis by Goldman Sachs (2003). This study shows how actual monetary policy in the United States has sharply deviated from a Taylor Rule prediction over the past few years. The Taylor Rule posits that a central bank should set short-term interest rates based on an equation containing the expected rate of inflation, the value of the "neutral" short-term rate, the inflation gap, and the output gap. As applied to the US Federal Reserve, the equation becomes:

$$\text{Fed funds rate} = \text{expected inflation} + \text{neutral real fed funds rate} + 0.5 * \text{inflation gap} + 0.5 * \text{output gap}$$

The inflation gap is defined as the difference between the Fed's preferred measure of inflation and its inflation target. The output gap is defined as the difference between actual and potential output. Using values of 2 percent for both the Fed's (implicit) inflation target and the neutral real short-term interest rate, the Taylor Rule does a credible job in tracking movements in short-term interest rates for much of the 1980s and 1990s. Table 6.1 shows, however, the large deviations between actual policy and policy predicted by the Taylor Rule.

The most striking element of these results is that actual policy deviated substantially from the Taylor Rule policy at exactly the times when the economy was showing persistent sluggishness and needed an additional stimulus—in the early 1990s and again in 2001–03.

Ninety-nine percent of the time an automatic pilot will fly an airliner as well as or maybe better than the pilot. But when some really exceptional situation arises, the pilot needs to be in control. This analogy illustrates how the Fed has helped the US economy. There have been several excep-

---

52. Blinder's comments can be found in Frankel and Orszag (2002).

Table 6.1   Actual monetary policy and the Taylor Rule, 1985–2003
(year-over-year percentage changes for output and CPI)

Year	Federal funds rate Actual	Taylor Rule	Gap	Core CPI	Output gap
1985	8.1	7.1	1.0	4.4	−0.9
1986	6.8	6.7	0.1	4.1	−0.7
1987	6.7	6.7	−0.1	3.9	−0.3
1988	7.6	8.1	−0.5	4.4	0.9
1989	9.2	8.6	0.6	4.5	1.7
1990	8.1	8.8	−0.7	5.0	0.5
1991	5.7	7.1	−1.4	4.9	−2.5
1992	3.5	5.6	−2.0	3.7	−1.8
1993	3.0	5.1	−2.0	3.3	−1.8
1994	4.2	5.0	−0.8	2.8	−0.5
1995	5.9	5.2	0.6	3.0	−0.6
1996	5.3	5.0	0.3	2.7	0.0
1997	5.5	5.0	0.5	2.4	0.9
1998	5.4	5.3	0.0	2.3	1.8
1999	5.0	5.3	−0.3	2.1	2.4
2000	6.3	5.8	0.5	2.4	2.2
2001	3.9	4.5	−0.6	2.7	−1.1
2002	1.7	3.7	−2.1	2.3	−1.5
2003	1.0	1.9	−0.9	1.3	−2.1

CPI = consumer price index

Source: Goldman Sachs (2003).

tional circumstances in recent economic history when the Federal Reserve was able to respond in a way that helped the economy adjust to changes in economic variables that would not have been included in any likely Taylor Rule ex ante. The stock market crash of 1987, the Asian financial crisis, and the collapse of the Russian domestic debt bonds (GKOs) and long-term capital management fund (LTCM) are examples. The economic downturn that began in 2000 and intensified in 2001 is another example. The Federal Reserve realized the severity of the situation quickly even though unemployment remained very low. The federal funds rate was reduced to its lowest level in years, while the ECB, by contrast, was dragging its feet, using its inflation target as a justification for less aggressive rate moves. The ECB has maintained its refinancing rate well above the federal funds rate, despite the fact that the euro has risen against the dollar, and the euro economy looks weaker than both the US and the world economy. The ECB should have done more to improve economic performance in Europe in the past two or three years.

Macroeconomic Policy to Support Reform

European policymakers have been caught in a dilemma for many years about the extent to which macropolicies can be used to stimulate faster economic growth and the extent to which microreform is necessary for growth. Central bankers are usually supporters of microreform, pressing for greater labor-market flexibility and less government involvement in the private sector. When they are pressed to follow more expansionary policies, the bankers argue that such policies would only be inflationary, given that microreform has not yet been achieved. Thus, the lack of microreform becomes a reason, or an excuse, for the failure to act more aggressively to stimulate growth.

The policymakers charged with effecting microreform measures argue, in turn, that with economic conditions so weak, they have to protect existing firms in order to protect jobs. They cannot cut back on income support programs if unemployment is already high and jobs are scarce.

The result has been a stalemate in which neither side was willing to move aggressively on growth policies. That stalemate now shows some signs of being broken as reform programs move forward—as described elsewhere in this book. But the nature of the reforms is still affected by economic weakness. Budget pressures and the need for increased work incentives have played a role in reducing the level of support for retired workers and the unemployed. However, more needs to be done. The second phase of reforms that Europe must follow includes a shift to much greater economic flexibility and in order to achieve this goal, a short-term increase in structural unemployment may occur. That would be much easier to deal with if overall growth in Europe were stronger and aggregate demand were expanding more strongly.

Europe today has a strong currency and is not fighting an inflation battle. *It is an appropriate time to follow growth-promoting policies since there is emerging progress on microreform.* The ECB, while keeping its independence clear, should be willing to take a strong growth-promoting stand in its monetary policy and take an active role on center stage rather than waiting on the sidelines. Without help from the macropolicy side, the full potential of microreform in Europe will be much harder or even impossible to achieve.

7

Are Current Reform Efforts on the Right Track?

We must be the change we wish to see in the world.

—Mahatma Gandhi

A growth-oriented agenda for economic reform was set out in chapter 1, and the economic analysis of this agenda has been the subject of subsequent chapters. This agenda was based on improving work incentives (for employers to create jobs and for workers to accept jobs); increasing competitive intensity in product and labor markets; and providing supportive macroeconomic policy. This book has recognized that stable but expansionary macroeconomic conditions are a prerequisite for growth, and chapter 6 discussed the monetary and fiscal policies and institutional arrangements that would create these conditions. The main focus of the book, however, has been on structural policies to improve incentives and increase competition, and these policies will also be the focus of this concluding chapter. Specifically, we will look at the reform efforts now under way in Europe to increase competitive intensity and make labor markets more flexible.

One of the European Commission's (Commission) main initiatives is to increase competitive intensity by creating a competition authority with the power to enforce EU-wide procompetition laws with companies that engage in cross-border activities in the region. The chapter starts, therefore, with a description and assessment of competition policy at the EU level. Although there is considerable value in having an EU competition policy, we argue that the broad reform agenda in Europe—encompassing social policies and product-market regulations—must be implemented at the national or member-state level since they have the power to bring about change. Throughout the book we have examined a number of reform policies and recommended proposals that should be followed. We have also assessed the extent to which the large European economies are on track to implement these reforms. It is valuable to summarize this information so we recap the highlights of Britain, France, Germany, and Italy in this last chapter. We then look at the issue of whether reform should be undertaken all at once or incrementally, before ending with a short conclusion.

Where Does EU Competition Policy Stand Now and What More Is Needed?

EU competition law is implemented at the EU and the member-state level, with the European Commission enforcing EU legislation and national competition authorities enforcing national laws. The national authorities may also be used to enforce EU regulations where these preempt national legislation.

Competition policy is an area in which developments at the EU level have driven progress at the member-state level. In some cases it has established new national legal frameworks and enforcement institutions where none previously existed—an important and positive effect.

European competition policy can be divided into four distinct areas: mergers and acquisitions, antitrust, liberalization, and state aid.

Mergers and Acquisitions

Since 1990, the European Commission has had exclusive power to approve European mergers and acquisitions of a certain size, removing the requirement for companies to seek approval at several national competition authorities. The exclusive power of the European Commission covers mergers where the aggregate worldwide turnover of all the undertakings concerned is more than €5 billion or where the aggregate EU-wide turnover of each of at least two of the undertakings concerned is more than €250 million—unless each of the undertakings concerned attains more than two-thirds of its aggregate EU-wide turnover within one and the same member state.

Competition policy's focus, therefore, is on large, cross-border mergers and acquisitions, and the first criterion is explicitly extraterritorial, which gives the Commission authority over non-EU companies operating in the European Union. Since 1990, the Commission has been notified of 2,508 mergers and acquisitions cases (as of June 30, 2004), and has cleared about 90 percent of these. Most of the remaining 10 percent of cases have been referred to member-state authorities. The European Commission has blocked a total of only 18 cases to date.[1] However, some of these have been very high-profile cases, for which the European Commission has received significant criticism—especially in the cases of Volvo/Scania (2000), GE/Honeywell (2001), Schneider/Legrand (2001), and Tetra Laval/Sidel (2001). The parties involved in the latter two cases undertook legal proceedings in the European Court of Justice (ECJ) against the European Commission, and in both cases the ECJ subsequently annulled the European Commission's decision and harshly criticized the basis for the Commission's ruling (the GE-Honeywell case still awaits an ECJ decision).

In response to the criticisms of its actions and the legal defeats it has suffered, in December 2002 the Commission made changes in its merger decision-making process. It increased the level of communication with the corporate parties hoping to merge in order to allow due opportunity for them to defend their proposed action. The Commission also increased the "economic foundation" of its decisions by appointing a chief competition economist and an internal Commission peer-review committee for all cases. The Commission also split up the centralized Merger Task Force (MTF) into separate sectoral units to facilitate expeditious review of pending cases.

Antitrust Policy

The European Commission must, under Article 81 (1) in the EU Treaty, act to prevent any agreements or practices that may affect trade *between* member states and that have as their objective or affect the prevention, restriction, or distortion of competition within the common market.[2] EU Treaty Article 82 states that the European Commission should prevent any abuse by one or more companies of a dominant position within the common market (or in a substantial part of the market). Such abuse must be prohibited if it affects trade *between* member states.[3] Thus, the mandate of the EU antitrust policy applies only to cross-border antitrust issues—roughly the equivalent in the United States of rules that apply to companies engaged in interstate commerce. Note, however, that EU Treaty Article 81 is intended to prevent price discrimination agreements within the European

---

1. So-called Article 8 (3) decisions. The Commission has also approved conditionally—i.e., with particular conditions and/or obligations attached for the parties involved, a little fewer than 200 cases. For specific data, see www.europa.eu.int/comm/competition/mergers/cases/index/#by_decision_type.html.

2. EU Treaty Article 81 (1), available at www.europa.eu.int/comm/competition/legislation/treaties/ec/art81_en.html.

3. EU Treaty Article 82, available at www.europa.eu.int/comm/competition/legislation/treaties/ec/art82_en.html.

Union. Companies cannot legally stop imports of low-price goods or services from one EU country into another EU country where prices are higher.

In May 2004, European companies were freed from their obligation to notify and seek clearance with the Commission for relevant business agreements that they enter into. Obviously, companies must still ensure that their agreements do not violate EU or national competition law, but removing the automatic necessity of notification should ease the administrative hurdle of many particularly smaller European mergers and acquisitions and must therefore be welcomed. It should also free Commission resources to pursue serious competition offenders, rather than process frequently routine filings. To some degree it is testimony to the raised level of knowledge of (though not necessarily adherence to) competition policy issues among European businesses that authorities can now to a greater extent rely on businesses knowing where the red lines are themselves, rather than require them to file a notification no matter what.

On the other hand, the Commission also on May 1, 2004, got increased powers of inspection and the power to intervene against all types of anticompetitive mergers (within its jurisdiction). It can annul any agreement it deems violates EU competition laws (with possible recourse to the ECJ) and fine companies involved in anticompetitive behavior up to 10 percent of global turnover. While the Commission has possessed antitrust powers since 1962, it is only in recent years that significant action has been taken this field. In 2001 and 2002 fines of €1.8 billion and €1 billion were imposed, respectively.[4] In addition, since 2001 the European Commission has taken action against at least three companies—Deutsche Post, Michelin, and DSD—for abuse of a dominant market position. Microsoft was fined €497 million and ordered to unbundle its media player from Windows. Microsoft has appealed the verdict.

Significant sectors of the European economy[5] are partially covered by the so-called block exemptions, which grant immunity for some types of collusion between firms, if they are deemed to improve overall competition through, for instance, improved distribution or technology transfer. As part of the changes in applications of Article 81 on May 1, 2004, older block exemptions were replaced with new regulations. Instead of imposing on companies positively the things they could do (under the old block exemptions), the new rules create a "negative list" of prohibited violations—such as price fixing, market sharing—as well as a safe harbor for all other agreements. According to EU Competition Commissioner Mario Monti, the aim of these reforms to block agreements is to limit market distortions and allow more freedom for businesses to make desired com-

---

4. Data available at www.europa.eu.int/comm/competition/citizen/cartel_stats.html.

5. Including, for instance, transportation (road, rail, sea, and air), telecommunications, and insurance.

mercial decisions. While it is still early days, we support the intent and direction of these reforms to competition policy.[6]

On balance, European competition policy has strengthened antitrust enforcement in recent years, despite the effective gaps remaining from excluded sectors. At the same time, national authorities have gained a more prominent role as their regulatory capabilities have increased. This development is foreseen to continue after May 1, 2004, with the new European Competition Network (ECN), comprising both the Commission and national authorities in an informal though institutionalized group (informal in that one actor cannot force a decision on another). In part, this reflects increased capabilities among national authorities and healthy decentralization of decision-making authority, but given the political sensitivity of many antitrust cases, attempts at member-state "power grabs" cannot be ruled out. Such attempts, however, must be resisted, as too wide a disparity of competition policy enforcement among entities in a single market—seeking, for instance, to protect national champions—would cause significant market distortions and harm overall levels of competition.

Liberalization of Former Government Monopolies

Traditionally, many European economies had placed large industrial sectors under state-controlled companies, especially industries deemed essential or those with significant economies of scale and high fixed costs—telecommunications and electricity, for example. As a result of changing technologies that allow efficient operation at smaller scale and changing attitudes, there has been a shift toward privatization and competition. The sale of government-owned assets has also been a source of revenue to fill budget gaps.

At the EU level, five Commission directives in the telecommunications, transport, postal services, gas, and electricity sectors were intended to introduce competition by separating infrastructure from commercial activities. These directives have come in part out of the EU's Lisbon agenda.

The efforts to privatize government monopolies and introduce competition have encountered enormous political opposition from member states, especially France. This opposition, in turn, is fueled by fierce resistance by the employees of the state companies, who fear the effect of competition on their jobs, wages, and pensions. Because of this opposition, implementing the directives has been slow, and very long transitional periods have frequently been the result.

A key issue is whether the most important step in liberating government monopolies is privatization or whether it is sufficient to create

---

6. For Commissioner Monti's full comments and additional information, see European Commission Competition Policy Newsletter, Special Edition May 2004. Available at www.europa.eu.int/comm/competition/publications/cpn/special_edition.pdf.

effective competition for a state-run enterprise. In this regard, EU Treaty Article 86 (2), which covers *Services of General Economic Interest*, is of particular interest. It states that:

> Undertakings entrusted with the operation of services of general economic interest or having the character of a revenue-producing monopoly shall be subject to the rules contained in this Treaty, in particular to the rules on competition, in so far as the application of such rules does not obstruct the performance, in law or in fact, of the particular tasks assigned to them. The development of trade must not be affected to such an extent as would be contrary to the interests of the Community.[7]

In principle this article is intended to make sure that state ownership is not used as a way of limiting competition within the European Union. However, in reality the article has been subject to "political interpretation." Some EU governments, notably the French, have argued that it is necessary to provide essential services to isolated and/or poorer regions of their economies, which requires either continued state ownership or limits on competition for formerly state-owned companies. The French government has argued that companies facing the full competitive pressures of a liberalized European utility service market, for example, would face too few incentives to expand service coverage to such poorer regions. They have called for significant exemptions for former state-owned utilities with respect to EU competition and common market rules.

Currently, the European Commission is drafting new legislation, aimed at clarifying the scope of "services of general economic interest" (see European Commission 2003e). Such legislation was a condition for the French government's acceptance of partial liberalization of the European energy markets at the 2002 Barcelona Summit.

Thus, while significant progress has been made in Europe toward privatization and increased competition, much more needs to be done and political resistance is blocking progress. The specifics of liberalizing state monopolies in the bigger EU countries are discussed later in this chapter.

State Aid

In an effort to create a level playing field for competition, EU Treaty Article 87 prohibits any state aid that distorts competition in the European Union, and tasks the European Commission to enforce this ban. There are exemptions to this ban, however, allowing state aid for small- and medium-sized enterprises (SMEs) and for the provision of training. In addition, the Commission can grant exemptions on a case-by-case basis, provided aid does not adversely affect the "common interest."

---

7. EU Treaty Article 86 (2), available at europa.eu.int/eur-lex/en/treaties/dat/C_2002325EN.003301.html.

Despite the good intentions of Article 87, state aid sparks frequent debates, and the overall level of state aid remains high in the European Union. The Commission estimated that between 1996–98, the total level of state aid in the European Union was €93 billion, or €250 per capita (European Commission 2000b). The European airline industry has been subject to clashes between the Commission and member states aiding their national flag carriers. Air France, Alitalia, Sabena, and Olympic Airways are examples of companies ordered to repay illegal aid to their national government. However, the stubbornly high overall level of state aid in the European Union illustrates the persistence of this problem to EU competition policy.

Companies that are not meeting the competitive test should either restructure or improve their operations, or they should be taken over or closed down. State aid slows down the process of restructuring that is a vital part of overall productivity improvement.

Hostile Takeovers

The discussion so far has been about European competition policy on mergers and acquisitions and on agreements among companies. These cases focus on preventing the formation of anticompetitive dominant companies or anticompetitive practices by groups of companies. Of course the opposite problem may be of as great or even greater concern. Some industries in Europe have failed to consolidate, leaving a fragmented structure where companies neither achieve minimum efficient scale nor use information technology (IT) effectively. In other cases an entrenched management may be incompetent but they hang on to their jobs because shareholders do not have access to relevant information on company performance, which makes it difficult for them to act. In such situations, the capital market's ability to mount hostile takeovers may be important to improving productivity. Even the threat of such takeovers may be enough to force managers to improve their operations.

Until now the rate of hostile takeovers in the core European economies has been very low. A study by Rossi and Volpin (2003) examines all the mergers and acquisitions announced between January 1, 1990 and December 31, 1999 and completed as of December 31, 2002. The study reports (table 7.1) that the volume of takeovers over this period is pretty high for most of the developed economies but varies across countries. Volume is defined as the percentage of traded firms that are targets of successful mergers or acquisitions over this decade, and the figures include: 65.63 percent for the United States, 53.65 percent for Britain, 56.40 percent for France, and 35.51 percent for Germany. Turning to hostile cross-border takeovers, the differences by country are much greater. The figures are 6.44 percent for the United States, 4.39 percent for Britain, 1.68 percent for

Table 7.1 International mergers and acquisitions by target country (percent)

Country	Volume[a] (percent)	Hostile takeovers[b] (percent)	Cross-border ratio[c] (percent)
Australia	34.09	4.60	27.16
Austria	38.14	1.03	51.55
Belgium	33.33	0.56	45.14
Britain	53.65	4.39	23.46
Canada	30.05	2.73	22.66
Denmark	24.03	0.81	38.26
Finland	45.45	0.91	22.67
France	56.40	1.68	33.81
Germany	35.51	0.30	26.05
Greece	12.66	0.00	23.13
Ireland	28.90	4.62	52.73
Italy	56.40	3.04	36.13
Japan	6.43	0.00	13.25
Netherlands	26.49	1.32	43.43
New Zealand	49.82	0.70	46.15
Norway	61.24	5.86	36.76
Portugal	31.37	1.96	40.00
Spain	15.72	0.17	37.55
Sweden	62.06	3.74	35.48
Switzerland	38.48	1.43	43.59
United States	65.63	6.44	9.07

a. Volume is the percentage of traded companies targeted in a completed deal.
b. Hostile takeover is the number of attempted hostile takeovers as a percentage of domestic traded firms.
c. Cross-border is the number of cross-border deals as a percent of all completed deals.

Source: Rossi and Volpin (2003).

France, and 0.30 percent for Germany. In other words, German companies are virtually immune from hostile cross-border takeovers and French companies face only a very low rate of such takeovers.

In order to clarify European competition policy, all EU members endorsed a "Takeover Directive" in late 2003, after 14 years of negotiations. Although the directive generated EU-wide guidelines for company takeovers, especially hostile ones, it was a failure. Instead of providing an EU-wide level playing field that would facilitate outside pressure on company management, the new EU rules preserved the use of multiple voting shares and "poison pills" by incumbent managers as "options" against hostile takeovers without prior shareholder approval.[8] Managers seeking to pre-

---

8. See European Parliament Press Service, Takeover Directive Adopted, December 16, 2003, available at www2.europarl.eu.int/omk/sipade2?PUBREF=-//EP//TEXT+PRESS+TW-20031215-S+0+DOC+XML+V0//EN&L=EN&LEVEL=2&NAV=X&LSTDOC=N#SECTION13 (accessed January 13, 2004).

serve the status quo as well as groups maintaining the importance of pre-serving "national champions" will eagerly exploit these "legal options."

In the presence of strong product-market competition, pressure from the capital market—in the form of hostile takeovers—may not be needed. But many examples remain where all-out competitive pressure is lacking, or where incumbent companies are favored or subsidized by policymakers. In these situations, the case is strong for using capital-market pressure as an additional tool to facilitate industry consolidations and to oust ineffective managers. The European Union has clearly failed to provide this spur to greater competition and higher productivity.

Conclusions on the EU Competition Authority

Policymakers in Europe perceive that the European Union now has a strong force working to add competitive intensity in the region. The EU competition authority's decisions receive extensive coverage and are often of considerable interest internationally since they involve the actions of large multinational corporations. Nevertheless, competition policy from the European Commission so far has been far short of ideal.

Preventing mergers among existing large companies and punishing anticompetitive behavior are sometimes necessary. The Commission is like the policeman on the street corner keeping an eye on things in order to prevent crime. However, the legal setbacks and criticisms suffered by the Commission in the ECJ suggest that, at least until recently, there has not been an adequate reckoning of the costs and benefits of such mergers. Further, industry consolidation is often an important mechanism for improving productivity and creating stronger competitors, and the European Commission must ensure that the changes in its assessment procedures are sufficient to determine when a genuine threat to competition occurs.

The biggest limitation of European competition policy, however, is not that it has been too aggressive in some cases. Rather, it lacks the power to tackle the anticompetitive behaviors and regulations that limit competition in many of the EU economies. Moreover, as noted above, member states are working to undermine the authority of the Commission with regard to opening national markets in a number of industries—notably industries that are described as "services of general interest," which include some utilities but could more broadly be applied to other industries. Governments want to protect from competition. If competitive intensity is really to be increased in the European Union, national governments must change their positions and move proactively to encourage, not limit, competition.

Reform: Driven by Individual European Governments, Reinforced at the EU Level

Although there are strong common themes to reform that apply throughout the region, the idea of instituting a single European program of reform is not credible. The European economies remain distinct and companies operating in multiple countries continue to face very diverse national business environments. National social security systems still present the citizens of Europe with very disparate conditions, and the national political will to tackle the economic problems is unequally distributed among the continent's capitals. Many of the answers to solving individual European countries' idiosyncratic problems lie in the actions of the individual governments themselves. Some European countries have already enacted substantial social insurance reforms, while others have further to go.

Most of the structural policies required to radically transform the European economy not only to fulfill the Lisbon 2010 agenda but also to preserve European prosperity beyond that (fast approaching) date must be originated and implemented by national governments. Each country must also design, fund, and execute its own social insurance and labor-market policies.

In principle, competition policy is now made at the EU level, but as we have seen, in practice many of the regulations that affect competition are set at the national level. The EU authority applies only to larger companies that operate across borders. Furthermore, only with monetary policy is there a true eurozone decision-making process that applies to all participating economies. Fiscal policies are decided at the member-state level, and the Stability and Growth Pact's influence now seems to be much less than was envisaged when the euro area was formed.

Even though most policy reform actions occur at the member-state level, there are certainly "spillover" effects in one country from economic outcomes in other countries. For the most part, these spillovers are positive. For example, the German economy has been an important engine of growth throughout Europe. If there is successful reform in Germany and that economy achieves rapid economic growth going forward, this will make it much easier for Europe as a whole to grow rapidly. Negative spillovers could occur if some, particularly larger, European economies lag behind the reform process. Investment will flow within Europe to the most dynamic areas and people will also become increasingly mobile. Cultural differences and language barriers continue to exist in Europe, dampening internal cross-border migration, but for the skilled, multilingual segment of (particularly young) Europeans, these matters are less of an impediment to mobility. Hence, some countries or regions could become chronically depressed areas if they become unattractive locations for jobs and investment.

In short, while there are common problems among many of the European economies, the onus is on individual member-state governments to actually carry out the most important reform steps. The EU institutions, like the ECB and the EU competition authority, can only support the reform efforts.

That immediately raises the question of how the individual member countries are doing so far? Many of the answers to that question have been given throughout this book, but it is worthwhile to summarize overall progress in the four largest economies—Britain, France, Germany, and (very briefly) Italy.

A Summary of Reforms to Date in the Four Largest Economies

Britain

Policymakers seem well aware that the central problem in Britain is low productivity. Current Chancellor of the Exchequer Gordon Brown, in particular, together with the Ministry of Trade and Industry, has made productivity improvement a major feature of his economic agenda. Some of the positive steps that have been taken in this area include:

- Policy initiatives have been adopted to address regulatory barriers to productivity change. The Office of Fair Trading (OFT) has been given an aggressive mandate not only to address standard anticompetitive behavior but also to identify regulatory barriers that diminish competition.

- Britain has remained very open to foreign direct investment from around the world, bringing in capital, technology, and managerial capability.

- Brown recently suggested granting visas to managerial and professional talent to come to Britain—in order to overcome what is seen as a shortage of managerial skills.[9]

- The privatization program started under Thatcher has been sustained, and many industries have gradually become more competitive as new entrants have challenged the former government monopolies. (A recent study shows very large productivity gains from privatization.)[10]

---

9. David Turner and Della Bradshaw, "Doors Thrown Open to Overseas Managers," *Financial Times*, March 18, 2004.

10. Ed Crooks column, "Privatized Industries Show the Way for Reform," *Financial Times*, March 23, 2004.

- The labor market in Britain is much more flexible and less regulated than the labor market in continental Europe. There is an understanding among policymakers that flexibility and worker mobility are essential to a productive economy.

- Efforts to link universities and technology companies have shown some success, notably in the Cambridge area.

A comparison of these positives against the policy framework laid out in chapter 1 and the analysis of Britain in chapter 4 suggests that additional steps should be taken to improve productivity and competitive intensity.

- Land use policies and the regulations to protect historical buildings create a major obstacle to investment and economic growth in Britain. Political resistance to change has prevented the development of a more rational land use policy that would combine economic development while preserving the best of historical and rural Britain.

- Despite much talk about loosening regulations that limit competition and the mandate given to the OFT, the reality is that deregulation has been limited in scope. The OFT needs the resources to conduct a serious analysis of regulatory barriers to productivity increase and the government then needs to act on these conclusions.

- The high prices of manufactured goods and the continued existence of low-productivity manufacturing establishments indicate that British manufacturing is not fully open to global competition. Formal and informal trade barriers should be eliminated as far as possible under EU tariff rules.

- Part of the productivity gap in Britain has been attributed to lower usage of IT. The Organization for Economic Cooperation and Development (OECD) has documented the relatively high prices of IT hardware in the European Union generally, including in Britain.[11] Policymakers should aggressively seek out the reasons for the relatively high IT prices and deal with them. The problem may lie in the retail distribution channel or with manufacturers taking advantage of small market differences to set prices at a higher level in Britain.

---

11. As a check on this result, we conducted an Internet search of PC prices in the United States and Britain and found that comparable PCs were 25 to 100 percent more expensive in Britain at the prevailing exchange rate. Research assistant Gunilla Pettersson conducted the search. The value-added tax has been removed from the figures given above. Given the rather high rate of value-added tax relative to sales tax rates in the United States, price differences will actually be even greater. The price differentials may be smaller for corporate buyers, but it is absurd that an economy that is trying to raise productivity and increase IT use should allow such high computer prices to persist.

In terms of social and labor-market policies, the welfare state is not very generous in Britain, and its National Health Service is a bare-bones operation. Work incentives are strong enough in Britain that, once the macroeconomic situation improved in the 1990s, employment increased and unemployment fell to moderate levels. Creating jobs is an area of comparative success in Britain in recent years. The Working Tax Credit[12] was introduced to provide additional work incentives for low-wage workers and to provide them with higher net income. Assuming that Britain will continue to grow and improve productivity, it should evaluate how to improve its social services without undermining work incentives.

- There are policies proposed or enacted to improve educational quality in Britain, and we support the goals of these policy initiatives. (This book has not looked specifically at educational policies, so we will not comment on whether these initiatives are the right ones.) The lack of workforce skills should not be overstated or blamed solely for low productivity in order to avoid taking the needed steps to improve product-market competition. The industry case studies for Britain suggest there are many ways in which productivity can be increased with the existing workforce.

- Basic levels of income support are relatively low in Britain. Provided the economy grows, it may be possible to provide a stronger safety net for the poor or unemployed. If so, then wage insurance, or an expansion of the Working Tax Credit, should be implemented rather than increasing support for those who choose not to work.

- Historically, Britain has underinvested in social services. In health care underinvestment was a method of rationing treatment and overall cost control, but this approach introduced inefficiencies in treatment protocols.[13] It will be important to keep health costs under control in the future, especially given the demographic trends. However, cost-effective investment in technology and equipment can actually be cost saving as well as beneficial to patients.

France

France faces low employment, short work hours, and chronically high unemployment. Thus, improved incentives for job creation and acceptance

---

12. In April 2003, the Working Families Tax Credit program was replaced by the Working Tax Credit program, which was qualitatively similar but extended benefits to people without children.

13. For example, because advanced screening equipment and medical techniques were only slowly introduced, Britain's doctors were unable to determine which patients could be helped by different treatment protocols. Doctors used conventional surgery, which is more expensive and dangerous, rather than laparoscopic surgery to treat colon cancer patients.

are very high priorities. Productivity issues are also important, and in some cases the policies that would help productivity would also help job creation. But first a review of the positive steps France has undertaken in the labor market and its social programs.

- Payroll taxes were reduced for low-wage workers in 1993, and this plan was expanded throughout the decade. As noted earlier in this book, France experienced substantial employment growth in the late 1990s, part of which was attributable to the payroll tax policy.

- Public-sector pensions are very generous in France. The pensions previously allowed individuals to retire with virtually full pay after 37.5 years of service. The French government changed this benefit by extending the years of service to 40 years, which is in line with the pensions available to private-sector workers.

- In 2003, France implemented changes to its unemployment benefit system as part of agreed upon reforms by employers and unions (three of the five national ones) to the UNEDIC (Union Nationale pour l'Emploi dans l'Industrie et le Commerce) unemployment insurance (UI) program. The reforms drastically cut entitlement periods by up to two-thirds, from 15 or 21 months to 7 months (or to 23 months from 30 months).[14] Similarly, in January 2004 the French government cut the entitlement period for the "specific solidarity allowance" (*allocation de solidarité spécifique* [ASS]), which is available to people who have exhausted their unemployment benefits.[15] In addition the French government is acting in cooperation with other actors in the labor market to prevent people from moving among the different social programs and to actively seek a comprehensive overhaul of the incentives presented by the French social security system.

While these 2003 reforms were a step in the right direction, the government unfortunately backtracked in 2004, following local election defeats. The UI reform was annulled and benefits restored to 256,000 workers who had lost eligibility in January 2004. Much of the positive momentum gained in 2003 has now been lost again.

In addition to the dangers of losing progress previously achieved, some major problems in the labor market, which are not being adequately addressed, are offsetting these positive steps:

---

14. See EIRO (2003b).

15. Previously, the ASS benefit, which operates on a sliding scale based on income, could be extended indefinitely every six months, provided that the recipient was actively seeking employment. As of 2004, the entitlement period will become limited to two years (three years for existing recipients). See EIRO (2003f).

- Public-sector spending in France is well over 50 percent of GDP, which means that the overall tax burden is very high. Payroll taxes are very high on average, and the tax wedge is around 50 percent. There is a very large gap between the employer cost per worker and the amount the employee receives. It is likely that this level of taxation has had a negative impact on employment. As the demographics change, it will be hard to avoid increasing this tax wedge even more, creating the danger of pushing more and more people out of the workforce.

- Even though there were changes in unemployment benefit provisions, there are no effective (Danish-style) programs to "encourage" workers to retrain, relocate, or create a plan of action to obtain new employment. The PAP/PARE program instituted in 2001 does not include credible sanctions needed to induce job seekers to obtain new skills and is consequently unlikely to achieve its goals of improving employment and workforce job skills.[16] There is also no wage insurance program or financial incentive for those who take a new job at a lower wage.

- Pension provisions are generally very generous and will generate a huge burden on the working population in the years ahead. Reforms enacted in 2003 are not sufficient to ensure the future financial health of the French PAYGO pension system.[17] French leadership needs to clearly explain to its citizens the future economic situation and the need for change. Restraint in the growth of pension benefit levels[18] is reasonable, together with an increase in the retirement age. The decline in the average retirement age has stopped, but it has not reversed and moved upward.

- Despite increasing the required contribution period for all workers to 40 years, this pension system still provides many opportunities for

16. Started in July 2001, the Return-to-Work Plan (*Plan d'Aide au Retour à l'Emploi*, or PARE) applies to all newly unemployed persons. It includes an in-depth interview for assessing the job seeker's employability, which results in the creation of the Personal Action Plan (PAP). The PAP outlines the set of actions the job seeker must take to successfully find a job. After a six-month period, if the individual has not found a suitable job (defined as corresponding to the skills and professional capabilities of the job seeker), the PAP is updated. Unfortunately, this process is wholly voluntary, and no sanctions are imposed against job seekers without a PAP (Bertelsmann Foundation 2001).

17. The French government and the OECD (2003b) estimate that the proposed reform will cover only about one-third of the expected private-sector pension shortfall by 2020—assuming a halving of the unemployment rate to 4.5 percent in 2020. Similarly, public-pension estimates assume—incorrectly—that state-owned utilities are included in the pension reform, and even then the estimates conclude that only half of the expected shortfall in pensions will be covered.

18. Much has been made of the "equalizing effect" between public and private pension plans in France from the 2003 reform. However, while progress has been made, significant inequalities persist between public and private employees.

French workers to leave the workforce at a very young age. As part of the 2003 pension reforms, it was specifically stipulated that "people with long working lives" should be able to retire at the age of 56, provided that they had paid contributions for fully 42 years. While this is viewed as "required social justice," the direction of the plan is wrong. In principle, government programs in countries such as France—with very low employment—should not encourage people to leave the workforce at an early age. Instead, governments should encourage people to remain in the workforce as long as possible. The national French Old-Age Fund for Wage Earners (CNAVTS) estimates that up to 460,000 (out of 500,000 potential eligibles) will apply for such early retirement before the end of 2008 and add more than €11 billion to the pension burden (EIRO 2003c). In addition, workers in publicly owned utilities (EdF [power], GdF [gas], SNCF [railways], and RATP [Paris metro/buses]) are not included in the reform and, consequently, can retire earlier than after 40 years of work (and contributions).

- The government introduced and partially subsidized a 35-hour workweek as the standard, based on the erroneous belief that it would create work sharing and increase employment. In fact, there is no credible evidence to support the view that overall employment has increased as a result of the mandatory shortened workweek. France needs policies to increase the number of hours of work available, not policies to discourage people from working. However, it must be acknowledged that when the shorter workweek was introduced, provisions providing employers greater flexibility over work assignments and scheduling also accompanied it. Although this flexibility was a substantial positive for the French labor market, it was an expensive trade-off.

- Generally, despite the greater flexibility introduced with the 35-hour week, the French labor market remains very rigid both in terms of its wage structure and its difficult hiring and firing processes. Labor protection has become a straitjacket that essentially restricts employment. For example, the burdensome legal structure in France affects the hotel industry: low- and medium-price French hotels minimize the number of employees by eliminating many services available in comparable hotels elsewhere, such as staff to check a guest into the hotel (instead guests use a credit card to enter their rooms). We strongly support enacting the proposed (Virville Report) "assignment and project contracts" (*contrat de mission/projet*), which would enable companies to hire workers only for the duration of a particular project (EIRO 2004b). Such contracts could provide one avenue for alleviating the constraints of job creation in France. Similarly, we support moves under way to change the hierarchical relationships between collective agreements entered at the national, regional, and local levels. Introducing greater opportunities for company-level agreements to deviate from sector-level accords will enhance flexibility and companies' abilities to adjust.

■ France uses the courts and the legal system to regulate the labor market, much more so than in other countries. Verdicts favor employees 75 percent of the time. Labor law reform is needed to give employers greater ability to restructure their operations.

■ France has a high-quality healthcare system. But, France's public health insurance fund, which pays for the vast majority of French health expenditure (with small participation by private insurance funds) has a rapidly rising deficit. Funding of the system is through a combination of contributions from employers (12.80 percent of wages) and employees (0.75 percent of wages), together with a number of different taxes (European Commission MISSOC Database, accessed May 27, 2004).

Recognizing the unsustainable path of healthcare finances, the French government in the spring of 2004 presented proposals to reform its healthcare system. A small additional fee of €1 is to be paid by all but the poorest upon seeing a doctor, and specialist treatment without referral penalized by lower reimbursements.[19] While these attempts to raise new revenue and lower costs are welcome, the proposed reforms fail to introduce required financial incentives for both patients and providers to lower overall costs.

France has also made positive, productivity-oriented, product-market reforms:

■ France has privatized—or mostly privatized—companies such as Air France and Renault. Such actions have increased productivity and made the companies more competitive.

■ The mobile telecommunications industry was structured in a way that created a very productive industry (as described in chapter 3).

■ More broadly, many efficient and productive private French companies compete strongly with global best-practice companies. For example, Carrefour has been more successful in Brazil and China than Wal-Mart.[20]

---

19. See *The Economist*, May 13, 2004, "The Price of Popping Pills," and Agence France-Presse (AFP), May 18, 2004, "France Unveils Plan to Stem Health Spending, Unions Cry Foul."

20. The reasons for Carrefour's greater success are clear. Carrefour entered Brazil's and China's markets earlier than Wal-Mart and was free to choose better store locations. Car-

- The French government has initiated a program to reduce the amount of bureaucratic red tape faced by companies interested in entering the market. The government has also promoted the creation of new firms and their subsequent access to capital.[21]

However, these positive product-market reforms must not overlook some remaining problems. The French government retains control over all major network industries, since this area has not been included in the privatization of state-owned assets since the 1990s. In fact, France maintains a 100 percent government ownership of the former government-run monopolies in electric power (Electricité de France, with a national market share of 95 percent in 2002) and gas (Gaz de France, with a national market share of 90 percent in 2002). Following the European Commission's liberalization directives the electric power and gas markets (for all nonhousehold consumers) will be opened up in the European Union in 2004.[22] In response, France created an official sectoral electricity regulator (*Commission de Régulation de l'Energie*, or CRE). While sectoral regulators offer the possibility of rigorously enforcing competition policy, the reality is that France only opened up its energy markets with the minimum threshold of its commitments to its EU partners. By some measures France has the most closed markets in the European Union and some of the most expensive network access charges for independent producers (figure 7.1). Large government investments in nuclear power have traditionally provided France with plentiful and relatively cheap power, albeit not on commercially viable conditions.

In the gas market there are signs that competition is working for industrial users, where prices since liberalization in 2000 have been below the EU average. The opposite is true in the unliberalized (2007) household market (due to open in 2007).

The French government also remains a majority shareholder (63 percent) in the former telecommunications monopoly, France Telecom, which

---

refour has also been more adept at dealing with the complex, and sometimes corrupt, local bureaucracies in these countries. Wal-Mart made mistakes when it entered Brazil, setting up store layouts that were unfamiliar to Brazilians and stocking shelves with items that were not in demand. Wal-Mart has, in contrast, done very well in Mexico.

21. Measures to reduce red tape include, but are not limited to, proposals to: limit the 956 forms that companies may have to complete; introduce a single-counter interface between companies and social security agencies; reduce the costs of hiring part-time and temporary workers (*Cheque emploi associatif*); delay required social security contributions for new firms; and reduce taxes and administrative procedures associated with ownership transfers (OECD 2003b, 58–62).

22. Some encouraging signs that competition is gradually entering the French power sector exist: EdF has lost up to 17 percent of its eligible customer business to new suppliers in areas already liberalized (consumers using more than 7GWh/year). See Prospex Research French Power Market Report 2003, www.prospex.co.uk (accessed January 13, 2004).

Figure 7.1 Degree of competition in the EU's electricity markets, February 2003

percent of open market

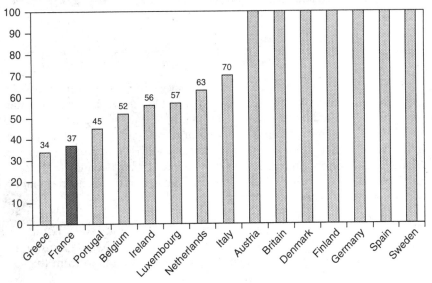

Source: European Commission (2003e).

retains an 80–90 percent market share in the fixed-line business. However, competition is increasing, with 28 operators sharing the total markets in local, long distance, and international calls in 2000. Competition has caused large price declines for businesses (22 percent from 1996–99), while consumers have enjoyed only a 6 percent decrease in the same period. Obviously, the high price of fixed-line telephony maintained by France Telecom is one reason for the low French use of the Internet.

We noted above that productivity is outstanding in mobile telecommunications in France, suggesting that if other network sectors were liberalized, substantial gains in productivity would occur and significant price declines could occur. However, workers and managers of the entrenched monopolies are resisting further privatization because of fears of job loss. Thus, further privatization and liberalization will be a considerable challenge.

■ Land use restrictions are very rigid in France and limit employment creation. The French retailing sector illustrates how land use restrictions have affected the evolution of a sector and limited employment opportunities. High minimum wages have also limited employment in the retail sector, despite reductions in payroll taxes (see chapter 3).

- The case study evidence for France suggests that barriers to productivity still exist in several industries. France, like Britain, needs a domestic competition agency with the mandate to identify regulations and other barriers to competition—including the barriers that keep manufacturing prices high.

Germany

As in France, raising employment is Germany's biggest priority, followed by improving productivity growth. By mid-December 2003 the German government signed its Agenda 2010 into law, and it is being implemented in 2004. The agenda is not a panacea and will not produce strong job growth (or higher productivity) in Germany without additional reforms. Nonetheless, it contains a number of sensible reforms similar to those in the Netherlands, Sweden, and Denmark. The agenda is focused on labor-market and social policy reform.

- The duration of unemployment benefits will be reduced to 12 months (up to 18 months if the unemployed is older than 55), depending on the age of the recipient, which is a significant reduction from the current range of 14–32 months.[23]

- The contribution-financed UI benefits will be renamed "unemployment benefit I" (*Arbeitslosengeld* I), while the former government-financed unemployment assistance (previously available after a means test was administered to those ineligible for unemployment benefits) will be merged with the government social assistance plan into a fixed-rate "unemployment benefit II" in 2005. All recipients of unemployment benefit II will be required to accept legal job offers, regardless of pay—even if the wage on the job is not based on collectively agreed rates.[24] Recipients who refuse a job offer will have their benefits cut by 30 percent, or stopped completely for three months if they are below the age of 25. People considered not fit to work will receive social benefits (*Sozialgeld*) at a rate similar to unemployment benefit II.

  In addition a modest wage insurance program was instituted to help older workers become reemployed. Thus far very few people have taken advantage of the program, but it represents a hopeful beginning to what could become an important program.

---

23. See German government (2004) and European Commission MISSOC Database, www.europa.eu/int/comm/employment_social/missoc/2003/missoc_238_en.htm (accessed May 29, 2004).

24. This decision to ignore collective-bargain agreements in the hiring decision—if locally demanded—sets a welcome precedent and should be introduced for much wider implementation across the German labor market. See description of "opening clauses" later in this section.

- German wage taxes will also be cut in 2004, which should increase labor supply. Low-income groups (earning less than €20,000 per year) will see a noteworthy decline of 10–40 percent in wage taxes, which will generate significantly larger incentives to create and accept employment.[25]

- Small employers are exempt from some of the rules that make German labor markets so rigid. The size of companies whose new hires are exempt from these rigid rules was increased from 5 employees to 10 employees.

- In October 2003 the German government announced that pension benefits for 2004 would be frozen in euros, eliminating the upward indexing that would otherwise have occurred.[26] Simultaneously, pensioners had to pay the full amount of contributions into an old-age care plan, part of which had hitherto been paid by the government. As such, German pensions were de facto cut.

- The government introduced the idea of a "sustainability factor" (*Nachhaltighkeitsfaktor*) in the pension system. If implemented, this would ensure that the total pension payout would be held equal to or below a contribution level of 20 percent of wages in 2020 (the current figure is 19.5 percent). It could rise to 22 percent of wages by 2030. Implementation would require either cuts in pensions, relative to the historical trend rate of growth, or an increase in the retirement age. It would, however, ensure the sustainability of the German pension system—albeit at very high rates of contribution. At present, however, this is only a rather vague proposal, and it is doubtful if appealing to an abstract idea like the "sustainability factor" will be sufficient to carry through such a politically difficult measure.

Reforms of the German health system have been very gradual, despite the fact that the high contribution rates (2003 average rates of 14.30 percent of wages, split evenly between employers and employees) add much to excessive German labor costs, and contributed to a combined €3 billion cash shortfall for sickness insurance funds (*Krankenversicherung*) in 2002. As part of Agenda 2010, beginning in January 2004, a quarterly €10 fee for visits to general practitioners and dentists will be charged. Of potentially more far-reaching cost containment consequences is the new Act on

---

25. Data for the *Entlastung der Lohnteuer/Solidaritatszuschlag* in 2004 from the German government, www.bundesregierung.de/Anlage578309/Steuertabelle.pdf (accessed December 19, 2003). According to the tax tables only low-income single parents with one child (*Alleinerziehende mit 1 Kind*) will not see major tax rebates in 2004.

26. This move was not part of Agenda 2010. It was caused by an acute cash shortage faced by the German government PAYGO pension system, since the government was not willing to let pension contributions increase to more than 19.5 percent of wages.

Diagnosis-Related Flat Rates (*Fallpauschalengesetz*) that stipulates that from January 2004, sickness insurance funds will pay hospitals according to a diagnosis-related flat rate, rather than simply the hospital charges so far in use. As patients retain their free choice of hospitals, this may lower costs substantially. However, it does not necessarily eliminate the potential financial incentive for German hospitals to keep patients hospitalized longer than strictly medically required. While these reforms are welcome, it is too early to properly gauge their effect on reining in German healthcare costs.

Even though these reforms are modest, sensible, and helpful, they have proven very unpopular. The political position of Chancellor Schröder has weakened significantly as has the position of his party, the SDP. Therefore, it is very unlikely that he will propose further reforms any time soon. The prospects for additional reform over the longer run are not quite so bleak, however, because both major political parties recognize that further changes will be needed.

- It is disappointing to note that increases in collective bargaining flexibility at the local level were postponed.[27] However, it is encouraging to note the increased use of company-level collective agreements,[28] as well as the wider use and more inclusive nature of so-called "opening clauses" in industry-level agreements.[29] Both instruments are facilitat-

---

27. It is our understanding that the possibility of government-regulated liberalization of collective bargaining remains possible, should Germany's traditional self-regulating social partners fail to agree upon increased flexibility within the next 12 months.

28. In September 2003 the German Institute for Labor Market and Employment Research (*Institut für Arbeitsmarkt- und Berufsforschung*, or IAB) published new figures that showed that only 61 percent of West German workers (and 35 percent of East German workers) were now covered by industrywide collective agreements. However, as many companies without an industry-level agreement "orient" themselves to the industry-level agreement, the true importance of these agreements is somewhat higher than indicated by these percentages. Seven percent of West German employees and 15 percent of East German workers were covered by company-level collective-bargain agreements. See EIRO (2004), Coverage of Collective Agreements and Works Councils Assessed, www.eiro.eurofound.eu.int/2004/01/feature/de0401106f.html (accessed December 18, 2003).

29. The use of "opening clauses" (*Öffnungsklauseln*) in industry-level collective bargaining inserts an instrument of differentiation and flexibility into the otherwise rigid German collective-bargaining system. The opening clauses come in numerous varieties, but at least three main categories should be mentioned for illustrative purposes: 1) Opening clauses on pay are defined as agreements between social partners that generally allow divergence from the collectively agreed payments, in case of dire economic circumstance. The most well-known example is the "general clause" in the German metalworking industry, which explicitly allows local bargaining parties to agree on other standards in order to avoid bankruptcy. 2) Opening clauses on working time are possibly the most widespread type and generally increase companies' flexibility with respect to flexible working hours. 3) Opening clauses for particular groups of employees or companies are a residual category that en-

ing much-needed flexibility in the German labor market (for example, the agreement obtained by Siemens in June 2004 to raise working hours). A legislative initiative making such company-level agreements and opening clauses the standard, rather than the exception to the norm, would be beneficial to German employment.

■ Rather than being abolished—or at least moved up to a much higher company employee threshold—Germany's strict job protection rules were preserved for companies with more than 10 employees.[30]

■ Foreseen with the introduction of the so-called Hartz Laws[31] the reductions in both employers' and employees' social security contributions are a move in the right direction, but seem too small to have much impact on German unemployment (Ich AG and "mini-" and "midi-jobs" will not lead to substantial drops in German unemployment[32]).

As in France, despite changes in unemployment benefit provisions, there are not *effective* (Danish-style) programs to encourage workers to retrain, relocate, or create a plan of action to obtain new employment. The so-called Job-AQTIV Act of 2002 was intended to mobilize the unemployed by offering improved job counseling in return for a more active job search by the unemployed. This will not have much effect, however, unless sanctions are imposed on those unwilling to truly participate in the program.

The new wage insurance program and other financial incentives for the unemployed to take a new job at a lower wage are limited to those over 55 years of age and are not being publicized or promoted. Workers who accept wage insurance have to give up the opportunity to collect alternative and more attractive benefits. The apprenticeship model historically

---

compasses opening clauses valid for specific groups of companies or employees, below the industry level of opening clauses. Examples include only small companies (15 employees or fewer) or specific employees—say, newly hired employees in the West German chemicals industry. See EIRO (1997).

30. Increasing the threshold to 10 employees is simply a reversal of earlier actions by the Schröder government in 1998, when—as one of its first measures—it overturned an earlier attempt to raise the threshold (also to 10 employees) by the previous center-right CDU/ FDP government. See EIRO (2003e).

31. The Hartz Laws were named after Peter Hartz, the chairman of the Hartz Commission. The Hartz Commission published a government-sanctioned report on German labor-market reforms in late 2002.

32. "Ich AG" refers to the unemployed, but hoping to become self-employed, who through the Federal Employment Agency can receive up to a €1,200 subsidy. Mini-jobs refer to small-scale employment paying less than €4,800 a year, which is exempt from income taxation and has only fixed-rate social security contributions attached. Midi-jobs refer to employment paying between €4,800 and €9,600 a year, on which employer social security contributions increase incrementally up to the full rate (German government 2004).

has provided Germany with a highly skilled workforce and has served as a substitute for other active labor-market policies. But it does not function as well in today's rapidly changing global economy. In fact, many of the unemployed have been through apprenticeship programs.

- Public-sector spending in Germany is as high as in France, exacerbated by continuing transfers to East Germany, which means that the overall tax burden is very high. The comments above regarding French public spending—including the need for fundamental pension reform— apply equally to Germany. The continuing east-west split in Germany is a separate issue. West Germany has generously provided sustained support to the east. However, the price of that generosity was applying union-set wages in both the west and the east. Combined with generous social-support payments, this has resulted in chronically high unemployment in the east and created an excessive tax burden on the west. It is impossible to replay history, but the situation in the economic east gives increased urgency to reforms of unemployment insurance, pensions, and the wage-setting process.

Turning to product markets, we look first at the privatization of the utility sector. Since the early 1990s, Germany has privatized a significant number of network industries, and thus competition policy has been brought to the forefront, as authorities have struggled to avoid merely privatizing former government monopolies. In particular, the telecommunications, electric power, and gas sectors have experienced dramatic changes.

- In telecommunications, the former government monopoly Deutsche Telekom (DT) was partly privatized in the mid-1990s, and the sector liberalized in accordance with EU directives. As a result, prices for various telecommunications services have declined drastically. However, local phone calls are an important exception since local service is not subject to competition and thus prices have been flat since 1997. Moreover, even though prices have fallen for many services, average German telecommunication prices are still among the highest in the European Union.[33] As we noted earlier, there is less competition and lower productivity in mobile phone service in Germany than in France. Therefore, significant competitive improvements can still be achieved in the German telecommunication sector.

---

33. The Eurostat Structural Indicators lists Germany as the EU country (together with Italy) with the highest price level for a 10-minute national call in 2003 and the fifth highest rate for local calls in the European Union. In contrast, Germany has the third lowest rate for international calls. Data from Eurostat Structural Indicators (Eurostat 2004b).

Figure 7.2   Household electricity prices in the European Union
(euro per kilowatt hours)

electricity price,
Germany = 100

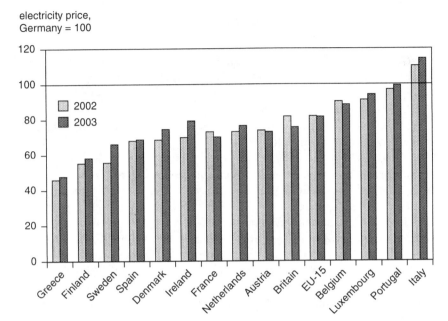

Source: Eurostat (2004b).

■ In principle, the electricity sector in Germany should be completely liberalized and subject to competition, as a result of German law passed in 1998. In practice, this sector is dominated by vertically integrated, regional conglomerates that control the majority of both generation and distribution assets. The detailed regulation of the sector has been laid down in two "Associations' Agreements," approved after the Federal Cartel Office enacted demanded changes. The privatization has been helpful. We saw earlier that productivity had improved even in anticipation of privatization, and the sector has seen price declines since 1998 of approximately 15 percent for industrial producers (although none for consumers).[34] As with telecommunications, however, Germany has persistently high relative power prices (figure 7.2), which indicates that significant competition advances can also be made in this sector. Furthermore, there are still significant problems with third-party access to the distribution networks, and Germany has

---

34. Data from Eurostat Structural Indicators (Eurostat 2004b).

by far the highest network access charges in the European Union.[35] The fact that Germany will create an energy sector regulator (covering both power and gas) in 2004—after six years of sector self-regulation—indicates that the German government may be forced to confront the competitive problems in the sector.

■ Germany's gas sector is very similar to its electricity sector, dominated by a few large firms that control the distribution network. Since 2000, the industry has also been regulated by an Associations' Agreement, which regulates third-party access and transmission charges to the distribution network. Significant problems still remain in this area and limit the effect of competition.

Looking at other aspects of product markets, relatively little has been done to increase flexibility and competitive intensity or really open up the economy for new job creation. The basic problem, as we noted earlier, is that Germany's economic system is designed to preserve existing companies and jobs, and not adept at allowing establishments to fail or flexible enough to create a more dynamic platform for future growth. The current economic system worked well for many years, but is struggling today as economic conditions change. The German economy is still heavily based in manufacturing—a sector where employment has been declining for years among developed economies.

The interlocking network of manufacturing companies, suppliers, unions, regional and local government, and banks remains largely intact and is protected from full competition by formal and informal barriers. Making use of highly skilled workers and strong technologies,[36] many companies in the manufacturing sector have remained strong exporters—providing unique and high-quality products to global markets. In the face of increased competition within the European Union and globally, and as a result of disruptive new technologies, it will be hard—maybe impossible—to maintain employment and investment in this sector.

■ To repeat a familiar theme, Germany's land use restrictions are inhibiting the expansion of the service sector and the creation of new service-sector employment.

---

35. This problem is aggravated by the fact that most local grids are owned by small municipalities and regional governments, which have a financial interest in maintaining monopolies since they have generated rents to them as the industry has consolidated. See European Commission (2003e, 13, graph 1).

36. Incremental technological innovation in Germany remains strong in traditional areas of manufacturing. Innovation in start-ups and brand new technologies is weaker.

- The banking system suffers from having too many small banks that are protected by regulation or owned by local governments. Germany needs financial-sector reform to provide it with a more modern financial sector to direct the country's savings toward new opportunities and away from state-guaranteed loans automatically provided to traditional borrowers.

- Germany—like Britain and France—needs a strong national competition authority with a mandate to tackle not just the anticompetitive behavior of companies but also anticompetitive regulations—such as the water purity law used to protect local breweries.

Italy

This book has not emphasized policies and economic performance in Italy to the same extent as Britain, France, and Germany, therefore this section will be brief. Another reason for the section's brevity is that Italy has not embarked on any significant reforms. Innumerable reforms have been proposed in Italy in recent years for social institutions as well as labor and product markets, but Prime Minister Silvio Berlusconi—despite his professed market orientation—has not been willing to tackle the unpopular issues of opening the labor market and dealing with social insurance issues. That is particularly unfortunate because with a debt to GDP ratio of over 100 percent, high payroll taxes, and the prospect of one worker per retiree by 2030, Italy faces severe challenges. The country must be applauded, however, for recent reductions in total payroll taxes, which have declined since 1996 from over 50 percent to "only" 45 percent for the average worker.[37]

An important issue for Italy is that it is de facto divided into two parts. Northern Italy is prosperous and has a (mostly) dynamic private sector, with many successful and relatively flexible small- and medium-sized enterprises, and moderate unemployment. Some flagship companies, such as Fiat, face difficult futures, but, overall, the region has great strengths. However, southern Italy is very different. Employment is low, and unemployment is high. Organized crime remains a serious problem as well, that is as much a consequence of poor economic performance as it is a barrier to future progress. A major feature of Italy's reform should be to change the structure of social insurance, income transfers to the south, labor laws and institutions, and pensions in a way that increases employment in the southern half of the country.

---

37. Defined as single, without dependents, and earning the average industrial wage (OECD 2004b).

A Big Push or a Slow and Incremental Approach to Reform?

Some of the social and competition policy issues highlighted above cry out to be part a reform package, rather than separate policies to be enacted individually. For example, no European government will be able to create a sustainable national pension system if it does not raise its employment level to near the Lisbon goals. This point is made by the recent *Joint Report by the Commission and the Council on Adequate and Sustainable Pensions* (European Commission and ECOFIN 2003), in which the Netherlands, Sweden, and Denmark—countries whose labor-market reforms we have examined in chapter 5—get "passing grades" in terms of the sustainability of their pension reforms.[38]

Restructuring industries to make them more productive must be accompanied by increased incentives for workers to take new jobs and a better environment for job creation. Otherwise, restructuring will lead to higher unemployment rather than lower unemployment. On the economic side, the case for a comprehensive program of reform is, therefore, pretty strong.

On the political side, there is an obvious risk that the sheer scale of the required economic reforms could cause unrelated national special-interest groups to form a "status quo–preserving coalition" against governments trying to implement simultaneous reforms to such systems as pension, the labor market, and social welfare. Counterbalancing this, perhaps, is the idea that if reform is comprehensive it reinforces in people's minds that the status quo cannot be maintained and a range of interest groups will have to make sacrifices in the short run in order to improve the situation for everyone in the long run. Change is sometimes said to be easier if "everyone's ox is being gored."

Election cycles and particular issues in individual European countries will determine the approach any given national government must take to successfully steer economic reforms through their legislative process. Some political systems with numerous stakeholders, decision-making bodies, and frequent elections—such as the German federal system—will favor big reform packages, where multiple issues can be traded against each other to satisfy all the different political actors involved. Other political systems with "a less constrained majority executive"—like Britain or

---

38. The report states, "The Dutch pension system performs well in terms of adequacy" (European Commission and ECOFIN 2003, 152) while "the reformed Swedish pension system should be able to deliver adequate pensions in a financially sustainable way" (European Commission and ECOFIN 2003, 169). The Danish pension system is also well structured: "In sum, the pension system seems to be financially sustainable in the long term under present policies with a fairly equitable sharing of the burden between generations" (European Commission and ECOFIN 2003, 116).

France when the president and the majority in parliament are from the same party—will facilitate reform less inhibited by outside actors.

If political considerations make a big-push reform effort impractical, then it may be possible to get a reform snowball rolling with incremental or local reforms. Specific firms or industries may break away from national rules, if their survival is threatened. Regions or localities may become easier on zoning rules if their economic base is eroding. Investors may move money overseas if local companies fail to restructure. Economic necessity can become the mother of invention in the area of reform.

Given the priorities listed above, Europe's main goal is to raise the employment level by finding jobs for the unemployed. This should occur naturally during 2004, since a worldwide cyclical recovery seems to be taking place (although the rising euro may limit the pace of expansion). This makes the present an ideal time for structural reforms to add reductions in structural unemployment to the reductions occurring in cyclical unemployment. It would be a tragedy if a cyclical recovery became an excuse to avoid further structural reforms.

The US economy has suffered a sharp drop in employment since 2000, but employment is now recovering strongly. We have acknowledged the many problems faced by the United States, but its economy is also a prime example of how a flexible labor market and a competitive product market benefit both employment and productivity. It is also important to remember that the Netherlands, Sweden, and Denmark show that "European-style" labor-market reforms also are effective in raising employment. Britain also has created a more flexible labor market, and generated solid employment growth and a relatively low rate of unemployment. In short, there are many examples from Europe (and around the world) to demonstrate that economic reform can succeed.

Conclusion: Progress Has Been Made, but Much More Is Needed

This chapter started with the question: Is the reform process on the right track? The overall answer is a qualified yes. Policymakers have said that work incentives must be increased to make work pay for individuals and make employment profitable for companies. There are now examples of countries within Europe that have instituted social policy reforms and been rewarded with rising employment. There are reform efforts under way in most of the major European economies—with Italy a notable exception.

On the product-market side, opening the single market has increased competitive intensity, and the pressure to privatize and open markets to competition is producing concrete results in higher productivity in some sectors. The fact that the mobile telecommunications industry started at a time when competition was being introduced has produced a very different outcome for that industry than would have occurred had it developed 20 years earlier.

Thus far, however, reforms have not been broad enough or widespread enough to really transform the European economy. The looming demographic crisis makes it imperative that such a transformation occur. Reform is on the right track but is not moving fast enough or far enough. Europe needs to transform into a new economy where change is the norm and is facilitated, not restrained, by policies and institutions. Social policies must move people into new jobs and not trap them in unemployment or early retirement. If Europe is to really embrace its future as a single market, there is no place for policies that prop up national champions or preserve state-linked behemoths that enjoy protection from competition.

If Europe really embraces transformative change, it has the potential to have it all. It can achieve rapid growth and full employment, while maintaining a high standard of living and avoiding severe poverty. To achieve success, Europeans will have to give up some deep-seated beliefs about what is expected of workers and managers. However, this seems a small price to pay if the alternative is to allow productivity to remain stagnant as special interests resist competition, or to see fewer people working to support larger cohorts of retirees.

References

Aaron, Henry J., and William B. Schwartz, eds. 2004. *Coping with Methusaleh: The Impact of Molecular Biology on Medicine and Society.* Washington: Brookings Institution.

Abraham, Katherine G., and John Haltiwanger. 1995. Real Wages and the Business Cycle. *Journal of Economic Literature* 33, no. 3 (September): 1215–64.

Addison, John T., and Paulino Teixeira. 2001. *The Economics of Employment Protection.* IZA Discussion Paper 381. Bonn: Forschunginstitut zor Zukunft der Arbeit GmBH.

Adema, W. 2001. *Net Social Expenditure* (2d ed). OECD Labor Market and Social Policy Occasional Papers 52. Paris: OECD.

Agell, Jonas, Peter Englund, and Jan Sodersten. 1996. Tax Reform of the Century—The Swedish Experiment. *National Tax Journal* 49, no. 4 (December): 643–64.

Agell, Jonas, Peter Englund, and Jan Sodersten. 1998. *Incentives and Redistribution in the Welfare State: The Swedish Tax Reform.* New York: St. Martin's Press.

Ahmad, Nadim. 2003. *Measuring Investment in Software.* OECD Science, Technology, and Industry Department Working Paper 6. Paris: OECD.

Akerlof, George A., William T. Dickens, and George L. Perry. 2000. Near Rational Wage and Price Setting and the Long Run Phillips Curve. *Brookings Papers on Economic Activity* (June): 1–44. Washington: Brookings Institution.

Aronsson, Thomas, and James Walker. 1997. The Effects of Sweden's Welfare State on Labor Supply Incentives. In *The Welfare State in Transition*, ed. Richard B. Freeman, Robert Topel, and Birgitta Swedenborg. Chicago: University of Chicago Press.

Ashenfelter, Orley, Colm Harmon, and Hessel Oosterbeek. 1999. *A Review of Estimates of the Schooling/Earnings Relationship, with Tests of Publication Bias.* CER Working Paper WP99/20. Dublin: Centre for Economic Research.

Atkinson, A. B. 1999. *The Economic Consequences of Rolling Back the Welfare State.* Munich Lectures in Economics. Cambridge, MA: MIT Press.

Autor, David H., and Mark G. Duggan. 2001. *The Rise in Disability Recipiency and the Decline in Unemployment.* NBER Working Paper 8336. Cambridge, MA: National Bureau of Economic Research.

Autor, David H., Lawrence F. Katz, and Alan B. Krueger. 1997. *Computing Inequality: Have Computers Changed the Labor Market?* NBER Working Paper 5956. Cambridge, MA: National Bureau of Economic Research.

Autor, David H., Frank Levy, and Richard J. Murnane. 2001. *The Skill Content Requirement of Recent Technological Change: An Empirical Exploration.* NBER Working Paper 8337. Cambridge, MA: National Bureau of Economic Research.

Baily, Martin N. 1978. Some Aspects of Optimal Unemployment Insurance. *Journal of Public Economics* 10: 379–402.

Baily, Martin N. 1987. Aging and the Ability to Work: Policy Issues and Recent Trends. In *Work, Health, and Income among the Elderly,* ed., G. Burtless. Washington: Brookings Institution.

Baily, Martin N. 2001. *Macroeconomic Implications of the New Economy.* Working Paper 01-9. Washington: Institute for International Economics.

Baily, Martin N., and A. Chakrabarti. 1988. *Innovation and Productivity Crisis.* Washington: Brookings Institution.

Baily, Martin N., and Alan M. Garber. 1997. Health Care Productivity. *Brookings Papers on Economic Activity: Microeconomics* (June): 143–202. Washington: Brookings Institution.

Baily, Martin Neil, and Gordon, Robert, J. 1988. The Productivity Slowdown, Measurement Issues and the Explosion of Computer Power. *Brookings Papers on Economic Activity* 2: 347–97. Washington: Brookings Institution.

Baily, Martin N., and R. M. Solow. 2001. International Productivity Comparisons Built from the Firm Level. *Journal of Economic Perspectives* 15, no. 3 (Summer): 151–72.

Baily, Martin N., and James Tobin. 1977. Macroeconomic Effects of Selective Public Employment and Wage Subsidies. *Brookings Papers on Economic Activity* 2: 511–44.

Baldassarri, Mario, and Francesco Busato. 2003. *Full Employment and High Growth in Europe.* England: Palgrave Macmillan Ltd.

Ball, Laurence, and Robert Moffitt. 2001. Productivity Growth and the Phillips Curve. Johns Hopkins University, Maryland. Photocopy (January).

Barker, Kate. 2003. Review of Housing Supply—Securing Our Future Housing Needs. Interim Report (December). London: UK Treasury.

Barro, Robert J. 1997. *Determinants of Economic Growth.* Cambridge, MA: MIT Press.

Bartel, Ann, Casey Ichniowski, and Kathryn Shaw. 2002. New Technology, Human Resource Practices and Skill Requirements: Evidence from Plant Visits in Three Industries. In *The Future of Work,* ed. Eileen Applebaum, Annette Bernhardt, and Richard Murnane. Washington: Russell Sage Foundation.

Bartelsman, Eric, Stefano Scarpetta, and Schivardi, Fabiano. 2003. *Comparative Analysis of Firm Demographics and Survival: Micro-level Evidence for the OECD Countries.* OECD Economics Department Working Paper 348. Paris: OECD.

Basu, Susanto, John G. Fernald, Nicholas Oulton, and Sylaja Srinivasan. 2003. *The Case of the Missing Productivity Growth: Or Does IT Explain Why Productivity Accelerated in the US but Not the UK?* NBER Working Paper 10010. Cambridge, MA: National Bureau of Economic Research.

Basu, Susanto, John G. Fernald, and Matthew D. Shapiro. 2000. Productivity Growth in the 1990s: Technology, Utilization, or Adjustment? Paper prepared for the *Carnegie-Rochester Conference Series on Public Policy,* November 7, Pittsburg, PA.

Baumol, William J. 1967. Macroeconomics of Unbalanced Growth: The Anatomy of Urban Crisis. *American Economic Review* 62: 415–26.

Baumol, William J. 2002. *The Free Market Innovation Machine: Analyzing the Growth Miracle of Capitalism.* Princeton, NJ: Princeton University Press.

Bayoumi, Tamim, Douglas Laxton, and Paolo Pesenti. 2003. When Leaner Isn't Meaner: Measuring Benefits and Spillovers of Greater Competition in Europe. Federal Reserve Bank of New York. Photocopy (April).

BEA (Bureau of Economic Analysis). 2003a. Chain price index for personal consumption expenditure, excluding food and energy. www.bea.gov/bea/dn/nipaweb/NIPATable Index.htm (accessed October 8, 2003).

BEA (Bureau of Economic Analysis). 2003b. GDP by Industry Data. www.bea.gov/bea/dn2/home/gdpbyindy.htm (accessed October, 2003).

BEA (Bureau of Economic Analysis). 2003c. NIPA Tables Data. www.bea.gov/bea/dn/ nipaweb/NIPATableIndex.htm (accessed October 9, 2003).

Bean, Charles, and Nicholas Crafts. 1996. British Economic Growth since 1945: Relative Economic Decline … and Renaissance? In *Economic Growth in Europe since 1945*, ed. Nicholas Crafts and Gianni Toniolo. Cambridge: Cambridge University Press.

Begg, David, Fabio Canova, Paul de Grauwe, Antonio Fatas, and Philip R. Lane. 2002a. *Surviving the Slowdown. Monitoring the European Central Bank 4.* London: Centre for Economic Policy Research.

Begg, David, Fabio Canova, Paul de Grauwe, Antonio Fatas, and Philip R. Lane. 2002b. Monitoring the European Central Bank Update (December). London: Centre for Economic Policy Research.

Berman, Eli, John Bound, and Zvi Griliches. 1994. Changes in the Demand for Skilled Labor within US Manufacturing: Evidence from the Annual Survey of Manufactures. *The Quarterly Journal of Economics* 109, no. 2: 367–97.

Bertelsmann Foundation. 2000. International Reform Monitor, issue 2. www.reformmonitor. org/downloads/brochure/refmon_2e.pdf (accessed March 28, 2004).

Bertelsmann Foundation. 2001. International Reform Monitor, issue 4 (April). www.reform monitor.org/downloads/brochure/refmon_4e.pdf (accessed March 28, 2004).

Blanchard, Olivier J. 1999. *European Unemployment: The Role of Shocks and Institutions.* Baffi Lecture, January. http://econ-www.mit.edu/faculty/download_pdf.php?id=804.

Blanchard, Olivier J. 2004. *The Economic Future of Europe.* May version. http://econ-www. mit.edu/faculty/download_pdf.php?id=856.

Blanchard, Olivier J., and A. Landier. 2000. *The Perverse Effects of Partial Labor Market Reform: Fixed Duration Contracts in France.* http://econ-www.mit.edu/faculty/download_pdf. php?id=819.

Blanchard, Olivier J., and Lawrence H. Summers. 1987. *Hysteresis and the European Unemployment Problem.* NBER Working Paper 1950. Cambridge, MA: National Bureau of Economic Research.

Blanchard, Olivier J., and Jean Tirole. 2003. Contours of Employment Protection Reform. English adaptation of a report written for the French Conseil d'Analyse Economique: Protection de l'emploi et procedures delicenciement. *La Documentation Francaise* 44. http://econ-www.mit.edu/faculty/download_pdf.php?id=831 (accessed January 13, 2004).

Blanchard, Olivier J., and J. Wolfers. 2000. *The Role of Shocks and Institutions in the Rise of European Unemployment: The Aggregate Evidence.* NBER Working Paper 7282. Cambridge, MA: National Bureau of Economic Research.

Blank, Rebecca M. 2002. US Welfare Reform: What's Relevant for Europe? University of Michigan and NBER, prepared for the CESifo Area Conference on Employment and Social Protection, June 14–15, Munich.

Blinder, Alan. 2000. *The Internet and the New Economy.* Brookings Institution Policy Brief 60 (June). Washington: Brookings Institution.

Blomquist, Soren, Matias Eklöf, and Whitney Newey. 2001. Tax Reform Evaluation Using Nonparametric Methods: Sweden 1980–1991. *Journal of Public Economics* 79, no. 3: 543–68.

BLS (Bureau of Labor Statistics). 2001. Data release, USDL 01-125, May 3. Washington: Bureau of Labor Statistics.

BLS (Bureau of Labor Statistics). 2002. International Comparisons of Labor Productivity and Unit Labor Costs in Manufacturing. Report 962. Washington: Bureau of Labor Statistics.

BLS (Bureau of Labor Statistics). 2003a. Foreign Labor Statistics. Washington: Bureau of Labor Statistics. http://data.bls.gov/labjava/outside.jsp?survey=in (accessed October 8, 2003).

BLS (Bureau of Labor Statistics). 2003b. Labor Force Statistics from the Current Population Survey. Washington: Bureau of Labor Statistics. ww.bls.gov/webapps/legacy/cpsatab9. htm (accessed October 8, 2003).

BLS (Bureau of Labor Statistics). 2003c. Major Sector Productivity and Costs Index. Washington: Bureau of Labor Statistics. http://data.bls.gov/labjava/outside.jsp?survey=pr (accessed October 8, 2003).

BLS (Bureau of Labor Statistics). 2003d. *Non-Farm Business Labor Productivity Growth.* Washington: Bureau of Labor Statistics.

BLS (Bureau of Labor Statistics). 2004. Employment from the BLS Household and Payroll Surveys: Summary of Recent Trends. Washington: Bureau of Labor Statistics. www.bls.gov/cps/ces_cps_trends.pdf (accessed June 2, 2004).

Blundell, Robert, and Paul Johnson. 1997. *Pensions and Retirement in the UK.* NBER Working Paper 6154. Cambridge, MA: National Bureau of Economic Research.

Blundell, Richard, Rachel Griffith, and John Van Reenen. 1999. Market Share, Market Value, and Innovation in a Panel of British Manufacturing Firms. *Review of Economic Studies* 66: 529–54.

Boeri, Tito. 2003. The Current Italian Pension Reform: Another Partial Solution? Presentation at Watson Wyatt Pension Policy seminar at Fondazione Rodolfo DeBenedetti, Milan (October 22).

Boldrin, Michele, Sergi Jimenez-Martini, and Franco Peracchi. 1997. *Social Security and Retirement in Spain.* NBER Working Paper 6136. Cambridge, MA: National Bureau of Economic Research.

Borghans, Lex, and Bas ter Weel. 2003. *Computers, Skills and Wages.* MERIT Working Paper (July). Maastricht, the Netherlands: Maastricht Economic Research Institute on Innovation and Technology.

Borghans, Lex, and Bas ter Weel. 2004. Are Computers Skills the New Basic Skills? The Returns to Computer, Writing and Math Skills in Britain. *Labour Economics* 11: 85–98. London: Elsevier.

Borsch-Supan, Axel, and Barbara Berkel. 2003. *Pension Reform in Germany: The Impact on Retirement Decision.* NBER Working Paper 9913. Cambridge, MA: National Bureau of Economic Research.

Bosworth, Barry, and George L. Perry. 1994. Productivity and Real Wages: Is There a Real Puzzle? *Brookings Papers on Economic Activity* 1: 317–36.

Botero, Juan, Simeon Djankov, Rafael La Porta, Florencio Lopez-de-Silanes, and Andrei Schleifer. 2003. *The Regulation of Labor.* NBER Working Paper 9756. Cambridge, MA: National Bureau of Economic Research.

Boylaud, Olivier, and Guiseppe Nicoletti. 2001. Regulatory Reform in Retail Distribution. *OECD Economic Studies,* no. 32, 2001/1. Paris: OECD.

Bradford, Scott C., and Robert Z. Lawrence. 2004. *Has Globalization Gone Far Enough?* Washington: Institute for International Economics.

Brady, Chris, and Andrew Lorenz. 2000. *End of the Road: BMW and Rover—A Brand Too Far.* Financial Times/Prentice Hall.

Brand, Martin. 2001. *Historical Revisions to Computer Producer Prices.* London: UK Office of National Statistics.

Brandt, Nicola. 2004. *Business Dynamics in Europe,* 2004. OECD Directorate for Science, Technology, and Industry DSTI/DOC(2004)1. Paris: OECD.

Brewer, Dominic, Eric Eide, and Ronald G. Ehrenberg. 1996. Does it Pay to Attend an Elite College? NBER Working Paper 5613. Cambridge, MA: National Bureau of Economic Research.

Broadbent, B., D. Schumacher, and S. Schels. 2004 *No Gain Without Pain—Germany's Adjustment to a Higher Cost of Capital.* Goldman Sachs Global Economics Paper 103, revised version February 26, 2004.

Broadberry, S. N. 1998. How Did the United States and Germany Overtake Britain? Sectoral Analysis of Comparative Productivity Levels, 1870–1990. *Journal of Economic History* 58, no. 2 (June): 13–61.

Brunila, Anne. 2002. *Fiscal Policy: Coordination, Discipline, and Stabilization.* Paper prepared for the Group of Economic Analysis of the European Commission, April, Brussels.

Bryan, Lowell, Jane Fraser, Jeremy Oppenheimer, and Wilhelm Rall. 1999. *Race for the World*. Boston, MA: Harvard Business School Press.

Brynjolfsson, Erik, and Lorin M. Hitt. 2000. Beyond Computation: Information Technology, Organizational Transformation and Business Performance. *Journal of Economic Perspectives* 14, no. 4 (Fall): 23–48.

Brynjolfsson, Erik, and Shinkyu Yang. 2001. Intangible Assets and Growth Accounting: Evidence from Computer Investments. Draft working paper (May). http://ebusiness.mit.edu/erik/itg01-05-30.pdf (accessed October 16, 2003).

Buiter, Willem H., and Clemens Grafe. 2002. *Patching Up the Pact—Some Suggestions for Enhancing Fiscal Sustainability and Macroeconomic Stability in an Enlarged European Union*. CEPR Discussion Paper 3496. London: Centre for Economic Policy Research.

Buiter, Willem H., and Marcus H. Miller. 1983. Changing the Rules: Economic Consequences of the Thatcher Regime. *Brookings Papers on Economic Activity* 2: 305–79. Washington: Brookings Institution.

Burda, M.C., and J. Hunt. 2001. From Reunification to Economic Integration: Productivity and the Labor Market in Eastern Germany. *Brookings Papers on Economic Activity* 2: 1–72. Washington: Brookings Institution.

Burtless, Gary, and Holger Schaefer. 2003. *Earnings Insurance for Germany*. Brookings Institution Policy Brief 104 (July). Washington: Brookings Institution.

Buti, Marco, Sylvester C. W. Eijffinger, and Daniele Franco. 2003. *Revisiting the Stability and Growth Pact: Grand Design or Internal Adjustment?* European Economy, Economic Papers no. 180, January. Brussels: European Commission.

Buti, Marco, Jurgen von Hagen, and Carlos Martinez Mongay, eds. 2001. *The Behavior of Fiscal Authorities*. London: Palgrave.

Calmfors, Lars, Anders Forslund, and Maria Hemström. 2001. Does Active Labour Market Policy Work? Lessons from the Swedish Experiences. *Swedish Economic Policy Review* 85: 61–124.

Campbell, Mike, Simon Baldwin, Steve Johnson, Rachael Chapman, Alexandra Upton, and Fiona Walton. 2001. *Skills in England 2001:The Research Report*. London, UK: The Department for Education and Skills (November).

Card, David. 1999. The Causal Effect of Education on Earnings. In *Handbook of Labour Economics 3*, ed. Orley Ashenfelter and David Card. New York: North-Holland.

Card, David, and Richard B. Freeman. 2001. *What Have Two Decades of British Economic Reform Delivered?* NBER Working Paper 8801. Cambridge, MA: National Bureau of Economic Research.

Carling, Kenneth, Bertil Holmlund, and Altin Vejsiu. 2001. Do Benefit Cuts Boost Job Findings? Swedish Evidence from the 1990s. *Economic Journal* 11 (October): 766–90.

Casella, Allessandra. 2001. Tradable Deficit Permits. Efficient Implementation of the Stability Pact in the European Monetary Union. In *The Stability and Growth Pact*, ed. Anne Brunila, Marco Buti, and Daniele Franco. London: Palgrave.

CBO (Congressional Budget Office). 2002. *The Budget and Economic Outlook: An Update August 2002*. www.cbo.gov/showdoc.cfm?index=3735&sequence=0 (accessed October 9, 2003).

CEA (Council of Economic Advisers). 2000. *Economic Report to the President 2000* (February). Washington: Council of Economic Advisers.

CEA (Council of Economic Advisers). 2001. *Economic Report to the President 2001*. Washington: Council of Economic Advisers.

Center for European Policy Studies. 2002. Fiscal and Monetary Policy for a Low-Speed Europe. 4th Annual Report of the CEPS Macro Economic Policy Groups, June. Brussels: CEPS.

Clarida, Richard, and Mark Gertler. 1996. *How the Bundesbank Conducts Monetary Policy*. NBER Working Paper 5581. Cambridge, MA: National Bureau of Economic Research.

Clarida, Richard, Jordi Gali, and Mark Gertler. 1997. *Monetary Policy Rules in Practice: Some International Evidence*. NBER Working Paper 6254. Cambridge, MA: National Bureau of Economic Research.

Cohen, D., P. Garibaldi, and S. Scarpetta, S., eds. 2004. The ICT Revolution, Productivity Differences and the Digital Divide, Report for the Fondatione Rodolfo Debenedetti in association with The William Davidson Institute. Oxford: Oxford University Press.

Cohen, Linda R., and Roger G. Noll. 1991. *The Technology Pork Barrel*. Washington: Brookings Institution.

Crafts, Nicholas, and G. Toniolo. 1996. *Economic Growth in Europe since 1945*. Cambridge: Cambridge University Press.

Crafts, Nicholas, and Mary O'Mahony. 2001. A Perspective on UK Productivity Performance. *Fiscal Studies* 2, no. 3: 271–306.

Crandall, Robert W., and Clifford Winston. 2003. Does Antitrust Policy Improve Consumer Welfare? Assessing the Evidence. *The Journal of Economic Perspectives* 17, no. 4 (Fall).

Crepon, Bruno, and Rozenn Dezplatz. 2001. Une Nouvelle Evaluation des Effets des Allegements de Charges Sociale sur les Bas Salaires. *Economique et Statistique*, no. 348: 3024, (August): Paris: INSEE.

Criscuolo, Chiara, and Jonathan Haskel. 2002. *Innovations and Productivity Growth in the UK*. CERIBA Discussion Paper (October). London: Centre for Research into Business Activity.

Criscuolo, Chiara, and Ralf Martin. 2002. Multinationals, Foreign Ownership, and Productivity in UK Businesses. CERIBA Draft Paper. London: Centre for Research into Business Activity.

Criscoulo, Chiara, and Ralf Martin. 2003. Multinationals and US Productivity Leadership: Evidence from Great Britain. CERIBA Discussion Paper (September). London: Centre for Research into Business Activity.

Dang, T., P. Antolin, and H. Oxley. 2001. *Fiscal Implications of Ageing: Projections of Age-Related Spending*. OECD Economics Department Working Paper 305. Paris: OECD.

Danish Ministry of Labour. 1999. The Labour Market Reforms—A Status. www.bm.dk/english/publications/thelabourmarketreforms/reform_0.asp?id=Documents&mtop=4&mlft=1&thgt=0. Copenhagen.

Danish Ministry of Labour. 2000. Effects of Danish Employability Enhancement Programs. www.bm.dk/english/publications/effects/eodeep.asp?id=Documents&mtop=4&mlft=1&thgt=0, Copenhagen.

Davies, S. W., and B. R. Lyons. 1991. Characterising Relative Performance: The Productivity Advantage of Foreign-Owned Firms in the UK. *Oxford Economic Papers* 43 (October): 84–595.

Davis, Bob, and David Wessel. 1998. *Prosperity: The Coming Twenty-Year Boom and What It Means to You*. New York: Times Books/Random House.

Denison, Edward. F. 1967. *Why Growth Rates Differ*. Washington: Brookings Institution.

Djankov, S., R. La Porta, F. Lopez De Silanes, and A. Schleifer. 2001. *The Regulation of Entry*, third draft, June. http://econ.worldbank.org/files/2379_wps2661.pdf (accessed October 8, 2003).

Doms, Mark, and J. Bradford Jensen. 1998a. Comparing Wages, Skills and Productivity between Domestically and Foreign-Owned Manufacturing Establishments in the United States. In *Geography and Ownership as Bases for Economics Accounting*, ed. Robert E. Baldwin, Robert E. Lipsey, and J. David Richardson. Chicago: University of Chicago Press.

Doms, Mark, and J. Bradford Jensen. 1998b. Productivity, Skill and Wage Effects of Multinational Corporations in the United States. In *Foreign Ownership and the Consequences of Direct Investment in the United States: Beyond Us and Them*, ed. Douglas Woodward and Douglas Nigh. New York: Quorum Books.

Dow, J. C. R. 1964. *The Management of the British Economy 1945–60*. Cambridge, UK: Cambridge University Press.

Eichengreen, Barry, ed. 1995. *Europe's Postwar Recovery*. Cambridge, MA: Cambridge University Press.

EIRO (European Industrial Relations Observatory). 1997. Opening Clauses Increase in Branch-Level Collective Agreements. www.eiro.eurofound.eu.int/1997/09/feature/de9709229f.html (accessed March 28, 2004).

EIRO (European Industrial Relations Observatory). 1998. Italy's System of Social Shock Absorbers Examined. www.eiro.eurofound.eu.int/1998/02/feature/it9802319f.html (accessed March 28, 2004).

EIRO (European Industrial Relations Observatory). 2003a. Developments in Industrial Action, 1998–2002. www.eiro.eurofound.eu.int/2003/11/feature/fr0311104f.html (accessed January 5, 2004).

EIRO (European Industrial Relations Observatory). 2003b. Impact of Unemployment Insurance Reform Becomes Clearer. www.eiro.eurofound.eu.int/2003/07/inbrief/fr0307102n.html, (accessed December 18, 2003).

EIRO (European Industrial Relations Observatory). 2003c. Retirement Before 60 Introduced for People with Long Working Lives. www.eiro.eurofound.eu.int/2003/12/inbrief/fr0312102n.html (accessed March 27, 2003).

EIRO (European Industrial Relations Observatory). 2003d. Sickness Insurance Reform Postponed. www.eiro.eurofound.ie/2003/03/Update/TN0303104U.html (accessed March 19, 2004).

EIRO (European Industrial Relations Observatory). 2003e. Survey Finds that Statutory Protection against Dismissal Hurts Small Firms. www.eiro.eurofound.eu.int/print/2003/06/feature/de0306108f.html (accessed January 13, 2004).

EIRO (European Industrial Relations Observatory). 2003f. Unemployment Allowance Entitlement To Be Cut. www.eiro.eurofound.eu.int/2003/10/inbrief/fr0310102n.html (accessed December 18, 2003).

EIRO (European Industrial Relations Observatory). 2004a. Coverage of Collective Agreements and Works Councils Assessed. www.eiro.eurofound.eu.int/2004/01/feature/de0401106f.html (accessed December 18, 2003).

EIRO (European Industrial Relations Observatory). 2004b. Debate on introduction of "assignment contracts." www.eiro.eurofound.eu.int/2004/02/feature/fr0402108f.html (accessed March 27, 2003).

EIRO (European Industrial Relations Observatory). 2004c. Laws on Protection against Dismissal and Unemployment Benefits Amended. www.eiro.eurofound.eu.int/2004/01/feature/de0401205f.html (accessed March 27, 2003).

EIRO (European Industrial Relations Observatory). 2004d. Social Partners Respond to Bargaining Reform Plans. www.eiro.eurofound.eu.int/2004/01/feature/fr0401110f.html (accessed March 27, 2003).

EIRO (European Industrial Relations Observatory). 2004e. Court Rules in Favor of Unemployed People Hit by Benefit Cuts. www.eiro.eurofound.eu.int/print/2004/05/inbrief/fr405/oln.html.

Employment Taskforce. 2003. Jobs, Jobs, Jobs Creating More Employment in Europe. Report of the Employment Task Force (chaired by Wim Kok), Brussels.

Eur-Lex. 1997a. Council Regulation (EC) No 1466/97 of July 7. http://europa.eu.int/smartapi/cgi/sga_doc?smartapi!celexapi!prod!CELEXnumdoc&lg=EN&numdoc=31997R1466&model=guichett (accessed October 8, 2003).

Eur-Lex. 1997b. Council Regulation (EC) No 1467/97, July 7. http://europa.eu.int/smartapi/cgi/sga_doc?smartapi!celexapi!prod!CELEXnumdoc&lg=EN&numdoc=31997R1467&model=guichett (accessed October 8, 2003).

European Central Bank. 2003a. Background Studies for the ECB's Evaluation of its Monetary Policy Strategy. Frankfurt: European Central Bank.

European Central Bank. 2003b. Euro Area Statistics Download. www.ecb.int/ (accessed October 8).

European Central Bank. 2004. *Monthly Bulletin*, July. Frankfurt: European Central Bank.

European Commission. 1998. Communication of the Commission on Undeclared Work, COM (98) 219. Brussels: European Commission.

European Commission. 2000a. EU Public Finances 2000. www.europa.eu.int/comm/economy_finance/publications/publicfinance_en.htm (accessed October 8, 2003).

European Commission. 2000b. Competition Policy in Europe and the Citizen. www.europa. eu.int/comm/competition/publications/competition_policy_and_the_citizen/en.pdf (accessed January 13, 2004).

European Commission. 2001a. EU Public Finances 2001. www.europa.eu.int/comm/ economy_finance/publications/publicfinance_en.htm (accessed October 8, 2003).

European Commission, Economic Policy Committee. 2001b. *Budgetary challenges posed by ageing populations: The impact on public spending on pensions, health and long-term care for the elderly and possible indicators of the long-term sustainability of public finances*, Report 24 October, EPC/ECFIN/655/01-EN Final. Brussels: European Commission.

European Commission. 2002a. EU Public Finances 2002. www.europa.eu.int/comm/ economy_finance/publications/publicfinance_en.htm (accessed October 8, 2003).

European Commission. 2002b. Communication From the Commission to Council and Parliament: Strengthening the Co-ordination of Budgetary Policies. COM (2002) 668 Final. http://europa.eu.int/eur-lex/en/com/cnc/2002/com2002_0668en01.pdf (accessed October 8, 2003).

European Commission. 2002c. Co-ordination of Economic Policies in the EU: A Presentation of Key Features of the Main Procedures. Euro Papers no. 45 (July). Brussels: European Commission.

European Commission. 2002d. Report from The Commission to the Council and the European Parliament on the State of the Internal Market For Services. Brussels: European Commission.

European Commission. 2002e. Report requested by the Stockholm European Council: Increasing Labour Force Participation and Promoting Active Ageing. COM (2002) 9 Final. Brussels: European Commission (January 24).

European Commission. 2002f. *e*Europe Action Plan. www.europa.eu.int/information_society/ eeurope/2002/action_plan/mid-term_review/index_en.htm (accessed February 17, 2004).

European Commission. 2003a. Choosing to Grow: Knowledge, Innovation and Jobs In a Cohesive Society. Report to the Spring European Council, March 21, 2003, on the Lisbon Strategy of Economic, Social and Environmental Renewal. www.europa.eu.int/comm/ lisbon_strategy/pdf/5b_en.pdf (accessed January 13, 2004).

European Commission. 2003b. EU Public Finances 2003. www.europa.eu.int/comm/ economy_finance/publications/publicfinance_en.htm (accessed October 8, 2003).

European Commission. 2003c. Green Paper on Services of General Interest. COM(2003) 270 Final. Brussels: European Commission.

European Commission. 2003d. Internal Market Scoreboard no. 12. Brussels: European Commission.

European Commission. 2003e. Second Benchmarking Report on the Implementation of The Internal Electricity and Gas Market (updated report incorporating Candidate Countries) SEC(2003) 448. Brussels: European Commission.

European Commission. 2003f. European Merger Control—Council Regulation 4064/89— Statistics. www.europa.eu.int/comm/competition/mergers/cases/stats.html (accessed January 13, 2004).

European Commission. 2003g. Merger Cases by Decision Type—Article 8(3). www.europa. eu.int/comm/competition/mergers/cases/index/by_dec_type_art_8_3.html (accessed January 13, 2004).

European Commission. 2004a. Statistical Annex of European Economy (Spring). www. europa.eu.int/comm/economy_finance/publications/european_economy/statistical annex_en.htm (accessed October 8).

European Commission. 2004b. Communication From the Commission to the Council—Joint Draft Employment Report 2003/2004. COM (2004) 24 Final, January. www.europa.eu. int/comm/lisbon_strategy/pdf/COM2004_024_en.pdf (accessed March 16, 2004).

European Commission. 2004c. Report From the European Commission to the Spring European Council: Delivering Lisbon—Reforms for the Enlarged EU. COM (2004) 29. Brussels: European Commission.

European Commission. 2004d. Key Indicators for the Eurozone. www.europa.int/comm/economy_finance/indicators/key_euro_area/euroindic_en.pdf (accessed July 19, 2004).

European Commission. 2004e. Report on the Implementation of the Internal Market Strategy (Q003–2006). COM (2004) 22 Final. Brussels: European Commission.

European Commission. 2004f. *Internal Market Scoreboard* 13. Brussels: European Commission.

European Commission and ECOFIN. 2003. Joint report by the Commission and the Council on Adequate and Sustainable Pensions, 6527/2/03, ECOFIN 51, Brussels.

European Convention. 2003. Draft Treaty Establishing a Constitution for Europe. http://european-convention.eu.int/docs/Treaty/cv00850.en03.pdf (accessed October 8, 2003).

European Council. 2000. Presidency Conclusions, Lisbon European Council, March 23–24, 2000. http://ue.eu.int/Newsroom/LoadDoc.asp?BID=76&DID=60917&from=&LANG=1 (accessed January 13, 2004).

European Council. 2003. Guidelines for the Employment Policies of the Member States. *Official Journal of the European Union* L197/13. www.europa.eu.int/eur-lex/pri/en/oj/dat/2003/l_197/l_19720030805en00130021.pdf (accessed May 21, 2004). 2003/587/EC.

Eurostat. 2002. Continuing Vocational Training Survey (CVTS2), Luxembourg.

Eurostat. 2004a. NewCronos Database. www.europa.eu.int/newcronos/suite/display.do?screen=navigation&language=en&depth=1&root=/ (accessed January 28, 2004).

Eurostat. 2004b. Structural Indicators. www.europa.eu.int/comm/eurostat/Public/datashop/print-product/EN?catalogue=Eurostat&product=1-structur-EN (accessed January 13).

Fitoussi, Jean-Paul, and Jerome Creel. 2002. *How to Reform the European Central Bank*. Pamphlet (October). London: Centre for European Reform.

Foster, Lucia, John Haltiwanger, and C. J. Krizan. 2001. The Link Between Aggregate and Micro Productivity Growth: The Evidence from Retail Trade. Washington: Bureau of the Census (July).

Frankel, Jeffrey A., and Peter R. Orszag, eds. 2002. *American Economic Policy in the 1990s*. Cambridge, MA: MIT Press.

Freeman, Richard. 1980. The Exit-Voice Tradeoff in the Labor Market: Unionism, Job Tenure, Quits, and Separations. *The Quarterly Journal of Economics* XCIV, no. 4 (June): 643–73.

Freeman, Richard. 2002. US-European Trends in Welfare Systems, Labor Markets and Migration. Paper presented at the conference on Transatlantic Perspectives on US-EU Economic Relations, John F. Kennedy School of Government, Harvard University (April 11–12): 4.

German government. 2004. Antworten zur Agenda 2010, February 2004 www.bundesregierung.de/Anlage608361/Agenda2010_Neuauflage.pdf (accessed March 28).

German government. 2003. Germany Is Taking Action—An Overview of Agenda 2010. eng.bundesregierung.de/frameset/index.jsp (accessed December 19).

Giersch, Herbert. 1985. *Eurosclerosis*. Kiel Discussion Papers 112. Kiel, Germany: Kiel Institute for World Economics (October).

Goldman Sachs. 2003. *Goldman Sachs US Daily Financial Market Comment*, October 15. New York: Goldman Sachs Economics Research.

Gordon, Robert J. 2000. Does the 'New Economy' Measure up to the Great Inventions of the Past? *Journal of Economic Perspectives* 14, no. 4 (Fall): 49–74.

Gordon, Robert J. 2001. Panel presentation at the conference titled "Productivity Growth: A New Era." Federal Reserve Bank of New York (November 2).

Gordon, Robert J. 2002. *Technology and Economic Performance in the American Economy*. NBER Working Papers 8771. Cambridge, MA: National Bureau of Economic Research

Gordon, Robert J. 2003a. America Wins with a Supermarket Sweep. search.ft.com/s03/search/article.html?id=030819006291 (accessed August 19).

Gordon, Robert J. 2003b. *Hi-Tech Innovation and Productivity Growth: Does Supply Create Its Own Demand?* NBER Working Papers 9437. Cambridge, MA: National Bureau of Economic Research.

Green, F., D. Ashton, B. Burchell, B. Davies, and A. Felstead. 2000. Are British Workers Becoming More Skilled? In *The Overeducated Worker? The Economics of Skills Utilization*, ed. L. Borghans and A. De Grip. Cheltenham, UK: Edward Elgar.

Greenspan, Alan. 1996. Remarks at the Annual Dinner and Francis Boyer Lecture of The American Enterprise Institute for Public Policy Research, Washington, December 5, 1996. www.federalreserve.gov/boarddocs/speeches/1996/19961205.htm (accessed October 9, 2003).

Griffith, Rachel, and Helen Simpson. 2003. *Characteristics of Foreign-Owned Firms in British Manufacturing*. NBER Working Paper 9573. Cambridge, MA: National Bureau of Economic Research.

Griffith, Rachel, Stephen Redding, and John Van Reenen. 2000. *Mapping the Two Faces of R&D: Productivity Growth in a Panel of OECD industries*. IFS Working Paper 02/00. London: Institute for Fiscal Studies.

Griffith, Rachel, Rupert Harrison, Jonathan Haskel, and Mari Sako. 2003. The UK Productivity Gap and the Importance of the Service Sectors. Advanced Institute of Management Research, Briefing Note (December).

Gust, C., and J. Marquez. 2002. *International Comparisons of Productivity Growth: The Role of Information Technology and Regulatory Practices*. International Finance Discussion Paper 727 (May). Washington: Board of Governors of the Federal Reserve System.

Haacker, Markus, and James H. Morsink. 2002. *You Say You Want a Revolution: Information Technology and Growth*. IMF Working Papers 02/70. Washington: International Monetary Fund.

Hall, Bronwyn. 1998. Innovation and Market Value. In *Productivity, Innovation and Economic Performance*, ed. Ray Barrell, Geoffrey Mason, and Mary O'Mahony. Cambridge, UK: Cambridge University Press.

Hall, Bronwyn, Adam Jaffe, and Manuel Trajtenberg. 2000. *Market Value and Patent Citations: A First Look*. NBER Working Paper 7741. Cambridge, MA: National Bureau of Economic Research.

Hall, Robert E. 2000. E-Capital: The Link between the Stock Market and the Labor Market in the 1990s. *Brookings Papers on Economic Activity* 2: 73–118. Washington: Brookings Institution.

Hall, Robert E. 2001. The Stock Market and Capital Accumulation. *American Economic Review* 91, no. 5 (December): 1185–202.

Hansen, Bruce E. 2001. The New Econometrics of Structural Change: Dating Breaks in U.S. Labor Productivity. *Journal of Economic Perspectives* 15, no. 4 (Fall): 117–28.

Hallett, Andrew Hughes, John Lewis, and Jurgen Von Hagen. 2004. Fiscal Policy in Europe 1991–2003: An Evidence-Based Analysis. CEPR Report (May). London: Centre for Economic Policy Research.

Haskel, Jonathan E., and Sonia Pereira. 2002. *Skills and Productivity in the UK: Using Matched Establishment and Worker Data*. CERIBA Discussion Paper (October). London: Centre for Research into Business Activity.

Haskel, Jonathan E., and Matthew J. Slaughter. 1998. *Does the Sector Bias of Skill-Biased Technical Change Explain Changing Wage Inequality?* NBER Working Paper 6565. Cambridge, MA: National Bureau of Economic Research.

Henrekson, Magnus, and Mats Person. 2004. The Effects on Sick Leave of Changes in the Sickness Insurance System. *Journal of Labor Economics* 22, no. 1.

Hillage, Jim, Jo Regan, Jenny Dickson, and Kirsten McLoughlin. 2002. *Employers Skill Survey 2002*. Department for Education and Skills Research Report RR372. London: Department for Education and Skills.

HM Treasury. 2002. Pre-Budget Report. www.hm-treasury.gov.uk/Pre_Budget_Report/prebud_pbr02/prebud_pbr02_index.cfm (accessed September 8, 2003).

Hoxby, Caroline M. 1998. The Return to Attending a More Selective College: 1960 to the Present. Cambridge, MA: Harvard University.

IMF (International Monetary Fund). 1995. Challenges to the Swedish Welfare State, by Desmond Lachman, Adam Bennett, John H. Green, Robert Hagemann and Ramana Ramaswamy, Occasional paper 130. Washington: International Monetary Fund.

IMF (International Monetary Fund). 1999. The Netherlands—Transforming a Market Economy, by C. Maxwell Watson, Bas B. Bakker, Jan Kees Martijn, and Ioannis Halikias, Occasional Paper 181, Washington: International Monetary Fund.

IMF (International Monetary Fund). 2001a. *Sweden: Selected Issues—The Role of Government.* IMF Country Report 01/169 (September). Washington: International Monetary Fund.

IMF (International Monetary Fund). 2001b. *World Economic Outlook. Fiscal Policy and Macroeconomic Stability* (May). Washington: International Monetary Fund.

IMF (International Monetary Fund). 2002a. *Kingdom of the Netherlands—Netherlands: Selected Issues.* IMF Country Report 02/123 (June). Washington: International Monetary Fund.

IMF (International Monetary Fund). 2002b. *Sweden: Selected Issues.* IMF Country Report 02/160 (August). Washington: International Monetary Fund.

Inklaar, R., Mary O'Mahony, and M. Timmer. 2003. ICT and Europe's Productivity Performance Industry-Level Growth Account Comparisons with the United States. Groningen Growth and Development Centre, Research Memorandum GD-68. University of Groningen.

Institute for Employment Research. 2003. *Skills in England 2002.* Learning and Skills Council Report. London: Institute for Employment Research.

Issing, Otmar, Vitor Gaspar, Ignazio Angeloni, and Oreste Tristani. 2001. *Monetary Policy in the Euro Area: Strategy and Decision-Making at the European Central Bank.* Cambridge: Cambridge University Press.

Johansson, Per, and Morten Palme. 2003. Moral Hazard and Sickness Insurance. people.su.se/~palme/wabs2.pdf (accessed March 22, 2004).

Johnson, Simon, Daniel Kaufmann, and Andrei Shleifer. 1997. The Unofficial Economy in Transition. *Brookings Papers on Economic Activity* 2: 159–239. Washington: Brookings Institution.

Jorgenson, Dale W. 1995. Productivity, Volume 2, International Comparisons of Economic Growth. Cambridge, MA: MIT Press.

Jorgenson, Dale W. 2003. Information Technology and the G7 Economies. *World Economics* 4, no. 4 (October–December). Henley-on-Thames, UK: NTC Economic and Financial Publishing.

Jorgenson, Dale W., S. H. Mun, and Kevin J. Stiroh. 2001. Projecting Productivity Growth: Lessons from the U.S. Growth Resurgence. Paper prepared for the conference on Technology, Growth and the Labor Market, sponsored by the Federal Reserve Bank of Atlanta and Georgia State University (December 31).

Katz, Lawrence F. 2002. Comments to Juhn, Murphy, and Topel. In *Current Unemployment, Historically Contemplated,* ed., W. C. Brainard, and G. L. Perry. *Brookings Papers on Economic Activity* 1: 79–137. Washington: Brookings Institution.

Kellner, Martin. 2004. Tax Amnesty 2004/2005—An Appropriate Revenue Tool? *German Law Journal* 5, no. 4 (April).

Klapper, Leora, Luc Laeven, and Raghuram Rajan. 2004. *Business Environment and Firm Entry: Evidence from International Data.* NBER Working Paper 10380. Cambridge, MA: National Bureau of Economic Research.

Kletzer, Lori G. 2001. *Job Loss from Imports: Measuring the Costs.* Washington: Institute for International Economics.

Kletzer, Lori G., and Robert E. Litan. 2001. *A Prescription to Relieve Worker Anxiety.* Policy Brief 01-2. Washington: Institute for International Economics.

Krueger, Alan, and Orley Ashenfelter. 1994. Estimates of the Economic Return to Schooling from a New Sample of Twins. *American Economic Review* 84, no. 5 (December): 1157–73.

Landes, David. 1998. *The Wealth and Poverty of Nations.* New York: W.W. Norton & Company.

Lawrence, Robert Z., and Colin Lawrence. 1985. Manufacturing Wage Dispersion: An End-Game Interpretation. *Brookings Papers on Economic Activity* 1: 47–106. Washington: Brookings Institution.

Lawrence, Robert Z., and Robert E. Litan. 1986. *Saving Free Trade: A Pragmatic Approach.* Washington: Brookings Institution.

Lawrence, Robert Z., and Charles L. Schultze, eds. 1987. *Barriers to European Growth.* Washington: Brookings Institution.

Lawrence, Robert Z., and Matthew J. Slaughter. 1993. International Trade and American Wages in the 1980s: Giant Sucking Sound or Small Hiccup? *Brookings Papers on Economic Activity: Microeconomics* 2: 161–210.

Layard, Richard, Stephen Nickell, and Richard Jackman. 1991. *Unemployment: Macroeconomic Performance and the Labour Market.* Oxford: Oxford University Press.

Litan, Robert E., and A. M. Rivlin. 2001. *The Economic Payoff from the Internet Revolution.* Washington: Brookings Institution.

Mason, Geoff, and David Finegold. 1997. Productivity, Machinery and Skills in the US and Western Europe. *National Institute Economic Review* 162 (October): 85–98.

Mason, Geoff, Karin Wagner, David Finegold, and Brent Keltner. 2000. The "IT Productivity Paradox" Revisited: International Comparisons of Information Technology, Work Organization and Productivity in Service Industries. *Vierteljahrschefte zur Wirtschaftsforschung* 4: 618–29.

Mateman, S., and P. H. Renooy. 2001. Undeclared Labour in Europe: Towards an Integrated Approach of Combating Undeclared Labour, Final Report. Regioplan Research Advice and Information, Amsterdam.

Messerlin, Patrick A. 2001. *Measuring the Costs of Protection in Europe: European Commercial Policy in the 2000s.* Washington: Institute for International Economics.

MGI (McKinsey Global Institute). 1994. *The Global Capital Market.* Washington: McKinsey Global Institute (October).

MGI (McKinsey Global Institute). 1996. *Health Care Productivity.* Washington: McKinsey Global Institute (October).

MGI (McKinsey Global Institute). 1997. *Removing Barriers to Growth and Employment in France and Germany.* Washington: McKinsey Global Institute.

MGI (McKinsey Global Institute). 1998. *Driving Productivity and Growth in the UK Economy.* www.mckinsey.com/knowledge/mgi/reports/UKprod.asp (accessed July 29, 2003).

MGI (McKinsey Global Institute). 2001. *US Productivity Growth 1995–2000.* Washington: McKinsey Global Institute.

MGI (McKinsey Global Institute). 2002a. *How IT Enables Productivity Growth.* Washington: McKinsey Global Institute.

MGI (McKinsey Global Institute). 2002b. *Reaching Higher Productivity Growth in Germany and France.* Washington: McKinsey Global Institute.

MGI (McKinsey Global Institute). 2003. *Improving European Competitiveness: MGI Perspective.* www.mckinsey.com/knowledge/mgi/reports/pdfs/european_competitiveness/European.pdf (accessed October 14, 2003).

Mills, P., and A. Quinet. 2002. How to Allow the Automatic Stabilisers to Play Fully? A Policy-Maker's Guide for EMU Countries. In *The Behavior of Fiscal Authorities,* ed. Marco Buti, Jurgen von Hagen, and Carlos Martinez Mongay. London: Palgrave.

Mitchell, Olivia. 1999. *New Trends in Pension Benefit and Retirement Provisions.* NBER Working Paper 7381. Cambridge, MA: National Bureau of Economic Research.

Naastepad, C. W. M., and A. Kleinknecht. 2002. The Dutch Productivity Slowdown: The Culprit at Last? Delft University. www.tbm.tudelft.nl/webstaf/ron/EJ-0702.pdf (accessed May 29, 2004).

National Center for Education Statistics. 2003. Comparative Indicators of Education in the United States and Other G-8 Countries: 2002. US Department of Education, Institute of Education Sciences, NCES 2003–026.

Nickell, Stephen. 1996. Competition and Corporate Performance. *Journal of Political Economy* 104, no. 4 (August): 724–46.

Nickell, Stephen. 2002. Monetary Policy Issues: Past, Present, Future. Speech given at Leamington Spa, June 19. www.bankofengland.co.uk/speeches/speech173.pdf (accessed May 29, 2004).

Nickell, Stephen. 2003. Labour Market Institutions and Unemployment in the OECD Countries, chapter 3 in CESifo DICE Report 2. www.cesifo.de/servlet/page?_pageid=56&_dad=portal30&_schema=PORTAL30&pa_id=105828.

Nickell, Stephen, L. Nunziata, and W. Ochel. 2002. Unemployment in the OECD since the 1960s: What Do We Know? Paper for the Unemployment Conference at the London School of Economics (May 27–28).

Nicoletti, Guiseppe, and Stefano Scarpetta. 2003. *Regulation, Productivity and Growth: OECD Evidence.* OECD Economics Department Working Paper 347 (January). Paris: OECD.

Nicoletti, Guiseppe, Stefano Scarpetta, and Olivier Boylaud. 2000. *Summary Indicators of Product Market Regulation with an Extension to Employment Protection Legislation.* OECD Economics Department Working Papers 226. Paris: OECD.

Nordhaus, William D. 1972. The Worldwide Wage Explosion. *Brookings Papers on Economic Activity* 2:35. Washington: Brookings Institution.

Nordhaus, William D. 2001. *Productivity Growth and the New Economy.* NBER Working Paper 8096. Cambridge, MA: National Bureau of Economic Research. January

O'Mahony, Mary. 2002. Productivity and Convergence in the EU. *National Institute Economic Review* 180, no. 1 (April): 72–82.

O'Mahony, Mary, and Willem de Boer. 2002. *Britain's Relative Productivity Performance: Has Anything Changed? National Institute Economic Review* 179, no. 1 (January): 38–43.

O'Mahony, Mary, and Bart van Ark, eds. 2003. *EU Productivity and Competitiveness: An Industry Perspective. Can Europe Resume the Catching-Up Process?* Luxembourg: Office for Official Publications of the European Communities.

OECD (Organization for Economic Cooperation and Development). 1999. OECD Employment Outlook. In *Employment Protection and Labor Market Protection.* Paris: OECD.

OECD (Organization for Economic Cooperation and Development). 2000a. The European Union's Trade Policies and Their Economic Effects. http://oecdpublications.gfi-nb.com/cgi-bin/OECDBookShop.storefront/EN/product/112000181P1.

OECD (Organization for Economic Cooperation and Development). 2000b. *OECD Economic Surveys: United Kingdom.* (June). Paris: OECD.

OECD (Organization for Economic Cooperation and Development). 2000c. *Reforms for an Ageing Society.* Paris: OECD.

OECD (Organization for Economic Cooperation and Development). 2001a. *Education at a Glance—OECD Indicators 2001.* Paris: OECD.

OECD (Organization for Economic Cooperation and Development). 2001b. *OECD Economic Studies: Special Issue on Regulatory Reform,* no. 32. Paris: OECD.

OECD (Organization for Economic Cooperation and Development). 2001c. *The New Economy: Beyond the Hype.* Paris: OECD.

OECD (Organization for Economic Cooperation and Development). 2001d. Aging and Income: Financial Resources and Retirement in 9 OECD Countries. Paris: OECD.

OECD (Organization for Economic Cooperation and Development). 2001e. *Summary Indicators of Product Market Regulation with an Extension to Employment Protection Legislation.* Economics Department WP 226. Paris: OECD.

OECD (Organization for Economic Cooperation and Development). 2001f. Secretariat Data Compilation of Private Pension Fund Assets. www.oecd.org/dataoecd/20/41/2768608.pdf (accessed May 24, 2004).

OECD (Organization for Economic Cooperation and Development). 2002a. Netherlands. *Country Economic Report 2002.* Paris: OECD.

OECD (Organization for Economic Cooperation and Development). 2002b. OECD Social Indicators Database. Paris: OECD.

OECD (Organization for Economic Cooperation and Development). 2002c. *Ability and Disability: Policies to Promote Work and Income Security for Disabled People*. Paris: OECD.

OECD (Organization for Economic Cooperation and Development). 2002d. *Economic Outlook*, vol. 2002/2, no. 72 (December). Paris: OECD.

OECD (Organization for Economic Cooperation and Development). 2002e. Health Data 2002: A Comparative Analysis of 30 Countries: 2002 Edition CD-ROM version.

OECD (Organization for Economic Cooperation and Development). 2002f. Increasing Employment: The Role of Later Retirement. In *OECD Economic Outlook*, no. 72. www.oecd.org/dataoecd/56/43/2487116.pdf (accessed October 8, 2003).

OECD (Organization for Economic Cooperation and Development). 2002g. *Measuring the Non-Observed Economy*. Statistics Brief, no. 5. Paris: OECD.

OECD (Organization for Economic Cooperation and Development). 2003a. Economic Outlook, no. 73 June 2003 Database. www.oecd.org/document/61/0,2340,en_2649_34109_2483901_1_1_1_1,00.html (accessed November 17, 2003).

OECD (Organization for Economic Cooperation and Development). 2003b. Economic Survey of France, July. Paris: OECD.

OECD (Organization for Economic Cooperation and Development). 2003c. *Health at a Glance*. Paris: OECD.

OECD (Organization for Economic Cooperation and Development). 2003d. The Policy Agenda for Growth. Paris: OECD.

OECD (Organization for Economic Cooperation and Development). 2003e. *Seizing the Benefits of ICT in a Digital Economy*. Paris: OECD.

OECD (Organization for Economic Cooperation and Development). 2003f. The Sources of Economic Growth in the OECD Countries. Paris: OECD.

OECD (Organization for Economic Cooperation and Development). 2003g. The Policy Agenda for Growth: Overview of the Sources of Economic Growth in OECD Countries. Paris: OECD.

OECD (Organization for Economic Cooperation and Development). 2003h. Total Tax Revenue as Percentage of GDP. www.oecd.org/dataoecd/22/35/17103874.pdf (accessed October 28, 2003).

OECD (Organization for Economic Cooperation and Development). 2003i. Labor Force Indicators. www1.oecd.org/scripts/cde/members/LFSINDICATORSAuthenticate.asp (accessed December 18, 2003).

OECD (Organization for Economic Cooperation and Development). 2003j. Structural Analysis Database (STAN). www.oecd.org/document/15/0,2340,en_2649_34445_1895503_1_1_1_1,00.html (accessed October 8, 2003).

OECD (Organization for Economic Cooperation and Development). 2004a. Economic Surveys 2004. Paris: OECD.

OECD (Organization for Economic Cooperation and Development). 2004b. Taxing Wages 2002–2003. Paris: OECD.

OECD (Organization for Economic Cooperation and Development). 2004c. Social Expenditure Database. Paris: OECD.

OECD (Organization for Economic Cooperation and Development). 2004d. Economic Survey of the Netherlands. Paris: OECD.

OECD (Organization for Economic Cooperation and Development). 2004e. Economic Survey of Sweden. Paris: OECD.

OECD (Organization for Economic Cooperation and Development). 2004f. The Economic Impact of ICT: Measurement, Evidence, and Implications. Paris: OECD.

OECD (Organization for Economic Cooperation and Development). 2004g. Employment Outlook 2004. Paris: OECD.

OECD (Organization for Economic Cooperation and Development). 2004h. A Detailed Description of Employment Protection Regulation in Force in 2003. Paris: OECD.

OECD, ILO, IMF, and CIS STAT. 2002. Measuring the Non-Observed Economy: A Handbook. Paris: OECD.

Oliner, S. D., and D. E. Sichel. 2000. The Resurgence of Growth in the Late 1990s: Is Information Technology the Story? *Journal of Economic Perspectives* 14, no. 4 (Fall): 3–32.

Oliner, S. D., and D. E. Sichel. 2002. Information Technology and Productivity: Where Are We Now and Where Are We Going? Notes for a presentation at the conference on Technology, Growth and the Labor Market, sponsored by the Federal Reserve Bank of Atlanta and Georgia State University. Photocopy (January 7).

Olson, Mancur. 1984. *The Rise and Decline of Nations: Economic Growth, Stagflation and Social Rigidities.* New Haven: Yale University Press.

Oshio, Takashi, and Naohiro Yashiro. 1997. *Social Security and Retirement in Japan.* NBER Working Paper 6156. Cambridge, MA: National Bureau of Economic Research.

Oulton, Nicholas. 2001. ICT and Productivity Growth in the United Kingdom. Paper presented at CAN Seminar, November 21–22, Paris.

Pakes, Ariel. 2002. *A Reconsideration of Hedonic Price Indices with an Application to PC's.* NBER Working Paper 8715. Cambridge, MA: National Bureau of Economic Research.

Palme, Marten, and Ingemar Svensson. 1997. *Social Security, Occupational Pensions, and Retirement in Sweden.* NBER Working Paper 6137. Cambridge, MA: National Bureau of Economic Research.

Pisani-Ferry, Jean. 2002. *Fiscal Discipline and Policy Coordination in the Eurozone: Assessment and Proposals.* Paper prepared for the Group of Economic Analysis of the European Commission, April, Brussels.

Porter, Michael E., and Christian H. M. Ketels. 2003. *UK Competitiveness: Moving to the Next Stage.* DTI Economics Paper 3. London: Department of Trade and Industry.

Posen, Adam, S. 2003. *Is Germany Turning Japanese?* Working Paper 03-2. Washington: Institute for International Economics.

Posen, Adam S. 2004. The Euro, Stabilization Policy, and the Stability and Growth Pact. Presentation at Euro at Five: Ready for a Global Role, Institute for International Economics conference, February 26, Washington.

Posen, Adam S. Forthcoming. *Germany and the World Economy.* Washington: Institute for International Economics.

Private Banker International. Various issues (March 2002, January and July 2003). Lafferty Group, London.

Renooy, Piet, Staffan Ivarsson, Olga van der Wusten-Gritsai, and Remco Meijer. 2004. *Undeclared Work in an enlarged Union. An analysis of undeclared work: an in-depth study of specific items. Final report.* Brussels: European Commission.

Retsinfo. 2003. Lovbekendtgoreise No. 708 from 13/08/2003. www.retsinfo.dk/_GETDOCM_/ACCN/B20030051605-REGL (accessed October 25, 2003).

Roach, Stephen S. 1998. No Productivity Boom for Workers. *Issues in Science and Technology* XIV, no. 4 (Summer): 49–56.

Roberts, John M. 2001. Estimates of the Productivity Trend Using Time-Varying Parameter Techniques. Finance and Economics Discussion Series 200–08. Washington: Board of Governors of the Federal Reserve System.

Rosen, Howard, and Trade Directorate and Trade Committee. 2003. Structural Adjustment in Textiles and Clothing, Trade-Related Labor Adjustment Policies. TD/TC/WP (2003) 34. Paris: OECD.

Rossi, Stefano, and Paolo Volpin. 2003. *Cross-Country Determinants of Mergers and Acquisitions.* ECGI Finance Working Paper 25. Brussels: European Corporate Governance Institute.

Rurup Commission. 2003. Nachhaltigkeit In Der Finanzierung Der Sozialen Sicherungssysteme—Bericht Der Kommission, Bundesministerium Für Gesundheit un Soziale Sicherung. www.soziale-sicherungssysteme.de/download/PDFs/Bericht.pdf (accessed December 17, 2003).

Sapir, Andre. 2003. *An Agenda for A Growing Europe, Making the EU Economic System Deliver.* Report of an Independent High-Level Study Group established on the Initiative of the President of the European Commission, July. Brussels: European Commission.

Scarpetta, Stefano, and Thierry Tressel. 2002. *Productivity and Convergence in a Panel of OECD Industries: Do Regulations and Institutions Matter?* OECD Economics Department Working Paper 342. Paris: OECD.

Scherer, P. 2001. *OECD Labor Market and Social Policy.* Occasional Papers 49; *Age of Withdrawal from the Labour Force in OECD Countries.* www.olis.oecd.org/OLIS/2001DOC.NSF/LINKTO/DEELSA-ELSA-WD(2001)2 (accessed October 8, 2003).

Schneider, F. 2002. *The Size and Development of the Shadow Economies and Shadow Economy Labor Force of 21 Countries: What Do We Really Know?* IZA Discussion Paper 514. Bonn: IZA.

Schneider, F., and D. Enste. 1998. *Increasing Shadow Economies All over the World—Fiction or Reality?* IZA Discussion Paper 26. Bonn: Institute for the Study of Labor.

Schneider, F., and D. Enste. 2000. *Shadow Economies Around the World.* IMF Working Paper WP/00/26. Washington: International Monetary Fund.

Schröder, Gerhard. 2003. Courage for Peace and Courage for Change. Policy Statement by Federal Chancellor Gerhard Schröder in the German Bundestag Berlin, March 14, 2003. http://eng.bundesregierung.de/frameset/index.jsp (accessed December 8, 2003).

Schultze, Charles, L. 1987. Saving, Investment, and Profitability in Europe. In *Barriers to European Growth*, ed., Robert Z. Lawrence, and C. L. Schultze: 508–40. Washington: Brookings Institution.

Shavell, Steven, and Laurence Weiss. 1979. The Optimal Payment of Unemployment Insurance Benefits over Time. *Journal of Political Economy* 87, no. 6: 1347–62.

Shaw, Kathryn, Anne Bartel, and Casey Ichniowski. 2003. "New Technology" and Its Impact on the Jobs of High School Educated Workers: A Look Deep Inside Three Manufacturing Industries. In *Low Wage America*, ed. Eileen Appelbaum, Annette Bernhardt, and Richard Murnane. New York: Russell Sage Foundation.

Shiller, Robert J. 2000. *Irrational Exuberance.* Princeton, NJ: Princeton University Press.

Sims, Christopher. 1999. Comments on Katz and Krueger. *Brookings Papers on Economic Activity* 1: 66–89. Washington: Brookings Institution.

Sinn, Hans-Werner. 2003. Ist Deutschland Noch Zu Retten? Munich: Econ-Verlag.

Solow, Robert M. 1987. We'd Better Watch Out. *New York Times Book Review*, July 12: 36.

SSDA (Sector Skills Development Agency). 2003. *The Skills and Productivity Challenge. A Summary of the Evidence Base for the SSDA's Strategic Plan 2003–2006.* Report prepared by Mike Campbell and Lesley Giles. London: Sector Skills Development Agency.

Steedman, Hilary. 2000. Updating of Skills Audit Data 1994–1998. Report to the Department of Education and Employment. CEP Photocopy. London: Centre for Economic Performance.

Stiroh, Kevin J. 2002. Information Technology and the US Productivity Revival: What Does the Industry Data Say? *American Economic Review* 92, no. 5 (December): 1559–76.

Stock, James H. 1998. Comments on Gordon. *Brookings Papers on Economic Activity* 2: 334–41. Washington: Brookings Institution.

Swedish National Social Insurance Board (Riksförsäkringsverket). 2003. www.rfv.se/forsak/belopp/docs/aktbel03.pdf; www.rfv.se/forsak/famba/sgi/index.htm; and www.rfv.se/forsak/pension/alder/analys/index.htm (accessed October 29, 2003).

Taylor, John B. 1943. Discretion versus Policy Rules in Practice. *Carnegie-Rochester Conference Series on Public Policy* 39: 195–214, Pittsburgh, PA.

Taylor, John B. 2000. Reassessing Discretionary Fiscal Policy. *The Journal of Economic Perspectives* 14, no. 3 (Summer): 21–36.

Temin, Peter. 2002. The Golden Age of European Growth Reconsidered. *European Review of Economic History*, no. 6: 3–22.

Thakur, Subhash M., Michael J. Keen, Balazs Horvath, and Valerie Cerra. 2003. *Sweden's Welfare State: Can the Bumblebee Keep Flying?* Washington: International Monetary Fund.

Triplett, J. E., and B. P. Bosworth. 2002. "Baumol's Disease" Has Been Cured: IT and Multifactor Productivity in US Services Industries. Brookings Institution, Washington. Photocopy.

Truman, Edwin M. 2003. *Inflation Targeting in the World Economy.* Washington: Institute for International Economics.

UNICE. 2004. It's the Internal Market, Stupid! A Company Survey on Trade Barriers in the European Union, Brussels.

United Kingdom Department for Education and Skills. 2003. 21st Century Skills: Realising Our Potential. www.dfes.gov.uk/skillsstrategy/_pdfs/whitePaper_PDFID4.pdf.

United Kingdom Department of Trade and Industry. 2002a. *The 2002 R&D Scoreboard.* www.innovation.gov.uk/projects/rd_scoreboard/analysis/analysis.htm#1 (accessed October 14).

United Kingdom Department of Trade and Industry. 2002b. *Productivity and Competitiveness Indicators: Update 2002.* London: Department of Trade and Industry.

United Kingdom Office of National Statistics. 2000. Online database. www.statistics.gov.uk (accessed December 4, 2004).

United Nations Economic Commission on Europe. 2003. Non-Observed Economy in National Accounts: A Survey of National Practices. Geneva: UN Economic Commission on Europe.

US Census Bureau. 2003. *Statistical Abstract of the United States 2003.* Washington: US Census Bureau.

University of Groningen and the Conference Board. 2004. GGDC Total Economy Database 2004. www.eco.rug.nl/ggdc (accessed May 24, 2004).

van Ark, Bart, Robert Inklaar, and Robert McGuckin. 2002. "Changing Gear" Productivity, ICT and Services: Europe and the United States. Groningen Growth and Development Center, Research Memorandum GD-60. Groningen: University of Groningen.

Van Ours, J. C. 2003. *Has the Dutch Productivity Miracle Come to and End?* CentER Discussion Paper 2003-32. Tilburg University. http://greywww.kub.nl:2080/greyfiles/center/2003/doc/32.pdf (accessed December 19, 2003).

Visser, Jelle, and Anton Hemerijck. 1997. *A Dutch Miracle: Job Growth, Welfare Reform and Corporatism in the Netherlands.* Amsterdam: Amsterdam University Press.

von Hagen, Jurgen. 2002. *More Growth for Stability—Reflections on Fiscal Policy in Euroland.* ZEI Policy Paper (June). Bonn: Center for European Integration Studies.

World Bank. 2003. *Doing Business in 2004: Understanding Regulation.* Washington: World Bank Group.

World Economic Forum. 2002. *Global Competitiveness Report 2002–2003.* Geneva: World Economic Forum.

Wren-Lewis, Simon. 2000. The Limits to Discretionary Fiscal Stabilization Policy. *Oxford Review of Economic Policy* 16, no. 4: 92–105.

Wyplosz, Charles. 2002a. Fiscal Policy: Rules or Institutions? Paper prepared for the Group of Economic Analysis of the European Commission, Brussels. (April).

Wyplosz, Charles. 2002b. The Stability Pact Meets its Fate. Paper prepared for the Euro50 Group meeting, Paris (November).

Zysman, J. 1977. The French State in the International Economy. *International Organization* (Fall).

Index

China, 6, 64, 297
Cold War, 35
competition. *See also* competitive intensity;
     European economic reform
  anticompetitive coalition, 41
  agencies, 8
  industry-specific regulation for, 9
  job creation and, 202
  product-market, 200–02
competitive intensity
  effects, 117, 125
  increasing, 8–10, 30, 94, 281
construction industry, 174*b*–75*b*
corporate control, barriers to, 11
Czech Republic, PMR index, 176

demographics
  impact of, 81–82, 92
  life expectancy
     discussed, 23–24, 69–71
     rising life expectancy at retirement, 72*f*
  rising proportion of elderly, 72–74
Denmark, 300, 309
  average annual hours worked, 212*f*
  degree of competition in open electricity
     market, 299*f*
  disability benefit recipiency rates in 20 to 64
     year-old population 1980–99, 232*f*
  economic growth, 6
  employment protection legislation indicator
     1998, 227*f*
  healthcare spending, 184
     out-of-pocket patient financing as
        percent of total healthcare expenditure,
        185*f*
  household electricity prices, 305*f*
  labor-market reform, 2, 13, 29
     case study, 224–32
     youth employment, 230–31, 231*f*
  mergers and acquisitions, 288*t*
  passive measures and labor-market training
     expenditures 1990–2000, 229*f*
  percent of active labor force enrolled in
     training, 229*f*
  total assets of private pension funds, 192*f*
  UI program, 13, 226–27
     rights and duties, 228–30
  underground production, 238*f*, 240*t*
  unemployment and employment to population
     rates, 225*f*
deregulation. *See also* regulation
  effects on productivity, 2, 28, 292
  recommendations for, 7, 8–11
disability. *See also* healthcare, social policy
  benefit recipiency rates in 20 to 64 year-old
     population 1980–99, 232*f*
  Denmark, 231–32
  in general, 190
  reforming, 193–96, 212–14
  Sweden, 220–23

EC. *See* European Commission
ECB. *See* European Central Bank
ECJ. *See* European Court of Justice
ECN. *See* European Competition Network
ECOFIN Council, 247–48, 253
  *Joint Report by the commission and the Council on
     Adequate and Sustainable Pensions*, 308
economic growth, 4. *See also* productivity growth
economic reform. *See* European economic reform
education. *See also* knowledge, research and
     development, training
  relation to productivity, 20–21, 138, 153–55,
     155–59, 293
efficiency. *See also* productivity
  static efficiency, 117
employment. *See also* labor market,
     unemployment, workers
  comparative effect of post-1973 slowdown on
     productivity growth and labor utilization,
     45*f*
  overall employment protection legislation
     indicator 1998, 227*f*
  cyclical and structural sources, 60–62
  EU-15 employment growth 1992–2003 and
     Lisbon goals, 31*f*
  full employment requirements, 4, 99
  hiring/firing barriers, 12
  hours worked, 23–24, 211
     average annual hours worked, 212*f*
  job creation, 7, 100, 293
     competition and, 202
     post-1973, 51–53
  job mobility, 181
  model of employment and productivity, 88–92
  part-time work, 210–11
  public- and private-sector job growth
     1992–2001, 53*f*
  relocation, for, 13
  total hours worked per capita 1973–2003, 52*f*
  UK Employers Skill Survey, 155
EMU. *See* European Monetary Union
energy, 43–46, 47. *See also* utilities
EU-15
  cyclically adjusted budgetary position
     1999–2004, 257*f*
  government consolidated gross debt 1980–2005,
     256*f*
  government lending or borrowing 1991–2005,
     255*f*
  household electricity prices, 305*f*
  member states actual and cyclical budget
     position 2003, 258*f*
  euro, 11, 18, 205, 254*n*, 259, 267–68
  inflation target and, 276–77
Europe. *See also* European Union; eurozone;
     specific countries
  employment principles, 65–66
  European values, 180–82
  offshore assets, 194*b*–95*b*
  postwar growth, 33–40

part-time employment 1983–2002, 211*f*
producer prices relative to world's lowest
  prices, 95*b*, 96
productivity growth, 99
total assets of private pension funds, 192*f*
UI program, 13–14
  unemployment benefit recipients
    1970–2000, 213*f*
underground production, 238*f*, 241*t*
Wassenaar Agreement, 205–06, 211*n*, 54, 215
New Zealand
  employment protection legislation indicator
    1998, 227*f*
  mergers and acquisitions, 288*t*
  underground production, 238*f*
NOE. *See* nonobserved economy
nonobserved economy (NOE)
  development and origins, 242–43
  in general, 235–36
  undeclared work, 239–42
  underground production, 236–39, 238*f*
Norway
  overall employment protection legislation
    indicator 1998, 227*f*
  mergers and acquisitions, 288*t*
  producer prices, 96
  underground production, 238*f*

OECD. *See* Organization for Economic
    Cooperation and Development
Organization for Economic Cooperation and
    Development (OECD)
  deregulated markets, 175–77
  growth analysis implications, 95–102, 149–50
  The New Economy, 133, 137
  recommendations, 9, 27, 292
  Sources of Economic Growth in OECD Countries,
    93–94

pension. *See* retirement; social policy
PMR index. *See* product-market regulation
Portugal
  competition in open electricity market, 299*f*
  employment-based survivor rates of new firms,
    101*f*
  employment protection legislation indicator
    1998, 227*f*
  household electricity prices, 305*f*
  mergers and acquisitions, 288*t*
  productivity growth, 99
  total assets of private pension funds, 192*f*
  underground production, 238*f*, 241*t*
price stability. *See* inflation
privatization
  effects on productivity, 2, 143, 291, 297
  failures, 143, 172
  recommendations for, 7, 8–11, 285–86
product-market regulation (PMR), 175–77. *See also*
    regulation
  PMR index, 176*b*

productivity. *See also* efficiency; multifactor
    productivity; productivity growth
  1973–95 global growth slowdown, 43–46
  best-practice productivity, 38, 40, 155, 166–67,
    297
  comparative effect of productivity growth and
    labor utilization, 83*f*
  economic performance since 1995, 83–86
  economies of scale, 38–39, 120
  impact of slower growth, US lesson, 47–49
  improving, 7–11
  measurement issues, 84*b*–85*b*
  model of employment and productivity,
    88–92
  productivity growth pre- and post-1973, 44*f*
  relation to higher wages, 56–60
  relation to job growth, 85–86
productivity growth. *See also* GDP growth
  case studies, 113–15
  in general, 82–83, 92, 93–95
  labor productivity growth, 110–11
    by industry 1990–2000, 134*t*
  OECD growth analysis implications, 95–102
  productivity growth accounting pre- and post-
    1973, 105*t*
  role of IT, 104–16
  US experience, 102–104, 116–17

R&D. *See* research and development
recession, 198, 215
regulation. *See also* deregulation
  effects, 22, 120–21, 124, 125, 292
  labor market, 98
  national regulatory barriers limit competition
    in EU, 127*b*–29*b*
  product-market regulation, 175–77
  productivity-enhancing, 129–31
research and development (R&D). *See also*
    education
  average R&D expenditures as shares of output
    1973–98, 150*t*
  relation to growth, 98–99
    Britain, 144, 148, 149–51
retail sector. *See also* food retail sector
  Abercrombie and Fitch, 125
  Amazon.com, 202
  Carrefour, 124, 297
  Costco, 125
  employment and wages, 59–60
  labor productivity growth, 112, 113, 118–19, 124,
    130
  skill sets, 156
  The Gap, 115, 125
  The Limited, 115
  Wal-Mart, 113, 114, 115, 125, 297
retirement. *See also* life expectancy
  average retirement 1965–99, 71*t*
  early-retirement programs, 17, 121, 180, 183,
    193, 212
  in general, 71–72, 190, 294

utilities, 125–26, 130, 298. *See also* energy; monopoly
  degree of competition in open electricity market, 299f
  electric power case study, 171–72
  household electricity prices, 305f
  UK Electricity Act, 171

wages, 164
  declines in, 34, 46, 47, 48–49, 55–56, 153
  employer wage cost for alternative after-tax wage rates, 68t
  increases in, 34, 61
  inequality in, 65–66
  institutional-rate wages, 65
  market-rate wages, 34-35, 64, 68, 203–04
  minimum-wage rates, 15
  probability of layoff following wage increase, 199f, 201f
  real national income per employee, 36–37
  real wage compensation pre- and post-1973, 55f
  reforming, 14–15
  relation to hours worked, 54
  relation to labor demand, 77–78
  relation to productivity, 56–60
  skill differences affecting, 62–66
  sources of growth in real national income per person, 37t
  stagflation, 34, 46

tax wedge and direct wage cost 2003, 67f
wage distribution 1973–2000, 63f, 206
wage-gap hypothesis, 54–56
wage insurance, 13
wage-setting process, 197–200, 304
women, 196
  average retirement 1965–99, 71t
  disability, 214
  life expectancy, 69–71, 70t
    rising life expectancy at retirement, 72f
  part-time work, 210–11
work incentive, 26, 76, 198, 293.
  examples, 196–97
  increasing, 11–18, 22, 180, 181, 243
  work incentive ratio, 89, 92
workers. *See also* employment; labor market; training
  altering view of economy, 3
  auto industry, 156, 157, 164
  hours worked
    annual hours worked per capita, 36t
    total hours worked per capita 1973–2003, 52f
  low-skill workers, 34
  "labor upskilling", 96
  ratio of retirees to employees, 72–73f
  skill shortages, 153–55
  sources of growth in real national income per person, 37t
  worker mobility, 180, 203, 208

Other Publications from the Institute for International Economics

* = out of print

POLICY ANALYSES IN INTERNATIONAL ECONOMICS Series

1 The Lending Policies of the International Monetary Fund*   John Williamson
August 1982   ISBN 0-88132-000-5
2 "Reciprocity": A New Approach to World Trade Policy?*   William R. Cline
September 1982   ISBN 0-88132-001-3
3 Trade Policy in the 1980s*
C. Fred Bergsten and William R. Cline
November 1982   ISBN 0-88132-002-1
4 International Debt and the Stability of the World Economy*   William R. Cline
September 1983   ISBN 0-88132-010-2
5 The Exchange Rate System,* Second Edition
John Williamson
Sept. 1983, rev. June 1985   ISBN 0-88132-034-X
6 Economic Sanctions in Support of Foreign Policy Goals*
Gary Clyde Hufbauer and Jeffrey J. Schott
October 1983   ISBN 0-88132-014-5
7 A New SDR Allocation?*   John Williamson
March 1984   ISBN 0-88132-028-5
8 An International Standard for Monetary Stabilization*   Ronald L. McKinnon
March 1984   ISBN 0-88132-018-8
9 The Yen/Dollar Agreement: Liberalizing Japanese Capital Markets*   Jeffrey A. Frankel
December 1984   ISBN 0-88132-035-8
10 Bank Lending to Developing Countries: The Policy Alternatives*   C. Fred Bergsten, William R. Cline, and John Williamson
April 1985   ISBN 0-88132-032-3
11 Trading for Growth: The Next Round of Trade Negotiations*
Gary Clyde Hufbauer and Jeffrey J. Schott
September 1985   ISBN 0-88132-033-1
12 Financial Intermediation Beyond the Debt Crisis*   Donald R. Lessard, John Williamson
September 1985   ISBN 0-88132-021-8
13 The United States-Japan Economic Problem*
C. Fred Bergsten and William R. Cline
October 1985, 2d ed. January 1987
                           ISBN 0-88132-060-9
14 Deficits and the Dollar: The World Economy at Risk*   Stephen Marris
December 1985, 2d ed. November 1987
                           ISBN 0-88132-067-6

15 Trade Policy for Troubled Industries*
Gary Clyde Hufbauer and Howard R. Rosen
March 1986   ISBN 0-88132-020-X
16 The United States and Canada: The Quest for Free Trade*   Paul Wonnacott, with an appendix by John Williamson
March 1987   ISBN 0-88132-056-0
17 Adjusting to Success: Balance of Payments Policy in the East Asian NICs*
Bela Balassa and John Williamson
June 1987, rev. April 1990 ISBN 0-88132-101-X
18 Mobilizing Bank Lending to Debtor Countries*   William R. Cline
June 1987   ISBN 0-88132-062-5
19 Auction Quotas and United States Trade Policy*   C. Fred Bergsten, Kimberly Ann Elliott, Jeffrey J. Schott, and Wendy E. Takacs
September 1987   ISBN 0-88132-050-1
20 Agriculture and the GATT: Rewriting the Rules*   Dale E. Hathaway
September 1987   ISBN 0-88132-052-8
21 Anti-Protection: Changing Forces in United States Trade Politics*
I. M. Destler and John S. Odell
September 1987   ISBN 0-88132-043-9
22 Targets and Indicators: A Blueprint for the International Coordination of Economic Policy
John Williamson and Marcus H. Miller
September 1987   ISBN 0-88132-051-X
23 Capital Flight: The Problem and Policy Responses*   Donald R. Lessard and John Williamson
December 1987   ISBN 0-88132-059-5
24 United States-Canada Free Trade: An Evaluation of the Agreement*
Jeffrey J. Schott
April 1988   ISBN 0-88132-072-2
25 Voluntary Approaches to Debt Relief*
John Williamson
Sept.1988, rev. May 1989   ISBN 0-88132-098-6
26 American Trade Adjustment: The Global Impact*   William R. Cline
March 1989   ISBN 0-88132-095-1
27 More Free Trade Areas?*
Jeffrey J. Schott
May 1989   ISBN 0-88132-085-4
28 The Progress of Policy Reform in Latin America*   John Williamson
January 1990   ISBN 0-88132-100-1
29 The Global Trade Negotiations: What Can Be Achieved?*   Jeffrey J. Schott
September 1990   ISBN 0-88132-137-0
30 Economic Policy Coordination: Requiem or Prologue?*   Wendy Dobson
April 1991   ISBN 0-88132-102-8

SPECIAL REPORTS

DISTRIBUTORS OUTSIDE THE UNITED STATES

Australia, New Zealand,
and Papua New Guinea
D.A. Information Services
648 Whitehorse Road
Mitcham, Victoria 3132, Australia
tel: 61-3-9210-7777
fax: 61-3-9210-7788
email: service@adadirect.com.au
http://www.dadirect.com.au

United Kingdom and Europe
(including Russia and Turkey)
The Eurospan Group
3 Henrietta Street, Covent Garden
London WC2E 8LU England
tel: 44-20-7240-0856
fax: 44-20-7379-0609
http://www.eurospan.co.uk

Japan and the Republic of Korea
United Publishers Services Ltd.
1-32-5, Higashi-shinagawa,
Shinagawa-ku, Tokyo 140-0002 JAPAN
tel: 81-3-5479-7251
fax: 81-3-5479-7307
info@ups.co.jp
For trade accounts only.
Individuals will find IIE books in
leading Tokyo bookstores.

Thailand
Asia Books
5 Sukhumvit Rd. Soi 61
Bangkok 10110 Thailand
tel: 662-714-07402 Ext: 221, 222, 223
fax: 662-391-2277
email: purchase@asiabooks.co.th
http://www.asiabooksonline.com

Canada
Renouf Bookstore
5369 Canotek Road, Unit 1
Ottawa, Ontario KlJ 9J3, Canada
tel: 613-745-2665
fax: 613-745-7660
http://www.renoufbooks.com

India, Bangladesh, Nepal, and Sri Lanka
Viva Books Pvt.
Mr. Vinod Vasishtha
4325/3, Ansari Rd.
Daryaganj, New Delhi-110002
India
tel: 91-11-327-9280
fax: 91-11-326-7224
email: vinod.viva@gndel.globalnet. ems.vsnl.
net.in

Southeast Asia (Brunei, Cambodia,
China, Malaysia, Hong Kong, Indonesia,
Laos, Myanmar, the Philippines, Singapore,
Taiwan, and Vietnam)
Hemisphere Publication Services
1 Kallang Pudding Rd. #0403
Golden Wheel Building
Singapore 349316
tel: 65-741-5166
fax: 65-742-9356

Visit our Web site at:
www.iie.com
E-mail orders to:
orders@iie.com